The Asian Economies in the Twentieth Century

The Asian Economies in the Twentieth Century

Edited by

Angus Maddison, D.S. Prasada Rao and William F. Shepherd

Edward Elgar
Cheltenham, UK • Northampton, MA, USA

Published by
Edward Elgar Publishing Limited
Glensanda House
Montpellier Parade
Cheltenham
Glos GL50 1UA
UK

Edward Elgar Publishing, Inc.
136 West Street
Suite 202
Northampton
Massachusetts 01060
USA

A catalogue record for this book
is available from the British Library

Library of Congress Cataloguing in Publication Data
The Asian economies in the twentieth century / edited by Angus Maddison, D.S. Prasada Rao, William F. Shepherd.
     p.cm.
   Includes bibliographical references (p.) and index.
   1. Asia–Economic conditions–20th century. I. Maddison, Angus. II. Prasada Rao, D.S. III. Shepherd, William F.
HC412 .A756 2002
330.95'043–dc21

ISBN 1–84064–045–6

Printed and bound in Great Britain by MPG Books Ltd, Bodmin, Cornwall

Contents

List of Tables

List of Figures

List of Contributors

Boon Lee – University of New England

Angus Maddison – University of Groningen

Dirk Pilat – Organisation for Economic Co-operation and Development

D.S. Prasada Rao – University of New England

William F. Shepherd – Griffith University

Siva Sivasubramonian – Retired Statistician

Marcel P. Timmer – University of Groningen

Bart van Ark – University of Groningen

Pierre van der Eng – Australian National University

Harry X. Wu – Polytechnic University

1. Introduction: Measuring Asian Performance

Angus Maddison

Over the long run there have been very big changes in the performance of the Asian economies. In 1820 they accounted for about 60 per cent of world GDP and 68 per cent of world population. Thereafter, their per capita income growth lagged well behind that in the rest of the world, so that in 1950, when their share of world population was 58 per cent, their share of world GDP had fallen to 18.5 per cent. Since then, their income growth has been faster than that in the rest of the world, and their share of world GDP in 1998 was around 37 per cent. This new dynamism was also reflected in their share of world trade, which rose from 14 per cent in 1950 to 27 per cent in 1998.

Within the aggregate picture there have been significant differences. Between 1820 and the 1970s, Japan was the most dynamic Asian economy, but its performance was dismal after 1990. Chinese per capita income was substantially lower in 1950 than in 1820, but increased more than sevenfold by 1998.

If we look at the world ranking of countries in terms of real GDP, China is now the second biggest economy, Japan third biggest, India fourth, Indonesia twelfth, South Korea fourteenth and Taiwan twentieth. These countries are major players in the world economy and it is their performance which is analysed in this study. We also confront their experience with Australia and the USA – two of the richest countries of the advanced capitalist group. The six Asian countries represented three-quarters of the Asian economy in 1998, and the eight countries together, about 52 per cent of the world economy.

In order to understand the forces which have produced variations in performance over time and between major economies, we need measures of output and productivity which are comparable and consistent.

Without measurement, judgements on why some countries got rich, why others are poor, why some catch up and others fall behind, are bound to be fuzzy. Quantification sharpens scholarly discussion and contributes to the dynamics of the research process. If it is done transparently, the dissenting reader can augment or reject parts of the evidence or introduce alternative hypotheses.

For this reason, the contributions to this book devote a good deal of attention to problems of measurement. The risks of comparing unadjusted growth rates and levels of real income are obvious in the case of China. Its official statisticians have given up the old Soviet concept of material product, and switched to using the Western concept of gross domestic product when measuring aggregate economic activity. However, their statistical practice is rooted in the past, and their measures exaggerate Chinese growth. Conversely, the exchange rate understates the purchasing power of the Chinese currency by a factor of four or five. For a meaningful comparison of China and the USA, we need to convert the yuan by a purchasing power parity rather than the exchange rate. four or five.

Table 1.1   Our Eight Country Sample as a Percentage of the World Economy, 1913–98

	GDP in billion in 1990 PP dollars	Per capita GDP in 1990 PP dollars	Population million	% of world GDP	% of world population
1998					
China	3 873.4	3 117	1 242.7	11.5	21.0
Japan	2 581.6	20 410	126.5	7.7	2.1
India	1 702.7	1 760	975.0	5.0	16.5
Indonesia	627.5	3 070	204.4	1.9	3.5
South Korea	564.2	12 152	46.4	1.7	0.8
Taiwan	327.0	15 012	21.8	1.0	0.4
Australia	382.3	20 390	18.8	1.1	0.3
USA	7 394.6	27 331	270.6	21.9	4.6
8 country total	17 453.3	6 005	2 906.2	51.8	49.2
Other Asia	2 858.2	3 177	899.6	8.4	15.2
Rest of world	13 414.1	6 382	2 101.9	39.8	35.5
World	33 725.6	5 709	5 907.7	100.0	100.0
1950					
China	239.9	439	546.8	4.5	21.7
Japan	161.0	1 926	83.6	3.0	3.3
India	222.2	619	359.0	4.2	14.2
Indonesia	66.4	840	79.0	1.2	3.1
South Korea	16.0	770	20.8	0.3	0.8
Taiwan	7.4	926	7.9	0.1	0.3
Australia	61.3	7 493	8.2	1.1	0.3
USA	1 455.9	9 561	152.3	27.3	6.0
8 country total	2 230.1	1 773	1 257.6	41.8	49.8
Other Asia	272.8	958	284.8	5.1	11.3
Rest of world	2 833.2	2 885	982.1	53.1	38.9
World	5 336.1	2 114	2 524.5	100.0	100.0
1913					
China	241.3	522	437.1	8.9	26.4
Japan	71.7	1 387	51.7	2.7	2.9
India	204.2	673	303.7	7.5	17.0
Indonesia	45.2	904	49.9	1.7	2.8
Korea	14.3	893	16.1	0.5	0.9
Taiwan	2.6	747	3.5	0.1	0.2
Australia	27.6	5 715	4.8	0.9	0.3
USA	517.4	5 301	97.6	19.1	5.4
8 country total	1 124.3	1 124	1 000.4	41.6	55.9
Other Asia	84.9	734	115.6	3.1	4.4
Rest of world	1 495.6	2 216	675.0	55.3	39.7
World	2 704.8	1 510	1 791.0	100.0	100.0

Source: A. Maddison, *The World Economy: A Millennial Perspective*, OECD Development Centre, Paris, 2001. The GDP estimates are converted by a purchasing power converter (ICP Geary Khamis PPP).

When we confront China and the USA, the problem of comparing real income requires knowledge of price levels and quantities of output in the two countries. If we have enough information we can estimate the size of Chinese output at US prices or US output at Chinese prices. When we compare more countries the statistical problems are more complex than in such binary comparisons. These are issues which are explored in the contributions to this volume.

In looking at the causes of growth, our objective is to produce a framework of accounts which shows inputs of physical capital (equipment and structures) and human capital (i.e. labour augmented by education and training), as well as comparable measures of gross output and intermediate inputs. When this is done, it is possible to develop a growth accounting framework, measure total factor productivity, and get a rough idea of the pace of technical progress (in the lead country) or the pace of technological diffusion (the degree of catch-up) in the follower countries.

This study is the fruit of a research project started in 1993 by the editors of this volume with financial support from the Australian Research Council. Our main objective was to provide the statistical foundations for comparative research on economic performance in the Asia-Pacific region. Our COPPAA project (Comparison of Output, Productivity and Purchasing Power in Asia and Australia) is based in the University of New England in Armidale and Griffith University in Brisbane. It developed in close cooperation with the ICOP project (International Comparison of Output and Productivity) of the University of Groningen in the Netherlands. We benefited from the network of international contacts which ICOP had developed, from meetings of the International Association for Research in Income and Wealth, and from cooperation with statistical offices and scholars in the countries in which our research was conducted.

There are eight detailed contributions to this book.

Chapter 2 traces the intellectual history of growth accounting and real income comparisons from its origins in the seventeenth century when William Petty and Gregory King constructed the first measures of national income, capital and labour inputs for England, and crude measures of comparative macroeconomic performance in England, France and the Netherlands. It explains the development of measures of purchasing power parity and real expenditure pioneered by Colin Clark in 1940, Milton Gilbert and others in OEEC in the 1950s, Irving Kravis, Robert Summers and Alan Heston in the ICP (International Comparison Project) from the 1970s onwards.

It explains our own approach in measuring real output and productivity by major sectors of the economy, which was pioneered by Rostas in the 1940s, and has been further refined and greatly extended by the ICOP project in Groningen.

Chapter 3 demonstrates alternative techniques for measuring performance in the farm sector for seven countries. The statistical problems in measuring farm performance are relatively easy because the number of products is fairly small, intercountry variations in quality are relatively modest, and the available information is rather comprehensive. The chapter compares two alternative approaches to multilateral comparison, i.e. the Geary-Khamis method which was developed by Kravis, Summers and Heston for their work on real expenditure, which we think is also most appropriate for our work from the production side. The alternative EKS procedure is used by Eurostat in its estimates of aggregate output in European Union countries. They prefer it for political reasons because it gives all countries the same weight, whatever their size.

Chapter 4 demonstrates the procedure for making binary comparisons of real output and productivity for Australian and US manufacturing. Such measures are much more complex than for farming. The number of products is much greater (up to 15 000 products are specified in industrial censuses). The quality of products varies more, and input–output relationships are more complex. As a result the coverage of such exercises is smaller than for farming. The empirical results of the chapter are very interesting as they show the large variations in productivity levels that can exist within advanced capitalist countries.

Chapter 5 provides new annual estimates of Chinese industrial performance since 1949 which are adjusted to take care of the measurement problems already mentioned. It presents an authoritative view of the impact of the Great Leap Forward, the Cultural Revolution, and of progress since the 1978 reforms.

Chapter 6 presents new annual estimates of Indian economic performance from 1900 to 1997, with a detailed analysis of developments of output and productivity in 13 sectors for 1900–46 for prepartition India, and 15 sectors for 1946–97.

Chapter 7 provides new annual estimates of Indonesian GDP growth for four major sectors of the economy, analyses the impact of changing terms of trade, the regional distribution of product, and the growth of the capital stock.

Chapter 8 is a comprehensive survey of Japanese performance since 1885, with annual estimates of GDP, and growth accounts which are used to explain the reasons for Japan's achievement in catching up with the West, and its sluggish performance since 1990. It also provides a binary comparison of Japanese and United States performance for the whole period.

Chapter 9 provides a comprehensive new set of growth accounts for South Korea and Taiwan for 1960–98. These two countries had the fastest growth in Asia in this period. The analysis helps to explain how this was achieved, and confronts their performance with that of Japan and the United States. It includes new estimates of investment back to 1913 for each country and a fully transparent explanation of the derivation of the capital stock estimates.

The attached bibliography lists research papers produced in the COPPAA project. Two related publications are A. Maddison, *Chinese Economic Performance in the Long Run*, OECD Development Centre, Paris, 1998, and A. Maddison, *The World Economy: A Millennial Perspective*, OECD Development Centre, Paris 2001.

RESEARCH MONOGRAPHS OF THE COPPAA PROJECT

Pilat, D., D.S. Prasada Rao and W.F. Shepherd, *Australian and United States Manufacturing: A Comparison of Real Output, Productivity Levels and Purchasing Power, 1970–1989*, COPPAA, No. 1, 1993.

Szirmai, A.E., W.F. Shepherd, D.S. Prasada Rao, and G. de Jong, *Manufacturing Sector Output and Productivity in Indonesia: An Australian Comparative Perspective, 1975–1990*, COPPAA, No. 2, 1995.

Timmer, M. and B. Lee, *China's Manufacturing Performance From an Australian Perspective, 1980–1991*, COPPAA, No. 3, 1996.

Wu, H.X., *Reconstructing Chinese GDP According to the National Accounts Concepts of Value Added: The Industrial Sector*, COPPAA, No. 4, 1997.

Lee, B. and A. Maddison, *A Comparison of Output Purchasing Power and Productivity in Indian and Chinese Manufacturing in the Mid-1980s*, COPPAA, No. 5, 1997.

2. The International Comparison of Real Product and Productivity

Angus Maddison and Bart van Ark

INTRODUCTION

In order to make valid inter-country comparisons of macro-economic performance in quantitative terms, we need:

(a) consensus on the scope, meaning and coverage of national accounts;

(b) national statistical authorities or academic researchers who implement these general principles by making estimates of GDP and its components in real and money terms which follow the agreed guidelines;

(c) appropriate purchasing power parity converters to convert the estimates in different national currencies into a common *numeraire*.

Work on national accounts and international comparisons of real income levels started in the seventeenth century. In 1696, Gregory King used a mix of evidence for the three main facets of national accounts – income, expenditure and production – to make rough comparisons of performance in France, the Netherlands and the UK. His approach was further developed by individual scholars over a period of 250 years, with substantial clarification of what the scope of the accounts should be, a large accumulation of estimates for individual countries, and, in the twentieth century, several important steps forward in the provision of international purchasing power converters, e.g. the Board of Trade enquiries into working class cost of living in Belgium, France, Germany, the UK and USA in the UK in 1908–13 and Colin Clark's bold (1940) attempt to compare expenditure levels and productivity by major sector of the economy in 26 countries

The big step forward in international comparison came from OEEC in the 1950s. It produced the first standardised system of national accounts which was accepted by its member countries and also by the United Nations, it promoted close consultation between statisticians in Western Europe and North America to ensure that the guidelines were implemented, and it made a massive breakthrough in developing purchasing power converters and international real product comparisons.

All subsequent work in comparing levels of real product and purchasing power derive from (a) the Gilbert and Kravis (1954) expenditure comparisons and (b) the Paige and Bombach (1959) real product comparisons. There have been no comprehensive comparisons from the income side, but there are partial income comparisons most of which are concerned with wage income.

The expenditure approach, as developed by Kravis, Heston and Summers in the ICP (International Comparisons Project) programme since the 1960s, is basically a highly sophisticated pricing exercise. It assembles a coherent, articulate and complete set of carefully specified prices at the final expenditure level from statistical offices in the participating countries, together with supplementary studies of the cost of investment goods and government services. Kravis, Heston and Summers (1982 is their *magnum opus*) pioneered new techniques for providing multilateral measures at 'international' prices. Their preferred multilateral measure was the Geary Khamis PPP, but they continued to publish the three binary PPP variants which OEEC had used, i.e. the Paasche PPP (with own country quantity weights), the Laspeyres PPP (with quantity weights of the numeraire country – the USA) and the Fisher geometric mean of the Laspeyres and Paasche measures. The ICP converters were then applied to the values in the national accounts of 151 expenditure components. The interspatial differences in volume between countries were derived as the end product. For countries not covered by ICP, Summers and Heston (1991) devised short cut estimates which use price information from cost of living surveys (of diplomats, UN officials, and people working abroad for private business) as a proxy for the ICP specification prices.

The production approach as developed by the ICOP (International Comparison of Output and Productivity) project of the University of Groningen since 1983 is derived from Rostas (1948), Paige and Bombach (1959) and Maddison (1970). It is intended to be complementary to ICP, and we do not regard it as a substitute. It involves a comparison of real output (value added) in major sectors (agriculture, industry and services) and of branches within these three broad sectors, and in some cases measures for GDP as a whole. It takes an integrated view of output and input quantities, producer prices and the values derived from these prices and quantities. It includes labour productivity measures with labour input measured in working hours where possible. It has been used in conjunction with estimates of capital stock, to measure total factor productivity. As with the ICP, ICOP research has involved the merger of cross-country benchmarks with national time series estimates. It has been conducted on a transparent basis, making available diskettes, voluminous background memoranda, articulate source descriptions, full disclosure of sample sizes and aggregation techniques. A description of the ICOP methodology for manufacturing can be found in Maddison and van Ark (1988, 1989) and is further elaborated in van Ark (1993 and 1996) and in Van Ark and Pilat (1993). The ICOP comparisons have essentially been bilateral, with the USA as the numeraire country and also as the star country. When comparing an array of ICOP results we have generally considered either the Paasche or the Fisher PPP variants. However, Pilat and Prasada Rao (1996) applied multilateral techniques to our manufacturing comparisons; Maddison and Prasada Rao (1996) did the same for agriculture.

The ICOP research technique is different from that of ICP. Rather than special surveys, it uses information from production censuses, input–output tables, national accounts and, in some special cases, information for individual firms. Its integrated statistics of quantity, unit value, and values permit crosschecks not available to ICP. It identifies variations in the coverage of national accounts which ICP has not explored.

The major reason why the methods and sources used by the ICOP team have been different from those of ICP is that its research strategy and objectives are different. It has been conducted by a group of university researchers rather than by national governments or international organisations. Its research results are those of individuals rather than being institutional. It was created to provide a broad interactive framework for quantitative analysis of economic growth processes as well as levels of performance. We were just as interested in measuring productivity and the forces determining it as we were in price structures.

The interests of the ICOP group have been worldwide, but we never aspired to comprehensive coverage. We were satisfied to concentrate our efforts on relatively large countries which would provide a representative picture that covers about three-quarters of world population and output and a very wide range of income levels.

Our interest was not only macroeconomic, but involved close scrutiny of sectors where it was possible to get some appreciation of the processes of technical change. Hence our research has investigated productivity performance at a detailed industry level. We also gave considerable attention to intercountry diffusion of technology and to differences between the lead country (USA in the twentieth century, UK for a good deal of the nineteenth) and the follower countries, and to processes of catch-up, convergence or divergence. This is a major reason why we have emphasised star system binary comparison rather than multilateral techniques which were appropriate to the mondialist and maximalist aspirations of ICP.

ICP has thrown great light on a vast array of problems, and ICOP opens up areas which are related but different. It permits:

(a) analysis of real product and productivity by industry. Since the Physiocrats, Malthus and Ricardo, the breakdown between agriculture, industry and services has been considered of fundamental importance, and the relative productivity standing of the three sectors is notoriously different;

(b) structural analysis – stressed by Kuznets, Chenery and Denison – and fundamental to growth accounts. The 'structure' of GDP on the production side involves a bigger service component than on the expenditure side, where some important services such as distribution are 'disguised' (see Maddison, 1983) because they do not figure explicitly as final expenditure items;

(c) sharper analysis of the causes of economic growth and of patterns of divergence between nations in growth accounts, catch up and convergence analysis, exploration of lead country-follower country phenomena;

(d) analysis of the locus of technical progress. For this purpose we have supplemented sector analysis by micro-oriented investigation of variance in performance between industries and between average and best practice firms;

(e) analysis of the relation between productivity and competitivity.

The ICOP research programme can usefully be analysed under the following headings, work on (a) agriculture; (b) mining; (c) manufacturing; (d) services and (e) the whole economy.

Agriculture

Agriculture was the first sector on the ICOP research agenda because it has a simple commodity structure (about 200 products instead of up to 15 000 in manufacturing). The availability of standardised information on output, feed and seed inputs, farm prices and farm accounts from the Food and Agriculture Organisation (FAO) greatly facilitated the problem of assembling the basic data for multicountry analysis on a reasonably standardised basis. Problems of quality, product differentiation, and coverage are smaller than in other sectors and it is easier to deploy double deflation.

Van Ooststroom and Maddison (1984) replicated the methodological approach of Maddison (1970). Maddison had covered 29 countries for 1965, using FAO statistics for 89 farm commodities, and employed a rough double deflation approach to measure gross value added at US prices. The 1984 study covered 144 farm products for 14 countries. It covered most of the countries targeted for subsequent ICOP manufacturing studies, and the benchmark year was 1975 to provide a comparison with round three of ICP. Maddison and Van Ooststroom (1993) was an updated version of the 1984 study, with a critical review of the literature on comparisons of agricultural performance.

Maddison and Van Ooststroom used a Laspeyres volume index as more prices were available for the USA than for other countries, so this option minimised the use of shadow prices. They also felt that US prices were the most relevant for catch-up analysis.

Table 2.1 Maddison–van Ooststroom Benchmark Results for Agriculture in 1975, Using Paasche PPPs and Shadow Pricing to Fill Data Gaps

	Gross value added per person engaged (USA = 100)	Gross value added per head of population (USA = 100)	Gross value added per hectare (USA = 100)	Paasche PPP for gross value added units of natio-nal currency per dollar	Exchange rate
Argentina	43.9	157.7	48.0	13.17	36.57
Brazil	10.0	80.2	81.7	7.47	8.13
China	2.3	47.9	218.2	n.a.	1.86
India	1.9	31.4	212.4	7.70	8.65
Indonesia	2.4	33.3	275.6	326.64	415.00
Korea	3.6	32.9	1 015.5	682.99	484.00
Mexico	6.7	46.0	56.1	13.52	12.50
France	39.8	105.4	341.9	5.67	4.29
Germany	30.1	51.9	511.1	3.01	2.46
Japan	8.8	31.2	1 243.5	631.78	296.79
Netherlands	90.0	112.6	1 441.4	3.25	2.53
UK	54.7	42.5	256.1	0.50	0.45
USA	100.0	100.0	100.0	1.00	1.00

Source: A. Maddison and H. van Ooststroom (1993), using the shadow pricing technique (generally wheat relatives) for filling holes in the data. The figures underlying this table are all at US prices (with a Paasche PPP converter).

Maddison and Prasada Rao (1996), used the same data base to calculate Paasche, Laspeyres, Fisher and Geary-Khamis measures of agricultural output net of feed and seed, using the same technique as ICP for filling holes in the data array; they used the CPD (country product dummy) method invented by Robert Summers (1973), instead of shadow prices. Their results are shown in Table 2.2.

Table 2.2 Maddison-Prasada Rao Results for Agriculture in 1975, Using three PPP Variants and the CPD Technique for Filling Data Gaps

	Gross value added per person engaged (USA = 100)			PPP variants (units of national currency per US dollar)		
	Laspeyres volume index using US price weights	Paasche volume index own country price weights	Fisher geometric mean	Paasche PPP own country quantity weights	Laspeyres PPP US quantity weights	Fisher geometric mean
Argentina	44.0	43.9	44.0	13.03	13.05	13.04
Brazil	10.2	8.9	9.6	7.15	8.23	7.67
India	2.2	2.0	2.1	6.87	7.48	7.17
Indonesia	2.6	1.7	2.1	340.95	514.08	418.63
Korea	3.6	3.1	3.3	704.44	840.93	769.53
Mexico	6.9	5.3	6.1	13.61	17.78	15.56
France	43.6	38.6	41.0	5.67	6.41	6.03
Germany	30.6	22.5	26.2	2.74	3.73	3.20
Japan	9.2	8.8	9.0	629.06	661.31	645.00
Netherlands	84.3	42.9	60.1	2.83	5.56	3.97
UK	55.9	41.7	48.3	0.502	0.673	0.581
USA	100.0	100.0	100.0	1.00	1.00	1.00

Source: A. Maddison and D.S. Prasada Rao (1996), using the CPD technique for filling holes in the data in order to get complete matching. Columns 1 and 4 differ from the corresponding columns of Table 2.1 for methodological reasons. The data base was virtually identical.

The main results of the agriculture study are shown in Tables 2.1 and 2.2. It is clear that in our sample of countries, the USA was the productivity leader, and the Netherlands was the closest competitor. The UK was in third place with productivity about half of the US level. Some countries with high productivity levels in manufacturing had poor performance in agriculture e.g. Germany at well under a third of the US level. Japanese performance was abysmal (less than a tenth of the US level). In a similar study, Prasada Rao (1993) found two countries, Australia and New Zealand, with slightly higher labour productivity in agriculture in 1975 than the USA. A major reason for US productivity leadership is an abundant supply of land. In terms of land productivity, US performance was only one-fourteenth of that in the Netherlands. In fact, the only countries with lower levels of land productivity than the USA, in our sample, were Argentina, Brazil, and Mexico.

A comparison of the PPPs and the exchange rates shown in Table 2.1 shows that in all the European countries, Japan, Korea and Mexico the agricultural price level (i.e. the PPP divided by the exchange rate) was higher than in the USA, whereas in Argentina, Brazil, India and Indonesia, agricultural prices were lower. The extreme cases were Argentina (where prices were one-third of the US level) and Japan (prices twice the US level).

When international comparisons of performance levels are made, either by the ICP expenditure approach or the ICOP approach by industry of origin, it is now conventional to have only one summary set of results. In the ICP case, the preferred option has hitherto been the multilateral Geary Khamis indicator. In the ICOP studies, preference has been either for use of the Paasche or Fisher converter.

In binary comparisons the three most straightforward options are: (i) Laspeyres volume comparisons based on the prices (unit values) of the numeraire country; (ii) Paasche volume comparisons based on the prices (unit values) of the other country or countries in the comparison; or (iii) the Fisher geometric average of these two measures which is in effect a compromise measure. Conversely, the PPPs corresponding to these three volume options are: (i) the Paasche PPP (with 'own' country quantity weights); (ii) the Laspeyres PPP (with the quantity weights of the numeraire country); and the Fisher geometric average of the two measures. The difference between the Paasche and Laspeyres PPPs varies between countries and branches of the economy under investigation. The gap between the two measures is generally widest for comparisons between countries with very different income or productivity levels.

In the ICOP approach we have attempted to be as transparent as possible, so that our procedures can be easily replicated (or modified, by those with different research objectives). Hence we have generally presented all of the PPP options, as in Table 2.2, even where, for convenience, we put most emphasis on one of the indicators.

Mining

Mining was the second sector which the ICOP group tackled. The rough international comparison of Wieringa and Maddison (1985) covered the same countries as the agriculture comparisons for 1975, and used only US prices as the basis for comparison. The prices were generally taken from the *Statistical Abstract of the United States* and from the US *Minerals Yearbook* and trade sources. Production of 45 minerals in the 13 countries was generally taken from the UN *Yearbook of Industrial Statistics*.

Table 2.3 presents a modified version of the Wieringa–Maddison paper, with correction for an error in the price of manganese, and an adjustment to a value added basis. Like the agriculture study, our mining results were generally from secondary sources. Houben (1990) was a more sophisticated analysis of the mining sector in Brazil, Mexico and the USA from census material, and was similar in approach to our studies for manufacturing.

Mining productivity depends importantly on the luck of natural resource endowment, and on the geological research and prospection effort in the country. In both respects the US advantage is clear. It is better endowed with mineral resources than almost all other countries, and the efforts of the US geological service have been exemplary since the 1860s. As a result, US mining output per head of population was well ahead of that in all the other countries in our sample, the nearest competitors being the Netherlands which had only 56 per cent of the US level per head of population. In terms of labour productivity, the Netherlands and Indonesia were the only countries in our sample to surpass the USA in 1975. Mining output in the Netherlands is dominated by the production of natural gas in Groningen which is capital-intensive and requires very little labour.

Table 2.3 Wieringa–Maddison Benchmark Results for Mining in 1975

	Paasche PPP (units of national currency per US $)	Gross value added per person engaged (USA = 100)	Gross value added per head of population (USA = 100)	Gross value added (USA = 100)
Argentina	22.20	33.3	21.5	2.62
Brazil	5.34	22.2	6.4	2.75
China	n.a.	5.7	6.6	28.96
India	3.32	6.5	2.6	7.06
Indonesia	957.53	117.6	11.3	6.88
Korea	395.51	12.6	6.3	1.01
Mexico	15.98	16.2	18.5	5.21
France	12.16	11.5	10.2	2.69
Germany	3.64	17.3	28.8	8.21
Japan	1 077.05	9.3	3.9	1.97
Netherlands	6.61	333.9	56.3	3.55
UK	0.64	15.0	27.7	7.22
USA	1.00	100.0	100.0	100.00

Source: Revised version of P. Wieringa and A. Maddison (1985). The measure of levels of gross value added was based on a Paasche PPP converter as in Table 2.1. Laspeyres and Fisher PPPs were not estimated.

The relative standing of countries in mining productivity can change very rapidly, when new resources are developed. Thus the performance of Mexico and the UK has improved a good deal since 1975, because the two OPEC shocks led to very large increases in oil production.

Manufacturing

Before embarking on detailed binary comparisons for industry, we explored the possibilities of using international industrial data files, such as those of UNIDO, to see if they provided an opportunity for the same type of multi-country jumpstart which was possible for agriculture and mining. However, the commodity specification in UNIDO's *Industrial Statistics Yearbook* is not very detailed and is incomplete for many countries, it contains no information on prices or unit values, and very little information on industrial input structures.

The basic sources for our manufacturing comparisons were therefore industrial production censuses and surveys where the ingredients for measuring real output, prices and labour productivity are available in returns from the same establishment. The degree of detail is very substantial. In most but not all cases we were able to confront the census results with national accounts and input–output tables, which helped us to get a better judgement on the comparability of our sources. The only important weakness of censuses is that information on service inputs is usually incomplete.

So far the ICOP group and our associates have carried out 30 binary comparisons for manufacturing. In 13 cases the USA was the star country. The benchmark year was generally 1975 or 1987, with earlier or later years in some cases. The comparisons with the USA included Argentina, Australia, Brazil, China, Ecuador, France, Germany, India, Indonesia, Japan, Korea, Mexico, the Netherlands, Taiwan, UK and the USSR. We also made binary comparisons for Czechoslovakia/Germany (FR), East Germany (DR)/West Germany (FR), Hungary/Germany (FR), Poland/Germany (FR), Brazil/Mexico, Brazil/UK, France/UK, Netherlands/UK, Spain/UK, and Japan/Korea. Other scholars have adopted our approach in binary comparisons for Germany(FR)/UK (O'Mahony, 1992), France/Germany (FR) (Freudenberg and Ünal-Kesenci, 1994), Ireland/UK (Birnie, 1996) and Portugal/UK (Peres, 1994), Finland/USA and Sweden/USA (Maliranta, 1994) and Belgium/USA (Soete, 1994).

Table 2.4 shows the productivity results for the countries where our research has been most intensive. The benchmark estimates were extrapolated to other years using time series at national prices. It demonstrates that the US leadership margin is smaller in manufacturing than in agriculture, and has been substantially eroded since 1960. In 1960 the ten OECD countries behind the US (starting with Australia up to the Netherlands) averaged 49 per cent of US manufacturing value added per hour worked, and by 1996 89 per cent. Some OECD countries caught up very rapidly, in particular Japan and Spain, but other countries stagnated relative to the USA (Australia, UK) or have even lost ground (Canada).

The manufacturing productivity gaps between European countries and the USA are wider on a per person basis than per hour, because working hours are lower in the European countries. They varied in the 1980s from a low 1 500 in Dutch manufacturing to around 1 900 in the USA and up to 2 500 in East Asian countries like Korea and Taiwan. Figures on hours worked are not normally available in production censuses so in most cases we had to estimate total hours worked by merging data from various sources. The comparability of the hours estimates is still weak (see Van Ark, 1993).

For the rest of the world, the rapid catch-up in manufacturing productivity in Korea and Taiwan clearly stand out as success stories. Catch-up was virtually absent in the other Asian countries (India, China and Indonesia) until the late 1980s, but thereafter one can see some narrowing of the productivity gap with the USA. Latin American countries (Brazil and Mexico) showed much higher productivity levels in manufacturing than the Asian countries, but their growth slowed substantially after the debt crisis of 1982.

The results for the East European countries and the USSR are quite striking. For the pre-transition period we found much lower levels of productivity than had been previously thought. There were very high ratios of inputs to gross output in these countries, and other evidence of inefficiency in the form of unsaleable inventories. Since the early 1990s developments in Eastern Europe have been very diverse. Recovery was slow in Hungary and Poland, but extremely rapid in East Germany. In the latter case, however, employment in manufacturing was cut by two-thirds from 3 million around 1990 to 1 million in 1998, and manufacturing activities were helped by substantial capital flows from the West to the Eastern Länder (Van Ark, 1999).

Table 2.4 ICOP Estimates of Comparative Levels of Labour Productivity in Manufacturing using Census Concept of Value Added, 1950–96, USA = 100

	Value added per person engaged, Fisher geometric mean				Value added per hour worked, Fisher geometric mean			
	1960	1973	1987	1996	1960	1973	1987	1996
West European Core								
Belgium	42.1	57.6	78.5	80.7	42.2	67.0	99.8	104.0
Finland	47.9	53.2	65.9	86.4	45.5	56.1	74.3	103.5
France	51.8	67.6	71.2	75.4	49.8	71.4	84.0	91.2
Germany (West)	63.0	75.6	70.2	66.2	57.9	79.0	82.2	84.6
Netherlands	54.4	79.3	83.3	82.8	50.2	87.0	105.4	108.9
Sweden	53.6	73.0	68.4	83.1	55.3	88.3	87.4	99.4
UK	49.9	51.1	53.6	53.1	45.9	52.5	58.0	61.1
Southern Europe								
Portugal	15.0	24.2	24.5	23.2 i				
Spain	15.1	28.5	46.5	39.6				
Eastern Europe								
Czechoslovakia	27.7	23.9	24.0	18.9				
Germany (East-)	24.3	22.5	22.5	57.6	23.5			
Hungary	17.6	16.7	20.1	25.2				
Poland	23.9	24.9	21.2	18.5				
USSR, industry (d)	27.2	25.5	26.1	27.3	26.8	27.7		
USSR, manufacturing	24.8	26.3						
Western Offshoots								
Australia	40.7	43.1	48.4	45.5	39.6	43.8	49.9	47.3
Canada	80.4	83.9	77.5	73.0	80.2	86.0	79.4	77.4
USA	100.0	100.0	100.0	100.0	100.0	100.0	100.0	100.0
Latin America								
Brazil	41.8	46.3	32.7	21.9				
Mexico	36.8	35.3	25.5	25.4				
Asia								
China, all firms	4.5	6.4 j						
China, large firms (b)	5.7	4.9						
India, all firms	2.1	2.6 g	2.2	2.4 k				
India, registered firms (a)	6.7	7.0 g	8.4	10.8 k	6.8			
Indonesia, all firms	4.0 e	3.0	h	4.6	5.0 i			
Indonesia, medium and large (c)	8.0	11.2 i	6.3					
Japan	24.9	55.0	76.4	82.7	19.9	47.5	67.5	83.2
South Korea	9.8 f	15.0	26.5	40.6	6.9 f	10.9	18.4	31.7
Taiwan	11.8 f	19.5	26.6	34.7	8.1 f	14.0	20.4	28.3

Notes: (a) including mining and public utilities; (b) enterprises above township level; (c) establishments with 20 or more employees and those with between 10–20 employees using power; (d) establishments with 20 or more employees except those in oil and gas refineries; (e) 1961; (f) 1963; (g) 1970; (h) 1971; (i) 1995; (j) 1994; (k) 1993. Portugal/UK, Spain/UK, Hungary/W. Germany, Poland/W. Germany and East Germany/W. Germany comparisons are shown here with the USA as the base country for the benchmark year.

Sources: Benchmark year estimates for Belgium/USA from Soete (1994); Finland/USA (1987) and Sweden/ USA (1987) from Maliranta (1994); W. Germany/USA (1987) from van Ark and Pilat (1993); France/USA (1987) from van Ark and Kouwenhoven (1994); Netherlands/USA from Kouwenhoven (1993); UK/USA (1987) from van Ark (1992); Portugal/UK (1984) from Peres Lopes (1994); Spain/UK (1984) from van Ark (1995); Czechoslovakia/W. Germany and East Germany/W. Germany from van Ark (1995); Hungary/W. Germany (1987) from Monnikhof (1996); Poland/W. Germany (1989) from Liberda, Monnikhof and van Ark (1996); Poland/ Germany (1993) and East Germany/W. Germany(1992) are unpublished ICOP estimates (January 1996); USSR/USA (1987) from Kouwenhoven (1997); Australia/USA (1987) from Pilat, Rao and Shepherd (1993); Canada/USA (1987) from de Jong (1996); Brazil/USA (1975) and Mexico/USA (1975) from van Ark and Maddison (1994); China/USA (1985) from Szirmai and Ren (1998); India/USA (1983/84), Taiwan/USA (1986) and Indonesia/USA (1987) from Timmer (1999); Japan/USA and Korea/USA from Pilat (1994). Extrapolations from benchmark years using national accounts series on sectoral GDP, employment and hours in manufacturing from original publications, updated and extended with series from http://www.eco.rug.nl/ggdc/Dseries/ industry.htm.

Manufacturing output was converted to a common currency using average price ratios for sample products. The 'prices' for manufacturing were obtained by dividing ex-factory sales values by the corresponding quantities. It is therefore more accurate to call them 'unit value ratios' (UVRs), which identifies their nature more clearly than the traditional term 'purchasing power parities'. Unit values for individual products were weighted stepwise by the corresponding quantities to obtain the ratio for the 'industry' to which the product belonged. Industry UVRs were then reweighted by the corresponding value added or gross output and aggregated to get estimates at the 'branch' level (usually for 16 branches). The process was then repeated to get the result for total manufacturing. The major advantage of this stepwise procedure is that the original product UVRs are successively reweighted according to their relative importance in the aggregate.

Our approach is different from the direct comparisons of physical output of Rostas (1948). He weighted quantity relatives by value added or employment, assuming the quantity relatives for covered products to be representative for those not covered, whereas our approach (like that of Fabricant, 1940) assumes that the price relationships (UVRs) we can measure are representative for what we could not measure. The coverage problem is much greater in manufacturing than for agriculture. The smallest sample size we accepted was 10 per cent of all manufacturing sales (in the India/US comparison). In other cases our coverage was up to 40 per cent of total gross output. Sensitivity tests suggest that with our 'stepwise' procedure the apparently low coverage is not a source of great error in the estimates (see Van Ark, 1993; Timmer, 2000).

Unit value ratios cannot be obtained for all products for several reasons. Some products are unique e.g. sarees in India and spacecraft in the USA. For some products no information on sales value or quantity is reported, generally because to do so would breach confidentiality. The characteristics of some products vary a good deal between countries, and the information which censuses provide may not be adequate to permit matching. For example, in the case of cars, we consulted industry experts and trade journals to obtain a better judgement on the matching or to adjust for quality differences in the Brazil/USA and Mexico/USA comparison (Maddison and Van Ark, 1988), and in the France/UK comparison (Van Ark, 1990). There were several other industries where census results were supplemented from trade sources, factory visits or consultation of engineering expertise.

All our manufacturing comparisons have been of a binary nature, and are therefore based on weights of one of the two countries in each comparison. In most cases, the USA was the 'star' country which figured in each of the binaries. The UVR ratios which result from this procedure are either Laspeyres (if one uses the quantity weights of the USA – the 'numéraire' country) or Paasche (using the other country's quantity weights). In summarising our results we generally used the geometric mean of the two ratios (the Fisher index) but we have systematically presented the full range of binary comparisons on alternative weighting systems.

A disadvantage of 'star' system comparisons which link up a series of binary comparisons is that they are not transitive. For example, comparisons between Brazil and Mexico which one can infer from binary comparisons between Brazil/USA and Mexico/USA are not the same as one gets from a direct Brazil/Mexico comparison. We found after testing that this was not a big problem for countries which are similar in product mix and productivity level. However, we found bigger intransitivity between countries with very different products and levels of development.

Pilat and Rao (1996) dealt with the transitivity problem by using our ICOP results to derive multilateral measures at branch level. Recently, Rao and Timmer (2000) experimented with multilateralisation at product level. The aim of multilateralisation is to provide inter-country relationships which are transitive and not influenced by the choice of the base country. However, the multilateral results will depend on how many and which countries are included. Thus if one takes the multilateral Geary Khamis estimates for the 12 EU countries and then adds data for the USA and Japan, all the original Geary Khamis estimates will change, and change significantly, as Japan and the USA are very large countries.

As there are no index numbers which possess all desirable properties, we have so far preferred to base our key estimates on binary comparisons and the 'star' country system. Binaries are transparent and the easiest to calculate. They are the most 'country characteristic', i.e., their weights best reflect the relative price and quantity structure of the countries compared.

Industry of origin comparisons face a major problem not encountered in those from the expenditure side, i.e. the need to get UVRs for both output and input to arrive at value added. The double deflation procedure was reasonably satisfactory in our study of agriculture but produced some implausible and erratic results when applied in manufacturing. The input structure is much more heterogeneous, and the production censuses often provide inadequate information on the composition of material and service inputs. Input–output tables are of some help, and on one occasion we made use of them to adjust the comparisons for the food processing industry in Japan for their use of relatively expensive agricultural inputs (Van Ark and Pilat, 1993). However, we found that on the whole, even with very good information, double deflation easily leads to volatile and improbable results, particularly when intermediate inputs make up a large part of gross output or when the input/output structure is very different between countries (Szirmai and Pilat, 1990; Van Ark, 1993).

Instead of applying an incomplete and unsatisfactory double deflation procedure, we therefore followed the practice of earlier industry of origin studies. After deriving estimates for gross output, we moved to the value added measure by adjusting for the ratio of the value of inputs to gross output, i.e. we assumed the same UVR for output and input. This is an area where further experimentation and sensitivity analysis are necessary.

In many manufacturing censuses the concept of value added differs from modern national accounting practice. Traditionally these censuses correct for double counting by deducting raw materials, packaging and energy inputs from the gross value of output, but purchases of service inputs for repair and maintenance, advertising, accountancy etc. are not deducted. In Table 2.4 we used this traditional 'census concept' of value added for the benchmark comparisons, but in Table 2.5 the productivity estimates for 1975 conform to the 'present national accounts concept', where all service inputs are deducted, except bank charges which are deducted globally in present national accounting practice instead of separately for each sector of activity. Except for the service adjustment, the estimates in Table 2.5 are based on the same census information as Table 2.4.

Table 2.5 Gross Value Added Per Person Employed in Manufacturing in 1975 (present national accounts concept) Using Three UVR Variants

	Gross value added per person engaged (USA = 100)			UVR variant (Units of national currency per US dollar)		
	Laspeyres volume index using US price weights	Paasche volume index own country price weights	Fisher geometric mean	Paasche PPP own country quantity weights	Laspeyres PPP US quantity mean weights	Fisher geometric
Argentina	35.8	28.8	32.1	34.43	42.75	38.37
Brazil	54.3	42.7	48.1	6.91	8.77	7.79
India	9.5	5.0	6.9	6.70	12.77	9.25
Indonesia	12.3	8.6	10.3	374.99	535.29	448.02
Korea	12.4	9.3	10.7	436.50	584.80	505.20
Mexico	43.9	33.7	38.4	11.97	15.60	13.67
France	79.8	72.2	75.9	4.18	4.61	4.39
Germany	86.6	83.2	84.7	2.34	2.43	2.39
Japan	73.7	53.4	62.6	196.40	269.50	230.10
Netherlands	86.3	76.5	81.2	2.48	2.80	2.64
UK	52.6	46.0	49.2	.436	.499	.466
USA	100.0	100.0	100.0	1.00	1.00	1.00

Sources: As for Table 2.4, except for Japan and Korea (Pilat, 1993) and the UK (van Ark, November 1990). Value added is adjusted here to the 'present national accounts concept'; for Japan, Korea and the USA the adjustment was made by using the ratio of service inputs to census value added from the input–output tables for these countries (Szirmai and Pilat, 1990).

Table 2.5 shows the manufacturing results for 1975 using three alternative UVR variants, the Paasche (at own country prices and US quantity weights), the Laspeyres (US prices and own country weights) and the Fisher (geometric average of the Paasche and Laspeyres measures). One can see that the Paasche UVR is more favourable for the follower countries than the Laspeyres UVR. This is due to the well-known Gerschenkron effect, due to the inverse relation of relative prices and quantities (high prices reduce demand), which one also finds in Table 2.2 for agriculture and in ICP studies.

Construction

This industry is engaged in building and repairing houses, offices, hotels, schools, hospitals, factories, roads and other kinds of government and private infrastructure etc. Its output is very heterogeneous. Designs, standards, types of building materials vary more between countries than for products where there is more international trade. The relative importance of site preparation or demolition varies a good deal from project to project. The average establishment is relatively small. In 1986, there were 492 000 in US construction compared with 355 000 in manufacturing, but employment was four times as high in manufacturing. For these reasons Paige and Bombach (1959) acknowledged that the construction sector was the most difficult they tackled.

Expenditure studies have devoted a good deal of effort to get detailed and well-specified PPPs for different categories of construction. This careful approach was characteristic of the Gilbert-Kravis (1954) study and has continued with the ICP (see Kravis, Heston and Summers, 1982: 48).

Pilat (1994) applied the ICP PPPs as a proxy for ICOP PPPs in his Japan/USA, Korea/USA comparisons. But it would also be useful to apply double deflation for this sector using ICOP PPPs for inputs of building materials.

Services

The service sector is the activity which has been most 'measurement resistant' both for the ICP and for our ICOP studies. The ICOP effort has so far been concerned with only nine countries, information is generally poorer for this part of the economy, and our procedures still need improvement. O'Mahony (1999) is another major addition to this field. It incorporates estimates for the whole economy (including all services) for France, Germany, Japan and the USA, for six benchmark years for the period 1950–96.

There are some services where the problems involved in comparing value added, relative prices and productivity are similar to those for manufacturing, and where census sources of information may be available for prices and quantities. This is true of electricity, gas and water supply, and sometimes for transport and communication. Most other service activities are comparison resistant, because it is difficult to measure output. This is a field which poses major problems for the ICP approach and has necessitated changes in ICP methodology in successive ICP rounds (see Heston and Summers, 1992).

Transport and Communications

The transport and communication sector consists of a range of transport services (railways, road passenger and freight transport, water transport, air transport and other transportation services) and two major communication services (postal services and telecommunications). Quantity indicators for postal services are pieces of mail, and for telecommunication a combination access lines and number of calls. The best quantity indicators for transport are based on passenger and ton kilometres, but transport indicators should be adjusted for differences in the importance of terminal services. Transport includes not only movement of passengers and freight, but loading and unloading at stations, terminals, ports and airports. The terminal element increases in importance when the average distance over which freight and passengers are carried is shorter.

Pilat (1994) contains comparisons for Korea, Japan and the USA without terminal adjustment. Mulder (1999) covers Brazil/USA and Mexico/USA and includes a survey of previous comparisons for this sector. He distinguishes between the movement of freight and passengers and terminal costs. He makes adjustments for safety, comfort and reliability of travel. Mulder's approach has been replicated by Van Ark, Monnikhof and Mulder (1999) for Canada, France, Germany, the Netherlands, UK and the USA. Table 2.6 shows unit value ratios and labour productivity by industry in transport and communication for each country relative to the USA. The unit value ratios are implicitly derived from the quantity indicators described above and the corresponding values. The results for individual modes of transport show a substantial variation in productivity. Lower productivity in European railways is due largely to the greater share of passengers compared to freight transport relative to the USA. Rail passenger transport is much more labour intensive than rail freight.

Table 2.6 Gross Value Added Per Person Engaged and Unit Value Ratios in Transport and Communication in 1992 (census concept)

	Gross value added per person engaged (USA = 100), Fisher geometric mean				Unit value ratio (units national currency per US dollar), Fisher variant			
	Canada	France	Germany (b)	Nether-lands	Canada	France	Germany (b)	Nether-lands
Railways (a)	63.8	59.6	27.8	80.7	1.45	8.24	4.24	1.42
Road passengers	98.5	100.3	133.9	146.4	1.07	5.20	1.17	1.22
Road freight	118.6	83.1	63.8	141.2	0.82	7.23	3.57	1.43
Water transport	97.8	46.4	58.0	67.4	1.33	10.49	5.82	2.65
Air transport	100.4	88.5	106.9	106.5	1.06	7.74	2.98	2.37
Total (c)	107.1	71.4	66.3	111.6	1.02	9.16	3.07	1.68
Communication	97.8	79.0	63.1	88.1	1.02	5.27	2.11	1.76
Transport and Communication	101.2	76.4	65.8	97.8	1.03	7.21	2.63	1.70
Exchange rate					1.21	5.29	1.56	1.76

Notes: (a) adjusted for terminal element; (b) territory of Federal Republic; (c) includes ancillary activities.

Sources: Van Ark, Monnikhof and Mulder (1999), Table 3.

Wholesale and Retail Trade

When one looks at the economy from the expenditure side as the ICP approach does, the share of services is smaller than it appears from the production side. Distribution accounts for a good deal of this difference. It is 'disguised' in the ICP approach because its value added is incorporated in final expenditure. Thus ICP values consumption of bread, rice, butter, meat, eggs and milk at retail market prices whereas the ICOP approach allocates value added to three different sectors: agriculture, food processing, and distributive activity. Kravis, Heston and Summers (1982) assumed that distributive margins were the same in all countries. Their basic procedure was the potato-is-a-potato rule: 'A potato with given physical characteristics was treated not only as the same product, but also as the same quantity, whether it was purchased in the country or in the city, in January, or in June, by the piece or by the bushel, and whether it was purchased at a retail market or consumed out of own production' (p. 31).

Because of these ICP assumptions and procedures there is a basic difference of approach to this sector in ICP and ICOP. Mulder and Maddison (1993) is a survey of previous attempts to measure distributive performance both intertemporally and internationally. Many other attempts simply used ICP purchasing power parities for different categories of traded items and reweighted them as a proxy for measuring gross output in this sector. This procedure implies acceptance of the potato-is-a-potato rule. Mulder and Maddison (1993) compared it with the results of a double deflated approach in a comparison between Mexico and the USA. They converted traders' sales values by detailed category (from the relevant censuses) using ICP PPPs for the corresponding items, and converted traders purchases by PPPs derived from the relevant ICOP studies for agriculture and manufacturing. They applied the same procedure for other inputs such as transport. The results of the two methods, i.e. single and double deflation, showed a substantial discrepancy. This was also true for Brazil (see Mulder, 1999).

Van Ark, Monnikhof and Mulder (1999) used a variant of the Maddison and Mulder approach for Canada, France, Germany, the Netherlands, UK and the USA. They obtained information on gross margins, i.e. sales minus purchases of goods destined for resale and changes in inventories for some 30 to 50 individual industries in retail and wholesale trade. They applied a double deflation procedure to obtain the purchasing power parities for retail trade. The conversion factors for sales represent selected expenditure PPPs for goods. For purchases they used unit value ratios (UVRs) for manufacturing from earlier ICOP studies for these countries. For wholesale trade, a single deflation procedure, using ICOP UVRs, was applied for the gross margin. Table 2.7 shows results based on a further refinement of the procedure used by Van Ark, Monnikhof and Mulder. ICP expenditure PPPs and ICOP UVRs are applied to sales in retail trade and purchases in wholesale trade, respectively. The sales in wholesale trade as well as the purchases in retail trade are converted to US dollars by an intermediate PPP, which is derived from the mark-ups in both subsectors (see Table 2.7).

Finance, Banking and Insurance

Pilat (1994) measured financial services by the volume of monetary transactions. For this purpose he used the monetary indicator M2, which is the sum of cash in circulation, demand deposits and various kinds of time and savings deposits, which he converted using ICP GDP PPPs. His separate comparison for insurance was based on the total number of life insurance policies. Mulder (1999) applies a more sophisticated transaction approach, which quantified the volume of services performed by each banking function. For banking output he estimated the number of cheques cashed, demand deposits, time deposits and commercial loans. For insurance his indicators were life and health policies. Future work needs a further differentiation of the quantitative importance of these transactions.

Table 2.7 *Gross Margins Per Person Engaged and Unit Value Ratios in Retail and Wholesale Trade in 1992 (census concept)*

	Gross margins per person engaged (USA = 100), Fisher geometric mean				Unit value ratio (units national currency per US dollar), Fisher variant			
	Canada	France	Germany (a)	Nether- lands	Canada	France	Germany (a)	Nether- lands
Retail Trade	57.3	95.9	86.7	70.7	1.67	7.43	2.90	2.07
Wholesale Trade	50.4	75.5	62.9	71.3	1.86	6.44	2.66	2.65
Total Trade	55.3	90.1	80.9	78.3	1.76	6.91	2.84	2.38
Exchange Rate					1.21	5.29	1.56	1.76

Notes: (a) territory of Federal Republic. 'Gross margins' refer to the value of sales minus the value of purchases and inventory adjustment. UVRs are Fisher indexes, i.e. geometric averages of the UVRs at national weights and at weights of the USA. PPPs for retail trade and wholesale trade are obtained by separate weighting of sales and purchases in each sector. Retail sales are converted by ICP PPPs, wholesale purchases are converted by ICOP UVRs for manufacturing. Retail purchases and wholesale sales are converted by the geometric average of ICOP UVRs adjusted for intercountry differences in mark-ups in wholesale trade, and of ICP PPPs, similarly adjusted, for retail trade. Retail sales PPPs are adjusted, where appropriate, for value added or sales taxes. European statistics refer to 'enterprises', Canadian and US to 'establishments'. The US and Canadian wholesale figures relate only to merchant wholesalers, and exclude manufacturing subsidiaries and commission agents.

Sources: Revised version of Van Ark, Monnikhof and Mulder (1999), Table 6, with adjustments as described above.

Housing Services and Commercial Real Estate

For housing there is often information in population censuses, which breaks down the stock into different categories by type of building or access to water, electricity etc. The material in the housing censuses for Brazil, Mexico and the USA is more or less adequate to make quantitative comparisons with adjustments for quality and these can be used with national accounts information on rents or imputed rents to get purchasing power parities.

In his Japan/USA comparisons, Pilat (1994) used an estimate of housing stock in the two countries from Maddison (1992) which was based on the perpetual inventory technique. Information on the stock of commercial business premises is more difficult to assess.

Education

This is a sector where most of the value added consists of payment for labour services and where the discrepancy between the scope of the ICP expenditure measure and the industry of origin ICOP approach is not as great as in many others (though the difference between market price and factor cost valuations may be large because of subsidies). The ICP approach to this 'comparison resistant' sector has been to measure output by employment inputs or adjusted employment inputs. Pilat (1994) innovated in measuring output in this sector by using IEA measures of educational achievement to correct for differences in cognitive outcomes. These IEA measures are based on tests of thousands of pupils at primary and secondary levels in a number of subjects, and are a very useful basis for qualitative adjustment. However, for Brazil and Mexico, such studies are not available and the quality adjustment is based on drop-out rates, i.e. not counting pupils who effectively learn nothing by dropping out before they are literate or numerate.

Health

This is also a comparison resistant sector where ICP uses inputs (employment with some adjustment) as its proxy measure of output. This assumes more or less equi-productivity in different countries. Pilat (1994) used ICP PPPs as a proxy for ICOP purposes. The World Bank, *World Development Report 1993; Investing in Health*, provided a vast range of new material and a new measure 'DALY' (disability adjusted life year) which can be used in future studies as a quality adjustment for health analogous to that which Pilat (1994) used for education.

Defence and General Government

This is perhaps the most comparison-resistant sector, and ICP practice has generally been to use employment (weighted by education level) as an indicator for output. It is not easy to think of better measures though the US government has developed programmes for measuring public sector productivity (see Kendrick, 1989). In Maddison (1970) it was assumed that productivity in these services was related to that in commodity production. Pilat (1994) used ICP PPPs as a proxy for an ICOP measure.

Other Services

These are a mix of personal services – household and recreational, hotels and restaurants, tourism, etc. as well as business, legal and social services which are measurement resistant. Pilat (1994) used ICP PPPs as a proxy for ICOP PPPs in this instance.

The Economy as a Whole

For 1975 the ICOP research group has constructed a complete set of comparisons by industry of origin which add up to the total economy for five countries (Brazil, Korea, Japan, Mexico and the USA). Table 2.8 presents a comprehensive review of these results for major sectors for 1975. The estimates show labour productivity in Korea at less than one-fifth, Brazil and Mexico at about one-third, and Japan at about two-thirds of the US level. In fact the 1975 results are available with three alternative binary PPP options, i.e. Paasche, Laspeyres and Fisher. Our comparison is in terms of the Paasche PPP, but the ICOP and ICP results would be similar if the other binary PPPs had been used.

Table 2.8 Comprehensive ICOP Results for Five Countries, 1975

	Agriculture	Forestry & fishing	Mining	Manufac- turing	Services (a)	Total economy
(A) Value added (million international dollars converted with Paasche UV)						
Brazil	18 303	1 160	1 036	38 100	133 103	191 702
Mexico	6 024	225	1 964	14 043	66 818	89 074
Korea	2 524	814	379	3 614	29 032	36 363
Japan	7 569	3 553	744	184 885	406 695	603 446
USA	46 981	4 405	37 718	336 063	1 074 517	1 499 684
(B) Persons Engaged (000s)						
Brazil	12 468	805	93	3 824	18 550	35 740
Mexico	6 134	229	241	1 744	7 830	16 178
Korea	4 831	942	60	1 585	4 412	11 830
Japan	5 870	740	160	13 733	31 727	52 230
USA	3 208	299	752	18 302	65 465	88 026
(C) Productivity (Gross Value added in international dollars per Person Engaged)						
Brazil	1 468	1 441	11 138	9 962	7 175	5 364
Mexico	982	983	8 149	8 053	8 534	5 506
Korea	522	864	6 316	2 279	6 580	3 074
Japan	1 289	4 801	4 651	13 463	12 819	11 554
USA	14 645	14 732	50 157	18 362	16 414	17 037

Note: (a) includes construction and public utilities.

Source: First 4 columns from sources cited in Tables 2.1, 2.3 and 2.5. Col. 5 mainly from Mulder (1999) and Pilat (1994). These two studies contain a detailed analysis of all major economic activities.

In an earlier paper (Maddison and Van Ark, 1994) we provided a confrontation between the ICOP results and those of ICP (Kravis, Heston and Summers, 1982). These comparisons suggested that the ICOP output estimates, after conversion to US dollars, were substantially lower than those of ICP for Brazil, Korea and Mexico and about the same for Japan. Earlier studies by Maddison (1970 and 1983) reached a similar conclusion. However, given the small number of countries for which we have total economy estimates on an industry-of-origin basis, and with the remaining measurement problems in services, one cannot derive very firm conclusions on the possible causes for differences between ICOP and ICP estimates at this stage. In any case the ICP approach to international comparisons of service activity has undergone some change since 1975 (see Heston and Summer 1992, for a review of the treatment of services in successive ICP rounds). Our own research programme is strongly oriented to improvement of comparisons for the service sector.

CONCLUSIONS

In the past 15 years the ICOP methodology has been developed on a systematic basis so that it can be replicated by other investigators covering other countries. We have published detailed descriptions of our methodology for agriculture, manufacturing, transport, distribution and for some other service sectors. Our procedures are fully transparent and complete statistical appendices are generally available on request. All data, including the calculations, are on computer, so that they can easily be used to fill in data for other countries.

So far we have covered one or more sectors of the economy for 30 countries. Given the requirement of reasonably reliable production censuses or surveys we do not believe the ICOP approach can cover as many countries as ICP has done over the years. We have not yet found a good shortcut procedure for countries without adequate national statistics. Nevertheless, we know that the ICOP approach can probably be replicated for several more countries, which together with those already covered, would cover about three-quarters of world GDP.

ACKNOWLEDGEMENT

We are grateful for comments and suggestions from Dirk Pilat, Nanno Mulder, D.S. Prasada Rao and Eddy Szirmai on the present draft. We have drawn extensively on their research output and that of other members of the ICOP team, as acknowledged in the text and bibliography.

REFERENCES

Ark, B. van (1990), 'Manufacturing Productivity Levels in France and the United Kingdom', *National Institute Economic Review*, **133**, 71–85.

Ark, B. van (1990), 'Comparative Levels of Manufacturing Productivity in Postwar Europe – Measurement and Comparison', *Oxford Bulletin of Economics and Statistics*, November, 343–73.

Ark, B. van (1992), 'Comparative Productivity in British and American Manufacturing', *National Institute Economic Review*, November.

Ark, B. van (1993), *International Comparisons of Output and Productivity*, Groningen Growth and Development Centre, Monograph Series No. 1, University of Groningen.

Ark, B. van (1995), 'Produccion y productividad en el sector manufacturero español. Un analisis comparativo 1950–1992', *Información Comercial Española. La actividad empresarial en España*, **746**, Madrid, 67–77.

Ark, B, van (1996), 'Convergence and Divergence in the European Periphery: Productivity in Eastern and Southern Europe in Retrospect' in B. van Ark and N.F.R. Crafts (eds), *Quantitative Aspects of Post-War European Economic Growth*, CEPR/Cambridge University Press, 271–326.

Ark, B. van (1996), 'Issues in Measurement and International Comparison of Productivity: An Overview' in OECD (1996).

Ark, B. van (1999), 'Economic Growth and Labour Productivity in Europe: Half a Century of East-West Comparisons', *Research Memorandum*, GD-41, Groningen Growth and Development Centre.

Ark, B. van and N. Beintema (1992), 'Output and Productivity Levels in Czechoslovak and German (FR) Manufacturing', Groningen.

Ark, B. van B. and D. Pilat (1993), 'Cross Country Productivity Levels: Differences and Causes', *Brookings Papers on Economic Activity, Microeconomics*, 2, Washington, DC.

Ark, B. van and R.D.J. Kouwenhoven (1994), 'Productivity in French Manufacturing: An International Comparative Perspective', *Research Memorandum*, GD-10, Groningen Growth and Development Centre.

Ark, B. van and R.D.J. Kouwenhoven (1994), 'La productivité du secteur manufacturier français en comparaison internationale', *Économie Internationale*, 60, Centre d'Études Prospectives et d'Informations Internationales (CEPII), Paris.

Ark, B. van and A. Maddison (1994), 'An International Comparison of Purchasing Power, Real Output and Productivity in Manufacturing Industries: Brazil, Mexico and the USA in 1975', *Research Memorandum*, GD-8, Groningen Growth and Development Centre.

Ark, B. van, E. Monnikhof and N. Mulder (1999), 'Productivity in Services: An International Comparative Prospective', *Canadian Journal of Economics*, 32 (2), 471–99.

Barnett, G.E. (1936), *Two Tracts by Gregory King*, Baltimore: Johns Hopkins.

Beintema, N. and B. van Ark (1993), 'Comparative Productivity in East and West German Manufacturing Before Reunification', *Research Memorandum*, GD-5, Groningen Growth and Development Centre, Reprinted in *Discussion Paper Series*, London: CEPR, February 1994.

Birnie, J.E. (1996), 'Comparative Productivity in Ireland: the Impact of Transfer Pricing and Foreign Ownership', in K. Wagner and B. van Ark (eds), *International Productivity Differences. Measurement and Explanations*, Amsterdam: North Holland, 194–223.

Blades, D. and D. Roberts (1987), 'A Note on the New OECD Benchmark Parities for 1985', *OECD Economic Studies*.

Clark, C. (1940), *The Conditions of Economic Progress*, London: Macmillan.

Fabricant, S. (1940), *The Output of Manufacturing Industries 1899–1937*, New York: NBER.

Freudenberg, M. and D. Ünal-Kecensi (1994), 'France-Allemagne: prix et productivité dans le secteur manufacturier', *Economie Internationale*, 60, CEPII, 33–70.

Gersbach, H. and B. van Ark (1994), 'Micro foundations for international productivity comparisons', *Research Memorandum*, GD-11, Groningen Growth and Development Centre.

Gilbert, M. and I.B. Kravis (1954), *An International Comparison of National Products and the Purchasing Power of Currencies*, Paris: OEEC.

Heston, A. and R. Summers (1992), 'Measuring Final Product Series for International Comparisons', in Z. Griliches (ed.), *Output and Measurement in the Service Sectors*. NBER Studies in Income and Wealth, 56, Chicago: University of Chicago Press.

Houben, A. (1990), 'An International Comparison of Real Output, Labour Productivity and Purchasing Power in the Mineral Industries of the United States, Brazil and Mexico for 1975', *Research Memorandum 368*, Groningen: Institute of Economic Research.

Jong, G. de (1996), 'Canada's Postwar Manufacturing Performance. A Comparison with the United States', *Research Memorandum*, GD-32, Groningen Growth and Development Centre.

Kendrick, J. (1989), 'Appraising the US Output and Productivity Estimates for Government – Where Do We Go from Here?', paper presented at Lahnstein: IARIW.

Kouwenhoven, R. (1993), 'Analysing Dutch Manufacturing Productivity', M.A. Thesis, University of Groningen.

Kouwenhoven, R. (1997), 'A Comparison of Soviet and US Industrial Performance, 1928–90', *Jahrbuch für Wirtschaftsgeschichte*, 2, 107–44.

Kravis, I.B., A. Heston and R. Summers (1982), *World Product and Income: International Comparisons of Real Gross Product*, Baltimore: Johns Hopkins.

Kravis, I.B. and R.E. Lipsey (1991), 'The International Comparison Program: Current Status and Problems', in P.E. Hooper and J.D. Richardson (eds), *International Economic Transactions: Issues in Measurement and Empirical Research*, Chicago: University of Chicago Press.

Liberda, B.Z., E.J. Monnikhof and B. van Ark (1996), 'Manufacturing Productivity Performance in Poland and West-Germany in 1989', *Economic Discussion Papers* 25, Faculty of Economic Sciences, University of Warsaw.

McKinsey Global Institute (1993), *Manufacturing Productivity*, Washington, DC.

Maddison, A. (1970), *Economic Progress and Policy in Developing Countries*, London: Allen and Unwin.

Maddison, A. (1983), 'A Comparison of Levels of GDP Per Capita in Developed and Developing Countries, 1700–1980', *Journal of Economic History*, **43** (1), 27.

Maddison, A. (1992), 'Standardised Estimates of Fixed Investment and Capital Stock at Constant Prices: A Long Run Survey for Six Countries', paper presented at Flims: IARIW.

Maddison, A. (1998), *Chinese Economic Performance in the Long Run*, Paris: OECD Development Centre.

Maddison, A. and B. van Ark (1988), *Comparisons of Real Output in Manufacturing*, Policy, Planning and Research Working Papers 5, Washington, DC: World Bank.

Maddison, A. and B. van Ark (1989), 'International Comparison of Purchasing Power, Real Output and Labour Productivity: A Case Study of Brazilian, Mexican and US Manufacturing, 1975', *Review of Income and Wealth*, **35**, 31–55.

Maddison, A. and H. van Ooststroom (1993), 'The International Comparison of Value Added, Productivity, and Purchasing Power Parities in Agriculture', *Research Memorandum GD-1*, Groningen Growth and Development Centre.

Maddison, A. and D.S. Prasada Rao (1996), 'A Generalized Approach to the International Comparison of Agricultural Output and Productivity', *Research Memorandum*, GD-27, Groningen Growth and Development Centre.

Maliranta (1994), 'Comparative Levels of Labour Productivity in Swedish, Finnish and American Manufacturing', Helsinki School of Economics, mimeographed.

Mulder, N. (1994), 'Transport and Communications in Mexico and the USA: Value Added, PPPs and Labour Productivity, 1970–90', *Research Memorandum GD-18*, Groningen Growth and Development Centre.

Mulder, N. (1999), *The Economic Performance of the Service Sector in Brazil, Mexico and the USA: A Comparative Historical Perspective*, Groningen Growth and Development Centre, Monograph Series No. 4, University of Groningen.

Mulder, N. and A. Maddison (1993), 'The International Comparison of Performance in Distribution', *Research Memorandum GD-2*, Groningen Growth and Development Centre.

Mulhall, M.G. (1896), *Industries and Wealth of Nations*, London: Longmans Green.

OECD (1996), *Industry Productivity: International Comparison and Measurement Issues*, Paris.

O'Mahony, M. (1992), 'Productivity Levels in British and German Manufacturing Industry', *National Institute Economic Review*.

O'Mahony, M. (1999), *Britain's Relative Productivity Performance, 1950–1996: An International Perspective*, London: NIESR.

Ooststroom, H. van and A. Maddison (1984), 'An International Comparison of Levels of Real Output and Productivity in Agriculture in 1975', *Research Memorandum 162*, Groningen: Institute of Economic Research.

Paige, D. and G. Bombach (1959), *A Comparison of National Output and Productivity of the United Kingdom and United States*, Paris: OEEC.

Peres Lopes, R. (1994), 'Manufacturing Productivity in Portugal in a Comparative Perspective', *Notas Economicas*, **4**, Universidade de Coimbra.

Pilat, D. (1991), 'Levels of Real Output and Labour Productivity by Industry of Origin. A Comparison of Japan and the United States 1975 and 1970–87', *Research Memorandum 408*, Groningen: Institute of Economic Research.

Pilat, D. (1993), 'The Sectoral Productivity Performance of Japan and the United States, 1885–1990', *Review of Income and Wealth*, **39** (4), 357–76.

Pilat, D. (1994), *The Economics of Rapid Growth: The Experience of Japan and Korea*, Aldershot: Edward Elgar.

Pilat, D. and A. Hofman (1990), 'Argentina's Manufacturing Performance: A Comparative View', *Research Memorandum 374*, Groningen: Institute of Economic Research.

Pilat, D. and D.S. Prasada Rao (1996), 'Multilateral Comparisons of Output, Productivity and Purchasing Power Parities in Manufacturing', *Review of Income and Wealth*, **42**, no. 2, June, pp. 113–30.

Pilat, D., D.S. Prasada Rao and W. Shepherd (1993), 'Comparison of Real Output, Productivity Levels and Purchasing Power in Australian/US Manufacturing 1970–1989', COPPAA, *Research Paper Series* l, Brisbane: Centre for the Study of Australia-Asia Relations, Griffith University.

Prasada Rao, D.S. (1993), *Intercountry Comparisons of Agricultural Output and Productivity*, FAO Economic and Social Development Paper 112, Rome.

Prasada Rao, D.S. and M.P. Timmer (2000), 'Multilateralisation of Manufacturing Sector Comparisons: Issues, Methods and Empirical Results', *Research Memorandum* GD-47, Groningen Growth and Development Centre.

Ren, R. (1997), *China's Economic Performance in International Perspective*, Paris: OECD Development Centre.

Ren, R. and A. Szirmai (2000), 'Comparative Performance in Chinese Manufacturing, 1980–1993', *China Economic Review*, 1–34.

Rostas, L. (1948), *Comparative Productivity in British and American Industry*, Cambridge: NIESR.

Shinohara, M. (1966), *Japan's Industrial Level in an International Perspective*, Tokyo: Economic Affairs Bureau, Ministry of Foreign Affairs.

Soete, A. (1994), 'The Evolution of the Competitiveness of the Belgian Manufacturing Industry in the Long Run, 1880–1990', paper presented at the Economics Department of the Catholic University Leuven.

Summers, R. (1973), 'International Price Comparisons Based Upon Incomplete Data', *Review of Income and Wealth*, **19** (1), 1–16.

Summers R. and A. Heston (1988), 'A New Set of International Comparisons of Real Product and Price Level Estimates for 130 Countries 1950–1985', *Review of Income and Wealth*, **34** (1), 1–26.

Summers, R. and A. Heston (1991), 'The Penn World Table (Mark 5): An Expanded Set of International Comparisons, 1950–1988', *Quarterly Journal of Economics*, May, 327–49.

Szirmai, A. (1993), 'Comparative Performance in Indonesian Manufacturing 1975–90', *Research Memorandum*, GD-3, Groningen Growth and Development Centre.

Szirmai, A., B. van Ark and D. Pilat (1993), *Explaining Economic Growth: Essays in Honour of Angus Maddison*, Amsterdam: North Holland.

Szirmai, A. and D. Pilat (1990), 'Comparisons of Purchasing Power, Real Output and Labour Productivity in Manufacturing in Japan, South Korea and the USA, 1975–1985', *Review of Income and Wealth*, **36** (1), 1–31.

Szirmai, A. and R. Ren (1998), 'China's Manufacturing Performance in Comparative Perspective', in M. Fouquin and F. Lemoine (eds), *The Chinese Economy*, London: Economica, 49–64.

Timmer, M.P. (2000), *The Dynamics of Asian Manufacturing. A Comparative Perspective, 1963–1993*, Cheltenham: Edward Elgar.

United Nations (1986), *World Comparisons of Purchasing Power and Real Product for 1980*, New York.

United Nations (1994), *World Comparisons of Real Gross Domestic Product and Purchasing Power 1985*, New York.

Wieringa, P. and A. Maddison (1985), 'An International Comparison of Levels of Real Output in Mining and Quarrying in 1975', University of Groningen, mimeographed.

3. International Comparison of Farm Sector Performance: Methodological Options and Empirical Findings for Asia-Pacific Economies, 1900–94

D.S. Prasada Rao, Angus Maddison and Boon Lee

1. INTRODUCTION

The present chapter has two objectives. The principal empirical aim is to quantify and compare twentieth century farm sector performance in seven Asia-Pacific countries (Australia, China, India, Indonesia, Japan, South Korea and the USA) using 1987 as our benchmark. The methodological aim is to explain the main alternative procedures for derivation of valid multilateral comparisons.

2. DATA SOURCES

The main data source is the computerised reporting system of the Statistics Division of the Food and Agriculture Organization of the United Nations in Rome (FAOSTAT). FAO maintains a user-friendly web site (URL: www.fao.org) from which users are able to obtain agricultural statistics free of charge. Detailed commodity level information in the form of producer prices, output, feed, and seed were downloaded from the FAO database for four years: 1975, 1978, 1987, and 1994. Choice of benchmark years was largely determined by the need to align the present work with estimates for other sectors. Year 1961 was the earliest year for which we had detailed FAO information. However, data for China in 1961 are of doubtful quality.

2.1 Commodity Price and Production Tables

Appendix Tables A3.1 and A3.2 show detailed FAO estimates of 1987 commodity production and farm prices respectively. They specify 146 agricultural products grouped under 11 different commodity headings.

Table A3.2 shows producer prices for our 1987 benchmark There are 86 commodity items for which we have quantities but no prices. Of the 86 missing observations, five were for the US (5 per cent), six for Australia (6.7 per cent), 41 for China (28 per cent), 10 for India (11 per cent), 11 for Indonesia (15 per cent), five for Japan (6.5 per cent), and eight for South Korea (10 per cent).

Maddison and van Ooststroom (1995) plugged the price holes mainly by the shadow price method i.e., they used the relationship between the missing price to the wheat (or rice) price in another country and used this coefficient to derive their shadow price. In some cases they used proxy prices. Partly as a simplification, partly by analytic preference, they expressed all the values in US (plus shadow) prices (i.e., in 'Paasche' prices, using the jargon of ICP). The price estimates derived using this procedure are shown in boxes in Appendix Table A3.2.

3. METHODOLOGY

The main purpose of this section is to provide a simple exposition of the two major aggregation methods used to derive internationally comparable economic aggregates. We describe the Geary-Khamis (GK) and the Elteto-Koves-Szulc (EKS) methods for aggregating price and quantity data to obtain purchasing power parities for converting value aggregates into a common currency unit. We also provide an evaluation of the relative merits of the two approaches. Our own preference is for the GK method which we analysed in greater detail in Maddison and Rao (1996).

3.1 Geary-Khamis Method for Multilateral Comparisons

This is the most widely used aggregation or index number method for international comparisons (see Kravis et al., 1982; Rao, 1993 and Pilat and Rao, 1996). Geary (1958) provided the underlying framework based on the concept of the purchasing power parity (PPP) of a currency. The approach was further refined in Khamis (1972) which describes the many interesting mathematical and statistical properties of the method.

Let π_j represent the general price level observed in a country. Then the price index 1_{jk}, for country k with country j as the base can be defined as:

$$I_{jk} = \frac{\pi_j}{\pi_k} \tag{3.1}$$

If π_js are known, then the indices can be computed. It is easy to see from equation (3.5) that:

(i) the index numbers are transitive; and that:

(ii)   they do not change if each π_j is multiplied by the same constant.

This means that it is sufficient, for index number purposes, if the ratios of π_js are uniquely determined through the use of an appropriate method.

Geary (1958) defines purchasing power of currency j, denoted by PPP_j, as the reciprocal of the general price level in country j, π_j. Thus:

$$PPP_j = \frac{1}{\pi_j}; \text{ and}$$

$$I_{jk} = \frac{\pi_j}{\pi_k} = \frac{PPP_k}{PPP_j}$$

(3.2)

From equation (3.2) it is evident that if PPP_js can be determined then the necessary price index numbers can be computed.

PPP_j shows the number of currency units of j-th country currency equivalent in purchasing power to one unit of a reference or base country currency. Thus if the PPP of an Australian dollar in terms of the US dollar is A\$1.21 = \$1.00, this means that 1.21 Australian has the same purchasing power as one US dollar. Thus the PPP can be used as an alternative converter for expressing Australian value added in US dollars instead of the exchange rate.

The main question then is how to measure this PPP. The Geary-Khamis method derives PPPs using the observed price and quantity data. But the method introduces another concept known as the *'international average price'* of a commodity, denoted by p_i, for each i = 1,2, ...N. These international average prices are expressed in a common currency unit or a reference currency or a *numeraire* currency.

The Geary-Khamis method determines (for M countries and N commodities):

(i)   M purchasing power parities, $PPP_1, PPP_2, ..., PPP_M$; and

(ii) N commodity international average prices, $P_1, P_2, ...P_N$

using the observed price-quantity data.

The procedure provides an intuitively obvious set of interrelated equations to define the PPPs and the international prices.

International prices
Suppose the PPP_j's are known. Then international price of i-th commodity (i = 1,2, ..., N) is defined as:

$$P_i = \frac{\sum_{j=1}^{M} \left[p_{ij} q_{ij} / PPP_j \right]}{\sum_{j=1}^{M} q_{ij}}$$

(3.3)

The denominator of equation (3.3) is simply the total quantity of i-th commodity in all the M countries involved in the comparisons. The numerator is the total value of i-th commodity over all the countries, after each country's value, $p_{ij} q_{ij}$ is converted into a common currency unit using respective PPPs. This is repeated for all the commodities.

Purchasing power parities
With the Geary-Khamis method, the purchasing power parities, PPPs, are determined using the following equation. For country j, PPP_j, is defined as:

$$PPP_j = \frac{\sum_{i=1}^{N} P_{ij} q_{ij}}{\sum_{i=1}^{N} P_i q_{ij}} \qquad (3.4)$$

The numerator in equation (3.4) is the total of value of all quantities in country j, expressed in the currency units of country j; and the denominator represents the value of country j's commodity bundle valued at international average prices expressed in some selected reference country (common) currency units. Thus the ratio in (3.4) provides a PPP for country j's currency.

Solving the Geary-Khamis system
The Geary-Khamis system consists of the (M + N) equations, (3.3) and (3.4), in the unknown entities PPP_j (j = 1,2, ..., M) and P_i (i = 1,2, ..., N). Further, these equations are interdependent in that values of PPP_js depend upon international prices, P_is, which in turn depend upon the unknown purchasing power parities, PPP_j's.

The Geary-Khamis system is meaningful only if a unique positive solution exists for the unknown PPP_j's and P_i's. This was proved in Khamis (1972) where it was shown that a solution which is positive and unique up to a factor of scalar multiplication exists for the unknowns in the system.

Thus Khamis proved that if one of the PPP_j's is set to unity, then the rest of the unknown parities and international prices can be *uniquely solved*. This offers a choice as to which country's currency is set to unity. If PPP of country 1's currency is set to unity, then PPP's of all other countries will be expressed in terms of country 1's currency. Similarly all the international prices give international average price of different commodities expressed in country 1's currency.

In most empirical studies, the US dollar is used as the reference currency for which the PPP is set to unity. However, since the PPP's are unique up to a factor of proportionality, ratios of the form PPP_j/PPP_k are independent of the choice of the currency selected.

Now we outline a simple method to solve the Geary-Khamis equations.

Iterative method
This method is an intuitive procedure based on the circular nature of the equations (3.3) and (3.4). The following steps are involved.

Step 1:
Start with any positive values for PPP_1, PPP_2, ..., PPP_M with one selected currency unit as the reference currency. If country 1 is the reference country, then we choose any set of positive values with $PPP_1 = 1.0$. The most obvious starting point could be to set all PPP_j's to unity.

Step 2:
Use the starting values of PPP$_j$'s in equations (3.3) to compute international average prices. Use these resulting international prices to compute the next round purchasing power parities using equation (3.4).

Then repeat steps 1 and 2 until the values converge, making sure that at each stage the PPP's obtained are normalised to make PPP$_1$ = 1.0.

Convergence and uniqueness
This iterative procedure is useful provided it converges, and converges to the same values irrespective of the starting values used. Khamis (1972) established the viability of the iterative procedure just outlined.

In fact, the speed of convergence is amazingly fast. Even with a large number of countries, the procedure converges in 10 to 15 iterations.

A numerical illustration
The following numerical example illustrates the multilateral comparison problem for three countries, USA, India and Brazil. Let us consider a purely hypothetical array of price and quantity information for wheat, potatoes, milk and lamb meat.

Item	USA ($) Price	Quantity	India (Rs) Price	Quantity	Brazil (Cruzeiros) Price	Quantity
Wheat	1.42	30	22	20	4	26
Potatoes	1.1	50	17	26	3.2	42
Milk	2.85	120	40	43	8	80
Lamb	24	140	380	30	80	45
Total value		3 800		14 002		4 478.4

Step 1:
Starting values of PPP$_j$'s:

PPP$_1$ = 1.0   PPP$_2$ = 1.0   PPP$_3$ = 1.0

Step 2:
International Prices from equation (3.3) with the starting values are:

P$_1$ = 7.72   P$_2$ = 5.35   P$_3$ = 11.12   P$_4$ = 85.40

The next set of PPP's are calculated using (3.4) and the above international prices are:

PPP$_1$ = 0.2756   PPP$_2$ = 4.2004   PPP$_3$ = 0.8683

After normalising these parities so that PPP$_1$ = 1.0 (divide all PPPs by 0.2756) then

PPP1 = 1.0   PPP2 = 15.24   PPP3 = 3.5

Step 3:
In the next step. International prices, using the new normalised parities, are:

P1 = 1.37   P2 = 1.07   P3 = 2.71   P4 = 2.67

These international prices can be used in deriving the next step parities by substituting these prices into (3.8). Then

PPP1 = 0.9898   PPP2 = 15.48   PPP3 = 3.21

After normalising these parities so that PPP_1 = 1.0 (divide all PPPs by 0.9898) then

PPP1 = 1.00   PPP2 = 15.64   PPP3 = 3.24

In the next step the PPPs converge. The final values of purchasing power parities and international prices with US dollars as the reference currency are:

PPP's:

$1.0 = US$1.0 $1.0 = Rs. 15.64 $1.0 = Cruzeiro 3.24

International Prices:

Wheat = $1.35   Potatoes = $1.06   Milk = $2.67   Lamb = $24.18

Properties of the Geary-Khamis method
The following is a list of properties of the Geary-Khamis method which can be proved using simple algebra.

(1)   The price index numbers underlying the Geary-Khamis method are defined simply as the ratios of the purchasing power parities. Index for country k with country j as the base is defined as:

$$I_{jk}(\text{Price}) = \frac{PPP_k}{PPP_j} \tag{3.5}$$

It is easy to check that the price indices in (3.5) are transitive and base invariant. The price index from the Geary-Khamis system can be derived as an algebraic expression when the number of countries involved in the problem is equal to 2. i.e., M = 2. Then using simple algebra we can show that

$$I_{jk}(\text{Price}) = \frac{\sum_{i=1}^{N} P_{12} \dfrac{q_{12} q_{i1}}{q_{i2} + q_{i1}}}{\sum_{i=1}^{N} P_{11} \dfrac{q_{12} q_{i1}}{q_{i2} + q_{i1}}} \tag{3.6}$$

In this case there is no need to compute the purchasing power parities separately.

(2)   The quantity index numbers are defined as:

$$I_{jk}(\text{Quantity}) = \frac{\sum_{i=1}^{N} P_i q_{ik}}{\sum_{i=1}^{N} P_i q_{ij}} \tag{3.7}$$

Quantity index numbers in equation (3.7) are also transitive. An intuitive interpretation of the quantity index number in (3.7) is that it is the ratio of the quantities in countries k and j valued at a common set of international prices, p_i.

(3)   The price and quantity index numbers, defined respectively in equations (3.6) and (3.7) satisfy the factor test that:

$$I_{jk}(\text{Price}) \times I_{jk}(\text{Quantity}) = \frac{\sum_{i=1}^{N} P_{ik} q_{ik}}{\sum_{i=1}^{N} P_{ij} q_{ij}} = \frac{\text{Value in country k}}{\text{Value in country j}} \tag{3.8}$$

(4)   The Geary-Khamis international prices and purchasing power parities satisfy the property that:

$$\frac{\sum_{i=1}^{N} P_{ij} q_{ij}}{\text{PPP}_j} = \sum_{i=1}^{N} P_i q_{ij} \tag{3.9}$$

The right-hand-side of equation (3.9) represents the value of quantities in country j at international prices, expressed in a common currency unit, whereas the left-hand-side represents the value in country j converted into a common currency unit using the PPP for the country. The Geary-Khamis method guarantees the same value aggregate whether obtained through a currency conversion of the total value or through a revaluation of a country commodity bundle at international average prices. This is generally referred to as the property of additive consistency.

In view of these excellent properties the Geary-Khamis method was selected in the 1970s as the principal aggregation/index number procedure for use in the International Comparisons Project (ICP) of the United Nations. It is also the main method used in international comparisons of agricultural production aggregates (see Prasada Rao, 1993) by the FAO in Rome. OECD uses the procedure in deriving purchasing power parities of currencies of its member countries (see OECD, 1990).

3.2 Elteto-Koves-Szulc (EKS) Method

Historical background
The Elteto-Koves-Szulc method has recently been increasingly used as an alternative to the GK approach to international comparison. It was proposed independently by two Hungarian statisticians Elteto and Koves (1964) and the Polish statistician Szulc (1964). The method is named after all three and is known as the EKS.[1]

Though the EKS method was discussed in the international comparison literature for over two decades, it has been adopted for use relatively recently for international comparison work undertaken for 1990, 1993 and 1996 by the OECD and the EUROSTAT. The EKS procedure is the aggregation method used in Eurostat comparisons. OECD publishes results of both methods.

A simple interpretation of the EKS index
We begin the description of the EKS method with an illustrative example. Within the EKS method comparisons between two countries are derived by using various link countries and the Fisher index number formula.

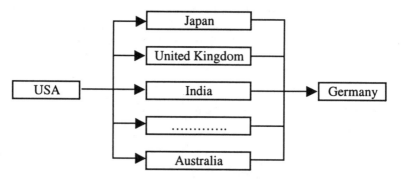

The figure above illustrates the basic structure of EKS comparisons. The method uses indirect comparisons between the USA and Germany derived using link countries, for example Japan, the UK, India or Australia. Comparisons involved in each of the links are derived using the Fisher formula. Since the Fisher index is not transitive, each indirect comparison produces a different numerical value for the comparison between the USA and Germany. There are M (equal to the number of countries involved) possible indirect comparisons between the two countries, but the EKS method uses an unweighted geometric average to yield a single comparison between the USA and Germany. Comparisons derived using this approach between different pairs of countries are then transitive.

Characteristicity and the EKS method

The EKS method has its foundations in the property of *'characteristicity'* discussed in Drechsler (1973). This property explicitly recognises the fact that multilateral methods for international comparisons which satisfy the *transitivity* property have a tendency to distort the binary comparisons involved. For example, if the USA and Germany are to be compared, the best or ideal way is to simply compare the price and quantity data for these two countries using any of the standard index number formulae (e.g., Fisher or Tornqvist indices). However, when these two countries are compared within a multilateral framework where transitivity is required, then comparisons between the USA and Germany should be consistent with other binary comparisons involving these two countries. For example, comparisons between the USA and Japan and between Japan and Germany should be consistent with the US-German comparison.

Drechsler (1973) concluded that transitivity necessarily influences the nature of all binary comparisons, thus leading to a loss in characteristicity. He suggested that such a loss in characteristicity resulting from the imposition of transitivity should be kept to a minimum. Preservation of characteristicity is the goal of the EKS method.

The EKS method – basic procedure

The EKS method in its original form used the Fisher formula, but a set of binary comparisons derived using the Fisher formula does not satisfy the transitivity property. Therefore, EKS derives a transitive set of comparisons using Fisher binary comparisons as building blocks in such way that the resulting comparisons *deviate* as little as possible from binary comparisons. Based on logarithmic distance, the sum of squares of the deviations of logarithms of Fisher indices, and the multilateral index numbers, the EKS method provides a formula for multilateral comparisons that satisfies the transitivity property.

For a pair of countries j and k (say USA and Germany), the EKS method uses the following formula:

$$\text{EKS}_{jk} = \prod_{\ell=1}^{M} \left[F_{j\ell} \cdot F_{\ell k} \right]^{1/M} \tag{3.10}$$

where $F_{\ell k}$ represents a binary comparison between countries ℓ and k using the Fisher formula. It is obvious that once the Fisher indices are known for all pairs of countries, the EKS indices can be calculated as the *unweighted geometric average* of all the comparisons between j and k derived through a chained comparison involving a link country ℓ $(1 = 1, 2, ..., M)$.

A numerical illustration

It is possible to illustrate the EKS method using the three-country and four-commodity example used for illustration of Geary-Khamis method in Section 3.1. The following matrices show all pairwise comparisons between USA, India and Brazil, as shown in Table 3.1.

Table 3.1 A Numerical Illustration of EKS

	Laspeyres	
1	9.779977	3.274029
0.081041	1	0.26191
0.302268	2.212939	1
	Paasche	
1	12.3395	3.308324
0.10225	1	0.451888
0.305434	3.818107	1
	Fisher	
1	10.98545	3.291132
0.09103	1	0.344026
0.303847	2.906757	1
	EKS indices	
1	10.49051	3.446407
0.095324	1	0.328526
0.290157	2.036757	1

Source: Indices derived using data from the example on Geary-Khamis method.

The four matrices above show the steps involved in the computation of the EKS indices. The first step is to compute the Laspeyres and Paasche indices using standard index number formulae. The Fisher index for each pair of countries (or element in the matrix above) is the geometric mean of the corresponding Laspeyres and Paasche index numbers. The EKS index numbers are then derived using the procedure described above. For example, if we wish to get the EKS index for India with USA as the base country (i.e. the first row – second column of the EKS matrix) then

$$EKS_{USA,INDIA} = \{[F_{USA,INDIA}F_{INDIA,INDIA}]\,[F_{USA,USA}F_{USA,INDIA}]\,[F_{USA,BRAZIL}F_{BRAZIL,INDIA}]\}^{1/3}$$

Now the corresponding Fisher indices can be substituted. Noting indices for countries with themselves as base are equal to 1, the above EKS index is then

$$EKS_{USA,INDIA} = \{(10.98545)(10.98545)(3.291132 \times 2.906757)\}^{1/3}$$

$$= 10.49051$$

Remaining elements of the EKS matrix can be similarly filled. EKS parities in the first row of the matrix of EKS indices are comparable to the Geary-Khamis parities calculated for the numerical illustration in Section 3.1.

3.3 The EKS versus the Geary-Khamis Approach: An Assessment of their Comparative Merits

Advantages of the Geary-Khamis method

The main advantages of the Geary-Khamis method are threefold. The first is that it provides an intuitively appealing framework to measure PPP's and international average prices. The purchasing power parities are defined using a formula that is very similar to the Laspeyres index. Average prices are defined as quantity weighted averages of prices observed in different countries. This approach is similar to that used in defining the average price of a commodity across regions of a given country. The principle underlying this kind of averaging process is known as *transactions equality*.

The second attraction is that the method produces PPPs for converting the principal aggregates, as well as international average prices, that can be used in defining internationally comparable aggregates at any desired level of aggregation.

The third and the most often cited advantage of the Geary-Khamis method is that it provides additive consistency. It provides internally consistent sets of internationally comparable national income accounts. The additive consistency property ensures that the total GDP when converted by the Geary-Khamis PPP is exactly equal to the value of all the quantities valued at international average prices. This property of additivity was the main reasons for the selection of the Geary-Khamis method as the main aggregation procedure in the International Comparison Project.

Criticisms of the Geary-Khamis approach

Over the last 20 years, the Geary-Khamis method has attracted a fair share of criticism.

(a) The major criticism is that the international average prices in the Geary-Khamis method are likely to be strongly influenced by large and rich countries. Since these prices are defined as quantity-weighted averages of national prices, it seems probable that international prices (and the relative price structure implicit in these average prices) will broadly reflect prices in larger and/or richer countries. While this problem is more obvious when only two countries are involved, it is not so obvious in comparisons involving many countries of different sizes and with varying levels of per capita income. An associated point is the possible presence of a Gerschenkron effect. If the international prices closely resemble prices in richer countries, then it seems likely that PPP adjusted output aggregates derived by the Geary-Khamis method will distort the levels for some of the poorer countries. Most empirical studies that attempt to measure these so-called distortions, e.g. overstatement of the real incomes of poorer countries, compare Geary-Khamis results with those derived from binary Fisher indices or EKS indices. Such attempts are somewhat flawed since they are based on the assumption that Fisher and EKS are true indices, an assumption that cannot be well justified.

(b) Some critics of Geary-Khamis argue that its theoretical foundations are weak. Diewert (1988) and Balk (1996) have shown that the Geary-Khamis method fails to satisfy some properties they consider relevant in testing the validity of multilateral methods for international comparison. Diewert (1988) proposed a comprehensive list of tests, in the spirit of Fisher's tests for index numbers, for selecting methods for international comparisons, and provided a comprehensive discussion of the performance of a number of main contenders including the GK and EKS methods.

Advantages of the EKS approach

Those who favour the EKS method generally argue that it has its roots firmly set in economic theory. This is the position of Caves, Christensen and Diewert (1982) who suggest that Fisher or Tornqvist binary index numbers are the most appropriate from an economic theoretic point of view. However, the Fisher formula does not provide transitivity property. So they suggest use of an EKS technique which generates multilateral index numbers that deviate least from their preferred but non-transitive Fisher indices.

The second advantage attributed to the EKS method is that it preserves characteristicity. This property came to prominence from the work of Drechsler (1973), and the EKS method sets this as its primary goal.

The third feature of the EKS method is that it offers equi-country weighting irrespective of the size of the country. Since the EKS index is a simple (unweighted) geometric average of all the linked or chained comparisons (irrespective of the link used), countries of all sizes and levels of development have an equal contribution to make in the construction of EKS indices. This was the main reason why EUROSTAT adopted the EKS method, because it is consistent with the political principles of equi-country treatment embodied in the constitution of the European Union.

Criticisms of the EKS approach

(a)   The major criticism of the EKS approach is that it does not have the 'international price' component. It is difficult to reconcile the EKS aggregates exactly with those for component subgroups because EKS does not have the property of additive consistency.

(b)   The second disadvantage relates the exaggerated importance attached to the principle of characteristicity. One of the basic premises underlying this requirement is that direct comparison of two countries provides the best possible outcome and a multilateral comparison should preserve this to the extent possible. However, when comparisons between fairly dissimilar countries are involved, a direct comparison is usually not very reliable. This can be easily seen from large gaps between the results of Laspeyres and Paasche indices. In such cases maintenance of characteristicity is not a virtue to be pursued at all costs. Recent research (Selvanathan and Rao, 1994; Hill, 1996) has established that it is feasible and desirable either to use a weighted averaging process to define PPPs or to use chained indices (based on the concept of a minimum spanning tree proposed in Hill, 1996). Both of these options are superior to the regular EKS index numbers.

(c)   A related point concerns the implications of according equal weight to all the countries. A consequence of this principle is that indirect comparisons derived using small countries like Liechtenstein, Andorra, Monaco and San Marino are given the same weights as those for the USA, China or Germany.

(d)   A further criticism is that the EKS method is the result of minimising the distance between the Fisher binary indices and transitive multilateral index numbers where distance is measured using the sum of squares of differences in logarithms of the indices involved (logarithmic distance between binary and multilateral indices). When distance is measured by an alternative procedure, e.g. simple Euclidean distance, the results are different.

3.4 Conclusions on the Merits of Geary-Khamis and EKS

In the present study, we have opted for the use of the Geary-Khamis method. It is particularly suited in instances where comparisons involve a revaluation of output quantities at selected prices. Historically, international comparisons of agricultural output have valued quantities using country prices (using either Laspeyres or Paasche indices) or have used wheat price relatives. This was the approach of Hayami and Ruttan (1985) who used a geometric mean of the prices in USA, Japan and India. The Geary-Khamis method is in fact superior to the Hayami and Ruttan approach (see Rao, Sharma and Shepherd. 1991). Further the Geary-Khamis method has the additional advantage of providing international average prices for all agricultural commodities which makes it possible to compute output aggregates for any sub-group of commodities with ease and flexibility which is not possible with the EKS method.

4. EMPIRICAL RESULTS

We focus on seven economies in the Asia-Pacific region which have been the focus of COPPAA research over the last few years. We cover the period 1961–94 in detail and extend the results to cover the period from 1900 using extrapolation methods. The primary source of data for 1961–94 is the FAO Statistics Division. The results presented here are all based on 1987 Geary-Khamis international prices, thus 1987 is the benchmark year for both the inter-country level comparisons as well as for the inter-temporal assessments.

Country Price Levels

In this section the PPP's and country price levels are presented for 1987 with United States as the numeraire country. Table 3.2 provides purchasing power parities (PPPs) and exchange rates for the benchmark year 1987. PPPs were derived by using shadow prices from Maddison and van Ooststroom (1995) to fill holes in the price data. PPPs are also presented at a disaggregated level for different commodity groups.

Generally, PPPs differ from the exchange rates. But a fascinating aspect of our tables is that the PPPs for India and China are reasonably close to the respective exchange rates[2]. Japan and Korea have PPPs much higher than the exchange rates, reflecting their high level of agricultural protection. A comparison of Japanese and Korean relative price levels (PPP/exchange rate) shows that both countries have high farm prices. Commodity specific PPPs and price levels are also quite useful in illuminating differences between farm products. For example, Table 3.2 shows that, in 1987, cereal prices were lower than the general level of farm prices.

Table 3.2 PPP and Country Price Levels for the Benchmark Year 1987

Commodity group	USA	Australia	China	India	Indonesia	Japan	South Korea
(PPPs = number of national currency units per international dollar)							
1 Cereals	0.73	1.02	3.07	13.24	1 106.06	1 919.38	3 880.55
2 Roots and tubers	1.07	2.86	2.44	20.76	1 264.05	1 132.11	3 655.14
3 Pulses	1.10	1.22	2.34	13.95	626.64	1 425.29	3 790.48
4 Nuts/oilseeds	0.85	1.01	3.06	15.12	1 640.15	830.34	4 338.11
5 Vegetables	1.27	2.33	2.15	16.35	2 623.53	807.12	1 413.66
6 Fruit	0.90	1.45	3.49	10.97	1 728.17	577.63	2 384.86
7 Other crops	1.61	1.16	2.49	11.31	1 540.79	1 085.58	2 053.41
8 Fibres	1.00	1.33	2.56	13.96	338.56	826.91	2 334.73
9 Milk and eggs	1.09	0.96	3.28	13.26	1 902.84	269.02	1 128.50
10 Meat	1.20	0.92	2.23	10.48	3 065.10	403.62	1 688.38
11 Honey, beeswax	1.56	0.82	1.84	11.11	–	2 242.55	8 210.43
Farm sector PPP	1.00	1.12	2.78	13.35	1 523.22	737.49	2 368.33
Exchange rate (USA = 1.00)	1.00	1.43	3.72	12.96	1 643.80	144.64	822.57
Country price levels (USA farm PPP = 100)							
1 Cereals	73.1	71.5	82.48	102.12	67.29	1 327.00	471.76
2 Roots and tubers	106.6	200.2	65.42	160.14	76.90	782.71	444.36
3 Pulses	109.9	85.8	62.75	107.60	38.12	985.40	460.81
4 Nuts/oilseeds	84.9	70.6	82.17	116.65	99.78	574.08	527.38
5 Vegetables	127.1	163.1	57.69	126.14	159.60	558.02	171.86
6 Fruit	90.4	101.8	93.87	84.64	105.13	399.36	289.93
7 Other crops	161.1	81.4	66.85	87.25	93.73	750.54	249.63
8 Fibres	100.3	93.5	68.81	107.68	20.60	571.70	283.83
9 Milk and eggs	108.9	67.6	88.05	102.26	115.76	185.99	137.19
10 Meat	119.8	64.7	59.92	80.85	186.46	279.05	205.26
11 Honey, beeswax	156.1	57.3	49.46	85.73	–	1 550.44	998.14
Farm sector PPP	100.0	78.5	74.61	102.99	92.66	509.88	287.92

Source: PPPs derived using Appendix Tables A3.1 and A3.2 using GK method. Exchange rates from IMF, *International Financial Statistics Yearbook 1996*. Washington, DC.

Performance of the Farm Sector in the Benchmark Year 1987

Gross output, inputs and value added for the farm are shown in Table 3.3.

All the aggregates for all the countries are shown in Table 3.3 at Geary-Khamis international prices calculated using the formulae described in Section 3.2. Feed and seed inputs were derived using FAO quantity data valued at international prices expressed in US or Geary-Khamis international dollars.

Table 3.3 Estimated Levels of Gross Output, Inputs and Value Added in Farming, 1987
(million 1987 Geary-Khamis international dollars)

	Gross output	Feed	Seed	Net output at farm gate	Non-farm inputs	Gross value added
Australia	15 204	446	185	14 573	6 840	7 732
China	156 020	10 647	2 415	142 959	29 805	113 154
India	77 090	954	2 550	73 586	7 288	66 297
Indonesia	18 763	261	113	18 389	2 532	15 857
Japan	15 956	1 967	60	13 929	3 765	10 164
South Korea	5 389	508	18	4 863	830	4 032
USA	133 893	15 492	1 078	117 323	32 407	84 916

Source: See text.

An alternative to our single deflation procedure would be double deflation of inputs and outputs, but application of such a procedure would require detailed price and quantity data on non-agricultural inputs. Single deflation was the main procedure used in all ICOP and COPPAA studies for manufacturing, and experiments for double deflation in manufacturing (where input ratios are much bigger) showed some odd results (including negative value added).

Table 3.4 shows the effect of using alternative aggregation methods to assess output and ranking of countries. The last three columns show differences in the results using Fisher, EKS and the Geary-Khamis methods.

Table 3.4 Alternative Measures of 1987 Gross Farm Output Using Different Aggregation
Approaches (million US$)

	Laspeyres	Paasche	Fisher	EKS	GK
Australia	13 245	14 685	13 947	12 674	15 204
China	147 893	178 662	162 551	170 730	156 020
India	83 567	75 188	79 267	81 859	77 090
Indonesia	16 453	17 401	16 920	19 093	18 763
Japan	17 435	18 946	18 175	16 342	15 956
South Korea	6 297	6 194	6 245	6 244	5 389
USA	133 893	133 893	133 893	133 893	133 893

Source: Gross output in national currencies derived from Appendix Tables A3.1 and A3.2, are converted into US dollars using PPPs compiled using different aggregation methods.

Several features in Table 3.4 are worth noting. The general ranking of the seven countries remains unaffected by the choice of the aggregation formula. This is hardly surprising given big differences in the size of the farm sector of the seven countries under consideration. Gross output values derived using the Geary-Khamis method are uniformly lower for all countries (except Australia) than those using EKS. Critics of the Geary-Khamis method have suggested that it has upward bias in assessing levels of real income or gross domestic product in low income countries. Exactly the opposite phenomenon is observed in our measures of agricultural output and value added. Finally, the EKS method is supposed to produce parities, and therefore value aggregates, closer to the Fisher parities and value aggregates. However, Table 3.4 shows that the GK method produces results closer to the Fisher measure than EKS in a number of instances, though EKS does produce results close to Fisher on the basis of all the binary comparisons taken together. These results demonstrate the need for care in interpreting the properties of the EKS method. As suggested in our conclusions at the end of Section 3.4, we recommend the use of the Geary-Khamis method. Therefore, the GK column in Table 3.4 is used for our empirical conclusions.

Farm Performance 1900–94

In the spirit of the other chapters included in the present volume, we have made aggregative extrapolations of our detailed value added aggregates 1961–94 to cover the period from 1900. In view of the difficulties in getting internationally comparable estimates of the amount of labour used in agriculture, farm sector performance is measured here in terms of value added per head of population. Table 3.5 shows the farm GDP and population figures and provides levels of agricultural production and per capita agricultural production from 1900 to 1994.

Table 3.5 Farm Gross Domestic Product, Population and Per Capita Product, 1990–94

				Farm GDP (a) (million 1987 Geary-Khamis international dollars)			
	USA	Australia (b)	China (c)	India (d)	Indonesia	Japan	South Korea
1900	–	1 130	–	23 312	2 912	3 504	–
1920	28 800	1 540	–	22 695	4 026	5 085	1 018
1935	31 529	2 807	47 347	26 964	4 973	5 732	1 265
1945	36 986	–	–	27 427	3 915	4 646	1 078
1961	45 298	5 820	37 737	37 692	6 680	7 049	1 634
1975	62 370	7 224	68 392	49 394	9 604	8 250	2 774
1978	73 568	9 426	71 379	54 912	10 500	10 161	3 422
1987	84 916	7 732	113 154	66 297	15 857	10 164	4 032
1994	91 319	7 016	151 210	86 915	19 502	9 464	4 886
			Population ('000 at mid-year)				
1900	76 391	3 741	400 000	235 729	42 746	44 103	8 772
1920	106 881	5 358	472 000	252 670	53 723	55 818	11 457
1935	127 859	6 732	505 292	297 808	65 192	69 238	14 738
1945	140 474	7 389	532 607	336 917	73 332	76 224	18 020
1961	183 691	10 508	660 333	444 000	97 085	94 890	25 566
1975	215 973	13 893	916 395	607 000	130 485	111 520	35 281
1978	222 585	14 359	956 165	649 000	140 425	114 920	36 969
1987	243 942	16 264	1 083 998	785 000	169 987	122 090	41 575
1994	261 558	18 012	1 191 835	913 495	191 524	125 188	44 501

Table 3.5 (continued)

Farm GDP per capita
(1987 Geary-Khamis international dollars)

	USA	Australia (b)	China (c)	India (d)	Indonesia	Japan	South Korea
1900	–	302	–	99	68	79	–
1920	269	288	–	90	75	91	89
1935	247	417	94	91	76	83	86
1945	263	–	–	81	53	61	60
1961	247	554	57	85	69	74	64
1975	289	520	75	81	74	74	79
1978	331	656	75	85	75	88	93
1987	348	475	104	84	93	83	97
1994	349	389	127	95	102	76	110

Sources: Population, unless otherwise stated, from A. Maddison, *Monitoring the World Economy 1820–1992*. pp. 104–15, Development Centre Studies, OECD, 1995, Paris. China 1994 from Maddison (1998: 169). India 1994 from FAO (1997). Indonesia 1994 from Van der Eng. South Korea 1994 from FAO (1997). 1961–94 estimates of gross farm output were derived from figures for each of these years on commodity output like those for 1987 in Table A3.1, with quantities for each year being multiplied by the 1987 prices shown in Table A3.2. Adjustment from gross output to value added was made for each year using the procedure demonstrated in Table 3.3. 1900–61 volume movement in farm GDP from sources cited below.
USA: Bureau of the Census, *Historical Statistics of the United States: Colonial Times to 1970,*. (Part 1), p. 232, US Department of Commerce, Washington, DC, 1975.
Australia: Butlin, N.G. Selected Comparative Economic Statistics 1900–1940: Australia and Britain, Canada, Japan, New Zealand and USA., *Source Paper No. 4*, ANU, Canberra, 1984 and Commonwealth Bureau of Census and Statistics, Rural Industries 1965–66. *Bulletin No. 4*, p. 163, Canberra.
China: Maddison, A., *Chinese Economic Performance in the Long Run*, p. 107, OECD, Paris, 1998.
India: Sivasubramonian, Chapter 6 of this study.
Indonesia: van der Eng, Chapter 7 of this study.
Japan: Yamada, S. 'The Secular Trends in Input–Output Relations of Agricultural Production in Japan, 1878–1978', p. 26 in Hou, C.M. and Yu, T.S. 1982. *Agricultural Development in China, Japan and Korea*, Academia Sinica, Taipei.
South Korea: Hayami, Y., Ruttan, V.W. and Southworth, H.M., *Agricultural Growth in Japan, Taiwan, Korea, and the Philippines*, p. 338–41, University Press of Hawaii, Honolulu, 1979.

All the countries in the study have increased farm GDP several fold since 1900. Per capita farm GDP has shown only moderate growth in five of the countries with a slight fall in India and Japan.

NOTES

1. However, the Italian statistician Gini had proposed this approach in 1924, so it may be appropriate to call it the Gini-EKS method.
2. This is in sharp contrast to the results from the International Comparison Program for GDP as a whole. The ICP results for GDP show PPPs for India, and other developing countries, to be well below the official exchange rates.

APPENDIX

Table A3.1 FAO Estimates of Farm Commodity Production in 1987 (metric tons)

	USA	Australia	China	India	Indonesia	Japan	South Korea
Cereals							
Wheat	57 361 800	12 287 000	85 900 000	44 322 900		863 700	3 374
Rice, paddy	5 879 000	549 000	174 260 000	85 338 700	40 078 200	13 284 000	7 595 760
Barley	11 354 300	3 417 000	2 800 000	1 669 400		352 900	717 139
Maize	181 142 000	206 419	79 240 000	5 721 300	5 155 680	1 000	127 390
Rye	495 980	26 010	1 000 000			35	1 183
Oats	5 424 400	1 733 000	500 000			6 030	
Millet (sorgh)	178 151	38 885	4 538 000	6 865 900		535	2 575
Sorghum	18 563 400	14 193 300	5 428 000	12 196 300		0	2 293
Buckwheat	33 867		1 600 000			18 400	11 627
Triticle		212 000	1 100 000				
Cereals, NES							5 352
Roots and tubers							
Potatoes	17 659 200	1 015 200	26 675 000	12 740 300	368 961	3 955 100	450 252
Sweet potatoes	527 400		4 682 114 440 000	1 490 600	2 012 850	1 423 000	542 617
Cassava			3 300 000	4 814 400	14 356 300		
Taro (coco yam)	2 860		1 200 000			391 500	0
Roots and tubers, NES			40 000		225 000	86 900	500
Pulses							
Dry beans	1 180 750	21 382	1 454 000	3 244 600	524 000	131 700	42 219
Broad beans		72 870	2 200 000			840	
Dry peas	208 000	486 840	1 652 000	388 000		1 830	2 366
Chick peas		54 066	0	4 531 800			
Cow peas	11 564	9 000				800	
Pigeon peas				2 271 500			
Lentils	77 000	0	48 000	659 300			
Pulses, NES			0	861 800	3 900	800	20 030
Nuts/oilseeds							
Cashew nuts			7 800	150 000	24 042		
Chestnuts			114 539			48 200	57 047
Almonds	500 000	4 864	15 000				
Walnuts	224 000	81	147 000	2 300			972
Pistachios	15 000		22 000				
Hazelnuts	19 780		7 200				
Areca nuts			61 414	219 000	10 000		
Nuts, NES	138 200	3 006	19 000				5 420
Soybeans	52 737 000	89 800	12 184 000	898 300	1 160 960	287 200	203 478
Groundnuts							
in shell	1 640 000	47 968	6 171 000	5 853 600	871 000	46 100	32 188
Coconuts			80 000	5 402 000	12 503 000		
Oil palm fruit			670 000				
Palm kernels			41 600		319 049		
Palm oil			166 600		1 506 060		
Olives	61 235	486	1 506				
Castor beans	0		330 000	195 200	1 400		24
Sunflower seed	1 183 000	137 487	1 241 000	635 300			
Rapeseed	12 250	65 914	6 605 000	2 604 700		1 970	7 803
Tung nuts	0		341 742				
Safflower seed	147 000	25 312	0	352 500			
Sesame seed	0		526 000	583 100		274	43 304
Mustard seed	25 954	283	0				
Melon seed			30 000				
Tallowtree seeds			680 000				
Vegetable tallow			102 000				

Table A3.1 (continued)

	USA	Australia	China	India	Indonesia	Japan	South Korea
Stillingia oil			102 000				
Kapokseed in shell					106 656		
Seed cotton	8 447 700		12 735 030				
Cottonseed	5 233 700	394 731	8 490 000	2 169 800	15 591		350
Linseed	189 000	7 781	460 000	316 600		0	
Hempseed			64 000				
Oilseed NES			519 000	179 300		30 000	28 118
Vegetables							
Cabbages	1 400 000	80 490	6 500 000	2 200 000	978 514	3 063 000	2 606 800
Artichokes	55 183						
Asparagus	106 460	6 145	1 260 000			35 000	
Lettuce	3 078 800	85 728	2 100 000			496 800	69 555
Spinach	176 000	2 752	2 145 000		89 950	400 100	64 926
Tomatoes	8 371 820	282 551	6 250 000	2 386 780	187 430	837 000	94 039
Cauliflower	334 500	112 240	1 400 000	2 900 000		140 700	0
Pumpkin, squash, gourds		80 360	1 000 000		190 847	276 800	60 266
Cucumbers, gerkins	576 470	15 550	5 760 000		267 976	1 026 000	173 226
Eggplants	34 500		3 850 000		158 285	607 200	20 537
Chillies, peppers	416 220	15 258	2 700 000		436 189	172 200	137 924
Onions and shallots, green			100 000			563 500	498 031
Onions, dry	2 046 290	181 711	4 700 000	2 700 700	412 522	1 307 000	525 321
Garlic	135 000		3 300 000	318 600	87 648		400 782
Leek, etc.			25 000		172 064		
Beans, green	116 000	32 728	420 000	46 000	112 605	99 000	
Peas, green	997 000	96 673	320 000	261 000		62 100	
Broad beans			61 482			14 000	
String beans	622 170		61 269				
Carrots	1 302 720	144 018	1 580 000		132 229	669 300	111 073
Green corn (maize)	3 311 000	52 418			220 000	404 300	
Mushrooms	278 700	18 258	275 000	1 500	3 500	80 900	13 895
Vegetables, fresh NES	2 500 000	106 333	51 500 000	43 000 000	550 000	3 830 000	3 244 000
Fruit							
Bananas	5 170	160 137	2 233 486	5 917 900	2 192 330	485	9 254
Oranges	7 157 000	478 918	998 126	1 500 000	559 000	354 700	
Tangerines, etc.	508 900	35 681	2 402 444			2 518 000	441 019
Lemons and limes	1 043 260	33 929	82 940	600 000			
Grapefruit and pomelo	2 346 000	33 170	82 170	70 000			
Citrus fruit, NES		145	181 180	85 000		423 300	3 571
Apples	4 872 600	324 741	4 265 000	861 404		997 900	556 160
Pears	851 400	144 582	2 489 000	72 676		476 740	144 856
Apricots	103 800	28 355	55 954	4 800			
Sour cherries	163 300						
Cherries	195 000	4 568		1 013		18 700	
Quinces		123	3 000				
Peaches, nectarines	1 253 700	67 836	630 000	90 300		212 400	137 774
Plums	886 000	27 976	670 000	33 995		66 800	37 088
Stone fruit, NES			2 600	1 000		10 900	
Strawberries	506 800	4 866	5 277			210 200	95 367
Raspberries	22 226	517					
Currants	45	491					
Blueberries	66 854						
Cranberries	153 900						
Berries, NES	20 135	373	3 300	1 000			

Table A3.1 (continued)

	USA	Australia	China	India	Indonesia	Japan	South Korea
Grapes	4 778 100	783 000	641 000	251 035		307 900	158 158
Watermelons	1 130 000	48 431	13 800 000			863 300	461 213
Cantaloupes, etc.	1 137 800	41 626	4 100 000	8 000		410 900	133 098
Figs	47 400	105	800	4 000			
Mangoes	13 610	6 991	315 000	10 113 300	515 949		
Avocados	189 600	9 798			56 600		
Pineapples	627 800	146 500	412 000	578 035	347 828	38 900	4 888
Dates	17 200		20 000				
Persimmons		233	820 000			290 200	75 677
Kiwi fruit	26 310	1 567				34 600	100
Papayas	30 800	4 473	117 412	276 346	321 000		
Fruit tropical, NES		4 536	1 167 783	1 131 000	957 000		
Fresh fruit, NES	25 677		267 193	5 700 000	1 500 000		32 140
Other crops							
Coffee, green	653		26 000	192 300	388 669		
Cocoa beans				7 000	50 199		
Tea			509 000	665 251	126 096	96 300	500
Hops	22 700	1 744	4 500			1 851	530
Pepper, white			4 000	31 340	28 976		
Pimeto, all spice	7 521		150 000	579 800	500	0	
Vanilla			250		1 836		
Cinnamon			20 000		27 033		
Cloves			500		56 970		
Nutmeg, mace, cardamons				9 270	15 404		
Anise, badian, fennel			16 000	28 000			
Ginger	0		63 067	142 840	53 000		7 500
Spices, NES			40 000	607 000	850		
Peppermint					1 900		
Straw, husks			12 000				
Tobacco leaves	539 260	12 160	1 943 000	461 800	112 691	104 400	78 039
Natural rubber			238 000	219 500	1 130 350		
Sugar cane	26 506 000	24 831 700	52 811 500	186 090 000	26 130 700	2 374 000	
Sugar beets	25 466 000		8 140 000			3 827 000	
Fibres							
Cotton lint	3 214 000	217 320	4 245 000	1 084 900	7 796		185
Flax fibre and tow		0	320 000			0	0
Hemp fire and tow			65 000	44 200		17	482
Kapok fibre					53 330		
Jute			300 000	1 042 700		0	
Jute-like fibres			269 000	177 300	22 641		
Ramie			567 000			0	42
Sisal			17 067		465		
Abaca (manila hemp)					424		
Fibre crops, NES		0	2 000	138 000			2 810
Wool, greasy	38 305	890 351	208 909	40 100	16 088	0	
Silk worm cocoons			116 988	73 000		34 726	7 203
Milk and eggs							
Cow milk, whole, fresh	64 731 000	6 363 000	3 301 000	21 200 000	235 000	7 334 940	1 413 130
Buffalo milk			1 800 000	24 123 000			
Sheep milk			487 000		66 000		
Goat milk			140 000	1 377 000	164 000		1 980
Camel milk			13 400				
Hen eggs	4 109 300	188 000	4 722 000	982 000	330 000	2 375 840	362 000
Eggs, excl. hen			1 180 000		122 000		1 715
Meat							
Cattle meat	10 734 000	1 541 110	671 441	1 147 430	167 420	549 514	208 228

Table A3.1 (continued)

	USA	Australia	China	India	Indonesia	Japan	South Korea
Buffalo meat			144 000	1 059 850	44 759		
Sheep meat	143 500	720 670	350 767	183 456	27 500	211	14
Goat meat		11 467	370 603	380 360	51 000	122	750
Pig meat	6 486 800	282 732	18 561 700	373 188	418 208	1 581 180	376 835
Duck meat	48 305	3 800	386 931		11 709		2 193
Geese meat			2 845 256				12
Turkey meat	1 679 200	21 000	4 420			33	
Chicken meat	7 145 000	355 250	1 572 630	194 709	377 099	1 425 930	215 804
Horse meat	71 536	27 482	49 800		1 198	4 766	
Ass meat			24 000				
Mule meat			22 500				
Camel meat			15 400				
Rabbit meat			101 002				3 598
Game meat	200 000						
Meat, NES			110 000	122 000		5 000	1 000
Honey, beeswax							
Honey	102 899	25 300	204 000	49 000		6 023	7 100
Beeswax	1 280	465	13 292	18 800			1 069

Notes: USA – 99 products; Australia – 89 products; China – 145 products; India – 91 products; Indonesia – 75 products; Japan – 77 products; and South Korea – 78 products.

Source: FAO 1997. *AGROSTAT*, Computer Data Base.

Table A3.2 FAO Producer Prices and Supplementary 'Shadow' Prices Received by Farmers in 1987

	USA	Australia	China	India	Indonesia	Japan	South Korea
Cereals							
Wheat	94	147	474	2 162		181 717	323 800
Rice, paddy	160	155	480	2 068	184 700	345 830	671 990
Barley	83	121	505	1 651	177 000	161 000	565 000
Maize	69	144	366	1 919	178 250	107 700	301 975
Rye	63	146	362		177 000	84 140	348 000
Oats	107	100	320	1 670	177 000	90 460	348 000
Millet (sorgh)	61	199	382	1 910		120 750	698 700
Sorghum	66	113	475	2 007		120 750	864 725
Buckwheat	52		412			311 111	897 500
Triticle		111	390				
Cereals, NES					177 000		1 00 000
Roots and tubers							
Potatoes	96	267	180	1 845	261 750	70 600	282 400
Sweet potatoes	220	651	170	2 190	169 000	160 500	293 600
Cassava			260	1 330	64 500		
Taro (coco yam)	158		200			134 800	304 530
Roots and tubers, NES			180		63 000	285 700	113 000
Pulses							
Dry beans	364	823	600	4 500	192 300	435 150	1 389 200
Broad beans		440	420			280 000	
Dry peas	154	213	543	4 500		440 000	665 700
Chick peas		250		4 070			
Cow peas	154	580				440 000	
Pigeon peas				5 085			
Lentils	203		420	5 000			
Pulses, NES				4 900	192 000	435 150	926 400
Nuts/oilseeds							
Cashew nuts			2 092	5 530	4 369 500		
Chestnuts			2 216			311 900	1 415 880
Almonds	2 315	6 398	2 092				
Walnuts	1 085	3 605	2 092	11 110			1 760 000
Pistachios	2 954		2 092				
Hazelnuts	1 069		2 092				
Areca nuts			2 092	5 530	4 369 500		
Nuts, NES	1 246	1 888	2 092				2 610 000
Soybeans	216	296	808	2 340	666 400	264 000	899 520
Groundnuts in shell	617	868	1 137	6 365	1 250 920	293 500	1 461 360
Coconuts			300	2 800	165 000		
Oil palm fruit			360				
Palm kernels			360		256 000		
Palm oil			670		425 000		
Olives	670	856	3 051				
Castor beans			3 051	5 683	250 000		797 000
Sunflower seed	183	247	866	8 220			
Rapeseed	179	241	980	6 140		222 000	469 000
Tung nuts			735				
Safflower seed	190	263		7 510			
Sesame seed			1 695	8 981	305 000	280 000	7 280 250
Mustard seed	165	450		6 124			
Melon seed			390				
Tallowtree seeds			390				
Vegetable tallow			390				
Stillingia oil			390				
Kapokseed in shell					107 900		
Seed cotton	610		2 842				

Table A3.2 (continued)

	USA	Australia	China	India	Indonesia	Japan	South Korea
Cottonseed	90	145	650	4 300	43 500		247 000
Linseed	129	246	750	6 320		122 870	
Hempseed			700			241 360	
Oilseed NES			700	7 510	250 000	163 474	557 000
Vegetables							
Cabbages	136	296	200	1 910	131 670	63 600	168 530
Artichokes	716						
Asparagus	1 274	1 600	240			736 500	
Lettuce	326	499	240			153 600	300 000
Spinach	348	411	240		336 920	247 800	273 600
Tomatoes	151	427	300	2 300	233 500	215 000	297 070
Cauliflower	549	360	200	1 910		135 200	
Pumpkin, squash, gourds	330	287	300		434 211	90 500	364 270
Cucumbers, gerkins	190	678	240		250 000	190 400	271 730
Eggplants	390		300		107 000	203 000	202 100
Chillies, peppers	520	717	300		1 228 500	257 200	220 000
Onions and shallots, green			400			147 570	168 270
Onions, dry	251	346	500	3 380	659 000	48 200	119 500
Garlic	490		1 800	4 500	1 286 494		708 000
Leek, etc.			240		659 000		
Beans, green	400	660	450	1 940	192 000	422 800	
Peas, green	247	279	450	1 940		591 600	
Broad beans			450			165 600	
String beans	403		450				
Carrots	185	317	300		229 000	89 200	392 270
Green corn (maize)	150	230			280 000	107 700	
Mushrooms	1 931	3 333	3 800	19 113	3 921 112	629 742	931 000
Vegetables, fresh NES	196	480	240	1 940	398 000	63 920	168 300
Fruit							
Bananas	653	791	911	1 860	352 000	122 670	1 639 887
Oranges	221	246	1 080	2 780	900 000	122 470	555 000
Tangerines, etc.	727	806	980			118 070	1 825 724
Lemons and limes	449	311	1 100	2 780			
Grapefruit and pomelo	193	240	728	2 780			
Citrus fruit, NES		300	980	2 780		134 710	610 468
Apples	209	624	1 757	2 170		106 200	445 530
Pears	214	529	1 362	2 170		189 300	596 733
Apricots	385	908	980	2 170			
Sour cherries	172						
Cherries	819	2 745		2 170		105 100	
Quinces		536	980				
Peaches, nectarines	300	738	984	2 170		262 900	446 200
Plums	340	1 082	700	2 170		386 800	729 000
Stone fruit, NES		1 080	980	2 170		262 900	
Strawberries	1 089	3 595	980			725 000	987 470
Raspberries	1 270	3 163					
Currants	1 650	744					
Blueberries	1 440						
Cranberries	980						
Berries, NES	1 140	1 400	980	2 170			
Grapes	274	248	800	6 850		686 000	653 600
Watermelons	100	238	259			99 000	394 400
Cantaloupes, etc.	230	790	370	2 510		264 100	255 730
Figs	331	1 756	980	2 140			
Mangoes	855	2 447	980	2 510	540 000		
Avocados	827	790			351 000		
Pineapples	158	292	984	2 140	180 000	118 000	396 787

Table A3.2 (continued)

	USA	Australia	China	India	Indonesia	Japan	South Korea
Dates	855		980				
Persimmons		536	980			195 100	188 917
Kiwi fruit	855	536				270 000	188 917
Papayas	362	770	980	2 140	200 000		
Fruit tropical, NES		274	980	2 140	252 640		
Fresh fruit, NES	280	274	980	2 140	252 640	284 000	260 000
Other crops							
Coffee, green	6 388		3 600	16 370	3 937 300		
Cocoa beans				17 000	2 427 800		
Tea			3 500	17 000	2 377 200	1 795 000	1 888 000
Hops	3 329	4 660	1 876			2 359 000	2 717 000
Pepper, white			2 850	39 507	7 228 500		
Pimeto, all spice	750		2 850	11 958	1 600 000	1 700 000	
Vanilla			1 760		4 463 800		
Cinnamon			5 323		2 481 300		
Cloves			5 323		6 147 300		
Nutmeg, mace, cardamons				54 000	3 333 700		
Anise, badian, fennel			2 850	26 800			
Ginger			2 397	7 825	1 051 182		834 861
Spices, NES			2 850	9 305	1 250 000		
Peppermint					1 250 000	3 950 000	
Straw, husks			2 000				
Tobacco leaves	3 467	5 350	2 000	8 769	3 096 300	1 963 000	2 750 000
Natural rubber			6 176	7 800	577 000		
Sugar cane	29	23	74	250	36 000	21 110	
Sugar beets	38		109			19 380	
Fibres							
Cotton lint	1 404	2 548	3 558	19 900	435 000		2 480 000
Flax fibre and tow			3 500			1 024 000	297 000
Hemp fire and tow			1 448	16 978		1 024 000	760 000
Kapok fibre					153 000		
Jute			500	2 390		355 600	
Jute-like fibres			500	2 252	324 000		
Ramie			12 800				1 443 000
Sisal			4 349	2 200	226 730		
Abaca (manila hemp)					291 600		
Fibre crops, NES			3 558	1 800	360 000		463 000
Wool	2 022	5 141	6 200	40 000	600 000		
Silk worm cocoons			4 879	22 254		1 457 000	4 223 000
Milk and eggs							
Cow milk, whole, fresh	276	204	536	3 130	357 000	89 700	322 000
Buffalo milk			530	4 150			
Sheep milk			468		357 000		
Goat milk			470	3 100	357 000		392 000
Camel milk			470				
Hen eggs	771	1 933	3 207	10 230	1 850 000	147 800	753 850
Eggs, excl. hen		2 000	3 207		1 699 500		690 000
Meat							
Cattle meat	2 435	1 739	4 300	10 320	5 500 000	1 178 000	3 298 680
Buffalo meat			3 800	10 320	4 150 000		
Sheep meat	2 808	1 030	3 164	28 090	4 144 000	1 180 000	3 600 000
Goat meat		1 030	3 259	28 090	4 300 000	1 180 000	3 600 600
Pig meat	1 822	1 718	2 150	18 990	3 607 600	464 893	2 403 020
Duck meat	970	1 769	3 209		1 832 900		2 975 500
Geese meat			3 209				3 100 000
Turkey meat	983	1 769	4 188			221 160	
Chicken meat	864	1 769	4 188	28 090	3 000 000	221 160	802 000
Horse meat	2 000	1 025	3 400		1 493 300	218 100	

Table A3.2 (continued)

	USA	Australia	China	India	Indonesia	Japan	South Korea
Ass meat			3 100				
Mule meat			3 100				
Camel meat			2 300				
Rabbit meat			2 100				1 791 800
Game meat	850	1 769					
Meat, NES		732	2 450	10 320	2 688 100	218 100	1 804 000
Honey, beeswax							
Honey	1 700	890	1 990	11 621		2 446 428	8 782 050
Beeswax	1 700	890	1 990	11 621			8 782 050

Notes: Prices in boxes are 'shadow' prices. These were used for products where quantities but no prices were available to these items. The procedure for deriving 'shadow' prices followed that of Maddison and van Ooststroom (1993) and Maddison and Rao (1996).

Source: FAO 1997. *AGROSTAT*, Computer Data Base.

REFERENCES

Balk (1996), 'Van Ijzeren's Method of International Price and Volume Comparison: An Exposition' in Rao, D.S.P and Salazar-Carrillo, J., *International Comparisons of Prices, Output and Productivity*, North-Holland, Elsevier.

Caves, D.W., Christensen, L.R. and Diewert, W.E. (1982), 'The Economic Theory of Index Numbers and the Measurement of Input, Output and Productivity', *Econometrica*, **50**, 1393–414.

Diewert, W.E. (1988), *Microeconomic Approaches to the Theory of International Comparisons*, mimeographed paper presented at the Expert Group Meeting on ICP Methodology, Luxembourg, 6–10 June.

Drechsler, L. (1973) 'Weighting of Index Numbers in Multilateral Comparisons', *Review of Income and Wealth*, **19**, 17–34.

Elteto, O. and Koves, P. (1964), 'On an Index Computation Problem in International Comparisons' (in Hungarian), *Statistztikai Szemle*, **42**, 507–18.

EUROSTAT (1982), *Multilateral Measurements of Purchasing Power and Real GDP*, Eurostat, Luxemburg.

Geary, R.C. (1958), 'A Note on the Comparison of Exchange Rates and Purchasing Power Parities Between Countries', *Journal of the Royal Statistical Society*, **121**(1).

Gerschenkron, A. (1951), *A Dollar Index of Soviet Machinery Output*, Rand Corporation, Santa Monica.

Hayami, Y. and Ruttan, V. (1985), *Agricultural Development: An International Perspective* (revised edition), John Hopkins University Press, Baltimore.

Hill, R.J. (1999), 'Comparative Price Levels Across Countries Using Minimum-Spanning Trees', *Review of Economics and Statistics*, **81**(1), 135–42.

Khamis, S.H. (1972), 'A New System of Index Numbers for National and International Purposes', *Journal of the Royal Statistical Society*, **135**(1).

Kravis, I.B., Heston, A. and Summers, R. (1982), *World Product and Income*, John Hopkins University Press, Baltimore.

Maddison, A. and Ooststroom, H. van (1995), 'The International Comparison of Value Added, Productivity and Purchasing Power Parities in Agriculture' in A. Maddison, *Explaining the Economic Performance of Nations: Essays in Time and Space*, Edward Elgar, Aldershot.

Maddison, A. and Rao, D.S.P. (1996), *A Generalised Approach to International Comparisons of Agricultural Output and Productivity*, Research Memorandum GD-27, Groningen Growth and Development Centre, University of Groningen, Groningen.

OECD (1990), *National Accounts – Main Aggregates 1960–1988*, vol. 1, Paris.

Pilat, D. and Rao, D.S.P. (1996), 'Multilateral Comparisons of Output, Productivity and Purchasing Power Parities in Manufacturing', *Review of Income and Wealth*, **42**, (June), 113–30.

Rao, D.S.P. (1993), *Intercountry Comparisons of Agricultural Output and Productivity*, FAO Economic and Social Development Paper, No. 112, Rome.

Rao, D.S.P., Sharma, K.C. and Shepherd, W.F. (1991), 'On the Aggregation Problem in International Comparisons of Agricultural Production Aggregates', *Journal of Development Economics*, **35**, 197–204.

Selvanathan, E.A. and Rao, D.S.P. (1994), *Index Numbers: A Stochastic Approach*, Macmillan, New York.

Szulc, B. (1964), 'Index Numbers for Multilateral Regional Comparisons' (in Polish), *Przeglad Statystyczny*, **3**, 239–54.

4. A Comparison of Real Output and Productivity Levels in Australian and United States Manufacturing, 1970–95

William F. Shepherd and D.S. Prasada Rao

1. INTRODUCTION

International comparisons of output levels, labour and capital inputs and productivity levels provide indicative benchmark standards for assessing countries' economic growth performance (Krugman, 1994; Young, 1995; Collins and Bosworth, 1996). Useful as are comparisons of rates of productivity growth between countries, they provide no indication of the levels of productivity from which growth rates are derived. Comparisons of productivity levels on the other hand enable assessment to be made of different countries' productivity standards at a given time and provide an indication of any industries within a particular sector of an economy in which productivity performance may be lacking by international benchmark standards. Nevertheless, all international comparisons face the same basic problem of how best to convert GDP and other sectoral aggregates expressed in national currencies into a common monetary unit or numeraire currency. Nominal exchange rates cannot be used for this purpose since they are strongly influenced by short term capital movements and merely indicate the purchasing power of national currencies over tradable goods and services.

Since exchange rates are biased for purposes of international comparisons, alternative methods are employed for derivation of conversion factors based principally on the concept of purchasing power parity (PPP) of currencies. Two major options are available. The bulk of international comparative studies has drawn on work of the International Comparison Programme/Project (ICP) of the United Nations (Kravis et al., 1982; UN, 1986; EUROSTAT, 1983; Ward, 1985) which estimates PPPs derived from final expenditure components in national accounts. These PPPs are then used to convert various GDP aggregates into a common currency unit. This final expenditure PPP approach permits meaningful comparisons of real output and expenditure levels among countries at a macroeconomic level. However, this approach cannot be used directly for sectoral analysis of labour or multifactor productivity comparisons since it does not produce real product by industry.

The alternative industry-of-origin approach is more appropriate for sectoral analysis and productivity comparisons since it employs PPPs by industrial sector of origin. This method, dating back to the work of Rostas (1948) and Paige and Bombach (1959), has been greatly extended by the International Comparison of Output and Productivity (ICOP) project at the

University of Groningen (Maddison and van Ark, 1988). More recently the ICOP industry-of-origin approach has been regionalised within the Comparisons of Output, Productivity and Purchasing Power in Australia and Asia (COPPAA) project (Pilat, Prasada Rao and Shepherd, 1993; Szirmai, Shepherd, Prasada Rao and de Jong, 1995; Timmer and Boon Lee, 1996; Wu, 1997; Boon Lee and Maddison, 1997). The COPPAA project is based in the University of New England in Armidale and Griffith University in Brisbane. As the name suggests, the project was established to undertake, in cooperation with the ICOP team, industry-of-origin comparisons of real output and productivity between Australia and her main trading partners in the Asia Pacific region.

The different outcomes that may arise from applying the approaches may be illustrated from recent studies of labour productivity in Australian and United States manufacturing. Drawing on ICP, GDP final expenditure based PPPs, and employing nominal exchange rates, the Australian Industry Commission (IC, 1997) estimated Australian manufacturing labour productivity (per person employed) to be some 66 per cent of the US level for the period 1990 to 1993. In contrast, Pilat, Prasada Rao and Shepherd (1993), using ICOP/COPPAA industry-of-origin PPPs estimated Australian manufacturing labour productivity to be some 48 per cent of the US level in 1988 and Pilat (1996), again using the same approach, produced an estimate of Australian manufacturing labour productivity of 52 per cent of the US level in 1993.

Highlighting the difference in productivity estimates that can arise from application of different methodological approaches is of interest in itself. It also offers additional perspective on the current view in Australia that policy induced structural adjustments from the mid-1980s have significantly raised productivity growth rates throughout the economy, in turn implying some catch-up in productivity levels between Australia and the world's leading economies Industry Commission (1996, 1997, 1997a), Productivity Commission (1998, 1998a) and Productivity Commission and Australian National University (1998). Consequently, the main objectives of this chapter are to illustrate and then draw on the ICOP/COPPAA approach to examine one element of this potential catch-up by comparing manufacturing sector productivity levels in Australia and the United States, the world leader in manufacturing sector productivity levels (The Conference Board Europe, Summer 1997, Winter, 1997). Detailed binary comparisons are made for the benchmark year 1987. Using appropriate national time series the 1987 benchmark is extrapolated backward and forward to derive productivity comparisons for the period 1970 to 1995.

The chapter is organised as follows. Section 2 reviews the industry-of-origin methodological approach to international comparisons, Section 3 describes the data sources, Section 4 provides a detailed discussion of the results and Section 5 concludes the analysis.

2. METHODOLOGY

This study adopts the ICOP methodology. Details of the ICOP approach may be found in Maddison and van Ark (1988), Szirmai and Pilat (1990), van Ark (1992), Pilat and van Ark (1992).

2.1 Price Comparisons at Sample Industry, Branch and Manufacturing Sector Levels

The initial step involves matching broadly comparable industrial products identified by the sample industries to which they belong. These industries correspond approximately to the four-digit International Standard Industrial Classification (ISIC) of the United Nations. These industries are then combined to form branches within the manufacturing sector, with the branches further aggregated to manufacturing sector level. The associated product prices are similarly aggregated through product, sample industry, branch and manufacturing sector levels. Prices for matched products – which are not specific prices but rather unit values – are obtained by dividing the sales value of the product (at the factory gate) by the quantity sold. These unit values are aggregated in each country and ratios of the aggregated unit values are used to produce a price index, or purchasing power parity (PPP), first for the sample industry, then using relevant ratios, for the branch and manufacturing sector levels in Australia relative to the United States as the base country. Output and productivity comparisons for industry, branch and manufacturing sector levels are then made on the basis of these industry-of-origin, sectoral purchasing power parities.

These procedures may be illustrated using the following notation and procedures. Let p and q represent commodity prices and quantities, with subscripts i and j referring, respectively, to the commodity and the industry to which the commodity belongs. Superscripts X and U refer to the two countries and m and n, in brackets, refer, respectively, to matched and non-matched industries. PPP^{XU} represents the purchasing power parity at sample industry, branch and manufacturing sector levels of country X (Australia) with country U (the US) as base. The various level PPPs may be computed by comparing prices in each country using country X quantity weights, i.e., to produce a Paasche price index, or country U quantity weights, i.e., to produce a Laspeyres price index, or by use of a geometric mean of these two price indices leading to the Fisher price index.

Sample industry PPPs
Given the above notion and procedures, purchasing power parity for sample industry j may be computed as

$$PPP^{XU(X)}_{j(m)} = \frac{\sum_{i=1}^{s_j} p^X_{ij} q^X_{ij}}{\sum_{i=1}^{s_j} p^U_{ij} q^X_{ij}} \qquad (4.1)$$

using quantity weights of country X (the Paasche price index), or

$$PPP^{XU(U)}_{j(m)} = \frac{\sum_{i=1}^{s_j} p^X_{ij} q^U_{ij}}{\sum_{i=1}^{s_j} p^U_{ij} q^U_{ij}} \qquad (4.2)$$

using quantity weights of country U (the Laspeyres price index). S_j refers to the number of commodities matched in sample industry j.

Once the PPP is computed using either formula it is assumed to represent the whole sample industry from which the commodities are matched, provided the matched products cover at least 25 per cent of the value of the output of the industry. For industries for which less than 25 to 30 per cent of output can be matched, the PPP of the branch to which the particular industry belongs is used as the PPP for the industry. Thus the PPP for a non-matched industry , j(n), is given by either

$$
PPP_{j(n)}^{XU(X)} = \frac{\displaystyle\sum_{j=1}^{b_k}\sum_{i=1}^{S_j} p_{ij}^X q_{ij}^X}{\displaystyle\sum_{j=1}^{b_k}\sum_{i=1}^{S_j} p_{ij}^U q_{ij}^X}
\tag{4.3}
$$

using quantity weights of country X, or by

$$
PPP_{j(n)}^{XU(U)} = \frac{\displaystyle\sum_{j=1}^{b_k}\sum_{i=1}^{S_j} p_{ij}^X q_{ij}^U}{\displaystyle\sum_{j=1}^{b_k}\sum_{i=1}^{S_j} p_{ij}^U q_{ij}^U}
\tag{4.4}
$$

at quantity weights of country U. Here b_k represents the number of sample industries that belong to the branch k.

Branch level PPPs

The branch level parities are obtained by a weighted averaging of the parities of the sample industries that belong to a given branch. The weights used are usually based on output shares, but since a single deflation procedure is used in this study, as in various ICOP studies, the branch level PPPs are defined using value added shares. The PPP for a given branch k is defined as

$$
PPP_{k}^{XU(X)} = \frac{\displaystyle\sum_{j=1}^{b_k} VA_j^{X(X)}}{\displaystyle\sum_{j=1}^{b_k} \frac{VA_j^{X(X)}}{PPP_j^{XU(X)}}}
\tag{4.5}
$$

using value added share weights of country X, and

$$PPP_k^{XU(U)} = \frac{\sum_{j=1}^{b_k} \left[VA_j^{U(U)} * PPP_j^{XU(U)} \right]}{\sum_{j=1}^{b_k} VA_j^{U(U)}}$$

(4.6)

at value added share weights of country U. In these equations, VA_j in equations (4.5) and (4.6) represents the value added of the j-th sample industry and PPP_j represents the j-th sample industry purchasing power parity based on equations (4.3) and (4.4), depending on whether or not appropriate matches are made. As before, if there are no matched products within a branch, the PPP for the remaining branches is assumed to hold for the branch. This is the case only for the branch entitled 'other manufacturing'.

Manufacturing sector PPPs
Following equations (4.5) and (4.6), value added weights for different branches can be used in defining purchasing power parity at the sectoral level. The following formulae are used.

$$PPP^{XU(X)} = \frac{\sum_{k=1}^{K} VA_k^{X(X)}}{\sum_{k=1}^{K} \frac{VA_k^{X(X)}}{PPP_k^{XU(X)}}}$$

(4.7)

using the value added share weights of country X, and

$$PPP^{XU(U)} = \frac{\sum_{k=1}^{K_k} \left[VA_k^{U(U)} * PPP_k^{XU(U)} \right]}{\sum_{k=1}^{K} VA_k^{U(U)}}$$

(4.8)

using the value share weights of country U. VA_k is the value added in branch k.

Fisher parities
In the definitions above, it is clear that price indices or parities based on US weights correspond to the Laspeyres formula, while the Australian weights lead to prices indices or parities based on the Paasche formula. As the own country and base country weights can be considered as two ends of a spectrum, a geometric mean of these two price indices, or parities, results in Fisher parities. These are defined at the different levels of aggregation, as

$$PPP^{Fisher} = \sqrt{PPP^{XU(X)} * PPP^{XU(U)}} .$$

(4.9)

In most of the tables in the empirical results sections below, parities resulting from all three formulae are presented, but for final comparisons of gross value added and productivity only the Fisher parities are used.

Price levels
Price levels at the different levels of aggregation, sample industry, branch or the sector as a whole, are defined as the ratio of the relevant purchasing power parity to the official exchange rate.

2.2 Real Output and Productivity Comparisons

Real manufacturing sector GDP or value added in the manufacturing sector is defined as the value added at own country prices, expressed in own country units, deflated by the purchasing power parity and converted into the currency of the base/numeraire country. A single deflation procedure is used to convert the value added into the base country currency units. In the present study, since the United States is the base country, real GDP in Australia is obtained by converting the manufacturing sector GDP in Australian dollars into US dollars using the purchasing power parities compiled at the manufacturing sector output level.

Labour productivity
Labour productivity is defined as the real value added or manufacturing GDP per person employed or per hour worked in the manufacturing sector or its branches. Labour productivity at the sectoral level is defined as

$$\text{PRODUCT}_{L_n}^{XU} = \frac{GVA^X / PPP_{XU}^{Fisher}}{L_n^X} \tag{4.10}$$

where $\text{PRODUCT}_{L_n}^{XU}$ represents the value added per person employed in country X expressed in the currency of country U. L_n^X represents the number of persons employed in the manufacturing sector of country X. The Fisher PPP is used in deflating the value added. Labour productivity in country U, expressed in country U currency, can be obtained by dividing GVA^{UU} by the number of persons employed in country U.

Labour productivity is measured by the real value added per hour worked in the manufacturing sector, using equation (4.10), but replacing the number of persons employed, L_n, by the total number of hours worked, L_h. Labour productivity can also be defined at branch or sample industry level using equation (4.10), by replacing the sectoral value added and PPP figures by the sample industry or branch level figures.

Joint-factor productivity
The concept of joint-factor productivity becomes relevant when more than one factor input is utilised in production. In most standard productivity comparisons it is necessary to account for different amounts of capital used in achieving a given level of production for a

given amount of labour input. To derive joint-factor productivity measures it is necessary to make certain assumptions regarding the nature of the underlying production function. In the present study, the well-known Cobb–Douglas form of the production function is utilised. Assuming constant returns to scale and using an unweighted average of the factor shares over the two countries X and U, a measure of relative joint-factor productivity is defined as

$$\ln \frac{A^X}{A^U} = \ln \frac{Y^X / L^X}{Y^U / L^U} - (1 - \alpha) \ln \frac{K^X / L^X}{K^U / L^U} \tag{4.11}$$

where Y, K and L, respectively, denote the level of output, labour and capital inputs. A and α are the parameters of the Cobb–douglas production function.

It is possible to define joint-factor productivity using more general forms of the production function such as, for example, the transcendental logarithmic production function. These alternative approaches are reviewed in van Ark (1992), Pilat and van Ark (1992) and Coelli, Rao and Battese (1998).

3. DATA

Census Information

Censuses of manufacturing serve as the basic data source in each country. With the exception of 1970–71 and 1985–86, the Australian manufacturing census was originally held every year. The Australian Bureau of Statistics (ABS) now holds full-sacle censuses every three years and smaller surveys in intervening years. It covers all establishments, although the smallest establishments are surveyed in less detail.

The Australian census is similar to the US census in most respects. It uses the US concept of value added, which includes service inputs. Employment includes working proprietors and head office employees. The Australian census also serves as the main source for industry estimates in the national accounts. The national accounts also provide an estimate for manufacturing derived from the income approach, but industry detail is based entirely on the census. The US manufacturing census is held every five years with an annual survey of manufactures giving a less complete account of manufacturing production for intermediate years. The quinquennial census is extremely detailed, including more than 450 industries and 11 000 products. The censuses also provide details on several thousand manufacturing products – some 3 000 in Australia and approximately 11 000 in the United States.

In most countries, manufacturing productivity may be derived from either the census of manufactures or the national accounts. However, for cross country comparisons the census is the preferred source. It is a primary source, which implies that all information is derived from a single survey. This further implies that information on employment and output is consistent, a crucial requirement for productivity comparisons. In contrast, the national accounts are a secondary source which combines information from different surveys into one integrated framework. For example, employment is derived from labour force surveys which are based on households, while output data are derived from either census information or from tax returns. Manufacturing censuses have an additional advantage for cross country comparisons in that the greater amount of included detailed information facilitates industry reclassification in the pursuit of greater comparability between any two countries. Census of manufactures are thus the preferred sources for cross country manufacturing sector productivity comparisons.

For the 1987 benchmark comparisons, Australian industry output information is derived from '1986–87, Manufacturing Industry: Details of Operations' (ABS Catalogue No. 8203.0, 1989). Product detail is from '1986–87 Manufacturing Commodities: Principal Articles Produced' (ABS Catalogue No. 8303.0, 1989). United States industry information is derived from '1987 Census of Manufactures: General Summary', and product information is contained in '1987 Census of Manufactures: Industry Reports', (both from Bureau of the Census, US Department of Commerce, 1990).

Labour and Capital Inputs

Labour productivity estimates are based on value added per person employed and per person employed adjusted for different hours worked in each country. Hours worked estimates for Australia are drawn from 'Distribution and Composition of Employee Earnings and Hours', (ABS Catalogue No. 6306.0, 1987). For the United States, more precise estimates are made on the basis of hours paid, drawn from the 'Monthly Labour Force Review', December 1988 and various after issues (Bureau of Labour Statistics, BLS), adjusted by ratios of hours actually worked to hours paid, from 'Ratio of Hours at Work to Hours Paid for Production and Non-Supervisory Employees, by Industry 1981–1988' (BLS, 1989). Hours actually worked are a more accurate reflection of labour than that based on paid hours. In this sense, the Australian data are less refined than those in the United States.

Australian capital stock estimates are derived from 'Capital Formation in Australian Manufacturing, 1945–1955 to 1987–1988', (Bureau of Industry Economics, 1989) and 'Australian National Accounts: Capital Stock' (ABS Catalogue No. 5221.0, various issues). US capital stock estimates are derived from 'Fixed Reproducible Tangible Wealth in the United States, 1925–1985, Bureau of Economic Analysis 1987' and various issues of the 'Survey of Current Business', Bureau of Economic Analysis (both US Department of Commerce).

Time Series

Time series of manufacturing sector output and employment are needed to extend the 1987 benchmark comparisons back to 1970 and forward to 1995. Since output is expressed in current prices, production censuses cannot be used to derive time series. Australia is an exception to this rule. Detailed time series for manufacturing can be derived from 'Constant Price Estimates of Manufacturing Production' (ABS Catalogue No. 8221.0, various issues). For the United States, time series for gross domestic product and value added by manufacturing branch may be derived from various issues of Survey of Current Business, Bureau of Economic Analysis.

Census and National Accounts Data – A Confrontation

Tables 4.1 and 4.2 show the manufacturing census and national accounts based estimates of manufacturing output and persons employed in Australia and the United States. For the reasons outlined above, these two sources provide fairly consistent estimates for Australia, although the census value added, (hence ultimately productivity per person employed) is some 9 per cent higher than the national accounts value added estimates according to the production method. No direct comparability exists in the two sources for manufacturing output in the United States in 1987, although the number of persons employed estimated in both sources are reasonably consistent.

4. EMPIRICAL RESULTS

4.1 Relative Size and Structure of the Manufacturing Sector

The manufacturing sectors in Australia and the United States have a similar structure although the size and the scale of the sector is much larger in the United States.

Table 4.3 shows the number of persons employed and the relative size of the manufacturing sector, by branch level, in Australia and the United States, expressed in national currencies, in the benchmark year 1987. The table also shows manufacturing sector output and value added expressed in US dollars converted using the PPPs. Using PPPs, the gross value of output in the Australian manufacturing sector is $79.1 billion ($82.5 billion at the official exchange rate) and for the United States $2,475.9 billion, some 31 times the size of the Australian manufacturing sector output (a bit less at the official exchange rates). Gross value added or GDP by the manufacturing sector in Australia, defined as gross output net of intermediate inputs, is $31.0 billion ($32.3 billion at official exchange rates) and in the United States $1,166 billion, some 38 times the gross value added by the Australian manufacturing sector. The manufacturing sector gross value added is 39 per cent of manufacturing gross output in Australia compared with 47 per cent for the United States. The Australian manufacturing sector contributed 17.4 per cent of total GDP and 14.7 per cent of total employment in 1987 while the United States had comparable figures of 19.5 per cent of total GDP and 16 per cent of all persons employed. Clearly, the use of PPPs produces different estimates of relative size and value added (hence ultimately, labour productivity per person) than does the official exchange rate.

In terms of structure, the largest contribution to gross output, value added and persons employed in Australia in 1987 were basic and fabricated metal products; food manufacturing; machinery and transport equipment; chemicals, petroleum and coal products; electrical machinery and equipment; and paper products, printing and publishing. For the United States, the largest contributors were machinery and transport equipment, chemicals, petroleum and coal products; food manufacturing; basic and fabricated metal products; and paper products, printing and publishing. Thus although the size order of branch contribution differed, the same five or six branches dominated manufacturing output and employment in each country in 1987.

Table 4.1   *Value Added, Employment and Hours Worked by Manufacturing Branch: Australia, 1987*

	Production Census			National Accounts			
	Census value added (A$M)	Employment (persons)	Census value added per person (A$)	Gross domestic product (A$M)	Employment (1 000 persons)	GDP per person (A$)	Annual hours worked per person employed
Food manufacturing	6 641	147 394	45 053	9 022	170	53 071	1 872
Beverages	1 482	18 805	78 819	(a)	(a)		1 872
Tobacco products	356	4 100	86 805	(a)	(a)		1 872
Textile mill products	1 858	47 634	39 008	1 208	34	35 529	1 863
Wearing apparel	1 234	48 636	25 370	1 706	75	22 747	1 863
Leather products and footwear	517	16 705	30 958	(b)	(b)		1 863
Wood furniture and fixtures	2 604	80 461	32 360	2 347	81	28 975	1 791
Paper printing and publishing	5 243	108 678	48 242	4 748	109	43 560	1 791
Chemicals, petroleum and coal products	4 164	54 266	76 739	3 324	54	61 556	1 827
Rubber and plastic products	1 898	43 355	43 774	(c)	(c)		1 827
Non-metallic mineral products	2 234	40 272	55 485	1 904	40	47 600	1 697
Basic and fabricated metal products	8 006	173 009	46 275	7 272	173	42 035	1 868
Machinery and transport equipment	6 309	165 222	38 185	3 878(d)	112(d)	34 625	1 881
Electrical machinery and equipment	2 746	67 204	40 865	4 533(e)	130(e)	34 869	1 859
Other manufacturing industries	941	25 955	36 265	2 330	63	36 984	1 908
Total manufacturing production approach	46 234	1 041 696	44 383	42 272	1 042	40 568	1 846
Total manufacturing income approach	–	–	–	44 664	1 042	42 864	

Notes: (a) Included in Food Manufacturing. (b) Included in Wearing Apparel. (c) Included in Other Manufacturing Industries. (d) Excludes General Machinery and Equipment. (e) Includes General Machinery and Equipment.

Sources: Census data from ABS, 1986–87 Manufacturing Industry, Details of Operations, Australia, Catalogue No. 8203.0, 1989. National Accounts from ABS, 1988–89 Australian National Accounts, Gross Product, Employment and Hours Worked, Catalogue No. 5211.0, 1989. Hours worked from ABS, *Distribution and Composition of Employee Earnings and Hours*, Australia, Catalogue No. 6306.0, Canberra, May 1987.

Table 4.2 *Value Added, Employment and Hours Worked by Manufacturing Branch: United States, 1987*

	Production Census		National Accounts (a)			
	Census value added (US$M)	Employment including head offices (persons)	Gross domestic product at market prices (US$M)	Gross domestic product at factor cost (US$M)	Persons engaged (persons)	Annual hours worked per person (b)
Food manufacturing	99 018.1	1 384 925	60 642	54 691	1 498 269	1 893
Beverages (c)	22 584.8	172 175	13 383	12 069	167 731	1 866
Tobacco products	14 263.8	63 500	15 486	10 798	55 000	1 853
Textile mill products	25 660.1	698 900	19 960	19 528	736 000	2 053
Wearing apparel	32 515.6	1 113 800	22 461	22 227	1 130 000	1 794
Leather products and footwear	4 377.9	135 700	3 298	3 239	151 000	1 843
Wood furniture and fixtures	48 975.0	1 235 100	42 690	41 915	1 351 000	1 964
Paper products printing and publishing	140 651.0	2 232 900	97 645	95 393	2 286 000	1 847
Chemicals and allied coal products	18 518.3	153 600	33 646	21 597	163 000	1 922
Rubber and plastic products	44 436.8	863 300	29 951	29 159	829 000	1 986
Non-metallic mineral products	33 383.1	554 300	27 501	26 646	604 000	2 003
Basic and fabricated metal products	121 078.4	2 228 900	96 755	93 376	2 168 000	1 956
Machinery and transport equipment	255 263.6	3 966 100	187 109	181 161	4 112 000	1 905
Electrical machinery and equipment	95 815.3	1 689 400	85 037	83 556	2 090 000	1 877
Other manufacturing industries	88 427.5	1 429 900	40 899	40 002	1 121 000	1 885
Total manufacturing	1 165 746.9	18 950 900	853 620	810 061	19 491 000	1 909

Notes: (a) These figures are not compatible with more recent revisions of Gross National Product at market prices in M.F. Mohr, 'Gross National Product by Industry, 1987–89', *Survey of Current Business*, April 1991. (b) Census basis, no adjustment is made for hours worked by self-employed persons. (c) In the US national accounts 'Beverages' is included in 'Food and Kindred Products'. Its national accounts employment and value added was calculated from the census shares.

Sources: Census data from US Dept. of Commerce, Bureau of the Census, *1987 Census of Manufactures, General Summary*. GDP from US Dept. of Commerce, Bureau of Economic Analysis, *Gross National Product by Industry and Type of Income in Current Dollars and by Industry in Constant Dollars, 1947–1986*, July 1987. Total persons engaged from US Dept. of Commerce, *Survey of Current Business*, July 1989. Hours worked based on actual hours worked from BLS, *Ratio of Hours at Work to Hours Paid for Production and Nonsupervisory Employees, by Industry, 1981–1988*. Hours paid from BLS, *Monthly Labor Review*, December 1988.

Table 4.3   *Gross Value of Output, Gross Value Added and Employment by the Manufacturing Branches: Australia and the USA, 1987 (national currencies and number of persons)*

Manufacturing branches	Australia (1986–87) A$			United States (1987) US$		
	Gross output (A$M)	Gross value added (A$M)	Persons employed (number)	Gross output (US$M)	Gross value added (US$M)	Persons employed (number)
Food manufacturing	20 627.2	6 640.6	147 394	282 398.2	99 018.1	1 384 925
Beverages	3 567.4	1 482.2	18 805	47 327.2	22 584.8	172 175
Tobacco products	655.3	355.9	4 100	20 757.1	14 263.8	63 500
Textile mill products	4 429.5	1 858.1	47 634	62 786.4	25 660.1	698 900
Wearing apparel	2 599.5	1 233.9	48 636	64 242.6	32 515.6	1 113 800
Leather products and footwear	1 322.9	517.2	16 705	9 082.4	4 377.0	135 700
Wood products furniture and fixtures	6 116.7	2 603.7	80 461	107 208.6	48 975.0	1 235 100
Paper products printing and publishing	10 551.5	5 242.9	108 678	245 184.3	140 651.0	2 232 900
Chemicals, petroleum and coal products	11 310.9	4 164.3	54 266	359 960.1	139 295.9	1 182 000
Rubber and plastic products	4 624.0	1 897.8	43 355	86 634.3	44 436.8	863 300
Non-metallic mineral products	5 433.1	2 234.5	40 272	61 476.6	33 383.1	554 300
Basic and fabricated metal products	22 939.9	8 006.0	173 009	267 614.3	121 078.4	2 228 900
Machinery and transport equipment	15 549.2	6 309.1	165 222	550 605.6	255 263.6	3 966 100
Electrical machinery and equipment	6 377.3	2 746.3	67 204	171 286.4	95 815.3	1 689 400
Other manufacturing industries	1 927.2	941.3	25 955	139 336.8	88 427.5	1 429 900
Total manufacturing	118 031.8	46 233.7	1 041 696	2 475 900.9	1 165 746.9	18 950 900

	(Australia) (in US$)		(United States) (in US$)	
	Gross output	Gross value added	Gross output	Gross value added
Total manufacturing at the official exchange rate A$/US$ = 1.43	82.5	32.3	2 476.0	1 166.0
Total manufacturing at PPP exchange rate A$/US$ = 1.492	79.1	31.0		

Notes: 1. Total value of the manufacturing sector includes the output of the establishments with employment less than four. 2. Australian GDP in 1986–87 was A$265.18 billion and in the United States, US$4,075.6 billion. The total number of persons employed in Australia was 7.042 million and in the United States 118.432 million.

Sources: ABS *1986–87 Manufacturing Productivity, Details of Operations*, Australia, Catalogue No. 8203, 1989. US Department of Commerce, *Census of Manufacturers*, Washington, DC, 1990. Exchange rates from Table 5.

4.2 Branch Level PPPs, Price Levels and Labour Productivity Comparisons

Matched output by manufacturing branch
Column 1 of Table 4.4 shows the unit value ratios (UVRs) for the number of matched products within each sample industry, aggregated to branch level. Columns 2 and 3 show the percentage of each branch's gross output which is covered by matched products in each country.

Table 4.4   Matched Output as a Percentage of Total Gross Value of Output by Manufacturing Branch: Australia/USA, 1987

	No. of UVRs	Australia	United States
Food manufacturing	54	40.73	32.79
Beverages	4	60.19	37.87
Tobacco products	1	89.43	81.64
Textile mill products	17	31.09	39.38
Wearing apparel	27	61.07	34.97
Leather products and footwear	8	48.02	52.02
Wood products, furniture and fixtures	8	25.29	7.56
Paper products, printing and publishing	3	5.84	11.13
Chemicals, petroleum and coal products	19	15.03	4.07
Rubber and plastic products	1	4.81	6.72
Non-metallic mineral products	7	44.65	25.80
Basic and fabricated metal products	11	9.15	7.60
Machinery and transport equipment	8	20.92	16.88
Electrical machinery and equipment	10	9.52	5.51
Other manufacturing industries	0	0.00	0.00
Total manufacturing	178	23.05	15.10

Source: Gross value of output by manufacturing branch from census sources quoted in Tables 1 and 2, matched output and number of UVRs from basic matching tables.

The number of matched products and the proportions of output matched in individual branches vary considerably, from a low of 4.81 per cent for rubber and plastic products to a high of 89.43 per cent for tobacco products for Australia, and from a low of 4.07 per cent for chemicals, petroleum and coal products to a high of 81.64 per cent for tobacco products for the United States. Overall, the total number of 178 matched products accounted for 23.05 per cent of total manufacturing sector gross output in Australia and for 15.1 per cent in the United States. Though these coverage ratios appear to be small, they are broadly comparable to coverage ratios attained in a range of ICOP comparative studies for other countries (see Pilat and van Ark, 1992). Moreover, sensitivity tests conducted by the ICOP group show that the average UVR for total manufacturing is not very sensitive to outliers, thereby suggesting that the results are robust to the matching coverage ratios. For a more detailed discussion of the quality problem in matching procedures and of results from sensitivity tests, see van Ark (1993: 32–50).

Branch level PPPs, price levels and productivity comparisons
Table 4.5 shows manufacturing sector branch PPPs and relative price levels for Australia
and the United States, for the benchmark year 1987. Table 4.6 shows gross value added, by
branch, in each country's manufacturing sector.

The PPPs produced using US and Australian quantity weights, in columns 1 and 2 in
Table 4.5 represent, respectively, the Laspeyres and Paasche indices. Column 3 shows the
geometric average PPP, or the Fisher index, for each branch. A relative price level for each
branch and for the sector as a whole may be calculated as the Fisher PPP/exchange rate
(× 100). A relative price level in excess of 100 indicates that prices in Australian
manufacturing branches are higher than in their corresponding branches in the United
States.

It is clear from Table 4.5 that for 1987 PPPs for eight branches are greater than the
exchange rate, i.e., textile mill products; wearing apparel; wood products, furniture and
fittings; paper products, printing and publishing; non-metallic mineral products; basic and
fabricated metal products; and electrical machinery and equipment and the other

Table 4.5   *Purchasing Power Parities and Comparative Price Levels by Major*
            Manufacturing Branch: Australia/USA (A$ to the US$)

	PPP (A$/US$)			Relative price level Australia (a) (USA = 100)
	at US quantity weights	at Australian quantity weights	Geometric average	
Food manufacturing	1.411	1.263	1.335	93.4
Beverages	1.211	1.232	1.222	85.4
Tobacco products	0.680	0.680	0.680	47.6
Textile mill products	1.639	1.523	1.580	110.5
Wearing apparel	1.639	1.523	1.580	110.5
Leather products and footwear	1.514	1.317	1.412	98.7
Wood products, furniture and fixtures	2.055	2.083	2.069	144.7
Paper products, printing and publishing	1.757	1.849	1.803	126.1
Chemicals, petroleum and coal products	1.652	1.073	1.1332	93.1
Rubber and plastic products	1.256	1.256	1.256	87.8
Non-metallic mineral products	1.479	1.490	1.485	103.8
Basic and fabricated metal products	1.654	1.498	1.574	110.1
Machinery and transport equipment	1.342	1.233	1.286	89.9
Electrical machinery and equipment	1.978	2.086	2.031	142.0
Other manufacturing industries	1.576	1.412	1.492	104.3
Total manufacturing	1.576	1.412	1.492	104.3
Exchange rate	1.430	1.430	1.430	100.0

Note: (a) The relative price level is the PPP divided by the exchange rate.

Source: Industry PPPs derived from basic matching tables and weighted with industry value added weights
derived from basic census sources quoted in Tables 1 and 2.

Table 4.6   *Gross Value Added (Census Concept) by Major Manufacturing Branch: Australia and the USA, 1987*

	At Australian prices			At US prices		
	Australia (A$M)	USA (A$M)	Australia/USA (per cent)	Australia (US$M)	USA (US$M)	Australia/USA (per cent)
Food manufacturing	6 640.6	139 743.0	4.75	5 256.4	99 018.1	5.31
Beverages	1 482.2	27 348.3	5.42	1 202.8	22 584.8	5.33
Tobacco products	355.9	9 702.1	3.67	523.2	14 263.8	3.67
Textile mill products	1 858.1	45 140.2	4.12	1 129.8	25 660.1	4.40
Wearing apparel	1 233.9	53 294.3	2.32	810.1	32 515.6	2.49
Leather products and footwear	517.2	6 626.6	7.80	392.7	4 377.9	8.97
Wood products furniture and fixtures	2 603.7	100 661.6	2.59	1 250.2	48 975.0	2.55
Paper products printing and publishing	5 242.9	247 164.9	2.12	2 835.3	140 651.0	2.02
Chemicals, petroleum and coal products	4 164.3	230 121.8	1.81	3 879.3	139 295.9	2.78
Rubber and plastic products	1 897.8	55 823.9	3.40	1 510.7	44 436.8	3.40
Non-metallic mineral products	2 234.5	49 367.8	4.53	1 499.2	33 383.1	4.49
Basic and fabricated metal products	8 006.0	200 238.0	4.00	5 343.1	121 078.4	4.41
Machinery and transport equipment	6 309.1	342 591.5	1.84	5 118.8	255 263.6	2.01
Electrical machinery and equipment	2 746.3	189 512.6	1.45	1 316.4	95 815.3	1.37
Other manufacturing industries	941.3	139 319.2	0.68	666.4	88 427.5	0.75
Total manufacturing	46 233.7	1 836 655.8	2.52	32 734.7	1 165 746.9	2.81

Source: Census value added in national currency from basic sources shown in Tables 4.1 and 4.2; converted with PPPs.

manufacturing industries category. Translated into relative price levels, this indicates higher prices in these branches relative to those in the United States. It is significant that those branches experiencing the highest relative price levels are those that have traditionally enjoyed highest protection levels in Australia. The notable exception here is the lower relative price level for the highly protected machinery and transport equipment branch. The PPP for this branch depends mainly on the product match for passenger cars. Since the match is adjusted for model and engine capacity, the most likely explanation for the unexpected outcome is that machinery and transport equipment are of much higher quality in the United States, qualitative differences which cannot be picked up by production censuses and matching procedures.

As could be expected, the manufacturing branches with low price levels in Australia are found predominantly in agriculture and mineral-based production – food; beverages; tobacco products; chemicals, petroleum and coal products; and, perhaps more surprising, in leather products and footwear and rubber and plastic products. For the most part, the comparatively disadvantaged manufacturing sector branches had relatively higher price levels, implying limited international competitiveness, while the comparatively advantaged agriculture and minerals-based industries enjoyed relatively lower price levels, implying at least a potential for a greater degree of international competitiveness. Moreover, Table 4.6 shows that gross value added in Australian manufacturing was very low, at either 2.5 or 2.8 per cent of that in the United States when valued at Australian or US prices, respectively. Of course, such wide disparities in gross value added owe more to absolute scale effects in manufacturing, reflecting the fact that the US population is nearly 20 times that of Australia, rather than solely productivity effects. Again, however, the branches registering higher than average gross value added are those in agriculture and minerals based industries, i.e. food manufacturing, beverages; tobacco products and non-metallic mineral products.

Labour productivity comparisons
Tables 4.7 and 4.8 show gross value added per person employed and gross value added per hour worked in manufacturing in Australia and the United States.

In terms of gross value added per person employed, Table 4.7 shows that the overall level of labour productivity in Australian manufacturing lay between 45.8 per cent and 51.1 per cent of that in the United States, depending upon which country's prices are used for valuation. Based on Fisher PPPs, the overall level of productivity was 48.4 per cent of that in the United States. There was substantial variation in labour productivity across branches, from a minimum of 35.5 per cent of the US level for electrical machinery and equipment to a maximum of 68 per cent for leather products. Gross value added per person was also higher, on average, in the most heavily protected industries: textile mill products; wearing apparel; leather products like rubber and plastic; non-metallic mineral products; and basic and fabricated metal products. Branches such as food manufacturing, beverages and machinery and transport equipment had relatively low gross value added per person.

To derive more accurate measures of labour productivity it is necessary to adjust for difference in the average number of hours worked per person employed. Tables 4.1 and 4.2 show that in 1987 the average number of hours per person worked in Australia was 1846 compared to 1909 hours in the United States. Table 4.8 shows that once allowance is made for the greater number of hours worked per person employed in the United States, Australian labour productivity increased marginally from 48.4 to 50.0 per cent of that in the United States. A higher productivity is observed for textile mill products; wood products; chemicals, petroleum and coal products; rubber and plastic; non-metallic mineral products and basic and fabricated metal products when gross value added per hour worked is used in place of the gross value added per person employed.

Table 4.7   *Gross Value Added (Census Concept) Per Person Employed: Australia and the USA, 1987*

| | At Australian prices | | | At US prices | | | Geometric average |
	Australia (A$)	USA (A$)	Australia /USA	Australia (US$)	USA (US$)	Australia /USA	Australia /USA
Food manufacturing	45 053	100 903	44.7	35 662	71 497	49.9	47.2
Beverages	78 819	158 840	49.6	63 964	131 174	48.8	49.2
Tobacco products	86 805	152 789	56.8	127 618	224 627	56.8	56.8
Textile mill products	39 008	64 587	60.4	23 719	36 715	64.6	62.5
Wearing apparel	25 370	47 849	53.0	16 656	29 193	57.1	55.0
Leather products and footwear	30 958	48 833	63.4	23 506	32 262	72.9	68.0
Wood products furniture and fixtures	32 360	81 501	39.7	15 538	39 653	39.2	39.4
Paper products printing and publishing	48 242	110 692	43.6	26 089	62 990	41.4	42.5
Chemicals, petroleum and coal products	76 739	194 689	39.4	71 487	117 848	60.7	48.9
Rubber and plastic products	43 774	64 663	67.7	34 845	51 473	67.7	67.7
Non-metallic mineral products	55 485	89 063	62.3	37 227	60 226	61.8	62.1
Basic and fabricated metal products	46 275	89 837	51.5	30 883	54 322	56.9	54.1
Machinery and transport equipment	38 185	86 380	44.2	30 982	64 361	48.1	46.1
Electrical machinery and equipment	40 865	112 177	36.4	19 589	56 716	34.5	35.5
Other manufacturing industries	36 265	97 433	37.2	25 677	61 842	41.5	39.3
Total manufacturing	44 383	96 917	45.8	31 424	61 514	51.1	48.4

Source: Gross value added from Table 4.6, employment from Tables 4.1 and 4.2.

On the basis of this evidence, surprisingly, labour productivity appears to be greater in the more protected manufacturing branches. This is particularly the case once allowance is made for the marginally lower hours worked in Australia. This may suggest that labour shedding in these industries in Australia, despite protection, helped these branches achieve higher levels of productivity. A significant decline in the number of persons engaged in various manufacturing branches occurred over the period 1970 to 1995, particularly in the industries that, historically, had received protection, i.e., textiles, clothing and footwear, and transport equipment and machinery.

Table 4.8　*Gross Value Added (Census Concept) Per Hour Worked: Australia and the USA, 1987*

	At Australian prices			At US prices			Geometric average
	Australia (A$)	USA (A$)	Australia /USA	Australia (US$)	USA (US$)	Australia /USA	Australia /USA
Food manufacturing	24.1	53.3	45.2	19.1	37.8	50.3	47.7
Beverages	42.1	85.1	49.5	34.2	70.3	48.6	49.0
Tobacco products	46.4	82.5	56.2	68.2	121.2	56.2	56.2
Textile mill products	20.9	31.5	66.6	12.7	17.9	71.2	68.8
Wearing apparel	13.6	26.7	51.1	8.9	16.3	54.9	53.0
Leather products and footwear	16.6	26.5	62.7	12.6	17.5	72.1	67.2
Wood products, furniture and fixtures	18.1	41.5	43.5	8.7	20.2	43.0	43.3
Paper products, printing and publishing	26.9	59.9	44.9	14.6	34.1	42.7	43.8
Chemicals, petroleum and coal products	42.0	101.3	41.5	39.1	61.3	63.8	51.4
Rubber and plastic products	24.0	32.6	73.6	19.1	25.9	73.6	73.6
Non-metallic mineral products	32.7	44.5	73.6	21.9	30.1	73.0	73.3
Basic and fabricated metal products	24.8	45.9	54.0	16.5	27.8	59.5	56.7
Machinery and transport equipment	20.3	45.3	44.8	16.5	33.8	48.8	46.7
Electrical machinery and equipment	22.0	59.8	36.8	10.5	30.2	34.9	35.8
Other manufacturing industries	19.0	51.7	36.8	13.5	32.8	41.0	38.8
Total manufacturing	24.0	50.8	47.4	17.0	32.2	52.8	50.0

Source: Gross value added from Table 4.6, employment and hours worked from Tables 4.1 and 4.2.

Trends in productivity levels, 1970–95

The benchmark results may be extrapolated from 1987 back to 1970 and forward to 1995 in order to highlight the major long run trends in exchange rates, manufacturing sector and

GDP purchasing power parities, relative GDP and manufacturing sector price levels and manufacturing sector productivity levels.

Table 4.9 and Figures 4.1 and 4.2 illustrate trends for nominal exchange rates and manufacturing sector and GDP relative prices levels and PPPs.

Table 4.9   Exchange Rates, Purchasing Power Parities and Relative Price Levels in Manufacturing and GDP

	Manufacturing PPP	Exchange rate	PPP for GDP	Relative price level manufacturing	Relative price level GDP
		(A$ per US$)		(US = 100)	
1970	0.83	0.89	0.75	93.38	83.99
1971	0.85	0.88	0.75	96.58	84.94
1972	0.89	0.83	0.77	105.74	91.78
1973	0.96	0.70	0.81	136.72	115.06
1974	1.07	0.69	0.88	153.82	126.26
1975	1.10	0.76	0.93	143.49	121.73
1976	1.16	0.81	0.99	141.38	121.03
1977	1.17	0.90	1.01	130.13	111.97
1978	1.14	0.87	1.01	131.00	115.56
1979	1.13	0.89	1.02	126.69	113.97
1980	1.16	0.87	1.04	132.00	118.45
1981	1.17	0.87	1.04	134.04	119.54
1982	1.24	0.98	1.08	125.70	109.53
1983	1.33	1.11	1.13	119.92	101.80
1984	1.32	1.14	1.16	116.13	101.75
1985	1.42	1.43	1.19	99.49	83.10
1986	1.43	1.49	1.24	95.41	82.89
1987	1.49	1.42	1.29	104.48	90.34
1988	1.50	1.28	1.34	117.14	104.69
1989	1.54	1.26	1.38	121.73	109.09
1990	1.51	1.28	1.39	118.25	108.51
1991	1.49	1.28	1.37	116.02	106.70
1992	1.50	1.36	1.36	110.49	99.85
1993	1.52	1.47	1.35	103.05	91.77
1994	1.58	1.36	1.34	115.31	97.95
1995	1.66	1.34	1.35	122.71	100.07

Source: Pilat, Prasada Rao and Shepherd (1993) updated with OECD, ISDB database.

Manufacturing and GDP PPPs increased jointly over the period from 1970 to 1982, decreased sharply from 1982 through to the late 1980s then rose again from the early to mid-1990s, with the manufacturing sector PPP increasing at a faster rate in these sub-periods.

The manufacturing PPP also stayed above the exchange rate throughout the review period, apart from brief spells in 1970–71 and 1986–87. These trends suggest that the relative manufacturing sector price level rose faster than the GDP price level in Australia and relative to the US GDP price level, indicating in turn, the existence of a relatively higher Australian manufacturing sector price level almost throughout the entire period from 1970–95.

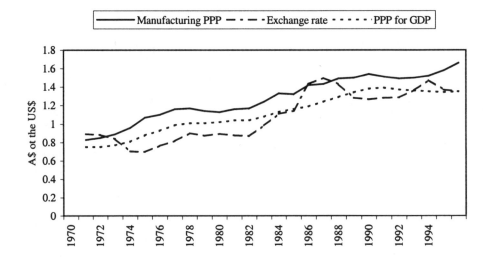

Source: Pilat, Prasada Rao and Shepherd (1993), updated with OECD, ISDB database.

*Figure 4.1   PPPs for Manufacturing and GDP, 1970–95 (Australia/United States,
A$/US$)*

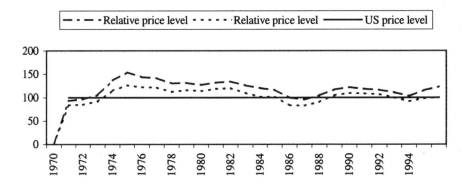

Source: Pilat, Prasada Rao and Shepherd (1993), updated with OECD, ISDB database.

*Figure 4.2   Implicit Price Levels for Manufacturing and GDP, 1970–95 (Australia/United
States, United States = 100)*

Trends in labour productivity

Based on Fisher PPPs, Table 4.7 shows that labour productivity, defined in terms of value added per person employed in Australian manufacturing was 48.4 per cent of the US level. Table 4.8 shows that once allowance is made for the greater number of hours worked in the United States (see Tables 4.1 and 4.2) labour productivity rose slightly to 50 per cent of the US level. In terms of trends in labour productivity, Table 4.10 and Figures 4.3 and 4.4 show that the Australian manufacturing sector operated at approximately half of the productivity level of the United States throughout the 1970–95 period.

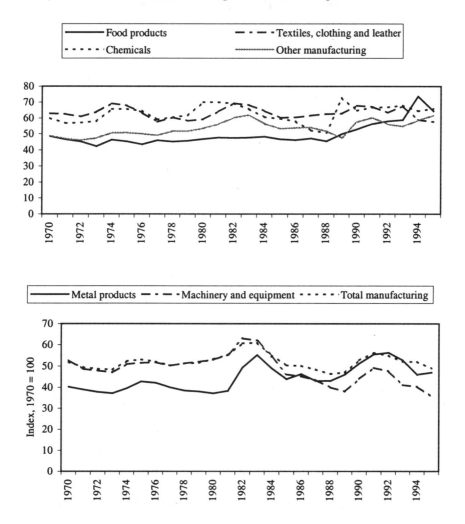

Source: Pilat, Prasada Rao and Shepherd (1993), updated with time series for the United States provided by Bart van Ark. Series for Australia derived from Industry Commission (1997a) and ABS sources.

Figure 4.3 Productivity Levels in Australian Manufacturing by Major Branches, 1970–95 (GDP per person engaged, USA = 100)

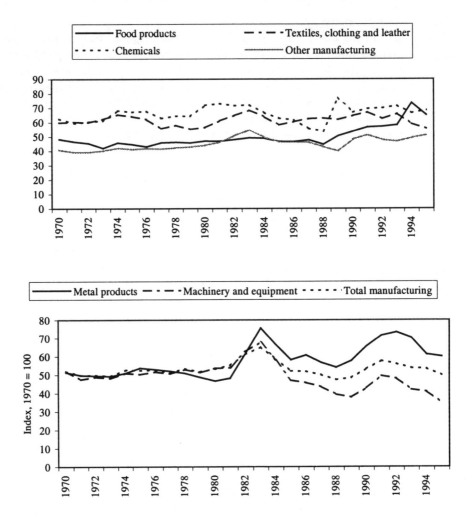

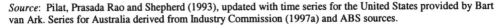

Source: Pilat, Prasada Rao and Shepherd (1993), updated with time series for the United States provided by Bart van Ark. Series for Australia derived from Industry Commission (1997a) and ABS sources.

Figure 4.4   Productivity Levels in Australian Manufacturing by Major Branches, 1970–95 (GDP per hour worked, USA = 100)

Labour productivity for the manufacturing sector improved slightly through the 1970s, deteriorated in the mid-1980s, improved again to the early 1990s, then deteriorated again to just less than 50 per cent of the US level in 1995.

It is equally clear that labour productivity also varied significantly both across branches and in different sub-periods. Table 4.10 shows that labour productivity levels for chemicals – including petroleum, coal products and rubber and plastic products – remained significantly and consistently higher than the manufacturing sector productivity levels throughout the review period. Textiles, clothing and footwear also recorded significantly higher than average manufacturing sector productivity levels through the period. On the other hand, labour productivity in food products – including food manufacturing, beverages and tobacco products, was below the sectoral average levels from 1970 to 1990 before registering strong growth through to 1995. Labour productivity in metal products exhibited better improvement while machinery and equipment – including transport and equipment and electrical machinery – sustained the largest decline in labour productivity, down from 52 per cent of the US level in 1970 to approximately 35 per cent in 1995.

Table 4.10 Trends in Labour Productivity by Major Manufacturing Branch (USA = 100)

Relative GDP per person, Australia/USA (USA = 100)						
Major branches	1970	1975	1980	1985	1990	1995
Food products	48.6	45.3	46.8	46.7	53.0	64.5
Textiles, clothing and leather	63.0	67.9	59.3	60.3	67.9	57.7
Chemicals	59.9	65.7	70.0	59.7	64.8	66.0
Other manufacturing	48.8	50.7	53.5	53.3	57.5	61.7
Metal products	40.2	42.7	37.2	43.9	51.2	47.0
Machinery and equipment	52.7	51.5	53.0	46.1	44.0	35.7
Total manufacturing	51.8	53.1	53.3	50.3	52.8	48.9

Relative GDP per hour worked, Australia/USA (USA = 100)						
Major branches	1970	1975	1980	1985	1990	1995
Food products	48.3	44.69	46.9	46.6	53.6	65.1
Textiles, clothing and leather	59.9	64.1	56.4	58.2	64.6	55.5
Chemicals	62.6	67.2	71.9	62.9	66.9	68.5
Other manufacturing	40.8	41.1	43.9	46.3	48.1	51.1
Metal products	51.3	53.7	46.7	58.2	65.5	60.0
Machinery and equipment	51.8	50.3	53.6	47.0	42.7	34.8
Total manufacturing	51.9	52.4	53.2	52.0	53.2	49.8

4.3 Joint Factor Productivity in Manufacturing

Table 4.11 and Figure 4.5 show the influence of capital stock on relative manufacturing sector productivity levels from 1970 to 1995. GDP per unit of capital stock – or relative capital productivity – registered just over 50 per cent of the US level throughout the 1970s, peaked at 59.3 per cent of the US level in 1980 then stayed around 55 per cent of the US level through to the mid-1990s – although with a sharp drop to 51.5 per cent of the US level in 1995. Allowing for the influence of capital stock produced a joint, or multi-factor productivity level of 52.6 per cent of the US level, on an hours worked basis, in the benchmark year 1987. This is a modest improvement over the labour productivity per hours worked basis, of 50.0 per cent and per person engaged of 48.4 per cent of the respective US levels recorded in the 1987 benchmark year. Joint factor productivity peaked at an equally modest 56.9 per cent of the US level in 1993, then declined to 51.5 per cent in 1995.

Table 4.11 Joint Factor Productivity, Australia and United States, 1970–95 (USA = 100)

	GDP per hour worked	GDP per unit of capital stock	Joint factor productivity
1970	43.5	53.6	47.2
1971	41.9	53.3	45.8
1972	42.5	50.9	45.7
1973	42.5	49.2	45.2
1974	42.9	50.7	45.9
1975	43.3	54.9	47.4
1976	44.2	52.2	47.3
1977	44.3	49.4	46.6
1978	47.7	50.4	49.4
1979	48.6	53.5	50.9
1980	51.0	59.3	54.4
1981	50.5	58.9	53.9
1982	49.0	57.3	52.3
1983	53.4	56.4	55.3
1984	54.0	55.5	55.4
1985	50.5	55.2	52.9
1986	51.1	56.1	53.5
1987	50.1	55.5	52.6
1988	49.0	54.9	51.6
1989	49.3	54.9	51.8
1990	49.5	54.8	52.0
1991	52.2	55.7	54.2
1992	52.7	56.0	54.7
1993	55.2	57.5	56.9
1994	52.8	54.5	54.3
1995	50.1	51.6	51.5

Source: Capital stock data are drawn from sources discussed in Section 3.

Tables 4.12 and 4.13 offer some explanation of the productivity gap between Australia and the United States for the 1987 benchmark year.

Table 4.12 shows that in 1987 some 39.3 per cent of the labour productivity gap between the two countries' manufacturing sectors was explained by the difference in capital intensity. However, the share of labour productivity explained by this factor varied considerably across branches. At one extreme, for textile mill products and leather products and footwear, capital intensity differences explained all of the productivity gap. This outcome suggests that once allowance was made for capital intensity in these branches in Australia, labour productivity was found to be higher than in the same branches in the United States. At the other extreme, the negative ratio for non-metallic products suggests that allowing for capital intensity actually widened the productivity gap for this branch. In turn, this suggests a very low level of labour productivity for non-metallic products in Australia in 1987.

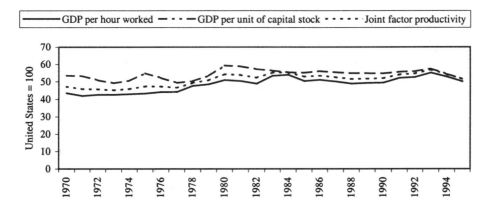

Source: Pilat, Prasada Rao and Shepherd (1993), updated with OECD, ISDB database. Hours worked United States provided by Van Ark and from Industry Commission (1997a).

Figure 4.5 Relative Productivity in Manufacturing, 1970–95 (Australia/United States, United States = 100)

Table 4.12 Relative Capital Intensity and Explained Labour Productivity by Manufacturing Branch: Australia/US, 1987

	1987 Relative gross capital stock (USA = 100)	1987 Gross capital stock per person (USA = 100)	1987 Share of labour productivity explained (%)
Food, beverages and tobacco	5.89	56.6	49.4
Textile mill products	3.08	47.8	123.7
Wearing apparel	4.92	117.9	22.5
Leather products and footwear	6.84	58.9	113.5
Wood products, furniture and fixtures	4.70	77.6	19.4
Paper products, printing and publishing	2.30	50.8	54.8
Chemicals, petroleum and coal products	2.32	52.0	53.9
Rubber and plastic products	3.74	78.9	48.2
Non-metallic mineral products	7.41	108.7	-12.3
Metals and machinery	4.46	81.0	24.0
Electrical machinery and equipment	1.84	43.4	65.9
Other manufacturing industries	1.62	88.0	10.8
Total manufacturing	3.75	69.0	39.3

Sources: Capital stock by branch, Australia from 'Capital Formation in Australian Manufacturing, 1954-55 to 1987-88', Working Paper No. 54, Bureau of Industry Economics, Canberra. Capital stock USA by branch from US Dept. of Commerce, BEA, *Fixed Reproducible Tangible Wealth in the United States*, 1925-1985, conversion with PPP for domestic capital formation from OECD (1989); employment derived from manufacturing censuses; labour shares in GDP derived from data supplied by Bureau of Economic Analysis, July 1987.

Table 4.13 attempts to explain part of the productivity gap by adjusting the original estimate of productivity per person employed to standardise for differences in branch distributions of employment and value added shares in each country. Table 4.13 shows that the unadjusted Australian labour productivity estimate rises to 53.5 per cent of the US level when Australian value-added shares are used. On the other hand, adjusting for US employment shares retained the same productivity level (or marginally lower at 47.3 per cent of the US level), but adjusting for the use of US value-added shares again raised the original unadjusted productivity level in Australia, from 48.4 per cent to 52.1 per cent of the US level. This suggests that if Australia had the same branch value-added shares as the United States, the labour productivity gap between the two countries would have been around 4 percentage points smaller. This further implies that Australian value added is typically concentrated in manufacturing branches with higher labour productivity than is the case in the United States.

Table 4.13   Gross Value Added Per Person Employed, Australia and the United States, 1987, Adjusted for Differences in Branch Labour Shares and Branch Value-added Shares

Australia/United States (%): Geometric Average	
Unadjusted estimate	48.4
At Australian employment shares	48.5
At US employment shares	47.3
At Australian value added shares	53.5
At US value added shares	52.1

Sources: Unadjusted comparison from Table 4.7, labour and value-added shares from Tables 1 and 2. The weighting procedure is as follows. The labour shares are applied directly to the branch GDP per person figures. The manufacturing totals are the sums of the reweighted branch figures. In the case of value-added shares, one applies the GDP proportions of one country to the GDP total in national currency of the other country to get reweighted GDP per branch. Subsequently one divides reweighted branch GDP by branch labour productivity figures to get reweighted branch employment. Total GDP at other country unit values divided by the reweighted employment total provides reweighted labour productivity at other country unit values.

Clearly, the preceding analysis demonstrates the existence of a considerable manufacturing sector productivity gap between Australia and the United States. The productivity gap is clear for both the 1987 benchmark year and for the full review period 1970–95. The addition of capital stock in the form of joint factor productivity produced only modest improvements in Australian manufacturing sector productivity levels *vis-à-vis* the United States, although adjusting for US value added shares did serve to reduce the productivity gap in the 1987 benchmark year.

5. CONCLUSIONS

This chapter outlines the methodology underpinning the ICOP/COPPAA industry-of-origin approach to international comparisons and provides comparative estimates of productivity levels in the Australian and United States manufacturing sectors for the period 1970 to

1995. Based on industry-of-origin PPPs, the present study has produced lower estimates of Australian manufacturing sector productivity levels for the early 1990s relative to the United States manufacturing sector levels than those based on exchange rates and ICP final expenditure PPPs produced by the Australian Industry Commission.

Despite this outcome, there is little doubt that sustained microeconomic reform policy-induced structural adjustments in the Australian economy since the mid-1980s has raised productivity growth rates and the threshold for non-inflationary growth of the Australian economy. Given this growth performance, the lack of significant catch up in Australian manufacturing sector productivity levels *vis-à-vis* the United States is more likely to have reflected the stronger non-inflationary growth and sustained productivity growth in the US economy and manufacturing sector rather than any significant deterioration in the productivity performance of the Australian manufacturing sector, at least from the late 1980s.

REFERENCES

Ark, B. van (1992), 'The ICOP: The Implications and Applicability' in A. Szirmai, B. van Ark and D. Pilat (eds), Explaining Economic Growth in Essays in Honour of Angus Maddison, North Holland, Amsterdam.

Ark, B. van (1993), International Comparisons of Output and Productivity – Manufacturing Productivity Performance of Ten Countries from 1950–1990. Groningen Growth and Development Centre, Minograph Series, No. 1, University of Groningen, Groningen.

Australian Bureau of Statistics (various issues), Australian National Accounts, Capital Stock, Catalogue No. 5221.0 ABS, Canberra.

Australian Bureau of Statistics (various issues), Constant Price Estimates of Manufacturing Production, Catalogue No. 8221.0, ABS, Canberra.

Australian Bureau of Statistics (1987), Distribution and Composition of Employee Earnings and Hours, Australia, Catalogue No. 6306.0, ABS, Canberra.

Australian Bureau of Statistics (1989), 1986–87 Manufacturing Industry, Details of Operations, Australia, Catalogue No. 8203.0, ABS, Canberra.

Australian Bureau of Statistics (1989), Manufacturing Commodities. Principal Articles Produced, Australia, Catalogue No. 8303.0, ABS, Canberra.

Australian Bureau of Statistics (1989), 1988–89 National Accounts, Gross Product, Employment and Hours Worked, Catalogue No. 5211-0, ABS, Canberra.

Boon, L. and Maddison, A. (1997), 'A Comparison of Output, Purchasing Power and Productivity in Indian and Chinese Manufacturing in the Mid-1980s'. COPPAA Series No. 5, Centre for the Study of Australia Asia Relations, Griffith University, Brisbane.

Bureau of Industry Economics (1989), 'Capital Formation in Australian Manufacturing 1945–55 to 1987–88', Working Paper 54.

Coelli, T., Prasada Rao, D.S. and Battese G. (1998), An Introduction to Efficiency and Productivity, Analysis, Kluwer, Academic Publishers, Boston.

Collins, S.M. and Bosworth, B.P. (1996), 'Economic growth in East Asia: accumulation versus assimilation', Bookings Papers on Economic Activity, 1996:2, pp. 135–203.

Eurostat, 1983, Comparison in Real Values of the Aggregates of ESA: 1980, Luxembourg.

Industry Commission (1996), 'Stocktake of Progress in Macroeconomic Reform', AGPS, Canberra.

Industry Commission (1997), 'Assessing Australia's Productivity Growth', AGPS, Canberra.

Industry Commission (1997a), 'Productivity Growth and Australian Manufacturing Industry, Statistical Annex', Staff Research Paper, AGPS, Canberra.

Kravis, I.B., Heston, A. and Summers, R. (1982), 'World Production and Income – International Comparisons of Real Gross Product', Johns Hopkin University Press, Baltimore, MD.

Krugman, P. (1994), 'The myth of Asia's miracle', Foreign Affairs, vol. 73, no. 6, pp. 62–78.

Maddison, A. and van Ark, B. (1998), 'Comparisons of real output in manufacturing' Policy, Planning and Research Working Papers, WP55, World Bank, Washington, DC.

Mohr, M.F. (1991), 'Gross National Product by Industry, 1987–89' Survey of Current Business, US Department of Commerce, Washington, DC, April.

Organisation for Economic Co-operation and Development (OECD) (1997), 'National Accounts, 1960–95, Paris.

Paige, D. and Bomback, G. (1959), A Comparison of National Output and Productivity, OEEC, Paris.

Pilat, D. (1996), 'Labour Productivity Levels in OECD Countries', Economic Working Paper 169, OECD, Paris.

Pilat, D. and van Ark, B. (1992), 'Productivity Leadership in Manufacturing: Germany, Japan, and the United States 1973–1989' Research Memorandum No. 456, Institute of Economic Research, University of Groningen.

Pilat, D., Prasada Rao, D.S. and Shepherd, W.F. (1993), 'Australia and United States Manufacturing: A comparison of Real Output, Productivity Levels and Purchasing Power, 1970–1989', COPPAA Series No. 1, Centre for the Study of Australia-Asia Relations, Griffith University, Brisbane.

Productivity Commission (1998), 'Annual Report 1997–98', AusInfo, Canberra.

Productivity Commission (1998a), 'Aspects of Structural Change in Australia', Research Paper, AusInfo, Canberra.

Productivity Commission and Australian National University (PC and ANU) (1998), Macroeconomic Reform and Productivity Growth, Workshop Proceedings, AusInfo, Canberra.

Rostas, L. (1948), 'Comparative Productivity in British and American Industry', National Institute of Economic and Social Research, Cambridge University Press, London.

Szirmai, A. and Pilat, D (1990), 'Comparisons of purchasing power, real output and labour productivity in manufacturing in Japan, South Korea and the USA, 1975–1985', Review of Income and Wealth, Series 36, no. 1, March, 1–31.

Szirmai, A, Shepherd, W.F, Prasada Rao, D.S. and de Jong, G. (1995), 'Manufacturing Sector Output and Productivity in Indonesia: An Australian Comparative Perspective, 1975–1990', COPPAA Series No. 2, Centre for the Study of Australia Asia Relations, Griffith University, Brisbane.

The Conference Board Europe (Winter 1997), 'Perspectives on a Global Economy: Technology, Productivity and Growth: US and German Issues'. The Conference Board Europe, Report No. 1206-97-RR, Brussels.

The Conference Board Europe (Summer 1997), 'Perspectives on a Global economy: Understanding Differences in Economic Performance'. The Conference Board Europe, Report No. 1187-97-RR, Brussels.

Timmer, M. and Lee, B. (1996), 'China's Manufacturing Performance from an Australian Perspective, 1980–1991', COPPAA Series No. 3 Centre for the Study of Australia Asia Relations, Griffith University, Brisbane.

United Nations (UN) (1986), World Comparisons of Purchasing Power and Real Product for 1980, Phase IV of the International Comparisons Project, UN, New York.

US Department of Commerce, Bureau of Economic Analysis (1987), 'Fixed Reproducible Tangible Wealth in the United States 1925–1985', US Department of Commerce, Washington, DC.

US Department of Commerce, Bureau of Labour Statistics (1988), 'Monthly Labour Force Review' December, US Department of Commerce, Washington, DC.

US Department of Commerce, Bureau of Labour Statistics (1989), 'Ratio of Hours at Work to Hours Paid for Production and Non-Supervisory Employees, by Industry 1981–1988', US Department of Commerce, Washington, DC.

US Department of Commerce, Bureau of the Census (1990), '1987 Census of Manufacturers – General Summary', US Department of Commerce, Washington, DC.

US Department of Commerce, Bureau of the Census (1990), '1987 Census of Manufacturers – Industry Reports', US Department of Commerce, Washington, DC.

US Department of Commerce, 'Survey of Current Business' (various issues), US Department of Commerce, Washington, DC.

US Department of Commerce, Bureau of Economic Analysis (1987), 'Gross National Product by Industry and Type of Licence in Current Dollars and by Industry in Constant Dollars, 1947–1986', US Department of Commerce, Washington, DC, July.

US Department of Commerce, Bureau of Labour Statistics (1988), 'Monthly Labour Review', US Department of Commerce, Washington, DC, December.

US Department of Commerce, 'Survey of Current Business' (1989), US Department of Commerce, Washington, DC, July.

Ward, M. (1985), 'Purchasing Power Parities and Real Expenditures in the OECD', OECD, Paris.

Wu, H.X. (1997), 'Reconstructing Chinese GDP According to the National Accounts Concepts of Value Added: The Industrial Sector, 1949–1994'. COPPAA Series No. 4, Centre for the Study of Australia Asia Relations, Griffith University, Brisbane.

Young, A. (1995), 'The tyranny of numbers: confronting the statistical realities of the East Asian growth experience', Quarterly Journal of Economics, vol. 110, August, pp 641–80.

5. Industrial Output and Labour Productivity in China 1949–94: A Reassessment[1]

Harry X. Wu

1. INTRODUCTION

China's economic reforms, started in 1978, have led to a rapid transition from central planning towards a more market-oriented system and integration into the world economy. The absolute size and rapid growth of the Chinese economy have attracted great attention from economists and politicians. A good deal of this interest has concentrated on the performance of industry because it has been widely believed that growth has been particularly exaggerated in this sector of the economy (Maddison, 1998; Ren, 1997; Woo, 1996; Keidel, 1992; Perkins, 1988).

There has long been a lack of proper measurement and assessment of China's long-term industrial performance. One reason is that in China statistical data were collected using the material product system (MPS) copied from Soviet practice and fundamentally different from the internationally accepted SNA system.[2] Another, more important reason, is that available data were quite inadequate for crosschecks and alternative assessments. In fact, during the 1960s and 1970s the Chinese authorities released no systematic statistics at all. Scholarly assessment by Western economists of China's growth performance was largely based on official statistics published in the 1950s. Some significant quantitative research was completed particularly in the 1960s, but such work gradually petered out in the 1970s.[3] Research on China's economic performance during the 1970s became more crude as systematic statistics were unavailable and widely scattered sources had to be used, including speeches of government leaders, editorials in official newspapers and unpublished data from a variety of sources.[4]

In the late 1980s, to facilitate the economic transition, China's State Statistical Bureau (SSB) adopted an SNA-type of national accounting system. In 1987, SSB established China's first SNA-type input–output table to estimate GDP. China's first-ever GDP estimates were released in 1988 with retrospective estimates of GDP to 1978. From then onwards, aggregate GDP with a breakdown by five major sectors[5] has been reported in SSB's annual publication *Statistical Yearbook of China*. However, the official techniques for measuring GDP performance are obscure. Accounts on an SNA basis have recently been pushed back to 1952 in a joint publication of SSB and the Institute of Economic Research, Hitotsubashi University (1997), but these new estimates are not convincing because their growth trend for industrial GDP is almost the same as that on the old NMP estimates.[6]

This chapter is a preliminary attempt to bridge the gap by constructing an independent index for Chinese industrial output from 1949 to 1995 based primarily on officially published data of physical output and China's 1987 Input–Output Table. It is organised as follows. In the next section previous studies by Western economists are briefly reviewed. Sections 3 and 4 discuss our methodology and data sources. Section 5 reports the results and contrasts them with official figures. Section 6 assesses long-run labour productivity performance based on an alternative estimation of China's industrial employment.

2. A REVIEW OF PREVIOUS WORK

The most important previous studies of economic performance under central planning were Liu and Yeh (1965) and Chao (1965) for the 1950s. Their research was motivated by the then widely accepted hypothesis that China's official output index contained upward biases which made it unreliable (Chao, 1965, p. 1). They attempted to construct independent indices of production and/or expenditure of the economy, because they believed that these were the most systematic and comprehensive methods of checking the plausibility and consistency of the official data. Liu and Yeh estimated China's national income both by industrial origin and final expenditure, while Chao based his estimate primarily on physical output.

Liu and Yeh covered 1933 and 1952–57, while Chao focused on 1949–59. Both studies covered manufacturing, mining and utilities, but included different product groups. Liu-Yeh covered 26 modern product groups and 45 traditional handicraft products in manufacturing, 32 mining products and three in utilities (Liu and Yeh, 1965, Table F-12, G-1 and H-1). Chao covered 72 product groups in manufacturing, one product in mining and one product for utilities (Chao, 1965, Table 11). Although Chao included non-factory products that were made by the handicraft sector, his focus was 'factory products', no matter how factories were powered, by machinery or by human labour.

Liu and Yeh went back to 1933 to compare the pre- and post-revolution periods but here I focus on the period 1952–57/59.

Given the quality and limited quantity of available Chinese data, constructing growth indexes was no easy task. Both studies had to deal with many aspects of the well known 'index number problem'. Great efforts were made to adjust official production, employment, wage and price data to derive proper weights reflecting a relatively more efficient and desirable system for the allocation of resources. Price data were the most troublesome. In the centrally planned economy of that time, all prices were set by the state rather than the market.

Chao used wage bills as branch weights to avoid the 'price effect', though he still had to use unit prices for intragroup weighting. Nevertheless, the price problem was not a big deal for Chao since he aimed to construct an industrial index based on physical factory output. Liu and Yeh were different because they attempted to construct an industrial index on a net value added basis, and thus depended heavily on the reliability of price data. In fact, they did not have much choice as there were only two official constant price benchmarks for 1952 and 1957 available from the Chinese State Statistical Bureau (SSB).

It is difficult to justify the findings of these studies. Generally Liu-Yeh show faster industrial growth than Chao and closer to the official (SSB) index. Particularly, for the period of the Great Leap Forward in 1958–59, Chao suggests much slower growth than official figures, supporting the generally accepted view that the industrial growth was then overstated by the authorities. However, even if we accept the assumption that China's official series had upward biases, it does not mean that the slower the growth, the closer to the truth. Exclusion of new products developed after 1952, which generally had higher prices because of high development costs was one of the factors that led to Chao's lower growth estimates.

3. METHODOLOGY

The methodology used in this study is based on a Laspeyres' quantity index with 1987 weights. The year 1987 was selected as the benchmark mainly because it was covered by China's first SNA-type input–output table which was available when this study began.

I attempt to establish an independent growth index for each branch of industry using physical output data. It is easy to estimate value added by each branch in 1987 prices, using the 1987 input–output table. There are three major steps involved in aggregating commodity-level quantity data to the standard branch level. The first step is to obtain 1987-based quantity indices at the industry (commodity group) level that exactly match the industry classification of the 1987 input–output table. The second step is to create a time series of real gross value added (GVA) in 1987 prices at the industry level using quantity indices. We assume that the ratios of gross value added to gross value of output remain constant over time, which implies that: (a) technology remains the same over time – essentially as given by the 1987 input–output table; and (b) the 1987 price weights are held constant over the entire period in question. These are strong assumptions, but there is no better alternative. Note that the second step makes industries (commodity groups) additive. The last step is to allocate gross value added by standard industrial branch and calculate the growth index for each branch.

The mathematical expression for the major steps of the estimation is given as follows. Let q_{ij} be the ith commodity or commodity group (i = 1, 2, ..., n) of the jth industry (j = 1, 2, ..., m) in quantity and w_{ij} be the weight for this commodity or commodity group, the physical output index for the jth industry based on a fixed period, i.e. 1987 in this study, $Q_{j,t}^{Index\,87}$, is defined by the following formula

$$Q_{j,t}^{Index87} = \frac{\sum\limits_{i=1}^{n} w_{ij} q_{ij,t}}{\sum\limits_{i=1}^{n} w_{ij} q_{ij,87}}. \qquad (5.1)$$

Equation 5.1 is in line with the approach of Laspeyres index, i.e. a fixed base-period weight index.

Clearly, as given by Equation 5.1, to compute the output index, quantities of commodities within each industry have to be aggregated by proper weights, which is called '*intra*-industry grouping'. Ideally, 1987 price data for these commodities should be used to decide the weights. However, for some commodities there is not even indirect information on prices. In cases where there is no information on prices, we assume that the prices of all i commodities within industry j are the same or similar in the year 1987, i.e.

$$P_{ij,87} \cong p \text{ for } i = 1, 2, ..., n,$$

then the Laspeyres quantity index is simplified to

$$Q_{j,t}^{\text{Index87}} = \frac{\sum_{i=1}^{n} q_{ij,t} P_{ij,87}}{\sum_{i=1}^{n} q_{ij,87} P_{ij,87}} = \frac{\sum_{i=1}^{n} q_{ij,t}}{\sum_{i=1}^{n} q_{ij,87}}. \tag{5.2}$$

The index for industry j given in Equation 5.2 is simply the ratio of the sum of the i quantities in period t to that of 1987. The only problem with this approach is that it is not independent of the unit of measurement. If the unit in which a particular commodity is measured changes, then the index changes. An unweighted geometric mean is often used to deal with this problem.[7] In this study, however, outside information is used to measure a commodity in a consistent unit over time. This is in line with the case where direct price or unit value data are available.

In cases where 1987 price data or unit value (UV) are available, the weight for the ith commodity of the jth industry is simply defined as

$$w_{ij,87} = \frac{UV_{ij,87}}{\sum_{i=1}^{n} UV_{ij,87}}. \tag{5.3}$$

Then the Equation 5.1 can be equivalently written as

$$Q_{j,t}^{\text{Index87}} = \frac{\sum_{i=1}^{n} UV_{ij,87} q_{ij,t}}{\sum_{i=1}^{n} UV_{ij,87} q_{ij,87}}. \tag{5.4}$$

The next step is to create a time series of gross value added (GVA) in 1987 prices for the jth industry by the following method

$$GVA_{j,t} = GVA_{j,87} \times \frac{\sum_{i=1}^{n} UV_{ij,87} q_{ij,t}}{\sum_{i=1}^{n} UV_{ij,87} q_{ij,87}}, \tag{5.5}$$

which can be rearranged as,

$$GVA_{j,t} = \frac{GVA_{j,87}}{\sum_{i=1}^{n} UV_{ij,87} q_{ij,87}} \times \sum_{i=1}^{n} UV_{ij,87} q_{ij,t} \qquad (5.5a)$$

$$= \begin{bmatrix} GVA \text{ to GVO Ratio} \\ \text{at the 1987 price} \end{bmatrix} \times \begin{bmatrix} GVO \text{ at the 1987} \\ \text{price in year } t \end{bmatrix}.$$

Finally, the estimated GVAs for each j industry of the kth branch are summed to obtain the GVA for the branch, that is,

$$GVA_{k,t} = \sum_{j=1}^{m} GVA_{jk,t}, \qquad (5.6)$$

based on which the growth index at constant 1987 prices for each branch can be derived.

4. DATA SOURCES AND PROBLEMS

Data on the physical output of each industrial commodity were obtained from various volumes of *China Industrial Economic Statistical Yearbook* published by the Department of Industry and Transportation Statistics (DITS) of SSB. Commodities included in the Yearbook are therefore called CIES items in this study. The number of available CIES items is about 200 but varies slightly from year to year. For example, there are 198 items reported in the 1994 Yearbook which covers the period 1949–93. Most of these items were updated to 1994 in the 1995 Yearbook.[8]

Gross value added data by industry were obtained from *China 1987 Input–Output Table* (DBNE and ONIOS, 1991). The GVA data are available at the industry level specified in the input–output table (called CIOT industries in this study). CIOT industries are allocated to branches according to the ISIC (international standard industrial classification) criteria.

Ideally, weights for intra-industry aggregation should be based on producer prices of all commodities of the relevant industry. In the absence of such price data, two approaches are used. One is to adopt 'common sense' 1987 weights for individual items in a particular CIOT industry, with the sum of the assumed weights equal to 100. The other is to aggregate all the items in quantitative units, i.e. impose a 1987 quantity weight. The latter approach is mainly used for industries whose products are relatively homogenous. Neither approach is satisfactory, but there are no alternatives. A top research priority in future will certainly be the estimation of more reliable intra-industry weights for benchmark years (see Wu 1997, Table A4).[9]

Not every CIES item could be used in constructing our quantity index. In the first stage of data processing, items with the following problems were dropped: (a) less representative items, which are difficult to allocate to a particular group; (b) significantly incomplete time series; and (c) absence of relevant price data for weighting. As a result, only 116 of the 198 available items were selected (Wu, 1997, Table A2). Most of the selected CIES items were available annually from 1949 to 1994. However, some start later than 1949, either because they were new products only available after 1949, or because they were not included in official statistics in the earlier period or the data had been lost. For items where there are data gaps, interpolation and/or extrapolation was used to reconstruct time series by following either their own trend or the trend of other relevant items, often obtained by regression.

Another problem is that in most cases the value of a CIOT industry could not be fully identified by the available CIES items. In such cases, the unidentified or non-covered part of the CIOT industry was assumed to follow the same trend as the identified part of the industry.[10]

5. RESULTS AND PRELIMINARY ANALYSIS

Following the methodology discussed previously, using available CIES quantity data and other information, the *intra*-industry grouping by weights for each CIOT industry is made (Wu, 1997, Table A4). The result of the *intra*-industry grouping exercise is the physical output index by CIOT industry. The GVA time series for each CIOT industry is extrapolated by applying the GVA from China's 1987 Input–Output Table to the estimated industrial output index. Then all the CIOT industries in GVA are grouped into relevant ISIC branches, assuming that the CIES-unidentified CIOT items moved along the same trend as that of the CIES-identified CIOT items. Table 5.1 reports the estimated GVA for 15 manufacturing branches, plus mining and utilities, for selected years. This table also presents GVA estimates for the industrial sector as a whole for 1987 under both Chinese and Western classifications.[11]

5.1 Growth Rate Performance

Figure 5.1 compares China's industrial growth from 1949 to 1994 as estimated here and in official sources. Table 5.2 shows rates of growth of my index by industrial branch for selected periods and compares my aggregate estimates with the official (SSB) estimates and the recent SSB-Hitotsubashi estimates mentioned earlier. My estimates for the industrial sector as a whole show slower growth. The differences are significant: nearly 2 percentage points for the pre-reform period 1952–78 (Mao Zedong's central planning era) and 3.5 percentage points for the post-reform period 1978–94 (Deng Xiaoping's market era). Contrary to the official estimates, our estimates show a slower industrial growth in the post reform than in the pre-reform period.

The only exception is in the Great Leap Forward years 1958–60 where my new estimates have almost no correction effect, even though the reported rate is unbelievably high. One possible reason is that the original reports on growth rate in these years were too high to be credited and the statistical authority adjusted them using a physical output approach similar to ours.[12]

Table 5.1 Estimated Gross Value Added (GVA) by Industrial Branch, Selected Years 1952–94 (million 1987 yuan)

	1952	1957	1960	1965	1970	1978	1987	1994
1. Food products	1 230.31	1 910.00	2 000.22	2 916.26	3 022.38	6 167.01	18 548.86	27 379.38
a. Identified by CIES items	908.08	1 409.76	1 476.35	2 152.47	2 230.80	4 551.82	13 690.77	20 208.51
b. Residual	322.23	500.24	523.87	763.79	791.59	1 615.19	4 858.09	7 170.87
2. Beverages	204.49	595.69	1 155.82	791.29	1 075.80	2 196.06	10 624.65	19 853.43
a. Identified by CIES items	165.26	481.40	934.06	639.47	869.39	1 774.71	8 586.17	16 044.28
b. Residual	39.23	114.29	221.76	151.82	206.41	421.34	2 038.48	3 809.14
3. Tobacco products	1 784.89	3 004.00	3 024.20	3 219.53	5 273.83	7 961.26	19 404.74	23 115.96
4. Textile mill products	5 949.30	8 738.54	10 889.31	11 998.28	17 768.46	22 321.23	42 591.72	54 603.00
a. Identified by CIES items	5 602.56	8 229.24	10 254.67	11 299.01	16 732.89	21 020.32	40 109.42	51 420.66
b. Residual	346.73	509.29	634.64	699.28	1 035.57	1 300.91	2 482.30	3 182.33
5. Wearing apparels	1 274.48	1 872.00	2 332.74	2 570.31	3 806.41	4 781.72	9 124.13	11 791.31
6. Leather products and footwear	203.71	495.94	771.04	362.11	901.13	1 680.64	4 523.09	17 523.44
7. Wood products, furniture fixtures	2 125.62	3 732.89	7 355.57	5 267.19	5 006.52	5 057.88	6 863.60	6 613.11
a. Identified by CIES items	805.10	1 413.88	2 786.01	1 995.01	1 896.28	1 915.73	2 599.67	2 504.79
b. Residual	1 320.51	2 319.02	4 569.56	3 272.18	3 110.24	3 142.15	4 263.93	4 108.32
8. Paper products, printing, publishing	462.77	1 138.17	2 251.33	2 163.78	3 014.28	5 490.74	14 270.92	26 740.78
a. Identified by CIES items	285.86	703.07	1 390.69	1 336.61	1 861.98	3 391.74	8 815.43	16 518.31
b. Residual	176.91	435.10	860.64	827.17	1 152.30	2 099.00	5 455.49	10 222.47
9. Chemicals, petroleum, coal products	1 317.24	3 228.00	6 548.57	9 240.13	14 710.39	34 000.57	62 226.62	102 478.42
a. Identified by CIES items	1 316.06	3 225.11	6 542.71	9 231.87	14 697.23	33 970.16	62 170.96	102 386.76
b. Residual	1.18	2.89	5.86	8.27	13.16	30.41	55.66	91.66
10. Rubber and plastic products	210.82	469.00	834.81	1 284.64	2 314.77	4 945.79	13 734.59	40 953.66
a. Identified by CIES items	1 243.53	3 504.73	4 457.08	4 693.22	6 091.34	13 149.48	32 795.76	70 064.97
b. Residual	604.89	1 704.81	2 168.06	2 282.93	2 963.02	6 396.31	15 952.86	34 081.74
11. Building materials etc.	638.64	1 799.92	2 289.02	2 410.29	3 128.33	6 753.17	16 842.90	35 983.22
a. Identified by CIES items	604.89	1 704.81	2 168.06	2 282.93	2 963.02	6 396.31	15 952.86	39 953.24
b. Residual	638.64	1 799.92	2 289.02	2 410.29	3 128.33	6 753.17	16 842.90	42 182.30
12. Basic and fabricated metal products	1 163.93	4 562.46	17 420.24	10 789.43	16 705.22	30 237.71	50 824.88	83 573.46
a. Identified by CIES items	803.66	3 150.25	12 028.19	7 449.80	11 534.48	20 878.29	35 093.16	57 705.14
b. Residual	360.27	1 412.21	5 392.05	3 339.63	5 170.73	9 359.42	15 731.72	25 868.32

Table 5.1 (continued)

	1952	1957	1960	1965	1970	1978	1987	1994
13. Machinery and transport equipment	810.03	2 926.76	14 335.99	5 647.36	15 387.51	28 182.26	61 183.35	143 194.49
a. Identified by CIES items	744.40	2 689.61	13 174.38	5 189.77	14 140.69	25 898.71	56 225.80	131 591.76
b. Residual	65.64	237.15	1 161.61	457.59	1 246.82	2 283.55	4 957.55	11 602.73
14. Electrical machinery and equipment	169.50	597.67	3 523.04	1 393.76	4 079.18	8 070.37	28 587.01	94 425.48
a. Identified by CIES items	165.81	584.65	3 446.29	1 363.40	3 990.31	7 894.54	27 964.20	92 368.28
b. Residual	3.69	13.02	76.75	30.37	88.87	175.82	622.81	2 057.20
15. Other manufacturing	1 218.50	2 212.52	6 033.28	4 514.42	6 600.61	9 990.08	14 768.55	23 722.50
a. Identified by CIES items	660.69	1 199.66	3 271.35	2 447.79	3 578.97	5 416.79	8 007.76	12 862.74
b. Residual	557.81	1 012.85	2 761.93	2 066.62	3 021.65	4 573.29	6 760.79	10 859.75
Total manufacturing	19 369.12	38 988.37	82 933.26	66 851.73	105 757.83	184 232.79	390 072.47	746 033.37
a. Identified by CIES items	15 536.28	30 632.38	64 435.55	52 824.72	86 792.18	152 478.54	326 002.75	631 077.35
b. Residual	3 832.84	8 355.99	18 497.71	14 027.01	18 965.65	31 754.24	64 069.72	114 956.02
Mining	1 865.38	4 018.33	11 917.54	8 461.68	14 593.30	34 889.29	46 420.13	59 325.09
a. Identified by CIES items	1 736.00	3 739.63	11 090.97	7 874.81	13 581.16	32 469.47	43 200.57	55 210.48
b. Residual	129.38	278.70	826.56	586.88	1 012.15	2 419.82	3 219.56	4 114.61
Utilities	358.91	948.89	2 920.42	3 323.58	5 698.26	12 615.83	24 449.93	45 630.36
a. Identified by CIES items	333.55	881.86	2 714.11	3 088.79	5 295.72	11 724.60	22 722.69	42 406.85
b. Residual	25.35	67.03	206.31	234.79	402.55	891.23	1 727.24	3 223.51
Total industry	21 593.41	43 955.59	97 771.21	78 636.99	126 049.40	231 737.90	460 942.53	850 988.83
a. Identified by CIES items	17 605.83	35 253.87	78 240.63	63 788.32	105 669.05	196 672.61	391 926.01	728 694.69
b. Residual	3 987.57	8 701.72	19 530.58	14 848.68	20 380.35	35 065.29	69 016.52	122 294.14
Forestry (1987 only)							6 448.39	
Repair and maintenance (1987 only)							5 463.48	
Total industry (Official definition for 1987)							472 854.40	

89

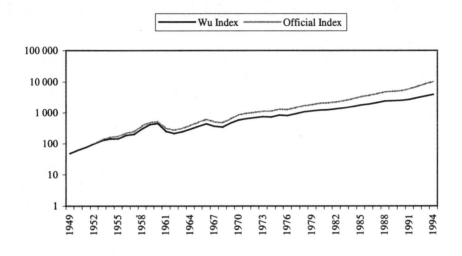

Source: Official estimates are as given in Table 5.2.

Figure 5.1 Summary Confrontation: Official Versus Wu's Growth Indices (1952=100)

In Table 5.2, three periods appear to be 'abnormal', including the 1949–52 recovery from the war, the Great Leap Forward years (1957–60) and its aftermath (1960–65). If these periods are excluded, the overall growth looks more 'normal'. In fact, the fifth column presents the annual compound growth rate of the period 1957–65 that ignores the sharp fluctuations particularly in 1958–62.

It is interesting to compare the two stages of the post-reform period. The first post-reform period (1978–87) saw a clear policy adjustment towards light consumer goods. As a result, light manufactures grew faster than heavy manufactures (9.55 compared to 8.16 per cent per annum) for the first time since 1949. The main contributor to this significant change was rural enterprises that were granted more freedom to develop labour-intensive manufacturing in a more market-oriented environment (Wu, 1994).

The second post-reform period (1988–94) saw a slight slow-down in the growth of light manufacturing, except for leather goods and footwear manufactures, while heavy manufacturing seemed to have regained a fast growth momentum. This should, however, be examined more closely. In fact, since the late 1980s the role of the market has become more important. As a result, the distinction between heavy and light industries does not always reflect the difference between producer and consumer goods. It is true that as Table 5.2 shows, industries mainly producing consumer goods, such as food, beverages, leather products, grew more rapidly in the post-reform than in the pre-reform period, while industries mainly producing producer goods, such as machinery, chemicals and metals, grew less rapidly in the post-reform than in the pre-reform period. But, some heavy industries moved towards concentration on consumer goods, such as building materials, electrical equipment and machinery industries. These industries have experienced fast growth since the reform, driven by increasing demand for household electrical goods and housing.

Table 5.2 Annual Average Compound Growth Rates of Gross Value Added by Industrial Branch, Selected Periods, 1949–94 (in percentages)

	1949 to 1952	1952 to 1957	1957 to 1960	1960 to 1965	1957 to 1965	1965 to 1970	1970 to 1978	1978 to 1987	1987 to 1994	1952 to 1978	1978 to 1994	1952 to 1994
1. Food products	30.75	9.20	1.55	7.83	5.43	0.72	9.32	13.02	5.72	6.40	9.76	7.67
2. Beverages	25.99	23.84	24.73	-7.30	3.61	6.34	9.33	19.14	9.34	9.56	14.75	11.51
3. Tobacco products	18.32	10.97	0.22	1.26	0.87	10.37	5.28	10.41	2.53	5.92	6.89	6.29
4. Textile products	25.77	7.99	7.61	1.96	4.04	8.17	2.89	7.44	3.61	5.22	5.75	5.42
5. Wearing apparel	25.77	7.99	7.61	1.96	4.04	8.17	2.89	7.44	3.73	5.22	5.80	5.44
6. Leather products, footwear	8.83	19.48	15.85	-14.03	-3.86	20.00	8.10	11.63	21.35	8.45	15.78	11.19
7. Wood products, furniture, fixtures	17.01	11.92	25.37	-6.46	4.40	-1.01	0.13	3.45	-0.53	3.39	1.69	2.74
8. Paper, printing and publishing	49.83	19.72	25.53	-0.79	8.36	6.85	7.78	11.20	9.39	9.98	10.40	10.14
9. Chemicals, petroleum and coal products	11.45	19.63	26.59	7.13	14.05	9.75	11.04	6.95	7.39	13.32	7.14	10.92
10. Rubber, plastic products	29.52	17.34	21.19	9.00	13.42	12.50	9.96	12.02	16.89	12.90	14.12	13.37
11. Building materials, etc.	33.21	23.03	8.34	1.04	3.72	5.35	10.10	10.69	11.45	9.50	11.02	10.07
12. Basic and fabricated metal products	95.66	31.42	56.30	-9.14	11.36	9.14	7.70	5.94	7.36	13.35	6.56	10.71
13. Machinery, transport equipment	61.84	29.29	69.83	-17.00	8.56	22.20	7.86	8.99	12.92	14.63	10.69	13.11
14. Electrical equipment	44.72	28.66	80.64	-16.93	11.16	23.96	8.90	15.09	18.61	16.02	16.62	16.25
15. Other manufacturing	52.94	12.67	39.71	-5.64	9.32	7.89	5.32	4.44	7.00	8.43	5.55	7.32
Total manufacturing	27.70	15.02	28.07	-3.98	6.97	9.61	7.18	8.69	9.71	9.05	9.13	9.08
Heavy manufacturing	38.11	24.90	42.55	-5.90	9.95	11.48	9.00	8.16	10.31	12.68	9.09	11.30
Light manufacturing	24.57	10.34	15.89	-1.73	4.54	7.55	4.62	9.55	8.76	6.23	9.20	7.36
Mining	27.14	16.59	43.67	-6.62	9.76	11.52	11.51	3.22	3.57	11.92	3.37	8.59
Utilities	19.29	21.46	45.46	2.62	16.96	11.39	10.45	7.63	9.32	14.67	8.37	12.23
A. Total industry (This study)	27.49	15.28	30.07	-4.06	7.54	9.90	7.91	7.94	9.15	9.56	8.47	9.14
B. Total industry (SSB: NMP/GDP)	n.a.	19.58	30.34	-2.47	8.73	12.56	8.68	10.40	13.83	11.46	11.89	11.65
C. Total industry (SSB-IERHU: GDP)	n.a.	19.84	28.11	-1.09	8.98	11.62	8.96	10.40	13.83	11.46	11.89	11.65
Over-estimation disparity (B-A)		4.30	0.27	1.59	1.19	2.66	0.77	2.46	4.68	1.90	3.42	2.51

Source: Branch estimates are from this study. Estimates for total industry A from this study; B the official NMP figures for the period 1952–77 and GDP figures for 1978–94 (SSB, 1993, p. 34; 1996, p. 42); and C the SSB-Hitotsubashi estimates of GDP for all years 1952–94 (SSB-IERHU, 1997, Table A10).

5.2 Structural Changes

Figure 5.2 shows structural changes in China's industrial sector, and demonstrates the continuing long-term emphasis on heavy industry. The pre-reform period saw a fast decline in the share of light industries and a rapid rise in the share of heavy industries. From 1952 to 1978, the light industrial share declined from 67 to 28 per cent, while the heavy industrial share increased from 33 to 72 per cent. During this period, however, there was temporary reversal following the collapse of the GLF: the heavy industrial share began to decline in 1960 and regained its 1960 level of 63 per cent only in 1970.

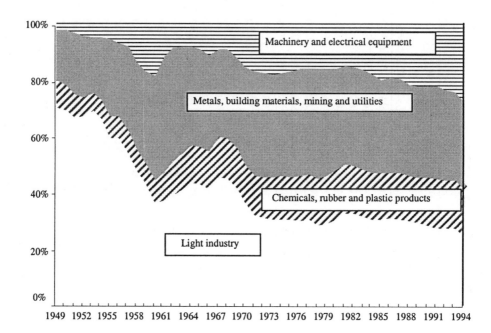

Figure 5.2 Structural Changes in Chinese Industry Value Added, 1952–94

The overall trend in the growth of heavy industry changed at the early stage of the economic reform. From 1978 to 1982, the share of light industries increased significantly by 5 percentage points from about 28 to 33 per cent. Although it declined afterwards, it maintained at a level of about 30–31 per cent until 1988. This was mainly due to the rapid development of market-driven, labour-intensive, small scale enterprises, most of which were located in rural areas, during this period (Wu, 1994).

The growth of the heavy industrial sector has speeded up since the 1990s, but heavy industry development in the post-reform period is perhaps somewhat healthier than in the pre-reform period because it has taken place in a more market-oriented environment. For example, one of the driving forces behind the fast growth of electrical equipment industries during this period came from consumer goods such as colour television sets and other household appliances. Another important sign of healthy development is that some heavy industries in which China apparently lacks a comparative advantage experienced a decline, such as chemicals, mining, basic metals and wood products. However, severe structural problems still exist and more significant adjustments are expected with further reform of the state sector.

5.3 Justification for the 1987 Price Weights

As stated before, the growth and structure indicators derived from the new estimates represent the movement of physical output indicators with price weights for the single year 1987 (i.e. a Laspeyres index). The 1987 price structure is likely to be less distorted than those of earlier years when central planning dominated resource allocation. Furthermore, our 1987 measure of gross value added is based on the SNA approach which characterised the 1987 input–output table.

However, it is possible that there have been changes in the aggregate input–output ratio for industry in the 45-year period covered. If the ratio of value added to gross output has been falling over time, our estimates will overstate the growth of value added and if the ratio has been rising, they will understate it.

Unfortunately, there is no adequate input–output table prior to that of 1987, hence it is impossible to estimate the extent to which the 1987 weights are biased. However, there are input–output tables for 1990 and 1992. A scrutiny of the aggregate ratios in these sources reveals a significant fall in the ratio of value added to gross output of the industrial sector between 1987 and 1990, and between 1990 and 1992, down from 34.5 per cent in 1987 (see Wu, 1997, Table A1) to 30.3 per cent in 1990 and 28.6 per cent in 1992.[13] If this increasing input ratio was characteristic for 1949 to 1994 as a whole, then our fixed 1987 weights will have overstated China's industrial growth.

Research on China and East Europe's centrally-planned economies has shown that their value added ratios in the late 1980s were significantly lower than in Western economies.[14] These centrally-planned economies made wasteful use of raw materials and other intermediate inputs because the price system did not encourage efficiency. Inputs of steel and energy were characteristically higher in these countries than in the West (van Ark, 1996). Apart from waste of inputs, these countries also tended to accumulate large unmarketable inventories.[15] Moreover, the ratios of these economies fell a good deal from pre-war levels to the 1990s. Research suggests that the Chinese economy was less wasteful of inputs than other former centrally-planned economies, but more wasteful than industrial economies.

There is another reason for thinking that the use of 1987 weights may exaggerate industrial growth. In general, smaller enterprises have lower value added ratios than larger ones. Since the size of the average enterprise has fallen in the process of economic reform mainly due to the fast development of labour-intensive rural enterprises, the value added ratio for the industrial sector must have fallen for this reason.[16]

On the other hand, there may also be factors that cause bias in the opposite direction. Post-reform decontrol and decentralisation of the economy probably means that the statistical authorities have not been able to record output as fully as in the past, especially in family-based rural enterprises. The possibility of increasingly lower coverage over time may have produced a downward bias which would to some extent compensate the effect of the upward bias due to increased input ratios. This downward bias effect should not, however, be exaggerated. In principle, SSB does not exclude any industrial activities, even though it is difficult to cover all small scale activities. Statistical coverage of industry has been generally improved since 1985 because of China's second national industrial census, and the 1987 weights used in this study are derived from the 1987 Input–Output Table based on a special survey attempting better coverage than the national SSB data collection network.[17]

5.4 Conclusions on the New Estimate of Gross Value Added

This exercise is a step forward towards a reconstruction of Chinese national GDP according to the national accounts concept of value added. It also provides a basis for international comparison of output and productivity for China using the ICOP approach developed in Groningen University.

The empirical results have a significant downward correction effect on the Chinese official growth rates. The results therefore support the hypothesis that the Chinese official growth index overstated China's industrial growth. The extent to which the official index may have overestimated growth performance varies over different periods and across different manufacturing branches and industries.

The Laspeyres index approach used in this study inevitably produces biases because it is subject to a fairly strong assumption that the 1987 price weights or the relationship between input and output prices remained unchanged over time. However, the evidence of rising input–output ratios over time in East European centrally-planned economies and China suggests that my study results may still exaggerate China's industrial output performance.

6. LABOUR PRODUCTIVITY PERFORMANCE

There is no reliable official assessment of China's industrial labour productivity performance because of problems in measuring both output and labour input. In fact, SSB has never collected or released any data on working hours in industry.

6.1 Inconsistencies in Current Official Industrial Employment Statistics

There are three major problems with China's official industrial employment statistics: (1) there is no unique published official source that has ultimate authority; (2) the definition of major employment indicators which are available is often obscure; and (3) the coverage of these indicators is inconsistent over time, particularly when used by different statistical authorities. These problems existed before the reform, but they have become more severe since the 1980s as the economy shifted from highly centralised planning towards a market system.

There are two basic concepts in Chinese employment statistics: 'staff and workers' or *zhigong*,[18] and 'persons engaged' or *congye renyuan*. The indicator 'staff and workers' was adopted in the early 1950s, along with the adoption of a central planning system, to refer to those who were allocated to a permanent position in state owned enterprises (SOEs) or urban collectively owned enterprises (COEs) by the nation-wide labour administration system within the planning framework.[19] These 'staff and workers' usually held urban or non-agricultural *hukou* (residential registration) status and were thereby entitled to subsidised rations for basic needs. The indicator 'persons engaged' was used under another name, 'social labourers' or *shehui laodongzhe*. This broader category included not only 'staff and workers' but also labourers outside the labour administration system, mainly in rural enterprises.[20]

One of the important consequences of the economic reform in the early 1980s was decentralisation of the labour administration system, which encouraged a rapid growth of outside-system employment. Important inconsistencies have therefore appeared in the official use of the two indicators. For example, two official sources, both belonging to SSB, have reported very different figures for the two indicators. These are the Department of Industrial and Transportation Statistics (DITS) and the Department of Population and Employment Statistics (DPES).[21] The DITS source reports that in 1994 the number of industrial 'staff and workers' was 83.3 million and the number of 'persons engaged' in industry was 150.6 million (1995, p. 85 and p. 5), while the DPES source gives the two indicators as 65.8 million and 107.7 million, respectively (1995, p. 18 and p. 11). The difference between the two sources is enormous. The DITS figures are about 27 and 40 per cent higher than the DPES figures, respectively.

However, on closer examination of the coverage of the indicators, one finds that both DPES and DITS have changed the definition of 'staff and workers' but in different ways. The DPES definition basically follows the previous principle that confines 'staff and workers' to cities and industrial areas. Therefore, in addition to employment in SOEs and urban COEs, for the post-reform period it also covers the employment in the recently emerged share-holding companies and foreign-funded enterprises (DPES, 1995, p. 639), most of which are located in newly established Special Economic Zones and Economic and Technological Development Areas. By contrast, the DITS definition includes employment in rural industry in addition to the DPES coverage, but is confined to employment in township – and above level enterprises (see DITS, 1992, p. 90).

For 'persons engaged', both the DPES and DITS figures seem to have followed the same definition, that is, they include anyone engaged in industrial employment no matter where the relevant enterprise is located and whether the job is administrated by the state labour administration system.[22] However, one may ask why, if the definition used is the same, the DITS figure is 40 per cent higher than the DPES figure? While the definition used by DPES has been published in all the DPES and SSB yearbooks, the definition used by DITS has never been clearly given. The author's interviews[23] with statisticians from DPES and DITS suggest that the key difference between the two departments is that DPES only includes those engaged in enterprises classified as 'independent accounting units' or *duli hesuan danwei*, while DITS also includes those employed by 'attached industrial units' or *fuying danwei* that are attached to 'independent accounting units' that are usually engaged in non-industrial activities (SDSB, 1993, pp. 107–108). Nevertheless, this certainly does not justify the 40 per cent difference between the DITS and DPES figures.

The above examples clearly suggest that China's statistical authorities have failed to develop employment indicators that not only reflect changes in the employment system but also maintain historical consistency. Furthermore, they have not even been able to explain the inconsistencies among various official sources. Clearly, any direct use of these official indicators without being aware of their significant inconsistencies can only produce meaningless analysis of labour input and productivity.

6.2 An alternative Estimate of Industrial Employment

Due to the inconsistencies in official industrial employment statistics, there is a need for an alternative estimate which reflects the *effective* labour input in industry. Such an estimate necessarily involves a quantitative judgement on the 'merits' of the available indicators, and adjustments to measure effective labour input.

The indicator 'persons engaged' is more problematic than that for 'staff and workers'. As China faces a severe unemployment problem, job creation has been one of the most important policy goals of the government. In the post-reform circumstances where marketisation encouraged the non-state sector to grow and forced the state sector to restructure, local officials understandably had strong incentives to exaggerate the numbers employed in the non-state sector and to underreport unemployment in the state sector. Since it is easier to supervise the urban and state sector than the rural and non-state sector, the overall net bias towards over-reporting will have more impact on the quality of 'persons engaged' than the quality of 'staff and workers'. This tendency is likely to be further strengthened by the way in which employment data are collected which involves attempts to simplify and standardise data collection in rural areas. As explained in an official statistical handbook, anyone is counted as *employed* as long as he or she worked at least for one hour during the week the survey was conducted (DPSSTS, 1998, p. 52). Local officials with strong incentives to exaggerate what they have achieved in promoting rural employment would understandably interpret this criterion in a loose way.[24] Due to this concern, although the above-mentioned 40-per cent difference between the DITS and DPES figures on 'persons engaged' is hardly to be justified given available information,[25] it is reasonable to select the DPES indicator instead of the DITS one.

If the indicator 'persons engaged' tends to exaggerate China's real industrial employment, can the DPES indicator for 'staff and workers' be used? By definition, this indicator is narrower in coverage than the indicator 'persons engaged'. However, this does not make it a reliable indicator of industrial employment. It underestimates employment because it totally excludes rural workers, though it tends to exaggerate the number of 'staff and workers' in state enterprises,[26] because local officials have an incentive to hide unemployment caused by their restructuring.

The DITS indicator of 'staff and workers' avoids the overestimation of 'persons engaged' and the underestimation of 'staff and workers' which one finds with the DPES indicator. There are two reasons for this: (a) township enterprises have a longer history, are larger and more stable than the rural smaller village and family enterprises; (b) the DITS indicator of 'staff and workers' comes with matching financial indicators, which characterise enterprises able to carry out basic accounting practices.

However, the DITS indicator is available only from 1987. To construct a comparable measure of 'staff and workers' before 1987 we need to add 'qualified' rural industrial labourers to the DPES series of 'staff and workers' for the urban sector to make it 'consistent' with the DITS series for the post-1987 period. Rural township enterprise employment is used as a proxy for 'qualified' rural industrial employment. Our labour input measure is shown in the third column of Table 5.3.

Table 5.3   *Alternative Measure of Labour Productivity in Chinese Industry: Gross Value Added Per Person Engaged, 1952–94*

		Labour Input		Labour Productivity	
Year	Gross value added by industry (million 1987 yuan)	Official/DPES persons engaged ('000)	Wu's alternative measure of persons engaged ('000)	Variant A per person engaged in 1987 yuan	Variant B per person engaged in 1987 yuan
1952	21 593	12 460	12 460	1 733	1 733
1953	27 319	13 730	13 730	1 990	1 990
1954	31 129	15 010	15 010	2 074	2 074
1955	31 499	14 000	14 000	2 250	2 250
1956	40 080	13 750	13 750	2 915	2 915
1957	43 956	14 010	14 010	3 137	3 137
1958	65 482	44 160	25 160	1 483	2 603
1959	90 285	28 810	22 680	3 134	3 981
1960	97 771	29 790	24 820	3 282	3 939
1961	53 989	22 240	19 940	2 428	2 708
1962	46 753	17 050	17 050	2 742	2 742
1963	53 226	16 320	16 320	3 261	3 261
1964	63 629	16 950	16 950	3 754	3 754
1965	78 637	18 280	17 914	4 302	4 390
1966	93 956	19 740	19 345	4 760	4 857
1967	78 939	20 320	19 914	3 885	3 964
1968	75 097	20 920	20 502	3 590	3 663
1969	99 512	23 650	23 177	4 208	4 294
1970	126 049	28 090	27 247	4 487	4 626
1971	140 148	32 330	31 360	4 335	4 469
1972	150 190	34 960	33 911	4 296	4 429
1973	162 013	37 040	35 929	4 374	4 509
1974	159 466	39 000	37 830	4 089	4 215
1975	182 230	42 840	41 126	4 254	4 431
1976	177 107	46 920	45 043	3 775	3 932
1977	201 411	48 090	46 166	4 188	4 363
1978	231 738	60 910	50 478	3 805	4 591
1979	250 093	62 980	52 618	3 971	4 753
1980	266 057	67 140	55 389	3 963	4 803
1981	269 507	69 750	57 753	3 864	4 667
1982	289 637	72 040	59 441	4 020	4 873
1983	312 558	73 970	60 722	4 225	5 147
1984	341 869	79 300	61 569	4 311	5 553
1985	386 072	83 490	66 045	4 624	5 846
1986	416 570	89 800	68 715	4 639	6 062
1987	460 943	93 420	72 980	4 934	6 316
1988	515 336	96 610	75 181	5 334	6 855
1989	532 330	95 680	75 460	5 564	7 054
1990	545 021	96 970	76 633	5 621	7 112

Table 5.3 (Continued)

		Labour Input		Labour Productivity	
	Gross value added by industry (million	Official/DPES persons engaged	Wu's alternative measure of persons engaged	Variant A per person engaged in 1987	Variant B per person engaged in 1987
Year	1987 yuan)	('000)	('000)	yuan	yuan
1991	591 379	99 470	79 652	5 945	7 424
1992	665 253	102 200	80 081	6 509	8 307
1993	749 229	104 670	82 999	7 158	9 027
1994	850 989	107 740	83 295	7 899	10 217

Source: Column 1 is my aggregate measure of gross value added in Chinese industry, see detailed figures for selected years in Table 5.1. Column 2 is the official labour input measure of the Department of Population and Employment Statistics (DPES) described in Section 6.1 above. Column 3 is my preferred measure of labour input, derived by adjusting the estimates of the Department of Industrial and Transport Statistics (DITS) as described in Section 6.2 above. Column 4 (Variant A) shows labour productivity derived by dividing Column 1 by Column 2. Column 5 (Variant B) is my preferred measure of labour productivity dividing Column 1 by Column 3.

6.3 Conclusions on Labour Productivity

My estimates of industrial gross value added for 1952–94 are used with both the official (DPES) indicator of labour input and my alternative estimates in order to derive alternative measure of labour productivity. The estimated results are reported in Column 5, Table 5.3, which contrasts another labour productivity measure (Column 4) based on official employment data.

My estimates show industrial labour productivity growing at 3.8 per cent in the pre-reform period and 5.3 per cent in the post-reform period, compared to 3.1 and 4.7 per cent per year, using the DPES denominator. My productivity result for the post-reform period is very close to that of Maddison in his recent study on China (5.2 per cent), but my result for the pre-reform period is higher (2.6 per cent) than his (Maddison, 1998, p. 81). My new estimates give further support to the expectation that market-oriented reforms have improved the efficiency of China's industrial production, though more sophisticated tests are needed to support this argument.

NOTES

1. Some of this study is based on research initiated when the author visited the University of Groningen in April–May 1996. Preliminary results of the research were published in the COPPAA (Comparison of Output, Productivity and Purchasing Power in Australia and Asia) Series and a University of Groningen Research Report (Wu, 1997). The author is very much indebted to Angus Maddison for detailed comments and very helpful suggestions. Initial financial support from the Research School of SOM, University of Groningen, is gratefully acknowledged. The new work described in this chapter was substantially supported by a Departmental Research Grant of Hong Kong Polytechnic University (No. S775). I alone am responsible for any errors or omissions.
2. See Wu (1997) for a detailed discussion of the problems in China's statistical practice.

3. For example, see Hollister (1959), Li (1959), Eckstein (1961), Liu and Yeh (1965), Chao (1965, 1968, 1970, 1974), Field (1980), Perkins (1975, 1980).

4. It should also be mentioned here that during the 1970s the US CIA carried out some work (by Michael Field) attempting to reconstruct Chinese industrial growth independently. But the method was rather crude, the data were poor and the work stopped after 1982. The CIA measures for China were published by the Joint Economic Committee of the US Congress (JEC) in 1972 (pp. 46–7), 1975 (pp. 42–3), 1978 (p. 231) and 1982 (p. 104).

5. Following the tradition of the MPS, the five sectors are agriculture, industry (manufacturing and mining), construction, transportation and telecommunication, and commerce.

6. A simple test for the relationship between the newly estimated industrial GDP and the old industrial NMP based on the equation, $\ln GDP_t = \alpha + \beta \ln NMP_t$, finds an almost identical growth trend of the two series with an adjusted R^2 of 0.9997. See Table 2 for a comparison of the SSB-Hitotsubashi GDP estimates with the SSB NMP-GDP estimates for selected years.

7. That is, $Q_{j,t}^{\text{Index87}} = \prod_{i=1}^{n} \left(\dfrac{Q_{i,t}}{Q_{i,87}} \right)^{y_n}$ which is independent of units of measurement.

8. See Wu (1997, Table A2) for CIES items of selected benchmark years. The full time series data used in the estimation are available from the author on request.

9. After a recent effort of data search, I have acquired 2000 detailed ex-factory price data for 1987 from Chinese statistical authorities which make it possible to crosscheck on my 'common sense' procedure, which seems to be pretty robust. Revisions incorporating the new estimates will appear in a subsequent article with updating to 1997.

10. See Wu (1997, Table A3) for the proportionate coverage by selected CIES items in each CIOT industry.

11. Due to limited space the complete GVA time series results could not be included in this chapter. They are available on request.

12. One way of adjusting for this obvious over-estimation is to constrain all industries to a maximum 30 per cent per annum growth rate. Such a constraint could produce an annual growth of 19.6 per cent for 1958–60.

13. Measured as ratio of gross value added to gross output using data from DBNE and ONIOS (1991 and 1993) and DNEA (1996).

14. See Wu (1997, Table 6) for a summary of these studies.

15. China News (CCTV International) reported on 2/12/1996, there were hundreds of millions of shirts remained in inventory because they were unsaleable.

16. The size of enterprises can be examined by looking at average labour employment per enterprise. As suggested by official data, the average size of industrial enterprises declined from about 140 workers in the mid-1970s to about 120 in the mid-1980s. Size increased again between the late 1980s and the early 1990s (DITS 1995, pp. 22 and 24). It should be noted that the official data exclude rural enterprises below the township level which are much smaller than other enterprises. Unfortunately, data for these enterprises are not available.

17. After the second national industrial census, SSB corrected its previous estimates of industrial gross value added. For 1987, the corrected figure was 4.4 per cent higher than the old figure (SSB, 1988, p. 36; 1992, p. 31). The 1987 Input–Output Table showed an increase in industrial output by 3.1 per cent.

18. In fact, this is an abbreviation for *zhiyuan* (staff) and *gongren* (workers) in Chinese.

19. The dominant proportion was SOE employment that accounted for about 75 per cent of total industrial 'staff and workers' at the end of 1970s, the eve of the reform (Table A6).

20. In 1977, for example, the share of 'staff and workers' and 'non-staff and workers' was about 85 and 15 per cent respectively (Table A6).

21. DPES has recently been renamed as Department of Population, Social, and Science and Technological Statistics in 1998 and still one of the SSB departments.

22. As given in DPES, total 'persons engaged' in industry include: (a) 'staff and workers' (note as defined by DPES), (b) owners and employees of private enterprises, (c) self-employed persons, (d) those engaged in rural township and village enterprises and (e) others not classified (1995, p. 639).

23. Several formal and informal interviews with the current and former directors as well as statisticians of DITS and DPES were held between April and October 1998 at China's State Statistical Bureau, Beijing.

24. An investigation in 1997, jointly run by several ministries including SSB, found 75 000 cases violating the state Statistical Law, most of them related to misreporting, tampering and fabricating data, and most of the worst cases related to rural industrial enterprises (*Outlook Weekly*, No. 15/1998, pp. 10–12).

25. Even after allowing for different coverage of 'independent units' and 'attached units', this gap cannot be justified. As suggested by China's Third Industrial Census, the ratio of all industrial units to 'independent

units' for 1995 is only 1.026 for employment and 1.022 for gross value of output, implying only 2-3 per cent difference (ONIC, 1996, pp. 3–4).
26. As instructed by the same official statistical handbook, due to the restructure those 'staff and workers' who have been forced to leave their posts but remained in the payroll list should still be counted as 'staff and workers' (DPSSTS, 1998, pp. 62–3).

REFERENCES

Bart van Ark (1996), 'Convergence and Divergence in the European Periphery: Productivity in Eastern and Southern Europe in Retrospect', in B. van Ark and N.F.R. Crafts (eds), *Quantitative Aspects of Post-War European Economic Growth*, CEPR/Cambridge University Press, pp. 271–326.

Chao, Kang (1970), *Agricultural Production in Communist China, 1949–65*, University of Wisconsin, Madison.

Chao, Kang (1974), *Capital Formation in Mainland China, 1952–1965*, University of California, Berkeley.

Chao, Kang (1968), The Construction Industry in Communist China, Aldine, Chicago.

Chao, Kang (1965), *The Rate and Pattern of Industrial Growth in Communist China*, University of Michigan, Ann Arbor.

DBNE (Department of Balances of National Economy of the State Statistical Bureau) and ONIOS (Office of the National Input–Output Survey) (1991), *Input–Output Table of China, 1987*, China Statistical Publishing House.

DBNE and ONIOS (1993), *Input–Output Table of China, 1990*, China Statistical Publishing House.

DITS (1995) (Department of Industry and Transportation Statistics, SSB), *China Industrial Economic Statistical Yearbook 1994*, China Statistical Publishing House.

DITS (1996), *China Industrial Economic Statistical Yearbook 1995*, China Statistical Publishing House.

DNEA (1996) (Department of National Economic Accounting), *Input–Output Table of China 1992*, China Statistical Publishing House.

DNEA (1997) (Department of National Economic Accounting), *Input–Output Table of China 1995*, China Statistical Publishing House.

DPES (1995) (Department of Population and Employment Statistics, SSB), *China Labour Statistical Yearbook*, China Statistical Publishing House.

DPSSTS (1998) (Department of Population, Social and Science and Technology Statistics), *Xinbian Laodong Tongji Shiyong Shouce (A New Handbook of Practical Labour Statistics)*, Beijing: China Statistical Publishing House.

DSS (1987) (Department of Social Statistics), Labour and Wage Statistics of China, Beijing: China Statistical Publishing House.

Eckstein, A. (1961), *The National Economy of Communist China*, Free Press.

ECCPY (Editorial Committee of China Price Yearbook) (1989), *Price Yearbook of China*. Beijing: Price Publishing House.

Field, R.M. (1980), 'Real Capital Formation in The People's Republic of China, 1952–73', in Eckstein, A. (ed.), *Quantitative Measures of China's Economic Output*, pp. 194–245, The University of Michigan Press, Ann Arbor.

Hollister, W.W. (1959), *China's Gross National Product and Social Accounts, 1950–1957*, Free Press, Glencoe.

JEC (1982) (Joint Economic Committee of the US Congress), *China Under the Four 'Modernisations'*, 2 vols., US Congress, August and December.

JEC (1978), *Chinese Economy Post Mao*, vol. 1, US Congress, November.

JEC (1975), *China: A Reassessment of the Economy*, US Congress, July.

JEC (1972), *People's Republic of China: An Economic Assessment*, US Congress, May.

Li, C.M. (1959), *Economic Development of Communist China*, Berkeley.

Liu, Ta-Chung and Yeh, Kung-Chia (1965), *The Economy of the Chinese Mainland: National Income and Economic Development, 1933–1959*, Princeton.

Maddison, Angus (1995), *Monitoring the World Economy 1820–1992*, OECD Development Centre, Paris.

Maddison, Angus (1998), *Chinese Economic Performance in the Long Run*, OECD Development Centre, Paris.

NCOTS (1995) (National Census Office for the Tertiary Sector, China), *The First Census on the Tertiary Industry in China: Summary Statistics*. Beijing: China Statistical Publishing House.

NICLG (National Industrial Census Leading Group, State Council) *China 1985 Industrial Census Data* (Simplified Edition). Beijing: China Statistical Publishing House.

ONIC (Office of National Industrial Census) (1996), *The Third National Industrial Census, The People's Republic of China 1995: Summary Statistics*. Beijing: China Statistical Publishing House.

Perkins, D.H. (1988), 'Reforming China's economic system', *Journal of Economic Literature*, Vol. 26. pp. 601–45.

Perkins, D.H. (1980), 'Issues in the Estimation of China's National Product', in Eckstein, A. (ed.), *Quantitative Measures of China's Economic Output*, pp. 246–73, The University of Michigan Press, Ann Arbor.

Perkins, D.H. (ed.) (1975), *China's Modern Economy in Historical Perspective*, Stanford University Press.

Ren, Ruoen (1997), *China's Economic Performance in An International Perspective*, OECD Development Centre, Paris.

RSEST (Rural Social and Economic Survey Team, SSB), *Rural Statistical Yearbook of China*, Beijing: China Statistical Publishing House.

SDSB (Shandong Statistical Bureau) (1993), *Tongji Shiyong Shouce (A Handbook of Practical Statistics)*, Beijing: China Statistical Publishing House.

SSB (State Statistical Bureau of China) (various issues), *Statistical Yearbook of China*, Beijing: China Statistical Publishing House.

Szirmai, Adam and Ruoen, Ren (1995), *China's Manufacturing Performance in Comparative Perspective, 1980–1992, Research Memorandum* 581 (GD–20), Institute of Economic Research, Groningen Growth and Development Centre, University of Groningen.

Woo, Wing Thye (1996), Chinese Economic Growth: Sources and Prospects, paper presented at Economics Discipline Seminar, RSPAS, Australian National University.

Wu, Harry X. (1997), Reconstructing Chinese GDP According to the National Accounts Concept of Value Added: The Industrial Sector, *COPPAA (Comparative Output, Productivity and Purchasing Power in Australia and Asia) Series* No. 4, Centre for the Study of Australia–Asia Relations, Griffith University, Australia, and *SOM Research Report* No. 97C24, University of Groningen, the Netherlands.

Wu, Harry X. (1994), Rural Enterprise Contribution to Growth and Structural Change, Chapter 3, in C. Findlay, A Watson and H.X. Wu (eds), *Rural Enterprises in China*, Macmillan Press, London.

Wu, Harry X. (1993), 'The "Real" Chinese Gross Domestic Product (GDP) for the Pre-reform Period 1952–77', *Review of Income and Wealth*, Series 39, no. 1.

6.   Twentieth Century Economic Performance of India

Siva Sivasubramonian

This chapter deals with an assessment of Indian economic performance in the twentieth century on the basis of estimates of real GDP growth, annual movements of per capita GDP and labour productivity. It provides a sector breakdown of GDP as the basis for structural analysis. For 1900–46, the estimates are by the author and refer to undivided India, i.e., the present territories of India, Pakistan and Bangladesh. From 1948 the estimates are from official sources and refer to contemporary India. The estimates of GDP and population are given for fiscal years centred on October 1st; hence 1900 refers to 1900–1901 and so on.

1. PERFORMANCE DURING 1900–46

For the pre-1947 period Mukherjee (1969: 52–53 and 110) listed 34 point estimates of per capita national income covering 16 years of this period. These are not comparable due to differences in concepts, coverage and methods of estimation. Very few were based on detailed analysis of basic data and many were superficial. When placed together they did not present a complete or coherent picture of the movements in national income in real terms.

Attempts have also been made to study the long-term trends in national and per capita income on the basis of time-series obtained by projecting backward and forward a well accepted estimate such as the estimate by Rao (1941: 186) for 1931–32 for British India (refers to Indian Provinces only and excludes native states) and/or estimate by the National Income Committee (NIC, 1951, 1954) for 1948–49 for Indian Union, using index numbers of business activity and sectoral production. Such attempts, summarised by Mukherjee (1969: 55–60), were subject to serious limitations arising from the applicability or otherwise of sectoral indices of production and general index of business activity for estimation of national income series of a country with a predominant unorganised sector.

The present study (Sivasubramonian, forthcoming) the most complete and comprehensive hitherto undertaken on the subject is a substantial revision of unpublished estimates made 30 years ago (Sivasubramonian, 1965) which have been widely used and commented upon. Amongst the important critics are Maddison (1971, 1985) and Heston (1982). On the basis of their criticisms and my own understanding of their deficiencies I have made significant revisions (see Sivasubramonian, 1997). Annual estimates of GDP at 1948–49 prices are presented in Table A6.1.

Trends in Real Output

Aggregate GDP at 1948–49 prices increased by 51.4 per cent between 1900 and 1946, that is, at a trend rate of 0.9 per cent per annum. In the meanwhile population grew at 0.8 per cent per year. Hence in the first five decades of the present century Indian per capita GDP was stagnant. It stood at Rs 224 (1948–49 prices) in 1900 and Rs 233 46 years later, a negligible increase of 3.7 per cent. A closer look at the annual figures reveals that per capita GDP ranged between Rs 245 and Rs 272 in 40 of the 47 years. In the first 16 years it rose at a trend rate of 0.9 per cent a year but due to the severe drought and famine of 1918 it suddenly dropped by 15 per cent. In the next 12 years it grew at an annual rate of 1.1 per cent reaching a level of Rs 272 in 1929, the highest in the first half of this century. From then on it gradually declined at 0.5 per cent per annum. One point worth noting is that it did not touch the initial level at any time later (see Figure 6.1). The pattern of movement of per capita GDP reveals alternating periods of growth and decline or stagnation. Each successive low point was generally higher than the previous one so also the peaks except the last one in 1943.

The annual growth of GDP by sector is presented in Table A6.2. Per capita GDP declined in 26 of the 47 years and aggregate GDP in 17 years. The variations are most noticeable in the primary sector (see Figure 6.2). Thus the big increases in 1902, 1909 and 1919 originated in the primary sector. Similarly, the sharp declines in 1907, 1918 and 1920 were caused by drought and famine. While the amplitudes of the variations were wider in the first quarter of this century, there were more years of negative growth in the second quarter. There were a number of years of drought and famine between 1900 and 1921 and an epidemic in 1918 which caused drastic declines in agricultural output. The second quarter of the century did not experience such severe conditions.

The acceleration of population growth in the latter half of the period caused a decline in per capita GDP in a number of years even though the rate of growth of GDP was almost the same as in the first half. The secondary sector recorded negative growth in 18 of the 47 years. Manufacturing output declined in 10 of the 18 years. To some extent this was an echo of agricultural performance with significant fluctuations in agro-based activity. The tertiary sector registered a fall in 14 of the 47 years. All the three sectors showed negative movement in four of the 47 years.

Both aggregate and per capita GDP exhibit considerable fluctuations in the rates of growth from decade to decade. The first and third decades witnessed growth rates of 1.3 per cent and 2 per cent in GDP but decline or slow growth in the others. The explanation for the alternating periods of growth and decline/stagnation can be traced largely to agriculture.

The GDP from agriculture increased by 17.3 per cent during the period. This is supported by two other studies, namely, Blyn's estimates (Blyn 1969: 316–17) according to which total yield of 18 crops increased by 12.2 per cent and Mukerji's index of agricultural production which registered an increase of 6.1 per cent (Mukerji, 1962: 18–19). My estimates of agricultural output at 1938–39 prices (Sivasubramonian, 1965: 99) showed an increase of only 10.8 per cent over the period. Heston (1982) and Maddison (1985) have pointed out that my 1965 estimates understated the growth of agriculture as well as the level of its contribution. The underestimation of growth was partly due to the procedure adopted by me to estimate the yield of crops such as jowar, bajra, barley, maize

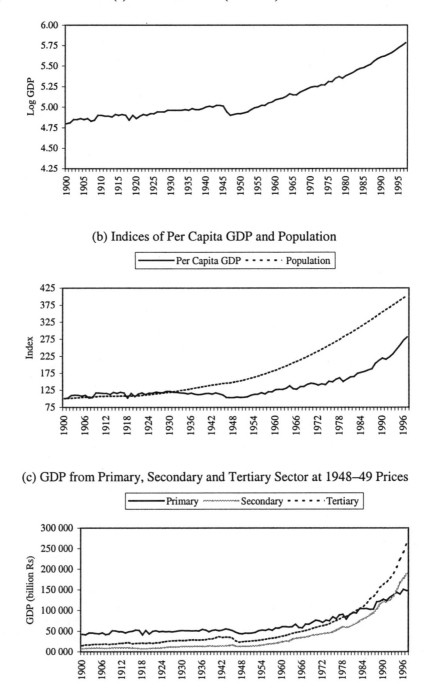

Figure 6.1   Indian Economic Performance in the Twentieth Century

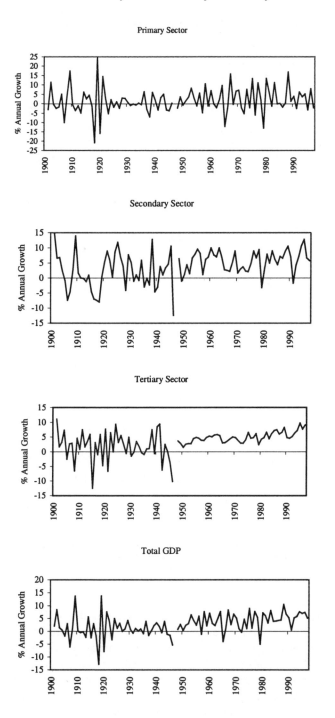

Figure 6.2 Fluctuations in Indian Economic Performance in the Twentieth Century, 1900–97

Table 6.1   Trend Growth Rates of GDP by Sector/Sub-Sector at 1948–49 Prices,
                1900–46

Sector/sub-sector	1900 to 1909	1910 to 1919	1920 to 1929	1930 to 1939	1940 to 1946	1900 to 1946	Index of growth to 1946 with 1900 = 100
(1)	(2)	(3)	(4)	(5)	(6)	(7)	(8)
Primary sector	1.0	−0.2	0.7	−	−0.1	0.4	122.2
Agriculture	0.9	−0.3	0.6	−0.1	−0.2	0.3	117.3
Livestock	1.2	0.4	1.2	0.5	0.1	0.7	140.9
Agriculture and							
livestock	0.9	−0.2	0.7	−0.01	−0.1	0.4	121.2
Forestry	1.3	1.4	0.9	3.7	1.4	1.7	256.6
Fishing	3.6	−1.6	0.8	0.8	0.5	0.6	149.4
Secondary sector	1.7	−3.5	5.6	0.9	2.6	1.5	212.4
Mining	5.0	2.5	2.6	3.8	−2.9	1.8	215.2
Manufacturing	5.7	1.6	4.8	7.1	4.3	3.8	728.2
Small-scale and							
cottage industries	0.5	−5.7	6.2	−2.3	2.0	0.4	123.6
Tertiary sector	2.1	0.4	3.4	1.3	−0.6	1.7	206.9
Railways and							
communications	5.9	5.4	1.4	2.0	6.6	2.6	481.8
Government services	1.7	1.5	3.2	2.4	−3.8	2.7	249.4
Other commerce							
and transport	2.6	−0.3	3.9	1.8	−1.3	1.6	199.1
Other services	1.2	0.2	3.3	0.1	−0.4	1.2	165.9
GDP	1.3	−0.4	2.0	0.6	−0.2	0.9	151.4
Per capita GDP	0.7	−0.5	1.1	−0.8	−1.3	0.1	103.7
Population*	0.6	0.1	0.9	1.4	1.2	0.8	145.9
GDP per person							
engaged	0.7	−0.2	1.9	−0.1	−1.3	0.7	125.7

Notes: Growth rates are estimated by fitting a linear trend line to logarithmic annual values of the given variable using the least-squares method. * Exponential end-point growth rate.

Source: Table A6.1.

and gram for which only area figures were available until 1911 and partly due to the method followed for estimating area under crops in 'non-reporting princely states' for the initial years. The underestimation of the level of contribution of agriculture was due to gross undervaluation of 'other crops' which consisted of costly items such as condiments and spices, fruits and vegetables, etc., and the omission of fodder crops, stalks and straw and rice husk and bran. These shortcomings when rectified, resulted in higher increases in agricultural output. Still the estimates are based on official yields per acre, which showed a declining trend over the years about which Heston has expressed scepticism (Sumit Guha,

1992: 1–34 and 100–26). The yield per hectare of certain crops for the initial and terminal years of the period 1900–46 and for the early post-independence years are shown below.

Table 6.2   Yield (Kgs Per Hectare) for Selected Crops

Crop	1900	1946	1950	1951	1952
(1)	(2)	(3)	(4)	(5)	(6)
Rice	1 068	859	668	653	763
Wheat	746	603	663	653	763
Bajra	335	355	288	247	296
Jowar	483	333	353	381	420
Maize	859	715	547	627	796
Gram	593	532	482	495	580

Sources: Columns (2) to (3) Sivasubramonian (1965). Columns (4) to (6) *Statistical Abstract of India, 1957.*

It is worth mentioning that yield rates did not decline steadily. They have been fluctuating. The yield per hectare of most of the crops in the early 1940s were much higher than those in 1946, sometimes even higher than the values relating to 1900. Thus rice was 957 kgs per hectare in 1943, wheat 740 in 1941, jowar and bajra 463 and 440 in 1943, maize and gram 886 and 452 in 1942 and so on. Apart from the deficiencies in the estimation of official (revenue) yield per acre, the declining trend can be attributed to some extent to the extension of cultivation to less fertile lands, slow progress in the spread of irrigation and lack of official support for the adoption of improved agricultural practices.

The gross area sown increased from 114 million hectares to 140 million hectares. There was little change in the relative shares of food and non-food crops. The share of four important cereals rice, wheat, jowar and bajra remained steady at around 68 per cent of the area under food grains. Only 23.1 per cent of the cultivated area (net area sown) was under irrigation in 1942 in undivided India; the corresponding percentage shares for Indian Union and Pakistan (including Bangladesh) were 18.9 and 45.2 (Fiscal Commission, 1949: 10). The area irrigated by wells in British India in 1902 was 11.6 million acres (4.7 million hectares) and 13.3 million acres (5.4 million hectares) in 1938 (Gadgil, 1971: 248). Irrigation by wells accounted for 25 per cent of the irrigated area; the other principal source was by canals (53.8 per cent) in 1939 in British India. The area under cultivation of foodgrains increased by 19.3 per cent, output of food grains moved up from 64 million tonnes to 69 million tonnes, that is by 7.8 per cent while population increased by 37 per cent. This led to a decline in per capita output of food grains by 22.8 per cent. This is corroborated by independent estimates of per capita food grains availability (including net imports) (Bhattacharjee, 1958: 222–23) which declined by 20.4 per cent between 1900 and 1944. The overall crop output increased only by 16.9 per cent while gross area under cultivation went up by 22.7 per cent. Thus while area under cultivation increased, output did not grow to the same extent. In other words, agriculture expanded but did not grow. Productivity per hectare declined by 12 per cent for food crops, 2 per cent for non-food crops and by 4.7 per cent for all crops. Another point indicative of the stagnation in agriculture is the fall in the proportion of land revenue from nearly half of the total tax receipts in 1900 to less than one-tenth in 1946 (Dharma Kumar, 1982: 928–29). GDP from agriculture (crops) increased at 0.3 per cent per annum during the period, livestock grew at 0.7 per cent and the combined agriculture-cum-livestock at 0.4 per cent.

Table 6.3   Indicators of Progress in Agriculture

	1900 to 1909	1910 to 1919	1920 to 1929	1930 to 1939	1940 to 1946
(1)	(2)	(3)	(4)	(5)	(6)
1. Gross area sown (million hectares)	114.2	124.3	128.7	134.5	140.1
2. Index of gross area sown	100.0	108.9	112.7	117.8	122.7
3. Area under food grains (million hectares)	88.9	95.1	96.4	99.5	106.1
4. Index of area under food grains	100.0	106.9	108.4	111.9	119.3
5. Area under food grains as % of total	77.9	76.5	74.9	73.9	75.8
6. Area under non-food (million hectares)	25.3	29.3	32.3	35.0	34.0
7. Index of area under non-food	100.0	115.9	127.9	138.7	134.5
8. Food grains production (million tonnes)	64.3	71.3	68.0	67.3	69.2
9. Index of value of output* – All crops	100.0	110.5	108.5	113.8	116.9
10. Index of value of output* – Food crops	100.0	109.7	103.7	104.5	105.8
11. Index of value of output* – Non-food crops	100.0	111.7	115.1	126.5	132.0
12. Index of population	100.0	104.0	109.0	122.6	137.1
13. Index of food output adjusted for population	100.0	105.5	95.1	85.2	77.2
14. Per capita availability of food (gms per day)	512	535	503	449	408
15. Index of per capita availability of food	100.0	104.4	98.9	87.3	79.6
16. Index of output per hectare – all crops	100.0	101.7	96.3	97.0	95.3

Note: * Based on values at 1938–39 prices.

Sources: Rows (1) to (13) and (16) based on Sivasubramonian (forthcoming). Rows (14) and (15) based on Bhattacharjee (1958: 222–3).

According to D.B. Meek (Meek, 1937: 363) mineral production increased at an average annual rate of 2.7 per cent between 1909 and 1935. This is reflected in the estimates of GDP presented here which show a trend rate of growth of 2.5 to 2.6 per cent for the period 1910 to 1929 and 3.8 per cent for 1930 to 1939. The increase in the number of joint stock companies from 58 in 1900 to 623 in 1946 and their paid-up capital from Rs 18 million to Rs 249 million over the same period lend support to the estimates. For the period as a whole, GDP from mining recorded a growth rate of 1.8 per cent per annum.

GDP from manufacturing increased nearly 7.3 times during the period while factory employment rose by five times. Manufacturing recorded continuous growth except for minor set backs due to unfavourable agricultural reasons and strikes in cotton mills at a trend rate of 3.8 per cent per annum. During the first decade industrial growth was 5.7 per cent, but there was sharp deceleration in the next probably due to the adverse effects of drought and famine. The performance of Indian industries between 1913 and 1938 was considered to be well above the world average (Rajat Ray, 1979: 16–17). According to the League of Nations Study *Industrialisation and Foreign Trade*, while the annual index of manufacturing production with 1913 = 100 stood at 182.7 in 1938 for the world, for India it reached a level of 239.7 (League of Nations, 1945: 135).

An interesting feature in the performance of manufacturing industries is that the growth rate during the depression decade was higher than the average for the first half of this century. Stimulated by protection, manufacturing grew at 7 per cent a year during the 1930s compared to 4.8 per cent in the 1920s and 4.3 during the 1940s.

Table 6.4   Average Annual Value Added (1938–39 Prices) and Employment

	Value Added (million Rs)			Average Number Employed ('000)		
Period	Cotton	Jute	Total Manufacturing	Cotton	Jute	Total Manufacturing
(1)	(2)	(3)	(4)	(5)	(6)	(7)
1900 to 1909	189	69	523	202	150	767
1910 to 1919	223	104	650	269	241	1 090
1920 to 1929	270	116	850	360	326	1 520
1930 to 1939	399	108	1 302	414	286	1 554
1940 to 1946	535	119	2 331	491	305	2 710
1900 to 1946	310	102	1 055	338	259	1 451

Source: Sivasubramonian (1977).

Average annual value added and employment in all industries except jute increased during the depression years. The rise was much more pronounced during the last seven years which included the war period. The jute industry recorded a decline in value added and employment during the depression decade due to its dependence on the export market.

Another aspect of the growth of industries is that the value added by non-traditional industries increased by 129 per cent during the last seven years compared to 32.5 per cent in the eight industries cotton, jute, sugar, paper, cement, woollen, textiles, iron and steel and matches for which basic data were separately available. Employment increased by 18.7 per cent in the eight industries referred above and by 137.4 per cent in the other industries in the same period. The value added by all industries increased 4.5 times between 1900 and 1946 on the basis of decennial averages. Cotton and jute together registered increases in value added by only 2.6 times and the remaining industries taken together 6.3 times during the period.

The changes in the structure of industrial output can be seen from Table 6.5.

The two most important industries cotton and jute which accounted for 45.9 per cent of the employment and 49.4 per cent of the value added in 1900 to 1909 declined gradually to 29.3 and 27.9 per cent respectively during the last seven year period. The changes in the relative shares became noticeable only in the last period indicating that diversification in any serious way took place only during the war period.

The tertiary sector recorded a trend growth rate of 1.7 per cent per annum, slightly higher than that shown by the secondary sector. Government services registered positive growth rates for the first four decades, the highest being during the 1920s. The negative growth recorded during 1940 to 1946 may be somewhat puzzling in the context of soaring government outlays. This is partly explained by the sudden sharp increase in the cost of living index used as a deflator by 170.3 per cent between 1940 and 1943 and partly due to post-war demobilisation and retrenchment of a million employees in 1945 and consequent fall in wages and salaries even in current prices. Two other sectors professions and liberal arts and domestic service for which cost of living index was used as deflator were also affected in a similar manner.

Table 6.5   Percentage Distribution of Net Output and Employment in Industries

	Net output			Employment		
Period (1)	Cotton (2)	Jute (3)	Other Industries (4)	Cotton (5)	Jute (6)	Other industries (7)
1900 to 1909	36.2	13.2	50.6	26.4	19.5	54.1
1910 to 1919	34.3	16.0	49.7	24.6	22.1	53.3
1920 to 1929	31.7	13.6	54.7	23.7	21.4	54.9
1930 to 1939	30.7	8.3	61.0	26.7	18.4	54.9
1940 to 1946	22.8	5.1	72.1	18.1	11.2	70.7

Source: Sivasubramonian (1977).

Real output of railways and communications was derived by using indicators of net ton–miles of goods carried and passenger miles for the former and number of letters, post cards etc., handled and number of money orders issued for the latter. Hence the growth in this sector reflects the movement in these indicators. An indicator not used in deriving output relates to the railway track mileage open for traffic which increased by 71.5 per cent during the period. For communications, the deflated value of money orders increased by 120.6 per cent, while the number of letters, postcards, etc., handled quadrupled. For other commerce and transport, the shipping tonnage cleared increased by 157.1 per cent between 1900 and 1939 but declined during the war period. Similarly a number of other indicators such as number and paid-up capital of joint stock companies, bank deposits, cheque clearances etc., all show substantial upward movements. Regarding professions and liberal arts indicators such as number of scholars in educational institutions, number of patients treated in hospitals etc., record signs of growth. Further the distribution of working force engaged in various professions and liberal arts showed a substantial change in its composition with educational, medical and legal services accounting for 47.6 per cent in 1951 compared to 14.1 per cent in 1901.

The tendency towards growth, though slow up to 1929, was also supported by an increase in public investment and public expenditure. The capital investment in the public sector grew from Rs 186 million in 1900 to Rs 827 million in 1927 at current prices after which it declined during the depression. Public expenditure grew from Rs 1022 million in 1900 to Rs 3178 million by 1929 at current prices. During the depression years it was around Rs 2500 million (Thavaraj, 1960: 219).

Table 6.6   *Distribution of Working Force under 'Professions and Liberal Arts'*

	1901	1911	1921	1931	1941	1951
(1)	(2)	(3)	(4)	(5)	(6)	(7)
Educational services	4.7	6.1	8.4	12.0	17.4	25.1
Medical services	4.8	5.7	6.0	7.2	8.6	13.3
Legal and business services, arts, letters and journalism	4.6	4.0	4.5	4.1	5.7	9.2
Barbers and beauty shops	25.0	22.0	21.7	21.5	18.2	15.8
Laundry services	27.1	27.7	28.4	26.8	26.4	17.5
Religious, charitable and welfare services	26.4	25.8	24.3	22.3	17.8	12.5
Recreation services	7.4	8.7	6.7	6.1	5.9	6.6
Total	100.0	100.0	100.0	100.0	100.0	100.0

Sources: Census *of India* 1901, 1911, 1921, 1931, 1941 and 1951. *Census of Pakistan* 1951.

Structure of GDP

The changes in the structure of GDP consequent to the variations in the rates of growth in value added of different sectors and sub-sectors and shifts in the composition of output are indicated in Table 6.7.

Table 6.7   *Structure of GDP at 1948–49 Prices, 1900 to 1946*

Sector	1900 to 1909	1910 to 1919	1920 to 1929	1930 to 1939	1940 to 1946
(1)	(2)	(3)	(4)	(5)	(6)
Primary sector	63.1	62.6	59.1	55.0	51.9
Agriculture	51.5	51.0	47.2	43.8	41.4
Livestock	10.7	10.5	10.9	10.2	9.5
Forestry	0.4	0.5	0.5	0.5	0.5
Fishing	0.5	0.6	0.5	0.5	0.5
Secondary sector	12.0	11.2	12.1	14.2	14.4
Mining	0.4	0.6	0.6	0.6	0.7
Manufacturing	2.4	2.8	3.3	4.6	7.5
Small-scale and cottage industries	9.2	7.8	8.2	9.0	6.2
Tertiary sector	24.9	26.2	28.8	30.8	33.7
Railways and communications	1.3	2.3	2.5	2.2	3.0
Government services	3.2	3.5	3.9	6.0	5.9
Other commerce and transport	11.7	11.6	12.8	12.4	16.0
Other services	8.7	8.8	9.6	10.2	8.8
GDP	100.0	100.0	100.0	100.0	100.0

Source: Table A6.1.

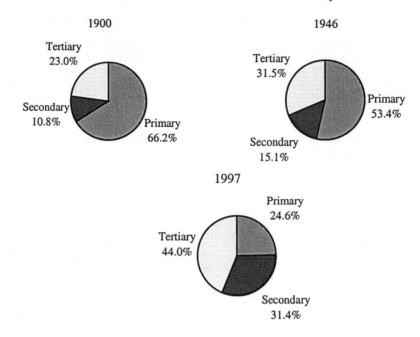

Figure 6.3(a) Sectoral Composition of GDP

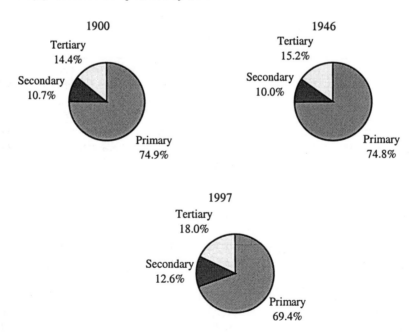

Figure 6.3(b) Sectoral Composition of Working Force

The share of the primary sector gradually declined while that of secondary and tertiary sectors rose (Figure 6.3). Considering the long time-span, the shifts from 63.1 to 51.9 per cent in the primary sector, from 12 to 14.4 per cent and from 24.9 to 33.7 per cent in the secondary and tertiary sectors cannot be considered very significant. Within the primary sector the share of agriculture declined from 51.5 to 41.4 per cent and that of other components remained more or less stable. The decline in the share of agriculture, was not accompanied by any appreciable increase in value added in absolute terms. While the share of manufacturing increased from 2.4 to 7.5 per cent, that of small-scale and cottage industries declined from 9.2 to 6.2 per cent. The increase in the share of the secondary sector was not sufficient to make the increase in commodity production commensurate with population growth.

Table 6.8   Growth Rates of Commodity and Non-Commodity Production

	Trend Rates of Growth		% Share in GDP		Non-commodity production as % of commodity production
	Commodity production	Non-commodity production	Commodity production	Non-commodity production	
1900 to 1909	0.9	2.1	75.4	24.6	23.6
1910 to 1919	−0.3	0.4	74.1	25.9	35.0
1920 to 1929	1.5	3.4	71.1	28.9	40.6
1930 to 1939	0.2	1.3	69.3	30.7	44.3
1940 to 1946	0.5	−0.6	66.4	33.6	50.6
1900 to 1946	0.6	1.7	–	–	–

Source: Table A6.1.

It has been found from the experience of other countries that in the early stages of economic growth the 'service' sector tends to grow faster than commodity production. In India it grew at 1.7 per cent per annum in the first half of this century compared to 0.6 per cent for the commodity producing sectors. The share of services increased from 24.6 to 33.6 per cent and that of commodities declined from 75.4 to 66.4 per cent. From around less than one-fourth in 1900 to 1909, services increased to half of the GDP of commodity producing sectors by the end of the period.

Structure of Working Force

The numbers engaged in the three sectors increased between 1900 and 1946, the increases in the primary, secondary and tertiary sectors being 20.2, 12.9 and 27.5 per cent respectively.

The shifts in occupational structure of the working force did not indicate even the slight improvement shown by the distribution of GDP. The share of the primary sector in the working force remained more or less the same and that of the secondary sector declined. There was a slight increase in the share of the tertiary sector. The working force during the 47 year period increased by 26.9 million i.e., by 20.5 per cent. This was not commensurate with the growth of population which increased by 45.9 per cent. The percentage of working force to total population showed a steady decline. Apart from conceptual changes, certain factors likely to have contributed to the decline in the working force participation rates were the decrease in the number of children employed in factories (International Labour Organisation, 1938: 42–3) and increase in school attendance.

Table 6.9   Structure of Working Force

As on Oct. 1st	Number of persons engaged (in millions)				% of total engaged			Working force as % of total population
	Primary	Secondary	Tertiary	Total	Primary	Secondary	Tertiary	
1900	98.4	14.0	18.9	131.3	74.9	10.7	14.4	46.2
1910	105.4	14.4	19.7	139.5	75.6	10.3	14.1	46.0
1920	105.6	13.0	19.1	137.7	76.7	9.4	13.9	45.0
1930	105.7	12.6	20.7	139.0	76.0	9.1	14.9	41.3
1940	109.2	15.0	23.8	148.0	73.8	10.1	16.1	38.3
1946	118.3	15.8	24.1	158.2	74.8	10.0	15.2	38.1

Source: Sivasubramonian (1965).

GDP Per Person Engaged

Only for mining, manufacturing and railways and communications are data relating to working force available from independent (other than population census) sources. For all the other sectors they are based on population census returns; hence productivity measurements based on the latter should be treated with some caution.

Based on quinquennial averages, it is found that for the primary sector as well as small scale and cottage industries GDP per engaged person increased at 0.1 per cent per annum. For manufacturing it increased by 0.5 per cent while for the service sectors, railways and communications, government services and other commerce and transport GDP per person engaged increased at 1.2 per cent per year. For mining it recorded negative growth. It may be noted that the organised sectors recorded substantial increases in productivity while unorganised sectors did not register similar gains.

In summing up the performance during 1900–46 one may recall the observations of Daniel Thorner, that 'some hold that twentieth century per capita income has been rising, some hold that it has not been rising. There is a third logical possibility that per capita income has been declining' (Thorner, 1955: 128). From the evidence presented above, it is clear that per capita GDP was stagnant. It was only marginally higher in 1946 than what it was in 1900. But there were periods of growth in between. Aggregate GDP increased at almost the same rate between 1930 and 1946 and 1900 to 1929. The acceleration of population growth led to decline in per capita GDP in the second quarter of the century. Agricultural output remained sluggish and food production lagged behind population growth. Manufacturing increased sevenfold. Commenting on the growth of manufacturing between 1913 and 1946 Goldsmith (1983: 68) has observed: 'The average rate of increase over the period as a whole of nearly 4 per cent and thus almost 3 per cent per head of the population, as well as near doubling of the share of manufacturing in national product and the tripling of the share in the labour force from 0.8 per cent in 1911 to about 2.3 in 1946, constitute significant progress in the process of industrialisation, even at this as yet low level'. The ton miles of goods carried by Indian Railways quadrupled and passenger miles increased over six times (Morris and Dudley, 1975: 209–12). Communications, government services and mining maintained moderate growth rates. But these were not enough to make an adequate impact on overall growth. In the meanwhile the literacy rate increased from 6.1 per cent in 1901 to 15.1 in 1941. The death rate declined from 37 per 1 000 in 1900 to 19 in 1946 and infant mortality rate from 205 per 1 000 in 1911 to 136 in 1946. The expectation of life at birth increased from 23.8 years at the beginning of the century to 32.1 by 1951. These were some signs of progress in the context of a stagnant per capita income. Hence it is but apt to use Rao's characterisation of the Indian economy (Rao, 1954) as 'a static economy in progress' to describe the performance in the first half of the century.

Table 6.10 Gross Value Added Per Person Engaged at 1948–49 Prices (Rs)

Sector/industry (1)	1900 to 1904 (2)	1942 to 1946 (3)	Average annual growth rate (4)
Primary sector	438	462	0.1
Secondary sector	586	961	1.2
Mining	1 824	1 050	−1.3
Manufacturing	2 249	2 812	0.5
Small-scale and cottage industries	489	515	0.1
Tertiary sector	874	1 369	1.2
Railways and communications	1 793	2 952	1.2
Other commerce and transport	930	1 581	1.3
Government services	677	1 133	1.2
Professions and liberal arts	474	547	0.3
Domestic service	248	266	0.2
All sectors	516	657	0.6

Source: Table A6.1. Sivasubramonian (1965) for working force

2. PERFORMANCE DURING 1947 TO 1997

Assessment of performance during the post-independence period is based on the revised estimates of GDP (new series) at current and constant (1980–81) prices for 1950 to 1995 issued by the Central Statistical Organisation (CSO, *National Accounts Statistics*, 1989 and subsequent annual issues up to 1997), on 'Quick Estimates' for 1996 (CSO, 1998(a)) and on 'Advance Estimates' for 1997 (CSO, 1998(b)). For 1948 and 1949 in the absence of GDP estimates by CSO, the author has made comparable estimates on the basis of conventional figures (refer to estimates made in the early years following NIC's recommendations). The gap 1947 was filled up by the NDP estimates of Chatterjee

(Chatterjee and Sinha, 1960) which were adjusted for comparability with our GDP measures. To provide an overlap for undivided India and contemporary India, estimates of GDP have been worked out for 1946 following a procedure similar to the one adopted for 1947, using the same sources. The estimates are shown at 1948–49 prices with sectors and sub-sectors in Table A6.3, for the period 1946 to 1997.

The process of economic planning was initiated in 1951 for which the reference base was 1950. The revised time-series on national accounts are also available from 1950. Based on the general trends in the growth pattern of GDP and the factors which influenced the movements, the period has been sub-divided into 1950 to 1964, 1965 to 1979 and 1980 to 1997 for further analysis. Data for the sub-period 1991 to 1997 are also shown alongside to focus on the developments in the post-reform phase.

Previous studies on the long-term growth of the Indian economy for the post-independence period, notably by Rao (1983) for 1950–80, Balasubramanyam (1984) for 1950–83, Sundrum (1987) for 1950–84 and Dandekar (1992) for 1950–90 have placed the average annual growth rate of real GDP between 3.5 and 3.7 per cent. The overall trend rate of growth has crossed the 4 per cent level due to the 7.3 per cent annual increase achieved during 1994–96.

Growth Rates of GDP

Aggregate real GDP doubled in 19 years starting from 1950, quadrupled in the next 18 years, (by 1987) and was 7.2 times the initial level by 1997. The trend growth rate was 4.1 per cent for the period 1950 to 1997. Population growth surged ahead from 1.7 per cent in 1951 to 2.3 per cent in the 1970s; so it took 39 years for per capita GDP to double. The First Five Year Plan aimed at doubling the national income by 1971 (in about 21 years) and per capita income by 1977 (in a period of 27 years) (*Second Five Year Plan: 3*). While the first goal was achieved in 19 years, the second was delayed by 12 years. If population growth had been contained at 1.5 per cent per year, the situation would have been very different. In 1947, per capita GDP was Rs 231.2 at 1948–49 prices – quite close to the estimate of Rs 232.7 for undivided India and Rs 232.0 for contemporary India in 1946. By 1997 the per capita GDP of Rs 627.9 was 2.7 times higher (Figure 6.1) than in 1947.

The pace of growth was neither steady or continuous. The acceleration from the 0.9 per cent annual growth in the colonial period to 4 per cent in 1950 to 1964 was indeed swift, smooth and remarkable. During the early years after independence, that is from 1947 to 1950 GDP grew at an average annual rate of 1.2 per cent not very different from the previous record. The picture changed considerably from 1951, the year the First Five Year Plan was launched. Despite the setbacks in 1957 and 1959 due to droughts, GDP registered a trend growth rate of 4 per cent for the period 1950 to 1964.

A series of droughts in 1965, 1966, 1972 and 1979, the oil price shocks of 1973 and 1979 and military conflicts in 1965 and 1971 affected the growth rate for 1965 to 1979 adversely which was lower at 3.6 per cent.

Consequent to policy changes introduced in the 1980s, GDP growth accelerated to a trend rate of 5.5 per cent for the period 1980 to 1997. The introduction of radical economic reforms in 1991 following a balance of payments crisis led to further acceleration of GDP growth to a trend rate of 6.6 per cent for the period 1991 to 1997.

Table 6.11 Trend Growth Rates of GDP by Sector at 1948–49 Prices, 1947 to 1997

Sector/Industry	1950 to 1964	1965 to 1979	1980 to 1997	1991 to 1997	1950 to 1997	1947 to 1997	Index of growth to 1997 with 1947=100
(1)	(2)	(3)	(4)	(5)	(6)	(7)	(8)
Primary sector	2.6	2.7	3.1	2.9	2.5	2.5	331.8
Agriculture	2.7	2.8	3.2	2.9	2.6	2.5	333.8
Forestry	1.1	0.6	–0.8	–0.5	0.4	0.6	161.4
Fishing	4.8	3.5	5.9	6.8	4.1	4.3	1 168.2
Secondary sector	6.8	4.3	6.8	8.5	5.5	5.5	1 511.5
Mining	5.6	3.3	6.4	4.1	5.4	5.4	1 754.7
Manufacturing – Total	6.7	4.6	7.0	9.5	5.5	5.5	1 549.0
Manufacturing – Registered	8.3	4.8	7.7	10.3	6.2	6.2	2 267.2
Manufacturing – Unregistered	5.2	4.4	5.8	8.0	4.6	4.6	967.1
Electricity, gas and water	11.4	7.7	8.5	7.1	9.0	9.0	6 797.3
Construction	6.7	2.6	5.0	5.2	4.6	4.6	918.7
Tertiary sector	4.5	4.3	6.5	7.7	4.9	4.8	1 135.2
Railways	5.5	3.4	3.3	2.4	3.9	4.0	766.8
Communications	7.2	6.1	8.4	14.9	6.9	6.8	3 136.1
Other commerce and transport	5.9	4.8	6.9	9.3	5.5	5.4	1 501.8
Banking and insurance	7.4	7.5	13.1	12.8	8.3	8.4	6 197.6
Real estate and business services	2.3	3.0	3.5	3.7	3.0	3.0	444.6
Public administration and defence	6.6	5.7	6.1	5.5	6.2	6.2	1 653.8
Other services	3.3	3.0	5.8	5.9	4.0	3.9	728.1
GDP	4.0	3.6	5.5	6.6	4.1	4.0	747.4
Per capita GDP	1.9	1.3	3.4	4.7	1.9	1.8	271.6
Population	2.0	2.3	2.0	1.8	2.1	2.0	275.1
GDP – Non-agriculture	5.1	4.2	6.5	7.9	5.2	5.1	1 202.6
GDP – Commodity production	3.7	3.1	4.8	5.8	3.6	3.6	590.0
Coefficient of variation of mean growth rates							
GDP – Total	0.7	1.2	0.5	0.5	0.8	0.8	–
GDP – Primary	1.6	3.3	2.0	1.5	2.4	2.5	–
GDP – Secondary	0.5	0.9	0.5	0.6	0.6	0.6	–
GDP – Tertiary	0.4	0.4	0.3	0.5	0.4	0.4	–

Source: Table A6.3.

The rate of growth of per capita GDP also varied over the sub-periods between 1.3 and 4.7 per cent, the average for the whole period (1947 to 1997) being 1.8 per cent.

An encouraging feature of the annual growth in the second half of this century is that GDP growth was negative for only four years (see Table A6.4). This is a great change from the experience in the first half of the century when it was negative for 18 of the 47 years (see Figure 6.2).

The primary sector recorded negative growth in 19 of the 50 years but its influence on GDP growth has diminished and that of secondary and tertiary sectors has increased. Negative growth was recorded for only three years in the secondary sector. In the tertiary sector growth has always been positive.

Structure of GDP

There has been a significant shift in the structure of the economy since mid-century. The share of the primary sector declined from 55 to 26 per cent while that of secondary and tertiary sectors rose from 16 to 31 per cent and from 30 to 43 per cent respectively on the basis of the three year averages.

Table 6.12 Structure of GDP at 1948–49 Prices (percentages)

Period (3 year average)	Primary	Secondary	Tertiary
(1)	(2)	(3)	(4)
1947 to 1949	54.5	15.9	29.6
1950 to 1952	53.6	16.0	30.4
1953 to 1955	53.6	16.8	29.6
1956 to 1958	51.3	18.3	30.4
1959 to 1961	49.3	19.8	30.9
1962 to 1964	45.7	22.1	32.2
1965 to 1967	42.2	23.7	34.1
1968 to 1970	42.9	23.6	33.6
1971 to 1973	41.1	24.1	34.8
1974 to 1976	40.0	24.3	35.7
1977 to 1979	37.9	25.7	36.3
1980 to 1982	36.9	25.8	37.3
1983 to 1985	35.5	26.9	37.6
1986 to 1988	32.1	28.2	39.8
1989 to 1991	30.7	29.2	40.1
1992 to 1994	29.7	29.2	41.1
1995 to 1997	25.8	31.4	42.8

Source: Table A6.3.

It should be noted that this fall in the share of agriculture has been accompanied by more than a three-fold increase in real gross value added. The non-agricultural sectors grew twice as fast as the agricultural sector over the period. Consequent to these changes in the relative shares and growth rates, the contribution of agriculture to overall growth declined from 34.5 per cent in the first period to 12.8 per cent during 1991–97.

Table 6.13 Percentage Contribution to GDP Growth

Period (1)	Agriculture (2)	Non-agriculture (3)	Commodity production (4)	Services (5)
1950 to 1964	34.5	65.5	65.5	34.5
1965 to 1979	29.0	71.0	58.1	41.9
1980 to 1997	21.2	78.8	55.4	44.6
1991 to 1997	12.8	87.2	52.0	48.0

Source: Table A6.3.

Dominated by agriculture, commodity production accounted for 71 per cent of the GDP in 1947. By 1997 the share of commodity production had declined to 56 per cent of the GDP. The service sectors have been growing faster than commodity production, the respective trend rates being 4.9 and 3.6 per cent for the whole period. The contribution of commodity production to overall growth declined from 65.5 per cent in the first period to 52.0 during 1991–97 and the services sector increased from 34.5 to 48 per cent.

Structure of the Working Force

Table 6.14 Structure of Working Force and GDP at 1948–49 Prices (percentages)

	Working force*			GDP		
Year (1)	Primary (2)	Secondary (3)	Tertiary (4)	Primary (5)	Secondary (6)	Tertiary (7)
1950	73.6	10.2	16.2	53.8	15.9	30.3
1960	72.9	11.3	15.8	49.8	19.7	30.5
1970	72.5	11.6	15.9	43.4	23.2	33.4
1980	70.5	13.4	16.1	37.5	25.3	37.2
1990	69.4	12.6	18.0	30.9	29.6	39.5

Note: * As on 1st October of the year.

Sources: Working force for 1950 and 1960. *Final Report of the National Income Committee*, February 1954, p. 108, *National Accounts Statistics*, 1978, p. 126, B.H. Dholakia, *The Sources of Economic Growth in India*, 1974, p. 97. For 1970, *Census of India*, Paper No. 3 of 1972, pp. 2–5. For 1980. *National Accounts Statistics, Sources and Methods*, 1989 p. 182–6. For 1990, *Census of India*, 1991, Paper No. 3 of 1991, p. 18. Pravin Visaria, *Work Force and Employment in India*, 1961–1994, IARNIW Conference paper (mimeographed) pp. 18–19 and p. 28. For share of GDP, Table A6.3.

Up to 1970, the structure of the working force remained more or less stable. But changes occurred between 1971 and 1981, with the decline in the share of the primary sector from 72.5 to 70.5 per cent and corresponding increases in the share of secondary and tertiary sectors. This trend continued through the 1980s but for a slight reversal in the case of secondary sector. The share of the primary sector in GDP declined from 43.4 per cent in 1970 to 30.9 per cent in 1990 and its share of the working force fell from 72.5 to 69.4 per cent. This is an indicator of structural change similar to what had taken place in the economies of developed countries of the world.

GDP Per Person Engaged

The changing structure of GDP and share in the working force have led to changes in the gross value added per person engaged.

Table 6.15 Index of Gross Value Added Per Person Engaged, 1960 = 100

	1950	1960	1970	1980	1990
(1)	(2)	(3)	(4)	(5)	(6)
Agriculture and allied industries (primary)	84.9	100.0	107.7	115.3	130.2
Mining and quarrying	64.7	100.0	121.1	148.7	263.8
Manufacturing – Total	61.9	100.0	138.8	162.3	287.2
Manufacturing – Registered	57.5	100.0	134.6	171.9	330.0
Manufacturing – Unregistered	68.1	100.0	126.4	148.5	232.6
Electricity, gas and water	–	100.0	123.9	149.3	279.9
Construction	–	100.0	152.2	140.2	170.4
Total secondary	71.2	100.0	140.7	160.2	269.3
Trade and transport services	63.8	100.0	114.9	153.5	204.5
Banking and insurance	–	100.0	79.4	92.1	184.3
Public administration and defence	52.6	100.0	158.1	221.8	277.4
Other services	103.4	100.0	158.5	204.5	254.5
Total tertiary	77.2	100.0	133.7	178.3	227.1
All sectors	79.4	100.0	122.8	148.2	199.8

Sources: Table A6.3, *National Accounts Statistics*, 1978. *National Accounts Statistics, Sources and Methods*, 1989. *Census of India*, Paper No. 3, 1972. *Census of India*, Paper No. 3, 1991.

The year 1950 could not be adopted as base due to the lack of comparability of working force data with later years. Registered manufacturing showed the highest increase in value added per person engaged, followed by electricity, gas and water. Value added per person engaged in agriculture and allied industries increased by 30.2 per cent between 1960 and 1990. In the secondary sector productivity increased 2.7 times the level in 1960. For the economy as a whole productivity doubled between 1960 and 1990. Compared to 1950 overall productivity was 2.5 times higher in 1990.

Primary Sector

Agriculture the dominant component of the primary sector, still has an important place in India's economy as it engaged 65 per cent of the working force according to the 1991 census and accounted for 23.6 per cent of the GDP of 1997. Forestry and fishery exhibited varying growth rates but their effect on the primary sector was only marginal. The growth rate of GDP from agriculture for the period as a whole was 2.5 per cent. The growth pattern varied over the period. It was around 2.6 to 2.7 per cent during the first and second periods and increased to 3.1 per cent in the third period. During the post-reform period growth rate of GDP from agriculture declined to 2.9 per cent.

Table 6.16 Selected Indicators of Progress in Agriculture (crops)

(a) Area under crops

	1950	1960	1970	1980	1990	1993
1. Net area sown (million hectares)	118.7	133.2	140.8	140.3	142.2	142.1
2. Gross area sown (million hectares)	131.9	152.8	165.8	173.3	185.5	186.4
3. Gross area sown as % of net area	111.1	114.7	117.8	123.5	130.5	131.2
4. Gross irrigated area (million hectares)	22.6	28.0	38.2	49.8	63.2	68.4
5. Gross irrigated area as % of gross area sown	17.1	18.3	23.0	28.7	34.1	36.7
6. Area under food grains (million hectares)	109.0	135.4	145.6	149.7	127.8	122.8
7. Area under food grains as % of gross area sown	82.6	88.7	87.8	86.4	68.9	65.9

(b) Rates of growth of selected indicators (percentage)

(1)	1950 to 1964 (2)	1965 to 1979 (3)	1980 to 1995 (4)	1950 to 1995 (5)
1. Gross area sown[a]	1.3	0.5	0.2^b	0.8^b
2. Gross irrigated area	2.2	3.2	1.9^b	2.7^b
3. Area under food crops	1.2	0.7	-0.1^b	0.6^b
4. Area under non-food crops	1.6	0.6	1.5^b	1.0^b
5. Fertiliser consumption	32.0	12.0	6.3	13.4
7. Gross capital formation	3.2	5.5	2.1	3.7

Notes: a Gross area sown = Net area sown + Area sown more than once. b Up to 1988–89 only.

Sources: *Agricultural Situation in India*, March 1992, pp. 964–70 and *Economic Survey*, 1996–97.

Before drawing any inferences from the figures it is necessary to note that 'agriculture' in CSO's national accounts include both crops and livestock. Recently the CSO (NAS 1997: 268) has provided GDP arising from livestock sector separately for the period 1980 to 1994, at 1980–81 prices. On the basis of this, the trend growth rate of GDP from livestock for the period was found to be 6.7 per cent per annum, while that for crops was 2.6 per cent. For agriculture including livestock the trend rate for the period was 3.3 per cent per annum.

Gross area sown increased from 132 million hectares in 1950 to 186 in 1993, an increase of 41 per cent. It increased at 1.3 per cent per annum during the first period, but tapered off subsequently, there being physical limits to further extension. The gross area under irrigation increased from 23 million hectares in 1950 to 68 in 1993, that is, from 17.1 to 36.7 per cent of the total cultivated area. The growth of area under irrigation accelerated during the 1970s during which period the new technology involving high-yielding variety seeds was introduced but declined subsequently. The rate of growth of gross capital formation which increased steeply to 5.5 per cent during 1965 to 1979 also declined drastically during the next phase. Area under food crops remained at 86 per cent of the total cultivated area until 1980 but declined thereafter with a deceleration in its growth rate. Area under non-food crops increased at a higher rate than area under food crops during the first and last periods. Fertiliser consumption initially increased at very high rates from the low levels of the early 1950s but declined subsequently giving an overall growth rate of 13.4 per cent. The impact of these on production and yield per hectare can be seen from Table 6.17.

Table 6.17 Increase in Production and Yield Rate

	Production (million tonnes)			Yield rate (Kg/hectare)		
			Index of Growth to 1996 with		1950	Index of Growth to 1996 with
	1950	1996	1950 = 100	1950	1950	1950 = 100
Food grains	50.8	199.0	391.7	522	1 604	307.3
Cereals	42.4	184.4	434.9	542	1 828	337.3
Pulses	8.4	14.6	172.6	441	624	141.5
Rice	20.6	81.2	394.2	668	1 897	284.0
Wheat	6.5	68.9	1060.0	663	2 651	399.8
Jowar	5.5	10.9	198.2	353	940	266.3
Maize	1.7	10.5	617.6	547	1 731	316.5
Bajra	2.6	8.2	315.4	288	818	284.0
Oil seeds	5.2	25.2	484.6	481	934	194.2
Sugarcane	57.1	276.8	484.8	33	68	206.1
Cotton[a]	3.0	14.3	476.7	88	280	318.2
Jute and Mesta[b]	3.3	11.0	333.3	104	1 833	175.7

Notes: a Million bales, bale = 170 kg. b Million bales, bale = 180 kg.

Sources: For 1950, *UI*, 1993–94, p. S–16 and S–18. For 1996, *UI*, 1996–97, vol. II pp. 22–23.

Wheat production increased tenfold and rice four-fold due to significant improvements in yield per hectare. The coarse cereals also doubled their yield rates. This is in stark contrast to the declining yield per acre during the pre-independence period. Pulses fared poorly, so also jute and oil seeds in terms of productivity increases.

The trend growth rates of area, production and yield per hectare of selected crops during the sub-periods as well as for the period as a whole are presented in Table 6.18.

1950 to 1964

During this period rice and wheat registered high growth rates in production of 4.3 per cent per year. The more important contributing factor for the former was yield rate while for the latter it was increase in area under cultivation. For inferior cereals jowar and bajra too the yield rate was the main contributing factor. Maize a relatively less important crop registered a very high rate of growth of output of 6.4 per cent per annum due to increase in area and yield rate at 2.7 and 3.6 per cent respectively. Pulses on the other hand depended much more on area expansion than productivity gains. Extension of area under cultivation was mainly responsible for the increase in output of oilseeds and jute. For cotton and sugar cane extension of area under crops as well as increase in productivity contributed more or less equally to the high growth rates in output.

Table 6.18   Trend Growth Rates of Area, Production and Yield per Hectare of Selected Crops (percentages)

Crop	1950 to 1964			1965 to 1979			1980 to 1996			1950 to 1996		
	A	P	Y	A	P	Y	A	P	Y	A	P	Y
(1)	(2)	(3)	(4)	(5)	(6)	(7)	(8)	(9)	(10)	(11)	(12)	(13)
Rice	1.4	4.3	2.9	0.9	2.9	2.0	0.5	3.2	2.7	0.8	2.8	2.2
Wheat	2.7	4.3	1.5	3.9	7.4	3.3	0.8	3.7	2.9	2.2	5.6	3.3
Jowar	0.9	3.1	2.2	−0.5	2.2	3.3	−2.5	−0.6	1.7	−0.7	1.0	1.7
Bajra	0.9	2.6	1.7	−1.0	0.6	2.0	−1.1	1.7	2.8	−0.2	1.6	1.8
Maize	2.7	6.4	3.6	0.9	1.1	0.2	0.2	2.4	2.3	1.2	3.0	1.7
Total cereals	1.3	3.7	2.4	0.7	3.6	3.0	−0.3	2.8	3.1	0.5	3.0	2.5
Gram	1.8	2.7	0.8	−0.1	1.1	1.4	−0.3	0.9	1.2	−0.7	0.0	0.7
Total pulses	1.8	2.2	0.4	0.1	0.6	0.2	a	1.3	1.2	0.1	0.6	0.5
Total foodgrains	1.4	3.6	2.3	0.6	3.2	2.6	−0.3	2.7	3.0	0.4	2.8	2.3
Total oilseeds	2.6	3.5	0.9	0.6	1.7	1.1	3.1	6.1	2.9	1.8	3.1	1.3
Cotton	1.9	4.2	2.3	a	3.4	3.4	0.6	4.3	3.8	0.2	2.7	2.5
Jute	2.6	4.0	1.4	0.8	1.4	0.6	−0.8	1.7	2.6	0.4	1.7	1.3
Sugarcane	3.2	6.6	3.1	2.0	2.9	1.2	2.1	3.5	1.3	1.8	3.5	1.7

Notes: A – Area. P – Production. Y – Yield per hectare. a: Negligible.

Sources: Based on data available in *Economic* Surveys. Report on Currency and Finance, Reserve Bank of India.

1965 to 1979

The most significant development during this period was the high rate of growth of output recorded by wheat, which is reported to have benefited from the new technology and HYV seeds. The rate of growth of area under cultivation of wheat was higher than in the previous period. With much higher gains in productivity, output grew at a record 7.4 per cent per annum. Extension of area under cultivation of rice slackened, productivity gains also became less and hence the growth rate was lower at 2.9 per cent during this period. The negative growth rate in area under jowar was more than compensated by the increase in yield rate to maintain a moderate growth of output. Bajra and maize fared very poorly, the former due to decline in area and the latter due to negligible gain in productivity. On the whole food grains recorded a lower rate of growth of output and area during the period. The gain in productivity was also not very different from the previous period. Cotton recorded higher rate of growth in productivity but lower growth rate in output due to stagnation in area under cultivation. For oilseeds expansion of area under cultivation was at a slower pace. With marginal improvement in productivity there was deceleration in the growth rate of output of oilseeds. Jute recorded much lower rates in area, output and productivity.

1980 to 1996

For food grains as a whole the rate of growth of area was negative and positive growth rate in production was only due to gains in productivity. Expansion of area under cultivation of rice slackened further and higher growth rate in production was achieved through increase in productivity. The deceleration in the growth of area under wheat was not compensated by productivity increase resulting in a substantial decline in growth rate of production from the record high of 7.4 per cent in the previous period to 3.7 per cent. Jowar recorded negative growth in area and production and decline in productivity. The decline in area under bajra continued but higher growth rate in output became possible due to increase in productivity. For maize too, the increased rate of growth was due to marked improvement in productivity. The most significant development during the period was the jump in the growth rate of output of oilseeds due to expansion in area and increase in productivity. There was a marginal increase in the growth rate of area under cotton but that under jute declined. The growth rates in production of cotton and jute increased due to gains in productivity. Both area and productivity contributed to the slight increase in the production of sugarcane. The disturbing trend is that the growth rate of production of food grains in the third period was distinctly lower than that recorded in the previous two periods.

The significant increase in production achieved during the latter half of the century was more due to the gains in productivity through the adoption of HYV seeds, increased use of fertilisers and extension of irrigation.

Some comparisons can now be attempted between the performance of agriculture before and after independence. The trend rate of growth for the composite group agriculture and livestock for 1900 to 1946 was 0.4 per cent. Compared to this the rate of growth of 2.5 per cent recorded for 1947 to 1997 is six times higher. Real GDP from agriculture multiplied 3.3 times between 1947 and 1997 while it grew by only 21.2 per cent between 1900 and 1946. Food grains output stagnated at 68 million tonnes before independence but it increased from 60.7 million tonnes in 1949 to 199.3 million tonnes in 1996, an increase at a rate of 2.6 per cent annum, slightly higher than the growth of population. Before independence food output lagged behind population growth which was much lower. The gap between growth rates of population and food grains production has however narrowed down in the 1990s. The break through from a stagnant agriculture and its progress towards a growth path caused by improvement in productivity is a significant achievement.

Secondary Sector

The share of the secondary sector in GDP increased from 15.9 per cent in 1950 to 31.4 per cent in 1997. In the meanwhile GDP originating from secondary sector multiplied nearly 15 times. One distinguishing feature compared to the pre-independence period is that the secondary sector grew faster than the tertiary sector. Changes in the structure of the secondary sector are shown in Table 6.19.

Manufacturing which accounted for 75.4 per cent of the GDP from secondary sector increased its share in total GDP from 12 to 24.4 per cent. There was a three-fold increase in the share of electricity, gas and water. All sub-sectors registered the same growth pattern, that is 5 to 8 per cent during the first period, then decline in the second and revival in the last period (Table 6.11).

Table 6.19 Composition of Secondary Sector

	% share in Total GDP		% share in Secondary sector GDP	
Sub-sector	1950	1997	1950	1997
(1)	(2)	(3)	(4)	(5)
Mining	0.7	1.2	4.6	3.8
Manufacturing – Total	12.0	24.4	75.4	77.5
Manufacturing – Registered	5.8	16.0	36.1	50.8
Manufacturing – Unregistered	6.2	8.4	39.3	26.7
Electricity, gas and water	0.3	2.1	1.8	6.8
Construction	2.9	3.7	18.2	11.9
Total	15.9	31.4	100.0	100.0

Source: Table A.3.

Manufacturing

During the period 1950 to 1997 GDP from manufacturing grew at a trend rate of 5.5 per cent per annum. Manufacturing is classified into two categories – 'registered' and 'unregistered'. The former covers all factories employing ten or more workers and using power and 20 or more workers but not using power. Units engaged in manufacturing and repair outside the above employment limits are covered under 'unregistered', which is more or less similar to the 'small-scale and cottage industries' mentioned in the first part of the chapter. Registered manufacturing grew at a trend rate of 6.2 per cent which cannot be considered high compared to the trend rate of 3.8 per cent for the first half of the century. Small-scale and cottage industries stagnated or even declined before independence. Hence the growth rate of 4.6 per cent for unregistered manufacturing is impressive.

Unregistered manufacturing accounted for 52.1 per cent of the GDP from manufacturing in 1950–51. As registered manufacturing grew faster, the share of unregistered manufacturing declined and became less than that of the registered manufacturing in 1959. In 1997 the relative shares of registered and unregistered manufacturing were 65.5 and 34.5 per cent respectively.

Between 1950 and 1990 GDP from registered manufacturing increased 12 times while factory employment increased only from 2.9 to 8.2 million persons, that is, a little less than three times. GDP from manufacturing, as a whole increased nearly 15 times between 1950 and 1997, registered manufacturing by 20 times and unregistered ten times. The growth of manufacturing industry has not been steady. The trend rates shown in Table 6.11 for the sub-periods, 1950 to 1964, 1965 to 1979, and 1980 to 1997 show growth during the first period, slackening of growth and stagnation during the second and revival during the third period.

Composition of Registered Manufacturing

The varying growth rates of different industrial groups over the period has brought about a substantial shift in the industrial structure. This is illustrated in Table 6.20 on composition of manufacturing output and value added.

Table 6.20   Composition of Manufacturing Output and Value Added (percentage share)
                (registered manufacturing)

Industry	Manufacturing Output				Value Added			
	1951	1970	1980	1994	1951	1970	1980	1994
(1)	(2)	(3)	(4)	(5)	(6)	(7)	(8)	(9)
Food, beverages and tobacco	28.8	19.9	15.6	18.0	16.2	9.3	8.6	11.8
Textiles	38.9	18.8	16.1	12.6	42.1	20.1	19.5	13.2
Rubber, chemicals and petroleum	6.0	16.0	24.4	27.0	7.5	17.3	19.5	28.6
Non-metallic minerals	2.0	3.0	2.9	3.4	3.6	4.0	3.8	4.0
Basic Metals	2.5	9.9	14.8	10.4	4.8	9.9	15.2	9.5
Engineering industries	7.6	19.9	18.1	18.9	10.8	24.9	23.0	20.9
All others	14.2	12.5	8.1	9.7	15.0	14.5	10.4	12.0
Total	100.0	100.0	100.0	100.0	100.0	100.0	100.0	100.0

Sources: Col. (2), (3), (6) and (7) are from V.N. Balasubramanyam, *The Economy of India*, 1984, p. 113. Col. (4), (5), (8) and (9) are based on *National Accounts Statistics*, 1997, by Central Statistical Organisation, Government of India, 1997 p. 207 and p. 209.

The traditional food and textile industries which accounted for 67.7 per cent of the output in 1951 claimed only 30.6 per cent in 1994. Rubber, chemicals and petroleum engineering industries and basic metals improved their share in total output as well as in value added. Only non-metallic minerals increased marginally. The figures reveal the extent of diversification achieved over the period.

Composition of Unregistered Manufacturing

NAS provides only value added figures for unregistered manufacturing. Certain changes are noticed in the relative shares of different industrial groups. Steep decrease was seen only in the case of food, drink and tobacco. The share of textiles declined only moderately from 32.2 per cent in 1950 to 26.5 in 1994, while in the case of registered manufacturing the fall was drastic from 42.1 to 13.2 per cent. This difference is due to the encouragement given by the government to handloom and small-scale industries. The share of metal and metal products moved up from 13.1 per cent in 1950 to 25.5 in 1994. The increase in the share in the miscellaneous group is illusory because of the wider coverage in 1994 including 'other repairs' under manufacturing hitherto excluded.

Table 6.21 Composition of Value Added in Unregistered Manufacturing

	Percentage share		
Industry	1950	1979	1994
(1)	(2)	(3)	(4)
Textiles and leather products	32.2	36.2	28.5
Wood and wood products	20.1	10.5	3.4
Metal manufacturing and engineering	13.1	14.2	25.5
Chemical and products	2.6	4.2	3.8
Food, drink and tobacco	21.4	10.6	6.4
Other industries	10.7	24.3	32.4
Total	100.0	100.0	100.0

Sources: Col. (2) and (3) from Rao, *India's National Income*, 1950–80. Col. (4) from *National Accounts Statistics*, 1997, CSO, p. 211.

Tertiary Sector

During the period 1900–47, the tertiary sector grew slightly faster than the secondary sector. This has now been reversed; the secondary sector has taken the lead. Among the service sectors, banking and insurance recorded the highest growth of 8.3 per cent for the period but its share in the GDP in the 1950s was relatively insignificant. During the period 1980 to 1997 when GDP recorded a growth of 5.5 per cent per annum banking and insurance grew at 13.1 per cent. Even during the post-reform period banking and insurance have maintained a high rate of growth of 12.8 per cent. Another sub-sector which has registered high growth is communications, especially during the post-reform phase, the growth rate for the period being 14.9 per cent per annum. Public administration and defence which recorded a growth rate of 6.2 per cent for the period as a whole, registered a sharp decline in the post-reform phase (1991 to 1996) to 3.4 per cent due to constraints in government expenditure. The implementation of the Pay Commission's recommendations in 1997 resulted in enhancing the growth rate of the sub-sector to 5.5 per cent for the period 1991 to 1997. The growth rate of GDP from railways declined from 5.5 per cent during the first period to 3.3 per cent in the third period. Between 1991 and 1997 its growth rate declined to 2.4 per cent. It may be noted that the investment in railways which increased at 11.5 per cent per annum between 1950 and 1964 registered a negative growth rate during 1965–79 but increased to 3.4 per cent during the last period. It was only 1.3 per cent during 1991–96. The growth rate of gross capital formation in railways was 1.5 per cent for the whole period. This has contributed to infrastructural problems. The GDP from tertiary sector increased 10.4 times during the period 1950 and 1997.

Rural/Urban Variations

Another aspect of interest in the structure of Domestic Product is the change, if any, in the relative shares of rural and urban areas, data for which are limited. The CSO has presented in *National Accounts Statistics* (1993: 216–17) a special table on the distribution of NDP (Net Domestic Product) by industry of origin in rural and urban areas for 1970 and 1980 at current prices.

Table 6.22 Net Domestic Product Originating in Rural and Urban Areas at Current Prices

Area	1970			1980		
	NDP (Rs billion)	Population (million)	Per Capita NDP (Rs)	NDP (Rs billion)	Population (million)	Per Capita NDP (Rs)
Rural	229.1	434.0	527.8	650.0	522.0	1 245.3
	(62.5)	(80.2)		(58.9)	(76.9)	
Urban	137.4	107.0	1 284.0	453.4	157.0	2 887.6
	(37.5)	(19.8)		(41.1)	(23.1)	
Total	366.5	541.0	677.4	1 130.4	679.0	1 625.0
	(100.0)	(100.0)	(100.0)	(100.0)	(100.0)	(100.0)

Note: Figures in brackets are percentages to total.

Source: National Accounts Statistics, 1993, pp. 216–17.

Rural areas accounted for 80.2 per cent of the population and 62.5 per cent of the NDP in 1970. These shares changed to 76.9 per cent for population and 58.9 per cent for NDP by 1980. There was thus a slight decline in the importance of rural areas. Urban per capita NDP was 2.4 times rural per capita NDP in 1970; this ratio also declined to 2.3 in 1980 indicating a marginal reduction in rural urban disparity. Urban per capita income was 3.4 times rural per capita income in British India in 1931–32 (Rao, 1941: 188).

Over 95 per cent of the NDP from agriculture originated in the rural areas. The share of rural areas in NDP increased significantly in the case of unregistered manufacturing, as a consequence of the development of small-scale and cottage industries. Increase in the share of rural areas was also registered in trade, hotels and restaurants and other services indicating the gradual opening up of the rural areas through increased communication and transport facilities. The share of the rural areas in construction, electricity, gas and water and real estate remained more or less the same. Considering the distribution of NDP by sector of origin in rural and urban areas the following picture emerges (see Table 6.24):

There has been a noticeable shift in the structure of NDP in rural areas, with the share of the primary sector declining from 72.5 per cent in 1970 to 64.4 per cent in 1980 and the secondary and tertiary sectors, increasing from 10.6 to 14.6 per cent and from 16.9 to 21 per cent. The share of NDP by major sectors did not exhibit any change in urban areas.

Table 6.23   Percentage Share of Rural and Urban Areas in NDP by Industry
            (at current prices)

	1970		1980	
	Rural	Urban	Rural	Urban
Agriculture	96.9	3.1	95.2	4.8
Mining and quarrying	61.0	39.0	54.8	45.2
Manufacturing	25.8	74.2	31.8	68.2
Registered	23.7	76.3	20.4	79.6
Unregistered	28.1	71.9	45.2	54.8
Construction	43.2	56.8	45.6	54.4
Electricity, gas and water	39.8	60.2	40.0	60.0
Transport, storage and communications	22.3	77.7	23.0	77.0
Trade, hotels and restaurants	18.2	81.8	30.3	69.7
Banking and insurance	19.3	80.7	15.7	84.3
Real estate and business services	48.4	51.6	50.0	50.0
Public Administration and defence	42.2	57.8	34.3	65.7
Other services	37.9	62.1	42.9	57.1
Total NDP	62.5	37.5	58.9	41.1

Source: National Accounts Statistics, 1993, pp. 216–17.

Table 6.24   Distribution of NDP from Rural and Urban Areas by Sector of Activity

	1970			1980		
	Rural	Urban	Total	Rural	Urban	Total
(1)	(2)	(3)	(4)	(5)	(6)	(7)
Primary	72.5	4.7	47.1	64.4	5.0	40.0
Secondary	10.6	37.7	20.7	14.6	37.7	24.3
Tertiary	16.9	57.6	32.2	21.0	57.3	35.7
Total	100.0	100.0	100.0	100.0	100.0	100.0

Source: National Accounts Statistics, 1993, pp. 216–17.

Interstate Differences

Data on Net State Domestic Product (NSDP) of different constituents of the Indian Union are presented in the *Economic Survey* (1997: S16–S17) at current prices only. Variations between states are studied in terms of their relative contribution to NDP and on the basis of the relation between per capita NSDP and per capita NDP. The percentage share of NSDPs in total NDP at current prices are shown in Table 6.25.

The states are ranked in Table 6.25 according to their share in NDP. The ranks in the last two columns relating to 1980 and 1993 do not exhibit any major changes. West Bengal and Andhra Pradesh have changed places at the 3rd and 4th position, Karnataka and Bihar in the 8th and 9th position and Haryana and Orissa in 13th and 14th places. Compared to 1960 there are considerable changes in the ranks, noticeable among them being Andhra Pradesh moving up from 6th to 3rd position and Bihar dropping from 5th to 9th. Maharashtra and Uttar Pradesh changed positions. Following a procedure similar to one adopted by Rao (1983: 90–93) the contributions of the top five states, and the middle five states and bottom six (leaving out Himachal Pradesh) are compared. It is found that the share of the top five states decreased marginally from 51.6 per cent in 1960 to 51.2 per cent in 1993. For the middle five states the share increased from 27.0 per cent to 28.4 per cent while the bottom six states, increased their shares from 15.2 per cent to 15.8 per cent. In view of the minor differences in the percentage shares there is no clear indication of widening disparity on the basis of this comparison.

Table 6.25 Percentage NSDP Share in NDP at Current Prices

	% NSDP share in NDP			Rankings		
	1960	1980	1993	1960	1980	1993
Maharashtra	12.0	14.4	15.9	2	1	1
Uttar Pradesh	13.8	13.2	11.8	1	2	2
West Bengal	10.0	9.1	7.8	3	3	4
Andhra Pradesh	7.4	6.9	8.2	6	4	3
Tamil Nadu	8.3	6.8	7.5	4	5	5
Madhya Pradesh	6.2	6.7	6.5	7	6	6
Gujarat	5.5	6.2	6.4	8	7	7
Karnataka	5.0	5.3	5.7	9	9	8
Bihar	7.5	6.0	5.2	5	8	9
Punjab	2.9	4.2	4.6	12	10	10
Rajastan	4.2	3.9	4.1	10	11	11
Kerala	3.2	3.6	3.2	11	12	12
Haryana	1.8	2.9	3.1	15	14	13
Orissa	2.8	3.3	2.6	13	13	14
Assam	0.7	2.2	2.2	14	15	15
Jammu and Kashmir	–	1.0	0.6	–	16	16
Himachal Pradesh	–	0.7	0.6	–	17	17
Total	93.8	96.4	96.4	–	–	–
All India	100.00	100.0	100.0	–	–	–

Sources: Economic Survey 1996, S–11. V.K.R.V. Rao, India's National Income, 1950–80, 1983: 91.

Per capita NSDP is shown as a percentage of per capita NDP for the years 1960, 1980 and 1993 in columns (2), (3) and (4) of Table 6.26.

The range of per capita NSDP as a percentage of per capita NDP increased over the period from 63.2 in 1960 to 129.7 in 1993 indicating widening disparity. Only five states had per capita NSDP higher than per capita NDP in 1993 as against seven in 1960 and 1980. The widening of income differences are also noticed on the basis of the percentage per capita NSDP to the highest per capita NSDP of the relevant year. The top position was occupied by Maharashtra in 1960 and by Punjab in 1980 and 1993. The range in the percentage variation of per capita NSDP's to the highest per capita NSDP was from 52.6 to 95.4 in 1960. This widened further in 1980 and 1993, the corresponding ranges being 34.3 to 91.1 in 1980 and 26.4 to 89.3 in 1993. This also points to the increasing differences in per capita income between states.

Table 6.26 Per Capita NSDP and Per Capita NDP and Their Relationship at Current Prices

(1)	% of per capita NSDAP to per capita NDP			% of per capita NDSP to the highest per capita NSDP		
	1960	1980	1993	1960	1980	1993
	(2)	(3)	(4)	(5)	(6)	(7)
Andhra Pradesh	89.0	84.9	96.2	67.2	51.6	54.7
Assam	102.6	79.0	76.4	77.0	48.0	43.3
Bihar	70.0	56.4	46.4	52.6	34.3	26.4
Gujarat	117.9	119.4	120.8	88.5	72.6	68.6
Haryana	106.5	145.8	146.4	80.0	88.6	83.1
Himachal Pradesh	–	104.9	96.0	–	63.7	54.4
Jammu and Kashmir	87.06	109.3	58.7	65.8	66.4	33.4
Karnataka	93.2	93.5	99.0	69.9	56.8	56.2
Kerala	84.4	92.8	86.4	63.3	56.4	49.1
Madhya Pradesh	84.7	84.0	76.3	63.6	52.4	43.3
Maharashtra	133.2	149.8	157.3	100.0	91.1	89.3
Orissa	70.7	80.9	64.2	53.1	49.1	36.5
Punjab	113.0	164.6	176.1	84.8	100.0	100.0
Rajastan	92.5	75.2	72.2	69.4	45.7	41.0
Tamilnadu	108.8	92.2	107.8	81.7	56.0	61.2
Uttar Pradesh	82.1	78.6	66.3	61.6	47.8	37.6
West Bengal	127.0	109.1	89.5	95.4	66.3	50.8
All India per capita NDP	100.0	100.0	100.0	75.1	60.8	56.8

Sources: Economic Survey 1996, S–12. V.K.R.V. Rao, India's National Income, 1950–80: 91.

The inter-state variations in the growth rates of real NSDP and per capita NSDP (at 1980–81) prices and the population between 1980 and 1995 are shown in Table 6.27.

At the lower end of the scale Assam, Orissa, Bihar, Madhya Pradesh and Uttar Pradesh recorded growth rates of per capita NSDP varying between 1.5 to 1.8 per cent far below the national average of 3.3 per cent. Maharashtra and Tamilnadu at the upper end of the scale experienced growth rates of 4.2 and 4.1 per cent. Population growth rate was lowest in Kerala and Tamilnadu (1.3 per cent) compared to the overall average of 2.1 per cent. Haryana, Madhya Pradesh, Maharashtra and Rajasthan exceeded the all India rate of growth.

Table 6.27   Rates of Growth of Population, NSDP and Per Capita NSDP at 1980–81
                   Prices, 1980 to 1995

	Population	NSDP	Per capita NSDP
Andhra Pradesh	2.0	4.3	2.2
Assam	2.2	3.7	1.5
Bihar	2.1	3.7	1.6
Gujarat	1.9	5.3	3.4
Haryana	2.3	5.4	3.0
Himachal Pradesh	1.9	4.6	2.7
Karnataka	1.8	5.0	3.2
Kerala	1.3	4.4	3.0
Madhya Pradesh	2.3	4.1	1.8
Maharashtra	2.2	6.5	4.2
Orissa	1.8	3.4	1.5
Punjab	1.8	5.0	3.2
Rajastan	2.4	6.0	3.5
Tamilnadu	1.3	5.5	4.1
Uttar Pradesh	2.1	4.0	1.8
West Bengal	2.0	4.9	2.8
All India	2.1	5.4	3.3

Source: Reserve Bank of India, *Report on Currency and Finance* (various issues).

CONCLUSIONS

The most significant aspect of the changes in GDP and structure is the transition from a stagnant economy during the colonial period to a high growth path in recent years. Stimulated by the economic plans and massive public investment, the economy grew at a moderate pace in the 1950s and early 1960s. A combination of factors such as severe droughts, the rise in oil prices, military conflicts, etc., depressed the growth of the economy and for the next 15 years the growth rates of GDP hovered around 3.6 per cent. The introduction of new technology, high yielding variety (HYV) seeds, extension of irrigation and use of modern inputs gave a boost to agricultural production. This was initially limited to wheat and specific regions but was subsequently extended to more crops and across other regions. Thus agriculture achieved higher growth in the 1980s and was less dependent on vagaries of weather. Industrial growth slowed down in the 1970s raising apprehensions of a structural retrogression, due to a variety of causes such as excess capacity, lack of demand, resource constraints and critical shortages of power and transport. The limited liberalisation of controls in the late 1970s and 1980s led to some pick up of industrial growth. Combined with 3.1 per cent growth rate in agricultural production, it placed the economy on a 5 per cent growth path in the 1980s. With the payments crisis in 1991, radical economic reforms led to relaxation of controls and restrictions. After a lag of two years industrial production surged forward to reach a record 13 per cent growth in 1995. GDP recorded a high growth rate of 7.3 per cent between 1994 and 1996. But the momentum gained has not been maintained. GDP growth has slipped to 5 per cent in 1997 (CSO, 1998(b)) caused mainly by 3.7 per cent decline in the index of agricultural production and a slowdown in the tempo of industrial growth from 7.1 per cent in 1996 to 4.2 per cent in 1997. The prospects for the closing years of the century are, however, not optimistic being influenced by several factors such as slow down in investment, unfavourable international economic environment resulting from economic sanctions and the fallout from the East Asian economic crisis and domestic political uncertainty. If agriculture in the wake of favourable monsoons maintain or exceed the trend growth rate of 2.5 per cent and industry and services increase by 8 and 7 per cent respectively, over all GDP growth may revive to 6 per cent during 1998 and 1999. Per capita GDP may then reach Rs 683 at 1948–49 prices by the end of the century, three times the initial level. It is also significant that per capita GDP which remained stagnant in the first half of the century, may double in the last 20 years.

The most significant achievement of the latter half of the century is in the agricultural front, in which the production of food grains increased four-fold from 50.8 million tonnes in 1950 to 199 million tonnes in 1996. Food production which lagged behind population growth during the pre-independence period had kept ahead of it. Yield rates which declined during 1900–46 increased dramatically and contributed to the increase in agricultural production far more than expansion in areas under cultivation. Equally significant is the declining influence of agriculture on GDP growth. On the industrial sphere too there have been spectacular achievements in the production of steel, cement, electric power and petroleum products. Unregistered manufacturing (i.e. small-scale and cottage industries) which declined or stagnated during the colonial period achieved average rate of growth over 4.6 per cent per annum between 1950 and 1997. Industrial productivity also increased considerably. The service sectors, transport, communications, banking and public administration expanded rapidly. All these have resulted in significant structural changes in output with the share of agriculture declining from 53 per cent in 1947 to 24 in 1997. The shifts in the distribution of working force by activity have not been so pronounced with nearly two-thirds still engaged in agriculture and allied industries. While there appears to be a marginal reduction in rural–urban disparity, inter-state differences have become more pronounced. Improvements in basic indicators of human development have been significant. The death rate declined from 27 per 1 000 in 1950 to nine in 1993, birth rate from 40 per 1 000 to 28.3 and infant mortality rate from 136 per 1 000 to 72. The life expectancy at birth increased from 32.1 years in 1950 to 62.4 in 1996. The literacy rate increased from 18.3 per cent in 1951 to 52.2 in 1991. That the benefits of these achievements could not result in amelioration of poverty has been the main drawback and concern. This has been mainly due to acceleration in population growth which has declined to 1.7 per cent per annum in the 1990s from 2.2 a decade ago. The continuation of this trend coupled with maintaining the tempo of growth at seven per cent in GDP achieved in the mid-1990s may lead to significant reduction of poverty in the foreseeable future.

Six to seven per cent growth in real GDP seemed unattainable a few years ago. Now that this has been realised during the last three years, and is expected to be achieved in the next two, despite the recent slow down the target of 8 to 9 per cent in the future seems to be within the realm of realisation given favourable domestic and external environment. India has tremendous economic potential, the proper mobilisation of which may lead to higher growth rates.

ACKNOWLEDGEMENT

I am grateful to Angus Maddison for his valuable suggestions and comments on an earlier draft of this chapter.

APPENDIX

Table A6.1 GDP by Industrial Origin at 1948–49 Prices, Undivided India, 1900 to 1946 (Rs million)

Year (1)	Agriculture (2)	Livestock (3)	Forestry (4)	Fishery (5)	Total primary (6)	Mining (7)	Manufac- turing (8)	Small-scale cottage industries (9)	Total secon- dary (10)
1900	34 752	6 887	235	348	42 223	269	970	5 646	6 884
1901	33 156	7 130	249	362	40 897	280	1491	6 117	7 888
1902	37 677	7 224	276	372	45 549	283	1579	6 543	8 405
1903	37 463	7 333	257	381	45 435	311	1628	7 035	8 974
1904	36 155	7 488	283	399	44 325	329	1697	7 159	9 184
1905	35 253	7 622	279	414	43 567	347	2006	6 746	9 098
1906	37 438	7 658	250	428	45 775	369	2056	6 004	8 430
1907	32 507	8 018	271	450	41 246	393	1804	5 836	8 033
1908	34 637	7 865	269	461	43 232	396	1808	6 046	8 250
1909	42 678	7 327	286	479	50 770	390	1954	7 056	9 400
1910	42 014	7 725	314	495	50 548	410	1859	7 284	9 554
1911	40 177	7 721	341	503	48 742	413	1866	7 276	9 555
1912	39 269	8 129	366	496	48 259	441	2204	6 894	9 540
1913	36 159	8 893	364	483	45 899	467	2066	6 891	9 425
1914	39 560	8 364	358	473	48 754	459	2118	6 930	9 507
1915	40 908	8 262	362	466	49 998	456	2294	6 323	9 073
1916	43 596	7 900	362	460	52 318	489	2245	5 705	8 438
1917	43 107	7 737	379	452	51 675	497	2196	5 120	7 813
1918	31 662	8 484	364	442	40 951	513	2085	4 593	7 191
1919	42 474	8 195	377	437	51 483	507	2214	4 491	7 212
1920	33 824	8 708	346	431	43 308	469	2370	4 749	7 587
1921	40 166	8 608	394	426	49 594	431	2427	5 402	8 260
1922	41 766	8 450	435	432	51 083	419	2406	5 923	8 747
1923	38 671	8 903	409	437	48 419	456	2036	6 269	8 761
1924	39 541	9 105	404	439	49 489	479	2673	6 372	9 525
1925	38 872	8 846	419	443	48 580	485	2748	7 411	10 644
1926	38 834	9419	414	447	49 114	500	3121	7 772	11 393
1927	37 854	9 250	422	450	47 976	526	3521	7 818	11 866
1928	39 373	9 263	394	455	49 484	525	2814	8 038	11 376
1929	40 408	9 656	408	462	50 934	553	3515	8 181	12 249
1930	41 194	9 314	387	465	51 360	522	3182	9 167	12 871
1931	40 814	9 267	393	468	50 943	480	3335	8 918	12 733
1932	40 716	9 305	396	471	50 889	441	3614	8 809	12 864
1933	40 406	9 288	407	471	50 573	445	3432	8 879	12 756
1934	40 336	9 508	431	479	50 754	504	3879	9 132	13 514
1935	40 187	9 396	457	485	50 526	548	4189	8 367	13 104
1936	43 439	9 453	453	489	53 835	558	4590	7 938	13 086
1937	41 802	9 502	491	489	52 284	639	4888	7 261	12 787
1938	38 013	9 661	530	495	48 698	619	5528	8 282	14 429
1939	40 896	9 722	507	498	51 622	639	5696	7 422	13 758
1940	42 141	9 488	507	504	52 641	779	5790	6 762	13 331
1941	40 168	9 706	503	507	50 885	872	6959	6 010	13 842
1942	41 955	9 556	529	507	52 547	920	7576	5 489	13 985
1943	44 258	9 875	574	512	55 219	830	8448	5 167	14 445
1944	42 904	9 384	613	516	53 417	628	8281	6 201	15 109
1945	40 877	9 622	438	518	51 455	639	8938	7 118	16 696
1946	40 773	9 704	603	520	51 600	579	7064	6 980	14 622

Source: See text p. 1.

Table A6.1 (continued)

Year (1)	Railways and commu- nications (11)	Govern- ment services (12)	Other commerce and transport (13)	Professions and liberal arts (14)	Domestic service (15)	House property (16)	Total tertiary (17)	Total GDP (18)	Popu- lation (million) (19)	Per capita GDP (Rs) (20)
1900	718	1 950	6 430	1 748	667	3 184	14 697	63 804	284.5	224.3
1901	777	1 971	7 822	1 849	695	3 212	16 326	65 111	286.2	227.5
1902	791	2 178	7 734	1 947	711	3 241	16 602	70 556	288.0	245.0
1903	844	2 384	7 825	2 043	769	3 269	17 134	71 543	289.7	247.0
1904	949	2 522	8 641	2 164	804	3 298	18 378	71 887	291.5	246.6
1905	995	2 347	8 467	2 040	746	3 326	17 921	70 587	293.3	240.7
1906	1 072	2 403	8 718	2 093	759	3 355	18 400	72 605	295.1	246.0
1907	1 181	2 321	9 190	2 107	747	3 384	18 930	68 209	296.9	229.7
1908	1 143	2 162	8 356	1 954	677	3 412	17 704	69 186	298.7	231.6
1909	1 127	2 418	8 594	2 186	752	3 445	18 522	78 692	300.5	261.9
1910	1 328	2 531	8 208	2 328	796	3 473	18 664	78 766	302.1	260.7
1911	1 436	2 735	8 991	2 554	868	3 479	20 063	78 360	303.1	258.5
1912	1 610	2 727	9 278	2 454	827	3 512	20 408	78 207	303.4	257.8
1913	1 656	2 601	10 124	2 372	820	3 549	21 122	76 446	303.7	251.7
1914	1 616	2 765	11 083	2 458	856	3 584	22 362	80 623	304.0	265.2
1915	1 751	2 648	8 387	2 363	801	3 623	19 573	78 643	304.2	258.5
1916	1 960	2 896	8 215	2 584	869	3 659	20 183	80 939	304.5	265.8
1917	1 989	3 066	7 777	2 571	887	3 700	19 990	79 478	304.8	260.8
1918	2 125	3 167	8 872	2 433	843	3 738	21 178	69 320	305.1	227.2
1919	2 122	2 672	8 961	1 967	678	3 781	20 181	78 875	305.3	258.4
1920	2 121	2 780	10 209	2 086	716	3 825	21 737	72 632	305.6	237.7
1921	1 958	2 691	8 862	2 156	744	3 881	20 292	78 147	307.3	254.3
1922	1 914	2 989	9 395	2 514	901	3 901	21 614	81 444	310.4	262.0
1923	1 955	3 350	8 376	2 911	1 097	3 924	21 613	78 793	313.6	251.3
1924	2 116	3 486	9 864	3 022	1 180	3 948	23 616	82 630	316.7	260.9
1925	2 048	3 328	10 657	3 128	1 254	3 968	24 383	83 608	319.9	261.4
1926	2 083	3 260	12 109	3 041	1 254	3 987	25 734	86 241	323.2	266.8
1927	2 217	3 402	12 255	3 159	1 350	4 023	26 406	86 248	326.4	264.2
1928	2 240	3 511	11 800	3 229	1 432	4 042	26 254	87 115	329.7	264.2
1929	2 249	3 816	12 534	3 337	1 562	4 050	27 548	90 732	333.1	272.4
1930	2 101	4 553	11 166	3 546	1 713	4 054	27 133	91 364	336.4	271.6
1931	1 881	5 139	10 732	3 549	1 710	4 075	27 086	90 762	341.0	266.2
1932	1 789	5 313	11 351	3 693	1 756	4 125	28 027	91 780	345.8	265.4
1933	1 850	5 743	11 107	3 851	1 808	4 176	28 535	91 864	350.7	261.9
1934	1 977	5 682	11 127	3 707	1 717	4 240	28 450	92 717	355.6	260.7
1935	2 011	5 696	10 841	3 642	1 687	4 330	28 207	91 837	360.6	254.7
1936	2 077	5 651	11 274	3 449	1 610	4 424	28 485	95 406	365.7	260.9
1937	2 237	5 657	11 527	3 326	1 523	4 520	28 790	93 861	370.9	253.1
1938	2 201	5 913	13 235	3 435	1 578	4 599	30 961	94 088	376.1	250.2
1939	2 279	6 081	12 915	3 272	1 524	4 714	30 785	96 165	381.4	252.1
1940	2 425	6 625	14 911	3 151	1 460	4 815	33 387	99 358	386.8	256.9
1941	2 671	6 583	18 131	2 901	1 349	4 896	36 531	101 258	391.7	258.5
1942	2 776	6 483	16 490	2 338	1 180	4 990	34 257	100 789	396.3	254.3
1943	3 089	4 863	19 565	1 712	783	5 087	35 099	104 764	400.3	261.7
1944	3 288	6 141	17 150	2 348	1 022	5 187	35 136	103 662	405.6	255.6
1945	3 508	6 214	14 928	2 756	1 142	5 297	33 845	101 996	410.4	248.5
1946	3 459	4 863	12 800	2 791	1 086	5 410	30 409	96 631	415.2	232.7

*Table A6.2 Annual Percentage Change of GDP at 1948–49 prices, Undivided India, 1900
              to 1946*

Year (1)	Primary (2)	Secondary (3)	Tertiary (4)	Total (5)	GDP (6)
1900					
1901	−3.1	14.6	11.1	2.0	1.4
1902	11.4	6.6	1.7	8.4	7.7
1903	−0.3	6.8	3.2	1.4	0.8
1904	−2.4	2.3	7.3	0.5	−0.1
1905	−1.7	−0.9	−2.5	−1.8	−2.4
1906	5.1	−7.4	2.7	2.9	2.2
1907	−9.9	−4.7	2.9	−6.1	−6.6
1908	4.8	2.7	−6.5	1.4	0.8
1909	17.4	13.9	4.6	13.7	13.1
1910	−0.4	1.6	0.8	0.1	−0.4
1911	−3.6	0.0	7.5	−0.5	−0.8
1912	−1.0	−0.2	1.7	−0.2	−0.3
1913	−4.9	−1.2	3.5	−2.3	−2.3
1914	6.2	0.9	5.9	5.5	5.4
1915	2.6	−4.6	−12.5	−2.5	−2.5
1916	4.6	−7.0	3.1	2.9	2.8
1917	−1.2	−7.4	−1.0	−1.8	−1.9
1918	−20.8	−8.0	5.9	−12.8	−12.9
1919	25.7	0.3	−4.7	13.8	13.7
1920	−15.9	5.2	7.7	−7.9	−8.0
1921	14.5	8.9	−6.6	7.6	7.0
1922	3.0	5.9	6.5	4.2	3.0
1923	−5.2	0.2	0.0	−3.3	−4.1
1924	2.2	8.7	9.3	4.9	3.8
1925	−1.8	11.8	3.2	1.2	0.2
1926	1.1	7.0	5.5	3.1	2.1
1927	−2.3	4.1	2.6	0.0	−1.0
1928	3.1	−4.1	−0.6	1.0	0.0
1929	2.9	7.7	4.9	4.2	3.1
1930	0.8	5.1	−1.5	0.7	−0.3
1931	−0.8	−1.1	−0.2	−0.7	−2.0
1932	−0.1	1.0	3.5	1.1	−0.3
1933	−0.6	−0.8	1.8	0.1	−1.3
1934	0.4	5.9	−0.3	0.9	−0.5
1935	−0.4	−3.0	−0.9	−0.9	−2.3
1936	6.5	−0.1	1.0	3.9	2.4
1937	−2.9	−2.3	1.1	−1.6	−3.0
1938	−6.9	12.8	7.5	0.2	−1.1
1939	6.0	−4.6	−0.6	2.2	0.8
1940	2.0	−3.1	8.5	3.3	1.9
1941	−3.3	3.8	9.4	1.9	0.6
1942	3.3	1.0	−6.2	−0.5	−1.6
1943	5.1	3.3	2.5	3.9	2.9
1944	−3.3	4.6	0.1	−1.1	−2.3
1945	−3.7	10.5	−3.7	−1.6	−2.8
1946	0.3	−12.4	−10.2	−5.3	−6.4

Source: Table A6.1.

Table A6.3 Gross Domestic Produce by Industrial Origin at 1948–49 Prices, India 1946 to 1997 (Rs million)

Year (1)	Agriculture (2)	Forestry (3)	Fishery (4)	Total primary (5)	Mining (6)	Registered manufacturing (7)	Unregistered manufacturing (8)	Total manufacturing (9)	Electricity gas and water (10)	Construction (11)	Total secondary (12)
1946	40 442	2 046	295	42 783	417	4 592	5 179	9 771	181	2 415	12 784
1947	42 161	1 965	296	44 422	411	4 208	5 200	9 408	187	2 425	12 431
1948	40 735	2 387	299	43 421	510	4 870	5 205	10 075	207	2 427	13 219
1949	41 843	2 760	392	44 995	543	4 781	5 148	9 929	216	2 402	13 090
1950	41 506	2 791	414	44 711	610	4 779	5 200	9 979	224	2 410	13 223
1951	42 187	2 785	439	45 411	685	4 905	5 389	10 294	250	2 575	13 804
1952	43 942	2 635	464	47 041	700	4 928	5 721	10 649	261	2 388	13 998
1953	47 893	2 550	474	50 917	711	5 145	6 325	11 470	282	2 462	14 925
1954	49 233	2 646	509	52 388	741	5 717	6 560	12 277	306	2 766	16 090
1955	48 504	2 752	550	51 806	753	6 418	6 826	13 244	339	3 291	17 627
1956	51 407	2 734	611	54 752	791	7 133	7 110	14 243	370	3 669	19 073
1957	48 795	2 744	626	52 165	843	7 466	7 327	14 793	426	3 220	19 282
1958	54 283	2 738	648	57 669	869	7 681	7 842	15 523	480	3 598	20 470
1959	53 491	2 834	658	56 983	914	8 456	8 125	16 581	552	3 845	21 892
1960	57 387	2 866	704	60 957	1 051	9 508	8 456	17 964	597	4 447	24 059
1961	57 202	2 980	724	60 906	1 111	10 377	9 123	19 500	682	4 603	25 896
1962	55 974	2 986	687	59 647	1 246	11 387	9 536	20 923	765	4 775	27 709
1963	57 023	3 166	751	60 940	1 280	12 675	10 232	22 907	904	5 358	30 449
1964	62 914	3 106	826	66 846	1 298	13 721	10 773	24 494	987	5 788	32 567
1965	54 440	3 521	826	58 787	1 451	14 172	10 556	24 728	1 090	6 175	33 444
1966	53 194	3 694	856	57 744	1 485	14 184	10 737	24 921	1 184	6 682	34 272
1967	62 275	3 678	893	66 846	1 528	13 721	11 286	25 007	1 314	7 163	35 012
1968	62 061	3 693	947	66 701	1 573	14 649	11 746	26 395	1 483	7 413	36 864
1969	66 559	3 684	970	71 213	1 651	17 194	12 052	29 246	1 616	7 643	40 156
1970	71 492	3 862	995	76 349	1 542	17 603	12 330	29 933	1 717	7 627	40 819
1971	69 588	4 032	1 059	74 679	1 582	17 921	12 985	30 906	1 856	7 660	42 004
1972	65 672	3 997	1 088	70 757	1 676	18 492	13 623	32 115	1 942	7 840	43 573
1973	71 206	3 885	1 119	76 210	1 698	19 404	14 142	33 546	1 986	7 331	44 561
1974	69 244	4 223	1 204	74 671	1 781	19 598	14 919	34 517	2 077	7 097	45 472
1975	79 073	4 340	1 278	84 691	1 997	19 796	15 444	35 240	2 379	8 109	47 725
1976	74 264	4 195	1 236	79 695	2 071	22 268	16 076	38 344	2 653	8 902	51 970
1977	83 558	3 714	1 236	88 508	2 133	23 763	16 970	40 733	2 779	9 803	55 448
1978	85 223	3 915	1 295	90 433	2 191	26 392	19 403	45 795	3 096	9 585	60 667
1979	73 836	3 567	1 287	78 690	2 214	25 801	18 489	44 290	3 134	9 079	58 717
1980	84 497	3 515	1 310	89 322	2 484	25 386	18 982	44 368	3 312	10 275	60 439
1981	89 828	3 583	1 331	94 742	2 819	27 343	20 585	47 928	3 622	10 833	65 202
1982	88 684	3 553	1 331	93 568	3 142	29 974	21 098	51 072	3 864	10 332	68 410
1983	98 996	3 448	1 604	104 048	3 227	34 373	21 789	56 162	4 141	11 052	74 582
1984	98 895	3 427	1 725	104 047	3 273	37 271	22 548	59 819	4 581	11 475	79 148
1985	99 199	3 428	1 681	104 308	3 453	38 144	24 058	62 202	4 958	12 072	82 685
1986	97 488	3 330	1 701	102 519	3 920	40 351	26 201	66 552	5 475	12 667	88 614
1987	98 012	3 218	1 756	102 986	4 055	43 206	28 212	71 418	5 907	13 073	94 453
1988	115 287	3 168	1 897	120 352	4 663	47 803	29 880	77 683	6 528	14 082	102 956
1989	116 536	3 443	2 133	122 112	5 004	54 438	32 333	86 771	7 208	14 801	113 784
1990	121 357	3 346	2 214	126 917	5 538	57 169	34 882	92 051	7 675	16 525	121 789
1991	118 188	3 322	2 328	123 838	5 742	55 860	32 793	88 653	8 413	16 885	119 693
1992	126 005	3 179	2 463	131 647	5 808	57 617	34 730	92 347	9 120	17 455	124 730
1993	130 753	3 105	2 659	136 517	5 925	64 310	35 905	100 215	9 763	17 675	133 578
1994	137 723	3 165	2 833	143 721	6 272	72 362	39 850	112 212	10 606	18 708	147 798
1995	133 056	3 159	3 009	139 224	6 800	82 570	45 318	127 888	11 382	20 523	166 593
1996	143 999	3 165	3 226	150 390	6 783	89 338	47 964	137 302	11 945	21 589	177 619
1997	140 753	3 171	3 458	147 382	7 212	95 404	50 291	145 695	12 711	22 278	187 896

Source: See text p. 10.

Table A6.3 (continued)

Year (1)	Railways (13)	Communi- cations (14)	Other transport and commerce (15)	Banking and insurance (16)	Real estate and business services (17)	Public adminis- tration and defence (18)	Other services (19)	Total tertiary (20)	GDP (21)	Popu- lation (million) (22)	Per capita GDP (Rs) (23)
1946	1 260	247	7 141	550	7 097	2 746	4 975	24 016	79 583	343	232.0
1947	1 268	266	6 347	617	7 087	2 645	4 896	23 126	79 979	346	231.2
1948	1 430	270	6 880	507	7 580	2 520	4 993	24 180	80 820	350	230.9
1949	1 575	262	6 937	608	7 747	2 505	5 236	24 870	82 955	355	233.7
1950	1 658	275	6 986	709	7 921	2 550	5 143	25 242	83 176	359	231.7
1951	1 682	291	7 173	731	8 088	2 610	5 310	25 885	85 100	365	233.2
1952	1 653	308	7 432	855	8 277	2 636	5 440	26 601	87 640	372	235.6
1953	1 668	325	7 723	826	8 467	2 751	5 583	27 343	93 185	379	245.9
1954	1 750	349	8 234	933	8 649	2 905	5 742	28 562	97 040	386	251.4
1955	1 934	380	8 813	1 066	8 838	3 020	5 901	29 952	99 385	393	252.9
1956	2 109	414	9 443	1 053	9 035	3 236	6 053	31 343	105 168	401	262.3
1957	2 322	421	9 686	1 180	9 232	3 490	6 247	32 578	104 025	409	254.3
1958	2 341	460	10 184	1 249	9 437	3 704	6 451	33 826	111 965	418	267.9
1959	2 516	494	10 809	1 391	9 649	3 944	6 668	35 471	114 346	426	268.4
1960	2 613	511	11 798	1 404	9 869	4 202	6 947	37 344	122 360	434	281.9
1961	2 734	556	12 574	1 586	10 097	4 471	7 221	39 239	126 041	444	283.9
1962	2 952	612	13 273	1 689	10 362	5 050	7 539	41 477	128 833	454	283.8
1963	3 127	684	14 207	1 768	10 635	5 614	7 861	43 896	135 285	464	291.6
1964	3 170	740	15 224	1 836	10 892	6 217	8 206	46 285	145 698	474	307.4
1965	3 413	785	15 400	1 917	11 181	6 439	8 550	47 685	139 916	486	287.9
1966	3 466	831	15 796	1 892	11 476	6 849	8 860	49 170	141 186	495	285.2
1967	3 568	874	16 477	1 943	11 787	7 151	9 184	50 984	152 842	506	302.1
1968	3 694	901	17 243	2 206	12 090	7 595	9 500	53 229	156 794	518	302.7
1969	3 825	949	18 199	2 409	12 408	8 258	9844	55 892	167 261	529	316.2
1970	3 941	1 028	19 096	2 626	12 742	8 955	10 206	58 594	175 762	541	324.9
1971	4 115	1 089	19 473	2 911	13 159	9 581	10 493	60 821	177 504	554	320.4
1972	4 285	1 149	19 824	3 094	13 530	9 931	10 810	62 623	176 953	567	312.1
1973	3 980	1 233	20 797	3 114	13 970	10 417	10 930	64 441	185 212	580	319.3
1974	4 169	1 284	22 058	2 818	14 394	10 821	11 514	67 058	187 201	593	315.7
1975	4 683	1 371	24 024	3 347	14 864	11 367	11 799	71 455	203 871	607	335.9
1976	5 012	1 486	25 012	4 055	15 304	11 847	12 005	74 721	206 386	620	332.9
1977	5 259	1 556	26 753	4 410	15 797	12 340	12 197	78 312	222 268	634	350.6
1978	5 221	1 659	29 131	5 105	16 289	13 251	12 437	83 093	234 193	648	361.4
1979	5 298	1 794	28 718	4 928	16 812	14 188	13 376	85 114	222 521	664	335.1
1980	5 449	1 922	30 365	4 923	17 298	15 122	13 660	88 739	238 500	679	351.3
1981	5 914	2 067	32 154	5 272	17 889	15 467	14 271	93 034	252 978	692	365.6
1982	6 045	2 229	33 909	6 091	18 738	17 090	15 066	99 168	261 146	708	368.9
1983	6 025	2 315	35 924	6 634	19 367	17 683	15 617	103 565	282 195	723	390.3
1984	6 142	2 522	37 984	7 443	20 057	19 434	16 310	109 892	293 087	739	396.6
1985	6 806	2 589	41 198	8 418	20 807	20 922	17 070	117 810	304 803	755	403.7
1986	7 339	2 765	43 744	9 666	21 611	22 986	18 527	126 638	317 771	771	412.2
1987	7 640	2 941	46 299	10 687	22 194	25 327	19 154	134 242	331 681	788	420.9
1988	7 562	3 102	49 759	12 455	22 945	26 993	20 242	143 058	366 366	805	455.1
1989	7 867	3 272	53 959	14 833	23 748	29 269	21 885	154 833	390 729	822	475.3
1990	8 129	3 509	56 760	16 133	24 680	29 566	23 528	162 305	411 011	839	489.9
1991	8 619	3 750	57 854	18 932	25 461	30 198	24 917	169 731	413 262	856	482.8
1992	8 522	4 155	61 607	20 021	26 295	31 764	26 101	178 465	434 842	872	498.7
1993	8 464	4 610	66 345	23 271	27 182	32 581	27 449	189 902	459 997	888	518.0
1994	8 580	5 352	73 385	26 260	28 228	33 044	28 795	203 644	495 163	904	547.7
1995	9 239	6 337	83 143	29 805	29 335	35 036	30 516	223 411	529 228	920	575.2
1996	9 521	7 443	90 081	33 338	30 381	37 349	32 409	240 522	568 531	936	607.4
1997	9 723	8 342	95 317	38 239	31 508	43 742	35 650	262 521	597 799	952	627.9

Source: See text p. 10.

Table A6.4 Annual Percentage Change in GDP by Sector at 1948–49 Prices, India 1947 to 1997

Year (1)	Primary (2)	Secondary (3)	Tertiary (4)	GDP (5)	Per Capita (6)
1947	3.83	–2.76	–3.71	0.50	–0.34
1948	–2.25	6.34	4.55	1.05	–0.13
1949	3.62	–0.98	2.85	2.64	1.20
1950	–0.63	1.02	1.50	0.27	–0.85
1951	1.57	4.39	2.55	2.31	0.63
1952	3.59	1.41	2.77	2.98	1.05
1953	8.24	6.62	2.79	6.33	4.36
1954	2.89	7.81	4.46	4.14	2.25
1955	–1.11	9.55	4.87	2.42	0.59
1956	5.69	8.20	4.64	5.82	3.71
1957	–4.72	1.10	3.94	–1.09	–3.02
1958	10.55	6.16	3.83	7.63	5.32
1959	–1.19	6.95	4.86	2.13	0.21
1960	6.97	9.90	5.28	7.01	5.04
1961	–0.08	7.64	5.07	3.01	0.69
1962	–2.07	7.00	5.70	2.22	–0.04
1963	2.17	9.89	5.83	5.01	2.74
1964	9.69	6.96	5.44	7.70	5.42
1965	–12.06	2.69	3.02	–3.97	–6.34
1966	–1.77	2.48	3.11	0.91	–0.93
1967	15.76	2.16	3.69	8.26	5.90
1968	–0.22	5.29	4.40	2.59	0.21
1969	6.76	8.93	5.00	6.68	4.46
1970	7.21	1.65	4.83	5.08	2.75
1971	–2.19	2.90	3.80	0.99	–1.38
1972	–5.25	3.74	2.96	–0.31	–2.60
1973	7.71	2.27	2.90	4.67	2.32
1974	–2.02	2.04	4.06	1.07	–1.14
1975	13.42	4.95	6.56	8.90	6.39
1976	–5.90	8.89	4.57	1.23	–0.89
1977	11.06	6.69	4.81	7.70	5.32
1978	2.17	9.41	6.11	5.37	3.09
1979	–12.99	–3.21	2.43	–4.98	–7.27
1980	13.51	2.93	4.26	7.18	4.81
1981	6.07	7.88	4.84	6.07	4.08
1982	–1.24	4.92	6.59	3.23	0.90
1983	11.20	9.02	4.43	8.06	5.82
1984	0.00	6.12	6.11	3.86	1.61
1985	0.25	4.47	7.21	4.00	1.79
1986	–1.72	7.17	7.49	4.25	2.09
1987	0.46	6.59	6.00	4.38	2.13
1988	16.86	9.00	6.57	10.46	8.12
1989	1.46	10.52	8.23	6.65	4.44
1990	3.93	7.04	4.83	5.19	3.06
1991	–2.43	–1.72	4.58	0.55	–1.45
1992	6.31	4.21	5.15	5.22	3.29
1993	3.70	7.09	6.41	5.78	3.88
1994	5.28	10.65	7.24	7.64	5.74
1995	–3.13	12.72	9.71	6.88	5.02
1996	8.02	6.62	7.66	7.43	5.59
1997	–2.00	5.79	9.15	5.15	3.38

Source: Table A6.3.

REFERENCES

Balasubramanyam, V.N. (1984), *The Economy of India*, p. 43.

Bhattacharjee, J.P., ed. (1958), 'Trend of Consumption of Food and Food Grains in India', *Studies in Agricultural Economies*, pp. 222–3.

Blyn, G. (1969), *Agricultural Trends in India*, pp. 316–17.

Census of India (1993), *Census of India*, Paper No. 3, 1991, p. 18.

Central Statistical Organisation (1978), *National Accounts Statistics*, p. 12.

Central Statistical Organisation (1989), *National Accounts Statistics*, Sources and Methods, pp. 182–84.

Central Statistical Organisation (1993), *National Accounts Statistics*, pp. 216–17.

Central Statistical Organisation (1997), *National Accounts Statistics*, p. 283.

Central Statistical Organisation (1998a), *Quick Estimates of GDP for 1996–97*.

Central Statistical Organisation (1998b), *Advanced Estimates of GDP for 1997–98*.

Chatterjee G.S. and Mira Sinha (1960), 'National Income Estimates of India, 1944–45 to 1947–48. A Review', *Second Indian Conference on Research in National Income* (mimeo).

Dandekar, V.M. (1982), 'Forty years after Independence' in Bimal Jalan ed., *The Indian Economy, Problems and Prospects*, pp. 33–8.

Daniel Thorner (1955), 'Long Term Trends in Output in India' in Simon Kuznets et al. ed., *Economic Growth of Brazil, India and Japan*, pp. 103–28.

Dharma Kumar (1982), 'The Fiscal System' in Dharma Kumar ed., *Cambridge Economic History of India*, vol. II, pp. 928–29.

Fiscal Commission (1949), *Statistical Information*, p. 10.

Gadgil D.R. (1971), *The Industrial Evolution of India in Recent Times*.

Goldsmith, R.W. (1983), *The Financing of Development in India*, 1860–1977, p. 68.

Government of India (1997), *Economic Survey*, 1996–97.

Heston, A. (1982), *'National Income'*, in Dharma Kumar ed., *Cambridge Economic History of India*, vol. II, pp. 376–453.

International Labour Organisation (1938), *Industrial Labour in India*, Studies and Reports Series A, no. 41, pp. 42–3.

League of Nations (1945), *Industrialisation and Foreign Trade*, p.135.

Maddison, A. (1971), 'Real National Income by Industrial Origin', *Class, Structure and Economic Growth: India, Pakistan and the Moghuls*, pp. 166–68.

Maddison, A. (1985), 'Alternative Estimates of Real Product in India, 1900–46, *Indian Economic and Social History Review*, vol. 22, no. 2, pp. 201–10.

Meek, D.B. (1937), 'Some Measures of Economic Activity in India', in *Journal of the Royal Statistical Society*, Part III, p. 363.

Ministry of Finance, Government of India (1951), *First Report of the National Income Committee*.

Ministry of Finance, Government of India (1954), *Final Report of the National Income Committee*.

Morris, M.D. and Clyde B. Dudley (1975), 'Selected Railway Statistics for India, Pakistan and Bangladesh in *Artha Vijnana* vol. 17, no. 3, pp. 209–12.

Mukherjee, M. (1969), *National Income of India, Trends and Structure*.

Mukerji, K. (1962), 'A note on Long-term Growth of National Income of India, 1900–01 to 1952–53', in V.K.R.V. Rao et al. (eds), *Papers on National Income and Allied Topics*, vol. I.

Planning Commission (1954), *Second Five Year Plan*.

Rajat, K. Ray (1979), *Industrialisation in India, Growth and Conflict in the Private Sector*, 1914–47, pp. 16–17.

Rao, V.K.R.V. (1941), *National Income of British India, 1931–32*.

Rao, V.K.R.V. (1954), 'Changes in India's National Income – A Static Economy in Progress', Reprinted in V.K.R.V. Rao et al. (eds), *Papers on National Income and Allied Topics*, vol. I, pp. 6–11.

Rao, V.K.R.V. (1983), *India's National Income, 1950–80*, p. 224.

Shetty, S.L. (1978), 'Structural Retrogression in the Indian Economy since the Mid-sixties', *Economic and Political Weekly,* Annual Number, Feb. 1978, pp. 185–244.

Sivasubramonian, S. (1960), 'Estimates of Gross Value of Output of Agriculture in Undivided India, 1900–1 to 1946–47 in V.K.R.V. Rao et al. (eds), *Papers on National Income and Allied Topics,* vol. I, pp. 231–46.

Sivasubramonian, S. (1965), 'National Income of India, Ph.D. Dissertation (mimeo), Delhi School of Economics, Delhi.

Sivasubramonian, S. (1977), 'Income from Secondary Sector in India, 1900–47, *Indian Economic and Social History Review,* vol. 14, no. 4, 1977, pp. 427–92.

Sivasubramonian, S. (1997), 'Revised Estimates of the National Income in India, 1900–01 to 1946–47', *Indian Economic and Social History Review,* vol. 34, 2, pp. 113–119.

Sivasubramonian, S. (forthcoming), National Income of India, 1900–1 to 1997–98, Sumit Guha, (1992), *Growth, Stagnation or Decline Agricultural Productivity in British India,* pp 1–34 and 100–26.

Sundrum, R.H. (1987), *Growth and Income Distribution in India, Policy and Performance Since Independence,* p. 350.

Thavaraj, M.J.K. (1960), 'Capital Formation in the Public Sector in India, A Historical Study, 1898–1938', in V.K.R.V. Rao et al. ed., *Papers on National Income and Allied Topics,* vol. I.

7. Indonesia's Growth Performance in the Twentieth Century

Pierre van der Eng

INTRODUCTION

Indonesia's high rates of economic growth during the last three decades has been regarded as part of the so-called East Asian miracle. It has also been argued that high growth in East Asia was not miraculous, but was simply due to the productive mobilisation of labour, human and physical capital, rather than technological change.[1] Those who take the latter position argue that, as Asian economies approach the international technological frontier, growth will slow down. Despite evidence of technological change in manufacturing in recent years, Indonesian producers are still a long way from international best-practice in most economic sectors (Szirmai, 1994). Given Indonesia's relative resource endowment and comparative advantage, its capacity to absorb technology from abroad may therefore have facilitated the long-term growth process.

The first section of this chapter presents consistent historical estimates of GDP in constant prices for 1900–97. These data reveal that economic growth in the early part of this century (1900–29) was much slower than in the well-documented recent era of high-growth (1967–97), but was nevertheless significant in historical and international perspective. The chapter then explores, in broad terms, three issues that may help to understand some of the differences in Indonesia's growth performance during these two periods of expansion and the intermediate period of stagnation. These are:

1. proximate sources of growth on the output side, *i.e.* the mobilisation of natural resources, labour and capital, and the possible role of technological change;
2. two proximate sources of growth on the demand side: foreign trade and domestic demand, due to public expenditure, private consumption and indirectly as a consequence of the integration and growth of a national market;
3. regional discrepancies in the distribution of production, productive capacity and income.

INDONESIA'S LONG-RUN GROWTH EXPERIENCE

The area we now know as Indonesia used to be a Dutch colony. During the nineteenth century, the expansion of colonial control radiated from the core island of Java to the rest of the country. Soon after 1900, all of Indonesia was brought under Dutch colonial administration, which gradually intensified during the ensuing 40 years. This process included a gradual expansion of economic contacts between different parts of the country, and with the rest of the world. Dutch colonial rule ended in 1942 with Indonesia's occupation by the Japanese. Three years of economic hardship followed, during which long-suppressed Indonesian nationalism came to the fore. Indonesian nationalists declared independence in 1945 and rallied opposition against a return to Dutch colonial rule. The ensuing war of independence postponed economic recuperation until full independence was granted in 1949.

Economic recovery stalled in the late-1950s and turned into decline in the 1960s with the development of political turmoil and poor economic management under the flamboyant left-leaning President Sukarno. The country experienced a nadir in 1965–66 when a Communist-inspired coup and a military counter-coup triggered widespread bloodshed until the military, directed by later President Soeharto, restored order. Economic recovery resumed and was supported by a rapid expansion of petroleum production for export and a boom in oil prices, particularly after 1973.

The oil boom ended in the mid-1980s, when oil prices decreased. However, economic growth continued because Indonesia embarked on a process of economic liberalisation. This contributed to a rapid expansion of domestic demand and of non-oil exports, particularly labour-intensive manufactures. The rapid economic expansion over-stretched the capabilities and lending capacity of the financial sector, which became burdened with bad debts in the early 1990s. Economic growth continued, as Indonesian companies gained ready access to international finance. However, by mid-1997 it appeared that too much had been invested in speculative ventures and that many Indonesian companies were unable to service their foreign liabilities. A run on the Indonesian currency sparked an economic crisis which was compounded by political uncertainty. The crisis led to the abdication of President Soeharto and to negative economic growth in 1998.

These broad trends are visible in Table 7.1, which summarises Indonesia's growth process during the twentieth century. The country experienced two broad phases of economic expansion: 1900–29 and 1967–97, when GDP (including oil and gas) growth averaged respectively 2.8 and 6.8 per cent per year and per capita growth was 1.6 and 4.6 per cent per year. The experience during the intermediate period was mixed. During 1934–41 and 1949–61 the country recovered from the set-backs of respectively the crisis of the early 1930s, and the Japanese occupation and war of independence. But, on balance, annual average GDP growth was a mere 1.0 per cent during 1929–67, while per capita growth was –0.6 per cent.

Compared with the experience since the 1960s, GDP per capita growth was slow during 1900–29. However, it was faster than in Western Europe, where GDP per capita increased during 1820–1913 by an average of 1.1 per cent per year (Maddison, 1995: 23). Growth of GDP per capita in Indonesia started in 1967 from a level of 1 025 1990 international dollars, while West European countries started in 1820 from an average level of 1 228 dollars (Maddison, 1995: 23, 205). It therefore appears that Indonesia's per capita economic growth during 1967–97 was fast by historical standards.

Economic growth induced structural change. Table 7.2 shows sector shares in non-oil GDP, as oil production will overstate the contribution of the industrial sector. It indicates that structural change during 1900–29 brought a gradual fall in the share of agriculture and a growing share of services, which was largely due to the development of trade and transport. The 1930s saw a remarkable rise of industrial output due to import-substituting industrialisation. Shares of the three sectors in output remained roughly constant during 1949–67. During 1967–97 industrial output increased much faster than output in agriculture and services, leading to an increase in the share of industry from 16 per cent in 1967 to almost 40 per cent in 1997, and a concomitant fall of the share of agriculture from 43 per cent to 16 per cent.

Table 7.1 Real GDP, Population and Real GDP Per Capita in Indonesia, 1900–97

	GDP (excluding oil and gas) (billion 1983 Rupiah)	GDP (including oil and gas) (billion 1983 Rupiah)	Population (x 1 000)	GDP per capita (including oil and gas) (1 000 1983 Rupiah)
1900	8 278	8 351	42 746	195
1913	11 501	11 877	49 934	238
1929	17 112	18 417	59 863	308
1941	21 709	23 494	71 316	329
1949	14 839	16 275	77 654	220
1967	20 632	26 762	109 343	245
1980	53 387	72 549	147 490	492
1997	173 938	191 516	201 354	951

Source: Van der Eng 1992, revised and updated as described in Appendix A.

Table 7.2 Main Sector Shares in Non-Oil GDP in Indonesia, 1900–97

	Agriculture	Industry	Services
1900	44.8	16.8	38.3
1913	41.7	16.5	41.7
1929	36.6	16.3	47.1
1941	36.1	21.9	42.0
1949	42.3	19.4	38.4
1967	42.9	16.4	40.7
1980	29.7	26.0	45.1
1997	16.3	39.2	44.6

Notes: Calculated from output data in 1983 constant prices. Agriculture includes food crops, animal husbandry, cash and estate crops, fisheries and forestry. Industry includes non-oil and gas mining, manufacturing, utilities and construction.

Source: Appendix A.

PROXIMATE SOURCES OF OUTPUT GROWTH

a. Natural Resources

Surface area per head of the population is a rough proxy for the availability of natural resources. During the twentieth century, population growth reduced the per capita availability of natural resources in Indonesia, but huge differences in resource endowment across the country remained. In densely populated Java surface area per capita decreased from 0.43 hectares in 1900 to 0.12 in 1995, while in the sparsely populated Outer Islands it decreased from 4.49 hectares in 1900 to 0.99 in 1995 (Van der Eng, 1996: 275; BPS, 1996). The frontier of land for agricultural production was reached in Java during the 1920s (Van der Eng, 1996: 24). Since then, increases in agricultural production in Java have been largely the result of increasing land productivity with complementary increases in reproducible capital.

The resource advantages of the Outer Islands have long drawn immigrants from elsewhere in Asia and from Java, resulting in a continuous expansion of cultivated land in the Outer Islands. This process accelerated after 1970 with the rapid expansion of small-holder production of lucrative cash crops such as rubber, coffee and cocoa, and concessions granted for palm oil plantations (Van der Eng, 1996: Appendix 4).

Surface area is an inaccurate indicator of mineral endowment. Most of the mineral deposits were situated in the Outer Islands. Their exploitation and the growth of mining output followed the establishment of colonial rule. Up to the late 1960s, tin and petroleum were the most important products. Oil production suffered little from the economic chaos after independence, but tin mining experienced a decrease in investment due to the nationalisation of foreign enterprise in 1958, the disadvantageous foreign exchange regime and several regional attempts to secede from the Republic of Indonesia. The removal of these sources of insecurity was a precondition for the expansion of foreign investment in a wide range of minerals, such as coal, nickel ore, bauxite and copper. Petroleum production increased rapidly during the 1970s, followed by production of a wide range of minerals during the 1970s and 1980s. Several provinces in the Outer Islands could have reaped windfall benefits from the expansion of mining output. The fact that they did not will be discussed below.

b. Demographic Change

Table 7.3 shows that population growth varied considerably during the twentieth century. In Java it fluctuated around 1.0 per cent per year up to 1949, doubled to 2.0 per cent in the 1970s, and decreased to 1.3 per cent in the 1990s. Population growth in the Outer Islands fluctuated around 1.6 per cent up to 1949, doubled to 3.0 per cent in the 1970s, and decreased to 2.2 per cent in the 1990s. The proximate causes of the post-war acceleration of population growth were a rapid fall of mortality and a lagged reduction in birth rates.

Changes in population dynamics had consequences for the development of the labour force. Table 7.3 shows that the activity rate fluctuated considerably during the twentieth century. In 1900–49 it increased in Java. It fell in Java and the Outer Islands from 1949 to 1980, but increased rapidly from 1980 to 1997. The increase in recent decades was due to a deceleration of population growth and an acceleration of labour force growth. The labour force increase was caused by three factors: cohorts of people born during the period of high population growth reached working age; increased life expectancy extended the gainful employment of older workers; and the female activity rate increased rapidly from 23 per cent in 1980 to 33 per cent in 1997.

Table 7.3 Population and Labour Force in Indonesia, 1900–97

	Population (millions)		Labour force (millions)		Crude activity rates (%)	
	Java	Outer Islands	Java	Outer Islands	Java	Outer Islands
1900	30.76	11.98	10.88	4.51	34	38
1913	35.26	14.67	13.20	5.60	36	38
1929	41.29	18.57	16.00	6.98	38	38
1941	48.00	23.30	18.59	8.56	38	37
1949	51.11	26.54	20.86	10.06	40	38
1967	70.54	38.79	25.77	13.62	36	35
1980	91.27	56.22	32.43	19.58	34	34
1997	117.75	86.60	53.14	35.20	43	42

Note: The crude activity rate is not corrected for changes in the age distribution.

Sources: 1900–90 from Van der Eng 1996: Appendix 3. 1991–97 interpolated and extrapolated with 1995 data from BPS 1996.

Economic growth wrought structural change in employment, as Table 7.4 shows for three census years. The share of agriculture decreased significantly after the 1960s, particularly in Java. Increasing numbers of people found gainful employment in industry and services. Employment in service sectors increased faster than in industry. A comparison of Tables 7.2 and 7.4 suggests that structural change in employment was less pronounced than in output. This indicates that the labour productivity gap between agriculture and non-agriculture increased, and that agricultural workers augmented their incomes with off-farm earnings.[2]

c. Human Capital

During recent decades educational facilities and average educational attainment have improved considerably. The share of population without schooling decreased sharply from 68 per cent in 1961 to 19 per cent in 1990 (Hill, 1996: 207). However, it is difficult to establish the degree of human capital formation before the 1960s. It is known that the intensification of colonial rule after 1900 was accompanied by a gradual improvement and expansion of educational facilities, which continued during the 1950s (Zainuddin, 1970).

Table 7.4 Sector Shares in Employment, 1930–90 (percentages)

	Males			Females			Both sexes		
	1930	1961	1990	1930	1961	1990	1930	1961	1990
Java:									
Agriculture	74.4[a]	71.2	43.3	72.9[a]	64.3	40.2	74.0[a]	69.2	42.2
Industry[b]	11.6	9.1	21.1	12.6	9.4	19.4	11.9	9.3	20.5
Services	14.0	19.7	35.6	14.5	26.2	40.4	14.1	21.5	37.3
Crude activity rates	53.1	50.5	53.1	17.9	18.2	28.7	35.1	34.0	40.7
Outer Islands:									
Agriculture	81.0[a]	79.9	62.1	79.0[a]	84.4	62.4	80.4[a]	81.1	62.2
Industry[b]	9.6	5.3	10.5	12.1	6.6	12.8	10.3	5.7	11.3
Services	9.4	14.8	27.4	8.8	9.0	24.8	9.3	13.2	26.5
Crude activity rates	46.6	48.3	49.3	18.2	17.7	28.0	32.4	33.1	38.7
Indonesia:									
Agriculture	76.3[a]	74.2	50.5	74.8[a]	71.2	48.9	75.9[a]	73.3	49.9
Industry[b]	11.0	7.9	17.0	12.4	8.4	16.8	11.4	8.0	16.9
Services	12.6	17.9	32.5	12.8	20.4	34.3	12.7	18.5	33.1
Crude activity rates	51.0	49.7	51.6	18.0	18.1	28.4	34.3	33.7	39.9

Notes: a. Includes 'insufficiently definable occupations'. b. Includes mining and construction. The crude activity rates are lower than in Table 7.3, because female labour participation and the female crude activity rates were underestimated in the original sources for 1930 and 1961, and have not been corrected in this table.

Sources: 1930 from Census 1936, Table 18. 1961 from Hugo et al. 1987, 262–4. 1990 from BPS 1992a, Table 30.3.

Table 7.5 contains an approximation of long-term changes in average educational attainment on the basis of primary and secondary school and university enrolments. The estimates in the last column resemble the census results in the first column, which suggests that they approximate the trend. Improvement in human capital was obviously a gradual process. Educational attainment grew fastest during 1900–29 at 6.8 per cent per year, because it started from a low base in 1900. It continued at a significant rate of 3.9 per cent per year during 1929–67 and 3.4 per cent during 1967–97. In the first half of the century, the gains were mainly due to the expansion of primary education. The share of secondary education increased after 1970, possibly in reaction to changes in the labour market where the demand for educated labour increased.

d. Physical Capital

There are no long-term time series of aggregate capital stock in Indonesia. For the colonial era there are several estimates of the stock value of all foreign-owned productive assets (Creutzberg, 1977: 60). These are not representative of all reproducible productive assets in the country, because they do not include Indonesian-owned assets, such as livestock, stocks of trees used for the production of perennial crops, equipment used in industry and transport, and dwellings. Nor do they include public infrastructure, such as irrigation works, roads, bridges, public buildings and harbour facilities. The only known estimate of pre-war total capital stock, including dwellings, suggests a total of ƒ10.2 billion (Sitsen, 1943: 12). This compares to an estimated value of the productive assets of foreign-owned and public enterprises of ƒ4.9 billion in the same year (Creutzberg, 1977: 25). The total suggests a capital-output ratio (COR) of around 2.

Table 7.5 Average Educational Attainment, 1900–98 (years of schooling per capita)

	Census bench-marks, total years of schooling	Estimated from enrolments				Census bench-marks, total years of schooling	Estimated from enrolments		
		Pri-mary	Secon-dary/ tertiary	Total			Pri-mary	Secon-dary/ tertiary	Total
1900	–	0.06	0.00	0.06	1967	–	1.73	0.13	1.86
1913	–	0.15	0.00	0.15	1971	2.47	2.02	0.18	2.20
1929	–	0.42	0.01	0.43	1980	3.07	2.54	0.37	2.91
1941	–	0.70	0.01	0.71	1990	4.31	3.43	0.84	4.27
1949	–	0.79	0.02	0.81	1998	–	3.95	1.31	5.26
1961	1.32	1.35	0.07	1.42					

Notes: The censuses (1961, 1970, 1980 and 1990 respectively) show type of education experience. Average educational attainment was calculated by assuming that those reported as having 'incomplete primary education' had an average of two years of schooling, those with primary education six years of schooling, completed secondary education nine years (six years plus three years for high school), and tertiary education 15 years (six plus three plus two years of college plus four years at university). Estimates in other columns are derived from data on primary, secondary and tertiary education enrolments from 1880 to 1998/99. Student years were accumulated on the assumption that the working life of a primary school graduate was 50 years, that of a secondary school graduate 45 years, and of a university graduate 40 years. The series of accumulated education in terms of student years were divided by population. This procedure assumes that all enrolled students actually went to school during the year, and makes no adjustment for quality differences between the types of schooling or between public and private universities.

Sources: 1961–80 census benchmarks from Hugo et al., 1987: 282. 1990 from BPS 1992a: Table 11.9. enrolments 1880–1997 from annual statistical series listed in Appendix A. 1995/96–1998/99 from the web-site of the Indonesian Department of Education and Culture, http://www.pdk.go.id

Figure 7.1 shows trends in investment during 1910–40 by the Dutch-owned enterprises which were nationalised in 1958, public enterprises and capital formation through public investment in irrigation works, harbour, transport and communication facilities. The chart indicates that the pre-war stock of productive assets increased fastest during the 1920s. Most of the investment flow was at that stage committed to plantation and mining ventures (75-80 per cent), followed by public works (5-10 per cent) and the merchant fleet (5 per cent). Even though the estimate of investment is incomplete, the ratio of investment and GDP was a lowly 4 per cent on average, decreasing to 2 per cent during the 1930s.

Post-war estimates of total capital stock are also hard to find. An elaborate approximation suggests a total of Rp 102 trillion in 1980, which implies a COR of 2.1

(Keuning, 1991: 101, 109). About 70 per cent of this capital stock consisted of structures, 22 per cent of imported machinery and equipment, and 8 per cent of domestically produced machinery and equipment. Most of the stock was employed in the service sector (49 per cent, or which 21 per cent in real estate), followed by mining (19 per cent), manufacturing (17 per cent) and agriculture (15 per cent) (Keuning, 1988: 41–42).

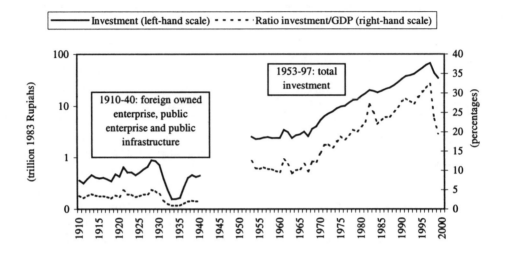

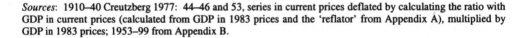

Sources: 1910–40 Creutzberg 1977: 44–46 and 53, series in current prices deflated by calculating the ratio with GDP in current prices (calculated from GDP in 1983 prices and the 'reflator' from Appendix A), multiplied by GDP in 1983 prices; 1953–99 from Appendix B.

Figure 7.1 Capital Formation, 1910–99 (trillion 1983 rupiahs)

Figure 7.1 shows trends in total investment during 1953–97. It indicates that the rate of capital formation stagnated in the 1950s and 1960s and accelerated after the 1960s. The share of investment in GDP rose from 10 per cent in the 1950s and 1960s to an average of 30 per cent over the 1990s. Figure 7.2 confirms that the role of capital in economic growth became more significant after the 1960s. The COR increased during 1952–67. During the 1950s a significant part must have involved private and public investment to rehabilitate infrastructure damaged during the Japanese occupation and the war of independence. In 1947 losses and damage were estimated at ƒ4.1 billion on the basis of pre-war replacement cost, or 40 per cent of total capital stock in 1940, of which some ƒ2.2 billion (half the capital stock of enterprises) consisted of damage to foreign enterprise (Fruin, 1947: 47; NIG, 1947: 86). The COR increased further during 1960–67, but this was largely caused by the contraction of GDP. *Vice versa*, the COR decreased during 1967–73, due to the acceleration of economic growth. Since 1973, the expansion of capital stock has been faster than economic growth. On the whole, the stock of productive assets increased by a factor of eight during 1973–99, with the biggest absolute increases in the 1990s. Figure 7.2 also shows that capital stock per worker has increased significantly since the 1960s, after two decades of slow recovery from the losses of the 1940s.

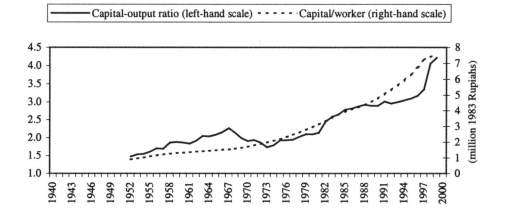

Source: Calculated from Appendices A and B, 1940 calculated with GDP in 1983 prices and an assumed Capital-Output Ratio of 2 (see main text).

Figure 7.2   Capital-Output Ratio and Capital Stock Per Worker, 1940–99

The role of physical capital in economic growth was clearly modest up to the 1970s. In broad terms, it was long confined to assisting the mobilisation of labour and natural resources for productive purposes (capital widening). Only in the 1970s did it start to enhance labour productivity (capital deepening).

Several factors explain why capital formation was low before the 1970s and why it accelerated thereafter. The main factor is that overall savings rates were low. In addition, most people did not accumulate savings in conventional ways, but in the form of non-productive assets such as precious metals and jewellery. Indeed, a capital market hardly existed in colonial Indonesia and colonial banks had limited financial resources (Van Laanen, 1990: 250). Foreign interests were on the whole reluctant to invest in colonial Indonesia and, by international standards, the country was a minor recipient of foreign direct investment. In fact, foreign enterprise was for about two-thirds financed by re-investing profits during 1820–1938 (Van der Eng, 1998: 309). The colonial government financed its investment in public enterprise and infrastructure by selling long-term debentures guaranteed by the Dutch government.

After independence Indonesia lost preferential access to the Dutch capital market at a time when its domestic savings were still low. Except for the petroleum industry, the political situation enhanced reluctance among foreign investors to commit resources to ventures in Indonesia (Jap, 1964). Foreign financial resources were mainly mobilised through government-guaranteed overseas borrowing. However, Indonesia's access to foreign credit remained restricted. The country received just US$ 1.4 billion in foreign aid and US$ 0.8 billion in concessional loans during 1950–65 (Rosendale, 1978: 104, 108, 112). By 1965 the country's foreign liabilities totalled a mere US$ 2.4 billion (Tan, 1967: 163).

The situation changed in the late-1960s, due to the economic stabilisation brought by the new government of President Soeharto, a more favourable attitude towards foreign investment, and the rapid expansion of petroleum exports. Of crucial importance was the bolstering of Indonesia's foreign exchange reserves. The reserves made it easier to service foreign liabilities, which reduced reluctance among foreign lenders and enhanced Indonesia's access to foreign capital. Indonesia's better relations with Western countries increased its access to foreign economic assistance and concessional loans. During the 1980s, net foreign direct investment picked up remarkably when the government reduced its inward-looking stance in economic policy and relaxed conditions under which foreign enterprises were admitted (Hill, 1992). This occurred at a time when large firms in East Asia started to take advantage of low labour costs in the ASEAN region by relocating parts of their ventures.

Table 7.6 contains a rough estimate of the sources of finance for capital formation. Using the current account deficit as a proxy measure, it shows that during 1967–76 12 per cent of total gross capital formation was financed with foreign savings, 11 per cent during 1977–86 and 9 per cent during 1987–96. The contribution of foreign savings to capital formation may have been more significant, because not all domestic savings were used for investment in tangible capital stock. The lower half of Table 7.10 indicates that, if all available foreign funds had been used for productive investment, during 1967–76 33 per cent of total gross capital formation may have been financed with foreign savings, 22 per cent during 1977–86 and 20 per cent during 1987–96. Table 7.6 suggests that access to foreign savings improved considerably, but also that domestic savings must have increased even faster during the last 30 years, financing most of capital formation. Domestic savings increased in accordance with rising average income and the rapid development of the domestic capital market.

Table 7.6 Capital Formation, Saving and Foreign Funding, 1967–96 (billion US dollars)

	1967–76	1977–86	1987–96
Total gross fixed capital formation	29.0	162.1	385.8
Current account deficit	–3.4	–17.6	–34.6
Domestic saving[a]	25.6	144.5	351.2
Grants in aid[b]	3.6	8.1	18.6
Net foreign direct investment	1.3	2.4	20.6
Net portfolio equity[c]	–	–	7.0
Net portfolio debt securities	–	1.1	7.2
Net long-term private loans	–0.4	2.5	14.9
Net long-term public loans	5.1	20.9	9.3
Total foreign finance	9.6	35.0	77.6

Notes: a. Residual. b. OECD estimates, includes development assistance without money transfers. c. 1993–96 only. Total gross fixed capital formation converted with official exchange rates.

Sources: *IMF International Financial Yearbook, IMF Balance of Payments Yearbook, Pendapatan Nasional Indonesia* and *Indikator Ekonomi* (various years).

e. Technological Progress

It is difficult to quantify technological progress, or increases in the efficiency with which land, labour and capital were used productively, and establish its contribution to Indonesia's long-term economic growth.[3] We therefore employ an intuitive approach.

During the twentieth century, mobilisation of labour and natural resources was the main force driving economic growth. The need for more capital-intensive production technologies beyond those embodied in imported capital goods was limited.

Before World War II, most venture capital was invested in private enterprise, in particular plantations, mining ventures and transport companies. Except for the sugar industry, plantation investment was mostly devoted to the conversion of largely unused land and to a lesser extent to the establishment of processing plants, storage and transport facilities. Mining companies invested in geological exploration and facilities for the storage and transport of produce. A large part of private investment in transport was devoted to the expansion of the inter-island shipping fleet and to road transport equipment. Most other capital formation in the transport sector was a consequence of public investment. The colonial government invested in the construction of roads, bridges and public transport, in particular the state railways in Java.

Technological change took place, but largely as a consequence of the use of technologies embodied in imported capital goods, such as construction materials, steam engines, steam ships, steam locomotives, diesel engines, cars and trucks, electricity generators, aeroplanes, weaving looms, and other mechanical equipment. These technologies were imported and employed when and where they were commercially viable. They may have been adjusted to suit local circumstances, and may have been operated at below-optimum rates. Given the ready access to foreign technologies, there was on the whole no urgent need for the development of home-grown innovations to address production bottlenecks for which foreign technology had no answers.

Home-grown innovations did emerge to improve efficiency in the use of land and labour and the movement of resources to more productive sectors. On the whole, however, such innovations did not require the mobilisation of large amounts of financial capital. For instance, the main location-specific sector which required home-grown innovations was agriculture, specifically food production and plantation crops, which generated new labour-absorbing techniques to address production constraints in land-scarce Java (Van der Eng, 1996: 69–93).

Access to imported technology was restricted during the 1950s and 1960s, due to the reduced availability of credit and foreign exchange for imports. A consequence of the fact that producers could no longer import near best-practice equipment as they required was that outdated pre-war technologies were preserved. This changed with the oil boom of the 1970s, which allowed the government to rehabilitate existing public infrastructure and expand it. This greatly enhanced the mobility of labour, natural resources and financial capital. The surge of investment was accompanied by a surge in imports, facilitated by increased export earnings. Best-practice, sometimes labour-replacing technologies were imported where these were commercially viable. Two prominent low-key examples are the small Japanese-made paddy hullers, which displaced female labour in the processing of paddy, and the replacement of handlooms by imported power looms in the weaving industry (Hill, 1998: 32–33).

The oil boom also enabled the government to intensify its import-substituting stance in economic policy, largely by supporting large-scale industrial ventures which were either operated as state companies or ventures owned by selected entrepreneurs. This development enhanced Indonesia's technical capabilities, albeit at a price. In reaction to the fall of international energy prices in the 1980s, the government took bold steps to address the situation through market deregulation and the adoption of a more outward-looking stance in economic policy. This furthered the importation of new embodied technologies for use when and where they were commercially viable.

The reduction of distortions in recent years enhanced a more efficient resource allocation in the economy as a whole, which generated stronger total factor productivity growth, particularly in manufacturing since the late-1980s (Timmer, 1999). However, such changes may again largely have resulted from the adoption and adaptation of imported technologies, embodied in imported capital goods. There have been several government-led initiatives to increase the pace of technological change, but there are few indications to support the view that Indonesia's industrial producers as a whole are engaged in pushing the production possibility frontier beyond the technology embodied in importable capital goods (Hill, 1998). On the other hand, it can be argued that Indonesia simply lived up to its yet unexhausted comparative advantage in labour-intensive production in Java and resource-intensive production in the Outer Islands, rather than knowledge-based production.

PROXIMATE SOURCES OF GROWTH ON THE DEMAND SIDE

a. Foreign Trade

It is often asserted that economic expansion during 1900–29 was largely generated by the growth of exports. Similarly, Indonesia's economic underdevelopment is often explained by suggesting that the impact of trade on economic growth was limited for a least four reasons: (a) the 'colonial drain'; (b) exports earnings were frittered away on imports of consumer products; (c) primary exports had few backward and forward linkages in the economy; (d) a structural fall in the barter terms of trade of exported primary commodities (Booth, 1990a, 1992, 1995). This section will address these four points.

Whether trade can be regarded as an 'engine of growth' depends largely on the ratio of exports and GDP and the rate of growth of exports. Table 7.7 indicates the direct contribution of exports to GDP growth during the three key phases of growth and during two sub-periods of recovery growth. During 1900–29 the volume of exports of a wide range of primary commodities, in particular sugar, tobacco, tin, rubber and palm oil, increased by a significant 5.6 per cent per year. The direct contribution of exports to GDP growth in this period was 42 per cent, compared with a mere 2 per cent during the period of economic stagnation 1929–67. Even during the sub-periods of economic recovery (1934–41 and 1949–61), the contribution of exports was low. In those years growth was driven by import-substitution. The volume of exports again increased at a high rate of 5.5 per cent per year during 1967–97, but its direct contribution to overall growth was lower at 20 per cent. Until the early 1980s export growth was largely fuelled by rapidly rising revenues from oil. With the fall of petroleum prices in the 1980s, the role of oil was taken over by manufactured exports.

Table 7.7 Broad Phases of Economic Growth in Indonesia, 1900–97

	1900–29	1934–41	1929–67	1949–61	1967–97
Population growth	1.1	1.5	1.5	1.9	2.1
Growth GDP	2.6	4.8	1.4	3.9	6.0
Growth GNP	2.5	5.4	1.4	3.9	5.9
Growth GDP per capita	1.5	3.3	–0.0	2.0	3.9
Growth GNP per capita	1.4	3.9	–0.0	2.0	3.8
Growth volume of exports	5.6	2.2	3.0	2.3	5.6
Average ratio of exports/GDP[a]	0.195	0.163	0.094	0.078	0.207
Direct contribution of exports to GDP growth[b]	42%	8%	2%	5%	19%

Notes: a. Calculated with exports and GDP in current prices. b. Calculated as: (average ratio exports/GDP) × (volume of exports growth / real GDP growth). Except for the ratio of exports and GDP, annual average growth rates calculated by fitting exponential regression curves onto the indicated data.

Sources: Population and GDP (in 1983 prices) from Van der Eng 1992, revised and updated as described in Appendix A; GNP (in 1983 prices) as estimated in Van der Eng 1993 and from *Pendapatan Nasional Indonesia*; volume and value of exports, 1900–19 from Van Ark 1988, linked for 1938–70 to Rosendale 1975, and for 1970–97 from *Pendapatan Nasional Indonesia*.

Table 7.7 shows that the direct contribution of exports varied during the twentieth century. Assuming an average multiplier of 1.3, the total contribution of exports may have been 55 per cent during 1900–29 and 26 per cent during 1967–97.[4] In the second period foreign trade was more a 'handmaiden' than an 'engine' of growth (Kravis, 1970). In both cases the expansion of production for domestic consumption also played a significant role in economic growth, perhaps more so in the second than in the first.

1. It is often assumed that the returns from primary exports mainly benefited investors in the foreign-owned enterprises during the colonial era, and that exports largely financed overseas remittances. Such casual suggestions misrepresent the actual situation. For instance, in 1925 the sugar industry in Java used 35 per cent of its gross revenues for payments to the indigenous economy in the form of wages, rents and payments for deliveries, around 10 per cent for tax payments, 15 per cent for dividend payments and the rest for the operation and depreciation of capital-intensive sugar factories, employment of senior personnel and financing research (Van der Mandere, 1928: 103–122). In addition, most exports were generated by foreign-owned companies, but the share of agricultural commodities produced by small farmers, such as rubber, copra and pepper, increased from 10 per cent in 1898 to 37 per cent in 1929. Both sets of figures

indicate that most of the export revenues benefited the Indonesian economy, as well as overseas investors.

Part of export earnings was used to finance overseas remittances. Throughout the twentieth century, Indonesia has had a merchandise trade surplus for that purpose. Net overseas remittances reflected the fact that Indonesia was a net importer of the services of foreign-owned productive resources. In the pre-war years this consisted of shipping, Dutch entrepreneurship and investment capital, and Chinese wage labour and entrepreneurship. After World War II, it consisted of shipping, foreign investment and entrepreneurship, and foreign loans. Table 7.7 shows that, when account is taken of all net overseas remittances, GNP growth during 1900–29 and 1967–97 was only slightly lower than GDP growth.

2. Most export earnings were used to finance merchandise imports. Before the mid-1930s, 50 to 60 per cent of imports consisted of consumer items. Their share decreased significantly after 1934 to less than 40 per cent, again during the 1950s to 30 per cent, and after the 1960s gradually to around 5 per cent in the 1990s.[5] This reflects trends in the efforts by the central government to boost import-substituting development. Given that high economic growth after the 1960s concurred with a falling share of consumer imports, were export earnings wasted on consumer items before the 1930s, rather than used for the importation of capital goods, semi-manufactures and industrial raw materials?

The implicit counterfactual is that the demand for consumer items could have been met with domestically produced goods and that the colonial government could have implemented import-substituting trade and industry policies at an earlier stage. This hypothesis ignores the fact that the import-replacing policy stance of later years raised costs and diminished the competitiveness of Indonesia's traditional exports (Hill, 1988). In addition, an almost constant 80-85 per cent of imported consumer goods was consumed by indigenous Indonesians, rather than the Europeans and Chinese in colonial Indonesia.[6] The costs of import-substitution would therefore largely have been borne by indigenous consumers in Indonesia.

3. It has been argued that, by supporting the development of primary exports, past governments failed to marshal productive resources into the development of export-oriented manufacturing industry with greater backward and forward linkages (Dick, 1993). However, the relevance of linkages applies mainly to a closed economy. Up to the 1930s, Indonesia's economy was open. Import tariffs were mainly used to raise public revenue, and non-tariff barriers hardly existed. In 1934 the colonial government raised import barriers to favour domestic production and combat the impact of the international crisis. Import-replacing policies were successful in the 1930s in terms of employment creation and import reduction. However, they set Indonesia on a path of import-substituting industrial development. These policies were extended during the 1950s and 1960s, and the degree of protection allotted to Indonesia's industries increased. Financial resources were scarce and employment creation was insufficient to absorb the accelerating increase of the labour force. Neglect of traditional export industries aggravated the shortage of foreign exchange earnings to finance the growing imports of raw and intermediate materials and capital goods which industries required. Only the oil boom of the 1970s brought relief in this respect.

Secondly, many preconditions for industrialisation had not been realised in colonial Indonesia. There was a surplus of unskilled labour, but transport and commercial infrastructure were long inadequate for large-scale industrial development. In addition, the size of the domestic market should not be overstated. Indonesia had more than 60 million people by 1930, but it was still a poor country with a vast mass of low-income earners whose interest may have been in cheap imported manufactures rather than relatively expensive domestically produced goods.

4. Figure 7.3 indicates a structural fall in Indonesia's barter terms of trade from 1914 to 1972. From 1973 to 1985 they improved dramatically, due to the rise in international energy prices. These changes in the terms of trade had a considerable impact on Gross Domestic Income (GDY), which measures the actual effective purchasing power of real GDP.

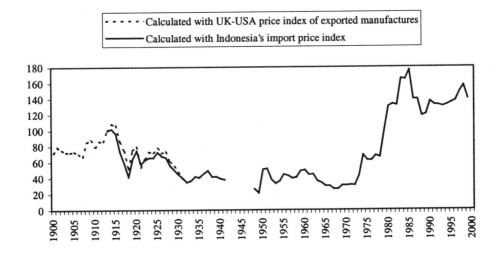

Source: Appendix C.

Figure 7.3 Barter Terms of Trade, 1900–99 (1913 = 100)

Figure 7.4 presents GDP per capita, corrected for the changes in the terms of trade, using two procedures which appear to yield similar results in the overlapping years. With 1913 as the 'pivot' year, GDY was significantly lower than GDP during 1916–41, and again during 1949–78. The annual average rate of growth of GDY per capita was just 1.1 per cent during 1900–29, compared to 1.6 per cent growth of per capita GDP in Table 7.1. The average level of GDY per capita during the 1950s and 1960s was broadly the same as during the 1930s. The annual average rate of growth of GDY per capita was 5.0 per cent during 1967–98, compared to 4.6 per cent growth of GDP per capita in Table 7.1, because Indonesia's barter terms of trade recovered to well above its 1913 level after the late 1970s.

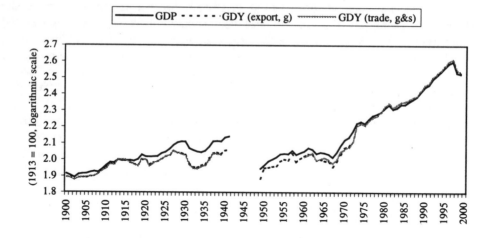

Notes: Due to the incompleteness of basic data, two approaches were used to estimate GDY, which yield a similar result. The 'trade, g&s' approach uses total goods and services trade in current prices. The 'export, g' approach uses only merchandise exports in current prices.

Sources: Appendices A and C.

Figure 7.4   GDP and GDY Per Capita, 1900–97 (1913 prices, 1913 = 100)

b. Domestic Demand: An Approximation

In the absence of complete and consistent estimates of expenditure on GDP, it is difficult to assess the development of domestic demand in quantitative terms. Table 7.8 approximates the shares of expenditure categories for the periods identified in Table 7.1. As expected, net exports of goods and services played only a minor role. Prior to World War I, total public expenditure averaged 8 per cent of GDP, increasing to an average of 15 per cent during the 1930s. This was a consequence of economic growth expanding the revenue base, the fact that the colonial government managed to find ways of tapping into new domestic sources for revenue, and improved access to the Dutch capital market to finance investment in public infrastructure (Booth, 1990b).

The momentum of expanding public expenditure was lost after World War II. Economic growth resumed, but the central government lost the ability to increase revenues while political uncertainty reduced its access to overseas capital markets. The new government installed in late 1966 had economic stabilisation and reconstruction as its first priority. It managed to increase public revenues, partly by diversifying the existing tax base, but largely because of the expansion of petroleum exports. Oil production increased after the introduction of production-sharing contracts in 1966, which ended a period of uncertainty about the position of foreign petroleum companies in Indonesia.

After 1973 the oil boom was carried by surging international oil prices, and the diversification of energy exports to natural gas. Production sharing contracts made the state company Pertamina the country's main petroleum and gas exporter, rather than the foreign companies which actually exploited the energy reserves. Table 7.9 indicates that

Pertamina's net profits and the income taxes paid by the private oil companies boosted the coffers of the central government. Together with foreign aid in the form of grants and concessional loans, oil revenues facilitated a dramatic expansion of public outlay. Consequently, the government was no longer tightly constrained by its budget and improved export performance enhanced access to overseas capital markets. Both allowed the pursuit of ambitious but pragmatic development plans. A large part of government expenditure was directed at the rehabilitation and further development of infrastructure and educational facilities in rural areas, and at agricultural development. Public expenditure rose from an average of 10 per cent of GDP per year during the 1960s to an average of 20 per cent during the last three decades.

Table 7.8 Categories of Expenditure on GDP, Annual Average Shares 1900–97 (percentages)

	Net exports		Public expenditure			Gross capital formation		Total ac-counted for	Private con-sump-tion[b]
	Goods only	Goods and ser-vices	Con-sump-tion	Gross capital forma-tion	Total	Private	Total		
1900–13	5.2	−0.9			7.8	±5.0		11.9	88.1
1914–29	9.5	−1.8			11.4	±5.0		14.6	85.4
1930–41	5.3	−0.4[d]			14.8	±5.0		19.4	80.6
1949–67	2.1	−0.2	5.6[a]	4.8[b]	10.4	−0.3[b]	4.5[c]	13.2	86.8
1968–80	4.6	1.3	8.6	8.3[b]	16.9	8.6[b]	16.9	25.4	74.6
1981–97	4.6	2.9	9.2	12.4[b]	21.6	13.3[b]	25.7	37.8	62.2
1900–29	6.9	−0.9			9.7	±5.0		13.8	86.2
1930–67	3.1	0.0			12.1	±5.0		17.1	82.9
1968–97	4.6	2.2	8.9	10.7[b]	19.6	10.7[b]	21.4	32.5	67.5

Notes: a. 1960–67 average. b. Residual. c. 1951–57 and 1960–67 average. d. 1930–39 average. The definitions of total public expenditure are not comparable over time.

Sources: Trade of goods (including ships) and services 1900–39 from Korthals Altes 1987, 1940–41 from *Economisch Weekblad voor Nederlandsch-Indië*, 1949–50 from *The Java Bank (De Javasche Bank): Report for the Financial Year 1950/51*, and 1951–82 from *IMF Balance of Payments Yearbook*; public expenditure from Creutzberg (1976) and annual statistical publications listed in Appendix A; total gross capital formation (current prices) 1951–57 from Muljatno (1960) and Djanin (1962), 1960–97 total gross capital formation and 1983–97 trade goods and services 1960–97 from *Pendapatan Nasional Indonesia* and *Indikator Ekonomi*. Private capital formation is estimated by deducting public capital formation from total capital formation. Public capital formation is estimated by deducting public consumption from total public expenditure. GDP in current prices estimated for 1900–82, using the constant price series and the 'reflator' from Appendix A.

The fall of the international energy prices in the early 1980s caused a slow-down of economic growth. Indonesia's external terms of trade fell by one-third and export earnings and public revenues declined. The government reacted aptly to falling public revenues by reducing expenditure. Real public service salaries decreased and development projects were shelved. Comprehensive tax reforms followed, inducing a diversification of public revenues away from oil, towards value-added, property and income taxes. Arguably more important were devaluations, a reduction of over-regulation, monopolies and protection in a range of sectors, and eradication of inefficiencies in resource allocation encouraged private investment. Figure 7.1 indicated that total gross capital formation increased from an average of 18 per cent of total GDP during the 1970s to 31 per cent in the 1990s. After the mid-1980s private investment overtook public investment.

Table 7.9 Exports and Government Revenue in Indonesia, 1960–97

	Export Revenue		Total Government Revenue		
Years[a]	(Million US$)	% Share of oil and gas	(Million US$)	% Share of oil and gas	% Share of ODA
1960–68	722	35	220	7	4
1969–73	1 637	47	1 615	25	24
1974–78	9 114	77	8 209	45	18
1979–83	21 636	78	18 377	57	14
1984–88	18 326	58	18 742	39	20
1989–93	29 553	35	27 696	27	18
1994–97	47 182	23	31 045	18	15

Notes: a. Except for 1960–68, years refers to fiscal years for government revenue (e.g. 1969 is 1969/70). 1997/98 concerns the most recent revised budget figures. Annual averages. Oil exports refer to crude oil and oil products. Government revenue calculated from fiscal year data with, for 1960–71, the free market exchange rate of the rupiah, rather than the controlled rate to approximate actual purchasing power. Government revenue from oil and gas refers to net oil profits and company tax. Overseas Development Assistance (ODA) refers to government-to-government grants and concessional loans.

Sources: Calculated from *Statistik Indonesia*; *Bulletin of Indonesian Economic Studies*, 34, No. 1 (1998) pp. 44–5. IMF *International Financial Statistics, UN Trade Yearbook, Pick's Currency Yearbook*.

It is difficult to assess long-term trends in private consumption. There is evidence to suggest that Javanese per capita consumption increased during 1921–29 by 1.2 per cent per year and, after a set-back in the early 1930s, by 2.2 per cent per year during 1935–39 (Van Laanen, 1979). Nothing else is known. For 1960–82, Indonesia's national accounts estimated private consumption as residual expenditure after capital formation, government consumption and foreign trade had been accounted for. Table 7.8 suggests that the contribution of private consumption to total expenditure on GDP may have been 80 to 85 per cent of GDP prior to the 1970s, decreasing to 60 to 65 per cent in the 1980s and 1990s. Hence, most of the growth of expenditure on GDP was due to changes in private consumption, particularly before the 1970s.

The key reason for stagnant or increasing consumption was stagnating or increasing real income. Given the restricted direct impact of production for export on the economy at large (Table 7.7), higher incomes were largely generated in production for domestic consumption. This must be reflected in an expanding domestic exchange of goods and services. No direct evidence on long-term changes in domestic trade is available. However, the expansion of trade could be regarded as a consequence of the development of domestic transport and communications infrastructure and the gradual evolution of a national economy.

c. Domestic Demand: The Contribution of Transport Development

Indonesia is an archipelago consisting of a large number of mountainous islands. The formation of Indonesia's national economy involved the integration of dispersed regional economies. This was a gradual process which took place over the twentieth century as a whole. The growth of transport and communications can be taken as a proxy measure of this process, which had three dimensions (Dick, 1996; Westermann, 1945): (a) an increase of the volume of goods and the number of people transported; (b) the expansion of the network of transport and communications across the country, first in Java and gradually encapsulating the Outer Islands; (c) a change from one means of transport to another, depending on the relative economic viability of transport technologies.

Table 7.10 suggests that the initial development of transport mainly benefited Java. Long-distance transport expanded due to the development of coastal shipping around Java. Railway construction accelerated in the 1890s and railways linked the main port cities of Jakarta, Surabaya and Semarang with the interior of Java. Up to World War I, railways were the main generator of change in land-based transport, as indicated by the rapid increase in passenger and freight transport by rail. After the war, the railway network was increasingly augmented by road transport. Roads were constructed and improved, cars, buses, trucks, motorcycles and bicycles appeared on the streets in increasing numbers. Road networks first evolved to feed railway stops, but in the late-1920s road transport started to compete with railways. The role of road transport increased in the 1930s, when trucks and buses competed the railways out of a significant share of the transport market. This development continued and accelerated after World War II, when the railway network ceased to expand.

Improvements of transport infrastructure in the Outer Islands took the form of better and regular shipping connections, which materialised with the gradual establishment of effective colonial rule in the Outer Islands. The Dutch-owned shipping company KPM maintained an increasingly dense network of main trunk lines connecting ports throughout the archipelago. This network was complemented by smaller companies, involved in shipping along the coast and up the main rivers in the Outer Islands, and by a large number of small *prahu* sailing vessels. The number of passengers carried by KPM expanded six-fold during 1900–29, while domestic freight shipped into Indonesia's many ports increased ten-fold. Shipping expansion stagnated during 1929–55, but it increased rapidly again after 1970.

Table 7.11 indicates that inter-island trade became increasingly important in Indonesia relative to foreign trade during the inter-war years. Part of its growth was generated by the diversion of trade from Singapore to Jakarta, which boosted the domestic transhipment of export commodities (Dick, 1990). Improved communications and, after 1934, restrictions on imports and the development of import-substituting industries in Java, further fuelled the expansion of inter-island trade. Table 7.10 shows also that the numbers of mailed items, telephone connections, radio and TV licenses increased over time, which underlines the improvement in communications during 1900–29 and again during 1970–95.

Table 7.10 Indicators of the Development of Transport and Communications, 1900–95

	1900	1913	1929	1940	1955	1970	1985	1995
Population (1900 = 100)	100	122	155	199	251	346	536	668
Road traffic								
Horses (× 1 000)	701	654	708	711	585	664	670	612
Passenger motor vehicles (× 1 000)	–	2	68	56	64	239	991	2 107
Buses (× 1 000)	–	0	6	7	10	24	227	688
Trucks (× 1 000)	–	0	16	11	45	102	845	1 336
Motorcycles (× 1 000)	–	2	15	15	77	440	4 795	9 077
Bicycles (× 1 000)	3	132	650	844	1 551	2 668	5 240	8 459
Length of roads (× 1 000 km)	37[a]		44[b]	68	79	84	207	327
Railway traffic								
Railway freight (million tons)	3.5	10.0	19.0	10.1	6.8	4.0	6.7	16.9
Railway passengers (million)	38.0	106.5	146.7	93.6	151.0	50.0	47.1	145.0
Domestic shipping								
Domestic freight shipping (million m^3)	16	78	164	122	125			
Freight at domestic ports (million tons)					10	23	85	315
Passengers domestic shipping (× 1 000)	197	663	1 203	502	796		925	2 000
Domestic air transport								
Freight (× 1 000 kg)	–	–	0.0	0.2	9.9	5.8	69.4	179.9
Passengers (× 1 000)	–	–	11	20	402	263	6 326	12 949
Communications								
Mailed items (million)	18.8	43.0	86.8	120.0	175.5	161.9	380.1	832.4
Telephone connections (× 1 000)	–	9	49	51	73	201	718	3 215
Radio licenses/radios (× 1 000)	–	10	50	102	495	3 477	*10 000*	31 943
TV licenses (× 1 000)	–	–	–	–	–	133	5 972	13 854

Notes: a. 1903. b. 1931. Motor vehicles are registered vehicles only. Domestic passenger shipping refers to passengers carried by KPM and PELNI liners only. Approximations are in italics.

Sources: Knaap (1989) and statistical sources listed in Appendix A. Stock of bicycles estimated with imports of bicycles from Indonesia's foreign trade statistics and bicycle production 1985–1995, assuming a working life of 30 years.

Table 7.11 Inter-Island and Export Trade, 1914–72

	Inter-island	Export	Ratio of inter-island and
	(million guilders/rupiahs)		export trade
1914	97	679	14
1921	323	1 195	27
1929	400	1 454	28
1940[a]	330	883	37
1955	10 970	10 618	103
1962	80 439	30 675	262
1962[b]	80 439	41 893	111
1969	281 468	279 160	99
1972	371 558	663 971	56

Notes: a. Trade between the Outer Islands estimated at ƒ70 million, which indicates that most inter-island trade was between Java and the Outer Islands. b. Exports estimated with the export exchange rate of Rp. 109 per US$, rather than the official exchange rate of Rp. 45 per US$. 1955–72 exports converted with overvalued official exchange rates.

Sources: Calculated from Korthals Altes 1991: 170–172, 1955 and 1962 from *Statistical Pocketbook of Indonesia*. 1969 and 1972 from *Lalu Lintas antar Pulau menurut Djenis Barang dan Sektor Pelajaran*.

Improvements in transport and communications enhanced the mobility of people, products, finance and information, and facilitated the gradual integration of markets in Indonesia, first in Java and later throughout the country. Reduced transport costs widened markets for a wide range of producers and encouraged specialisation of production. In so far as specialising producers were able to generate economies of scale, market integration may have reduced production costs and advanced production for domestic consumption.

GEOGRAPHICAL INCOME DISCREPANCIES

Increasing mobility of goods and people did not mean equalisation of incomes throughout Indonesia. The colonial state gradually imposed its authority throughout the archipelago after indigenous states had been subjugated. This brought about two countervailing processes: (a) an increasing reliance of the economy at large on exports generated in the Outer Islands; (b) a process of administrative and political centralisation, radiating from the core island of Java. Both processes led to an economic re-orientation of the Outer Island trade away from other parts of Southeast Asia (especially Singapore) towards Java. The introduction of a uniform monetary and fiscal systems and foreign trade regulations were part and parcel of this process.

On the whole, export production in the Outer Islands increased quickly. The exploitation of natural resources, in particular oil and tin, and the rapid development of agricultural exports after 1900 were all concentrated in the Outer Islands: tin in Bangka and Belitung, oil in Sumatra and Kalimantan, estate tobacco and rubber in North Sumatra, small-holder coffee in West Sumatra, small-holder copra in North Sulawesi and small-holder rubber in East Sumatra and West Kalimantan (Touwen, 1999). Java supplied 75 per cent of total exports around 1900, but its contribution fell to only one-third by 1940 (Korthals Altes, 1991: 70–75). On the other hand, Java continued to account for about two-thirds of Indonesia's imports. The regional imbalance in foreign trade was partly off-set by a growing flow of consumer goods from Java to the Outer Islands, such as rice, tobacco and textiles, especially after the colonial government introduced trade regulations to stimulate import-replacing development in Java in 1934. The precondition for this integration of regional markets were good communications, particularly domestic shipping.

The increasing share of the Outer Islands in exports continued after World War II and in 1955 represented 88 per cent of the Indonesian total. At that time export producers in the Outer Islands no longer received international prices, due to Indonesia's restrictive foreign exchange policies, which imposed additional tax on exports (Corden and Mackie, 1962). Moreover, export commodities increasingly had to be shipped through ports in Java, which increased handling costs.

Such centralising tendencies of the government in Jakarta fuelled allegations that import-consuming Java was 'draining' the export-producing Outer Islands. Regional discontent contributed to secessionist uprisings during 1956–58, which threatened the political and economic integration of the country. These regional uprisings were subdued with military force and have not been allowed to re-surface since, even though the extent to which the Outer Islands generated foreign exchange and revenues for the national government and for Java-based private companies increased further with the expansion of industries in the Outer Islands such as petroleum, natural gas, mining and forestry.

Provincial GDP data since the late 1960s have consistently indicated significant differences in GDP per capita between the provinces which are well endowed with natural resources and those which are densely populated and/or sparsely endowed with natural resources (Hill, 1991/92). Table 7.12 underlines the considerable regional economic differences in Indonesia. East Timor, East and West Nusatenggara are consistently at the lower end of the scale, while the operations of large mining companies place East Kalimantan and Irian Jaya at the top end.[7] The table reveals significant regional dynamics. GDP per capita in Riau, South Sumatra, Maluku, Bengkulu, North Sulawesi, Jambi and Southeast Sulawesi declined relative to the national average, while it improved in Irian Jaya, Bali, West Sumatra and most provinces in Java. On balance, the Gini ratio and the weighted coefficient of variation both indicate that the inequality of regional GDP has increased over time.

The evidence may confirm the thesis that during the process of economic development the spatial distribution of economic activity first concentrates and then disperses, thus causing the inequality of regional income distribution to first increase, due to the disequilibrating effects of factor mobility (Williamson, 1965). This is congruous with the fact that the degree of infrastructure development in the Outer Islands still lags behind Java. The Williamson thesis predicts that inequality will decrease at a later stage, as equalising forces of factor mobility take effect. The GDP data in Table 7.12 exclude value added in oil and gas production. If included, GDP in the provinces of Aceh, Riau and East Kalimantan would be significantly higher. The central government benefits most from the revenues these activities generate, and redistributes them in a way that bolsters the poorer provinces, particularly those in Java. The fact that public revenues have in recent decades been channelled into the development of manufacturing industry in Java has magnified the economic dichotomy between Java and some parts of the Outer Islands, and has prolonged the existence of relatively large interregional inequalities in non-mining GDP per capita (Akita and Lukman, 1995).

Table 7.12 Inequality of Regional Non-Oil GDP Per Capita, 1971, 1983 and 1996

Province	1971 National Av. = 100	Rank	1983 National Av. = 100	Rank	1996 National Av. = 100	Rank
Jakarta	247	(1)	328	(1)	372	(1)
East Kalimantan	247	(2)	218	(2)	222	(2)
Irian Jaya	99	(14)	108	(8)	168	(3)
Central Kalimantan	116	(8)	130	(4)	133	(4)
Bali	107	(11)	98	(11)	124	(5)
North Sumatra	158	(4)	103	(9)	104	(6)
South Kalimantan	111	(9)	109	(7)	102	(7)
Riau	139	(6)	116	(6)	102	(8)
West Kalimantan	101	(12)	90	(13)	96	(9)
East Java	88	(19)	99	(10)	95	(10)
Yogyakarta	75	(22)	75	(21)	92	(11)
West Sumatra	89	(18)	97	(12)	91	(12)
West Java	87	(20)	81	(18)	90	(13)
Aceh	96	(15)	119	(5)	89	(14)
South Sumatra	201	(3)	143	(3)	83	(15)
North Sulawesi	122	(7)	85	(16)	76	(16)
Maluku	106	(10)	88	(14)	72	(17)
Central Java	74	(23)	74	(22)	71	(18)
Jambi	150	(5)	84	(17)	67	(19)
Bengkulu	91	(17)	86	(15)	66	(20)
South Sulawesi	79	(21)	77	(20)	65	(21)
Central Sulawesi	56	(24)	73	(23)	64	(22)
Lampung	92	(16)	57	(24)	57	(23)
Southeast Sulawesi	99	(13)	81	(19)	54	(24)
West Nusatenggara	52	(25)	51	(25)	45	(25)
East Timor	–	(–)	49	(26)	42	(26)
East Nusatenggara	48	(26)	48	(27)	38	(27)
Gini ratio[a]	0.18		0.21		0.23	
CVw[b]	0.42		0.55		0.65	

Notes: a. Calculated with provincial totals of population and GDP, ranked by GDP per capita. The implicit assumption is that income is distributed equally within each province. b. Coefficient of variation weighted by population. GDP excludes Gross Value Added from oil and gas, and is not corrected for price differences between provinces.

Sources: Calculated with population data from *Statistik Indonesia*, and GDP data from BPS 1980, BPS 1992b and BPS 1997.

CONCLUSION

This chapter advanced some proximate reasons for Indonesia's growth performance during the twentieth century. Most of Indonesia's growth was a consequence of the simple mobilisation of productive resources; during the colonial era of land, labour and to some extent foreign capital, during the 1950s, 1960s and 1970s, mineral resources and labour, and during the 1980s and 1990s labour and domestic and foreign savings. Technological change did play a role in some sectors, but its role in the overall economy must have been modest. The contribution of technological change only became prominent with the growth of capital stock in the 1970s, particularly in manufacturing. It is likely that capital formation encouraged the importation of capital goods in which new technologies were embodied. On the whole, technological change in Indonesia appears to have revolved around the adoption and adaptation of imported embodied technologies, rather than the invention and adaptation of 'home-grown' produced technologies. Indonesia's capacity to absorb further embodied imported technologies is far from exhausted.

On the demand side, the development of foreign trade affected the GDP trend in two main ways. Its impact was modest during the period 1900–29 as a consequence of the limited backward and forward linkages of primary exports. In addition, changes in the barter terms of trade affected total disposable income. On the other hand, exports generated the foreign exchange required to finance the imported services of foreign capital, labour and entrepreneurship. It also helped to generate an expansion of public revenue and enhanced access by the colonial government to foreign capital markets. Consequently, domestic demand was bolstered by increasing public expenditure during 1910–29 and later during 1967–98, as a consequence of increasing returns from oil and gas exports. A large part of the increased revenues was used for infrastructures development, which enhanced the mobility of production factors and goods, integrated domestic markets and helped to create new income opportunities that are likely to have promoted average incomes.

Still, integration of the national economy was not fast enough to avoid an increase in economic inequality between the various provinces. In the provinces rich in natural resources or with abundant unskilled labour, productive resources were effectively mobilised. Provinces not so endowed or located in the periphery, experienced less dramatic economic change and have fallen behind.

ACKNOWLEDGEMENT

A preliminary version of this chapter was published as *Institute of Economic Research Discussion Paper – D99-1*, Hitotsubashi University, Tokyo, May 1999. The author thanks Angus Maddison and Hal Hill for their comments on previous versions of this chapter.

NOTES

1. See Dowling (1997) for a summary of this debate.
2. The 1995 population survey revealed that 64 per cent of farm households in Indonesia had mixed incomes, while 35 per cent earned most of their income from non-agricultural pursuits. In Java 90 per cent of farm

households had mixed incomes, while 51 per cent earned most of their income outside agricultural sector (BPS, 1996: Table 59.3).

3. The conventional way of doing this involves the calculation of the contribution of Total Factor Productivity (TFP) growth to economic growth. Several estimates of TFP growth exist for Indonesia (Dowling and Summers, 1998: 174, 183). They differ considerably, because the measurement of TFP is very problematic. Some of the key concerns are the weak database, variances in the definition of capital stock, the choice of the share of capital income in GDP, and business cycles effects. The data in Appendices A and B allow the estimation of TFP growth for 1953–97, but in the light of these problems, the exercise would be unavailing.

4. Perhaps a higher multiplier of 1.5 or 1.6 would be appropriate during the period 1986–97, because of the rapidly growing share in exports of manufactures with more significant backward linkages (Athukorala and Santosa, 1997: 85).

5. For 1900–60 the share of consumer items was approximated with: rice, wheat flour, soybeans, fish, dairy products, beverages, tobacco products, cloves, opium, soap, cosmetics, pottery, glassware, textile fabrics, garments, other textile products (except yarn), kerosene, matches, bicycles and bicycle tyres. After 1960 the share of consumer items is taken from Indonesia's foreign trade statistics: Korthals, Altes, 1991: 117–130; CKS, 1939: 28–35; *Indisch Verslag*, 1940: 350–354; *Statistik Indonesia* and *Indikator Ekonomi*.

6. Estimated, using the imported consumer items identified in footnote 6 and the corresponding shares of consumption by indigenous Indonesians from Meijer Ranneft and Huender (1926: 166–167).

7. Mining GVA cannot be excluded from provincial GDP in 1971. Without mining, East Kalimantan decreases to 4th and Irian Jaya to 14th position in 1996. In that case the Gini ratio is 0.23 and the coefficient of variation is 0.64. This is not different from Table 7.12, because both provinces have a low population weight.

APPENDIX A: ESTIMATION OF INDONESIAN GDP, 1900–99

Available official estimates of GDP in Indonesia are underestimated before 1983 (Van der Eng, 1992, 1997). For this reason, GDP for 1900–82 was re-estimated for 17 main sectors of Indonesia's economy, using broad indicators of productive activity and linked those to the official (at 1983 prices) for 1983–99. The aggregate results of this procedure are contained in Table A7.1. The detailed results are available from the author.

1-4. *Farm and plantation agriculture.* For the sectors food crops, farm cash crops, estate crops and animal husbandry, estimates of GVA in constant prices are from Van der Eng (1996). These are based on an old classification of farm cash crops and estate crops, which recorded the production of some farm cash crops (such as sugar produced from cane purchased from farmers) as estate production. The original GVA estimates for 'farm non-food crops' and 'estate crops' for 1983–89 were re-arranged. Estates are assumed to have produced 44.5 per cent (1982–83 average from the 1971–83 national accounts data) of GVA in the sectors 'farm non-food crops' and 'estate crops' together.

5. *Fisheries.* GVA in fisheries linked to the total landed fish catch for the years 1940 and 1951–82. Per capita production in 1940 (6.5 kg) was used to estimate fish production during 1900–39. For 1941 and 1949–50 fish catch is assumed to have moved parallel to real GVA from food crops.

6. *Forestry.* GVA in forestry linked to production of sawn wood, including firewood and charcoal for 1925–82. For 1900–24 forestry production was assumed to move parallel to real GVA of farm cash crops and estate crops.

7. *Mining and quarrying.* GVA in mining and quarrying (excluding oil and gas production) linked to an index of the physical production of six key mining products. The index was calculated with weights obtained by extrapolating GVA in 1980 from the old national accounts data to 1983, and by retropolating the value of gross output in 1985 from the newer national accounts data to 1983, and averaging the two sets of shares for each product. The 1983 weights were as follows: coal 0.027, tin 0.514, nickel 0.193, bauxite 0.021, copper 0.181, salt 0.064.

8. *Manufacturing.* A weak estimate was previously used (Van der Eng, 1992: 363–4), because of incomplete information on industrial output in manufacturing industry. In particular, aggregated data on output in the important small-scale and cottage industries are absent (Segers, 1988; Gordon, 1998). For this chapter, GVA in manufacturing was retropolated back to 1958 by linking it to GVA in manufacturing in constant prices from previous rounds of estimates of Indonesia's national accounts for 1958–60, 1960–71, 1971–83. The 1971, 1975 and 1980 Input–Output Tables were used to approximate the degree of underestimation in manufacturing GVA. The BPS estimate of GVA in manufacturing in 1971 was multiplied by 1.5, in 1975 by 1.2. In 1980 the degree of underestimation was negligible and no correction was introduced. It was assumed that the correction factor decreased during 1971–75 and 1975–80. For the intermediate years the correction factor was interpolated and the result used to inflate real GVA for 1971–80. The GVA series for 1958–60 and 1960–71 were used for retropolation without corrections. 1951–58 industrial output

(manufacturing, utilities and construction) linked to constant price series of industrial GVA from Suhartono (1967: 123), 1938 and 1951 linked to a series of industrial GVA from Mangkusuwondo (1975: 15); 1928–38 linked to constant price series of industrial output from Van Oorschot (1956: 93). Manufacturing GVA estimated by deducting real GVA in utilities and construction from total industrial output for 1928–57, and by assuming constant per capita output during 1900–28.

9. *Utilities.* GVA in utilities estimated for 1958–82 as for manufacturing GVA. The BPS estimate of GVA in utilities was multiplied by 2.25 in 1971 and 1.2 in 1975. 1940–57 GVA estimated by linking the 1958–89 series to the consumption of electricity, 1900–39 GVA estimated by linking to production of electricity and gas for public consumption with weights of 0.5 each.

10. *Construction.* GVA in construction estimated for 1958–82 as for manufacturing GVA. The BPS estimate of GVA in construction was multiplied by 1.5 in 1971 and 1.2 in 1975, Import and production of cement and real GVA in forestry, with weights of 0.75 and 0.25, were used as indicators of construction activity during 1900–57. For 1900–10 the volume of imported cement was estimated from the current value of imports, using the 1911 unit value.

11. *Trade.* GVA in trade estimated assuming that the following percentages of real GVA in the above sectors were marketed: food 30 per cent, animal husbandry 70 per cent, farm cash crops 70 per cent, estate crops 100 per cent, fisheries 90 per cent, forestry 80 per cent, manufacturing 100 per cent. Added was 100 per cent of imported commodities, converted to 1983 prices with the retail price index (see below). The total real value of marketed products was used to retropolate real GVA in trade.

12. *Transport and communication.* Two compound indicators were used to retropolate GVA in transport and communication. For 1943–82: 0.05 railway freight, 0.05 railway passengers, 0.50 registered trucks and buses, 0.20 and index of shipped freight (1900–57 domestic and international shipping in 1 000 m^3 net, 1957–83 cargo handled in Indonesian ports for domestic and international shipment in 1 000 tons), 0.15 mailed items and 0.05 telephone connections. For 1900–42: 0.175 railway freight, 0.175 railway passengers, 0.25 registered trucks and buses, 0.20 shipping index, 0.15 mailed items and 0.05 telephone connections.

13. *Financial services.* GVA in financial services estimated, using GVA in trade (sector 11) and the value of all circulated currency (M1), deflated with the retail price index (see below) as indicators for 1900–82, each with a weight of 0.5.

14. *Housing.* GVA in housing estimated, using population and the sub-total of sectors 1-13 as indicators for 1900–82, each with a weight of 0.5. The assumption is that growth of per capita income induces people to invest in the quality of houses, which increases the rental value of dwellings.

15. *Public administration and defence.* GVA in public administration was estimated, using gross public expenditure, deflated with the retail price index (see below) as an indicator for 1900–82.

16. *Other services.* GVA in the remaining sector was estimated, using the number of primary and secondary school children, population and the sub-total of the sectors 1-15 as indicators with weights of 0.25, 0.25 and 0.50 respectively.

17.   *Oil and gas.* The production of crude petroleum during 1900–82 was used to estimate GVA in oil and gas production.

Retail price index. The core of this index is an index of Jakarta retail prices. For 1913–41 and 1946–83 the index was estimated by linking monthly retail price indices and calculating annual averages. The following indices were linked:

Period	Based on	Reference period
Jan. 1916 – Dec. 1930	1922 survey (20 products)	1913
Jan. 1931 – Dec. 1938	1932 survey (38 products)	1913
Jan. 1939 – Dec. 1941	1938 survey (46 products)	July 1938
Apr. 1946 – Dec. 1953	1938 survey (19 products)	July 1938
Jan. 1954 – Dec. 1963	1938 survey (19 products)	1953
Jan. 1964 – Apr. 1968	1957/58 survey (62 products)	October 1966
May 1968 – Sep. 1979	1957/58 survey (62 products)	September 1966
Oct. 1979 – Dec. 1983	1977/78 survey (115–150 products)	April 1977–March 1978

The series was linked for 1913–15 to the annual retail price index (1913 = 100), and for 1900–12 to an index of the price of rice (Creutzberg, 1978: 45–7).

GDP 'reflator'. A GDP 'reflator' was constructed for 1900–67 to facilitate calculation of GDP in current prices. For 1968–98 the linked implicit GDP deflator from the Indonesian national accounts was used for that purpose. A long-term export price index was constructed by linking the implicit price indices of exports from the Indonesian national accounts for 1973–98, using 1983 as the base year. This series was linked to the export price index from Rosendale (1978). This series was based on prices in US$ and was therefore corrected for changes in the export exchange rate. The series was in turn linked in the overlapping years 1937–39 to the 1900–40 Paasche price index from Van Ark (1988). The index was extended to 1941 and 1949–50 with export price indices from *Economisch Weekblad voor Nederlandsch-Indië* and from *The Java Bank (De Javasche Bank): Report for the Financial Year 1950/51.* By attaching weights of 0.8 to the retail price index, and 0.2 to the Paasche unit value index of exported commodities.

Population and labour force. 1900–90 from Van der Eng (1996: Appendix 3), series with indigenous population in the Outer Islands estimated with 1.5 per cent annual growth. These series were extrapolated on the basis of the results of the 1995 inter-census population survey (BPS, 1996).

Extrapolation 1989–99. For each sector the series for 1983–89 in 1983 prices was linked to the series of GVA in 1993 prices for 1989–99. 1989–92 unpublished data from Badan Pusat Statistik in Jakarta, 1993–95 from *Pendapatan Nasional Indonesia* (1993–94) and *Indikator Ekonomi* (1997), 1996–99 from BPS website http://www.bps.go.id. The 1983–88 data were not corrected for the upward revision of GDP estimates for 1989–93. (Van der Eng, 1999).

Table A7.1 Key Indicators of Economic Change in Indonesia, 1900–99

	Gross Value Added at market prices									
	Agri-culture (1–6)	Indus-try (7–10)	Ser-vices (11–16)	Sub-total (1–16)	Oil and gas (17)	Total GVA	Popu-lation	Labour force	Retail price index	GDP 'reflator'
Year	(billion 1983 Rupiahs)						(x 1 000)		(1983 = 1 000)	
1900	3 715	1 392	3 171	8 278	73	8 351	42 746	15 400	0.208	0.218
1901	3 686	1 314	3 113	8 113	133	8 247	43 275	15 491	0.258	0.262
1902	3 564	1 296	3 184	8 044	85	8 129	43 810	15 666	0.239	0.242
1903	3 769	1 385	3 236	8 390	194	8 585	44 352	15 701	0.250	0.251
1904	3 839	1 324	3 381	8 545	219	8 763	44 901	15 918	0.224	0.231
1905	3 881	1 269	3 481	8 630	267	8 897	45 457	16 212	0.216	0.224
1906	4 060	1 281	3 564	8 905	267	9 172	45 993	16 438	0.229	0.235
1907	4 113	1 348	3 602	9 062	327	9 390	46 535	16 759	0.259	0.259
1908	4 037	1 372	3 667	9 077	341	9 417	47 085	17 087	0.273	0.283
1909	4 283	1 373	3 887	9 542	364	9 906	47 642	17 422	0.256	0.271
1910	4 523	1 498	4 183	10 205	364	10 569	48 206	17 764	0.256	0.264
1911	4 701	1 656	4 407	10 764	400	11 164	48 778	18 022	0.282	0.291
1912	4 697	1 746	4 455	10 898	365	11 263	49 358	18 282	0.325	0.327
1913	4 807	1 898	4 796	11 501	376	11 877	49 934	18 543	0.297	0.318
1914	4 889	1 752	4 840	11 481	376	11 857	50 517	18 808	0.288	0.315
1915	4 995	1 709	4 890	11 607	400	12 007	51 108	19 074	0.282	0.313
1916	4 931	1 860	4 987	11 778	413	12 192	51 705	19 346	0.304	0.332
1917	5 070	1 719	5 010	11 799	437	12 235	52 310	19 614	0.325	0.354
1918	5 283	1 720	5 093	12 096	424	12 520	52 334	19 801	0.416	0.417
1919	5 442	1 849	5 721	13 011	509	13 521	53 027	20 077	0.417	0.462
1920	5 137	1 897	5 740	12 774	582	13 357	53 723	20 357	0.678	0.701
1921	4 969	1 892	6 047	12 908	563	13 471	54 367	20 645	0.569	0.549
1922	5 347	1 931	5 842	13 120	567	13 687	55 020	20 937	0.495	0.484
1923	5 394	2 034	5 817	13 244	660	13 904	55 683	21 229	0.443	0.445
1924	5 698	2 084	6 185	13 967	680	14 647	56 354	21 532	0.408	0.416
1925	5 761	2 131	6 550	14 442	712	15 154	57 036	21 839	0.389	0.406
1926	6 064	2 342	6 876	15 282	706	15 988	57 727	22 151	0.388	0.397
1927	6 418	2 440	7 325	16 183	912	17 095	58 429	22 468	0.375	0.381
1928	6 520	2 557	7 769	16 846	1 067	17 913	59 140	22 534	0.368	0.359
1929	6 294	2 774	8 044	17 112	1 305	18 417	59 863	22 988	0.366	0.351
1930	6 528	2 821	7 815	17 165	1 387	18 551	60 596	23 346	0.357	0.334
1931	6 396	2 361	7 217	15 974	1 181	17 155	61 496	23 660	0.319	0.290
1932	6 419	2 231	7 010	15 660	1 296	16 956	62 400	23 979	0.267	0.238
1933	6 309	2 256	6 860	15 426	1 418	16 844	63 314	24 302	0.236	0.212
1934	6 025	2 551	6 817	15 394	1 546	16 940	64 246	24 631	0.217	0.198
1935	6 345	2 850	6 776	15 970	1 567	17 538	65 192	24 966	0.208	0.188

Table A7.1 (continued)

	Gross Value Added at market prices								Retail	
	Agri-culture (1–6)	Indus-try (7–10)	Ser-vices (11–16)	Sub-total (1–16)	Oil and gas (17)	Total GVA	Popu-lation	Labour force	price index	GDP 'reflator'
Year	(billion 1983 Rupiahs)						(x 1 000)		(1983 = 1 000)	
1936	6 655	3 284	7 212	17 150	1 662	18 812	66 154	25 306	0.201	0.186
1937	7 099	3 669	7 992	18 760	1 885	20 645	67 136	25 651	0.215	0.211
1938	7 101	3 795	8 254	19 150	1 905	21 055	68 131	26 002	0.220	0.206
1939	7 247	3 985	7 976	19 207	2 063	21 270	69 145	26 397	0.286	0.260
1940	7 563	4 478	8 699	20 740	2 060	22 801	70 175	26 721	0.230	0.225
1941	7 869	4 732	9 108	21 709	1 784	23 494	71 316	27 161	0.254	0.237
1949	6 272	2 873	5 694	14 839	1 436	16 275	77 654	30 935	2.782	2.599
1950	6 410	2 953	6 485	15 847	1 608	17 455	79 043	31 447	3.260	2.854
1951	6 858	3 406	6 649	16 913	1 843	18 756	80 525	32 010	5.436	4.716
1952	6 901	3 328	7 339	17 568	2 077	19 644	82 052	32 584	5.736	5.009
1953	7 054	3 428	7 645	18 128	2 494	20 621	83 611	33 016	6.095	5.235
1954	7 724	3 607	7 913	19 265	2 643	21 907	85 196	33 184	6.477	5.521
1955	7 473	4 144	8 035	19 652	2 857	22 509	86 807	33 135	8.577	7.308
1956	7 549	3 883	8 277	19 709	3 099	22 808	88 456	33 529	9.822	8.604
1957	7 558	4 469	8 554	20 581	3 785	24 366	90 124	34 044	10.781	9.578
1958	7 835	3 412	8 299	19 545	3 942	23 488	91 821	34 619	15.697	13.619
1959	8 222	3 315	8 435	19 972	4 525	24 497	93 565	35 298	18.978	16.721
1960	8 406	3 294	8 855	20 555	4 981	25 537	95 254	35 990	23.376	20.231
1961	8 523	3 679	9 863	22 065	5 146	27 211	97 085	36 727	32	27
1962	9 097	3 538	9 047	21 683	5 499	27 181	99 028	37 159	89	74
1963	8 474	3 274	9 007	20 755	5 385	26 139	101 009	37 597	199	169
1964	9 046	3 270	9 235	21 551	5 553	27 105	103 031	38 039	422	369
1965	9 029	3 322	9 196	21 546	5 829	27 375	105 093	38 485	1 708	1 428
1966	9 448	3 407	8 891	21 745	5 634	27 380	107 197	38 940	20	18
1967	8 811	3 409	8 413	20 632	6 129	26 762	109 343	39 395	53	46
1968	9 589	3 830	8 648	22 067	7 306	29 372	111 532	39 855	119	76
1969	9 921	4 549	9 516	23 986	9 003	32 988	113 765	40 327	139	93
1970	10 728	5 133	10 248	26 109	10 352	36 461	116 044	40 767	157	107
1971	10 767	5 868	11 003	27 637	10 819	38 457	118 368	41 261	163	109
1972	11 015	6 639	12 013	29 667	13 144	42 810	121 282	42 255	174	124
1973	12 201	7 333	13 395	32 930	16 233	49 163	124 271	43 308	228	165
1974	12 354	8 256	14 366	34 976	16 670	51 645	127 338	44 389	321	244
1975	12 273	8 670	14 866	35 810	15 845	51 655	130 485	45 499	382	274
1976	12 971	9 104	15 845	37 920	18 286	56 206	133 713	46 638	458	314
1977	13 213	10 149	16 777	40 140	20 449	60 589	137 026	47 808	508	354

Table A7.1 (continued)

	Gross Value Added at market prices								
Agri-culture (1–6)	Indus-try (7–10)	Ser-vices (11–16)	Sub-total (1–16)	Oil and gas (17)	Total GVA	Popu-lation	Labour force	Retail price index	GDP 'reflator'
Year		(billion 1983 Rupiahs)				(x 1 000)		(1983 = 1 000)	
1978	14 301	10 853	18 369	43 523	19 832	63 355	140 425	49 010	549	392
1979	14 669	12 024	20 817	47 510	19 293	66 803	143 912	50 243	661	505
1980	15 877	13 722	23 788	53 387	19 162	72 549	147 490	51 553	763	673
1981	16 803	15 094	26 183	58 081	19 456	77 537	150 657	53 016	829	741
1982	16 629	15 593	26 394	58 617	16 067	74 684	153 894	54 523	903	800
1983	17 696	15 812	29 065	62 573	15 103	77 676	157 204	56 362	1 000	1 000
1984	18 513	17 730	30 608	66 851	16 187	83 037	160 588	58 266		1 083
1985	19 300	19 267	32 002	70 569	14 513	85 082	164 047	60 238		1 140
1986	19 799	20 789	34 256	74 843	15 237	90 080	166 976	62 279		1 140
1987	20 224	22 679	36 396	79 299	15 219	94 518	169 959	64 393		1 321
1988	21 167	25 192	38 885	85 244	14 692	99 935	172 999	66 582		1 422
1989	22 267	28 227	43 007	93 502	15 422	108 924	176 094	68 850		1 649
1990	23 028	32 062	47 372	102 462	16 145	118 607	179 248	71 570		1 778
1991	23 756	35 983	47 143	106 882	17 718	124 599	182 223	74 016		2 006
1992	25 331	40 064	55 460	120 856	17 106	137 962	185 259	76 268		2 047
1993	25 792	44 963	59 570	130 324	17 124	147 448	188 359	78 592		2 237
1994	25 968	50 825	63 808	140 602	17 567	158 169	191 524	80 992		2 417
1995	27 184	57 074	68 715	152 972	17 567	170 540	194 755	83 468		2 665
1996	28 062	64 058	73 250	165 370	17 821	183 191	198 025	86 025		2 907
1997	28 149	67 921	77 284	173 354	17 716	191 069	201 354	88 344		3 285
1998	28 130	56 756	63 954	148 847	17 286	166 134	204 743	90 730		5 957
1999*	28 877	57 950	62 852	149 680	16 402	166 081	208 193	93 184		6 740

Note: * Preliminary data.

Sources: Data from a wide range of sources were used to compile the time series. The most important serials were: *Jaarcijfers van het Koninkrijk der Nederlanden – Koloniën* (1880–1921), *Statistisch Jaaroverzicht voor Nederlandsch Indië* (1922–30), *Indisch Verslag* (1931–40), *Statistik Indonesia* (1956–96), *Economisch Weekblad voor Nederlandsch-Indië* (1939–47), *Economisch Weekblad voor Indonesië* (1948–51), *Ichtisar Bulan Statistik* (1949–54), *Statistik Konjunktur* (1954–63), *Warta BPS* (1966–69) and *Indikator Ekonomi* (1970–99. Monthly price index data were also obtained from 'Prijzen, Indexcijfers en Wisselkoersen op Java.' *Mededeelingen van het Centraal Kantoor voor de Statistiek, No. 12, 19, 46, 88, 146* (1924–38) *and Statistik Ekonomi-Keunangan.*

APPENDIX B: ESTIMATION OF TOTAL CAPITAL STOCK, 1952–99

The estimation of total fixed capital stock (including residential structures) is based on data from Keuning (1988, 1991), Appendix A and *Pendapatan Nasional Indonesia* (various years). Keuning's capital stock data for 1975–85 are in 1980 prices, which have been converted to 1983 prices using the capital-output ratio (in 1980 prices) multiplied by GDP in 1983 prices in 1980. 1975–79 and 1981–85 are extrapolated by linking the 1980s estimate to Keuning's stock data.

Other years have been estimated with depreciation and investment in 1983 prices. Depreciation is 5 per cent of GDP (from Appendix 1), as in the Indonesian national accounts since 1983. Investment 1953–75 estimated on the basis of Keuning's investment series for 1953–85 in 1980 prices. The investment/GVA ratio (in 1980 prices) was multiplied by GDP (in 1983 prices) in 1980, to obtain investment in 1983 prices. The 1980 estimate was linked to Keuning's 1953–85 series and extrapolated. The investment series from the national accounts in 1983 prices was obtained by linking investment series in constant prices in overlapping years (1971, 1983, 1989). Fixed capital stock 1952–74 is estimated by deducting investment and adding depreciation in the previous year, working backwards from 1975, while 1986–99 is estimated by adding investment and deducting depreciation in the current year, working forwards from 1985.

Table A7.2 Estimation of Investment and Capital Stock in Indonesia, 1952–99

	Gross Fixed Capital Formation			Depreciation	Fixed Capital Stock	
	Keuning (1988: 16) 1980 prices)	Idem, converted to 1983 prices	National Accounts (1983 prices)	= 5% of GDP (1983 prices)	Keuning (1988: 39) (1980 prices)	Idem, converted and extrapolated (1983 prices)
1952						29 034
1953	1 719	2 547		1 031		31 581
1954	1 560	2 312		1 095		33 893
1955	1 578	2 338		1 125		36 231
1956	1 655	2 454		1 140		38 684
1957	1 701	2 522		1 218		41 206
1958	1 625	2 408		1 174		43 614
1959	1 624	2 407		1 225		46 021
1960	1 640	2 431	1 573	1 277		47 474
1961	2 350	3 483	2 260	1 361		49 903
1962	2 130	3 157	2 055	1 359		52 023
1963	1 625	2 409	1 568	1 307		53 440
1964	1 836	2 721	1 783	1 355		55 109
1965	1 915	2 838	1 855	1 369		56 886
1966	2 163	3 206	2 085	1 369		59 004
1967	1 762	2 612	1 701	1 338		60 521
1968	2 439	3 615	2 372	1 469		62 948

Table A7.2 (continued)

	Gross Fixed Capital Formation			Depre-ciation	Fixed Capital Stock	
	Keuning (1988: 16) 1980 prices)	Idem, converted to 1983 prices	National Accounts (1983 prices)	= 5% of GDP (1983 prices)	Keuning (1988: 39) (1980 prices)	Idem, converted and extrapolated (1983 prices)
1969	2 716	4 025	2 664	1 649		65 644
1970	3 594	5 327	3 535	1 823		69 497
1971	4 308	6 385	4 304	1 923		74 276
1972	4 834	7 165	5 124	2 141		79 609
1973	5 298	7 852	5 997	2 458		85 361
1974	6 098	9 038	7 149	2 582		92 151
1975	6 564	9 729	8 193	2 583	66 996	99 298
1976	6 842	10 141	8 684	2 810	73 082	108 318
1977	7 849	11 633	10 066	3 029	79 360	117 623
1978	8 784	13 020	11 582	3 168	86 451	128 133
1979	9 062	13 431	12 094	3 340	94 343	139 830
1980	10 476	15 527	14 378	3 627	102 484	151 896
1981	11 817	17 515	15 979	3 877	111 983	165 975
1982	13 650	20 231	18 055	3 734	122 756	181 942
1983	14 154	20 978	19 468	3 884	135 274	200 495
1984	12 735	18 875	18 297	4 152	148 223	219 687
1985	11 772	17 448	19 616	4 254	159 706	236 707
1986			21 422	4 504		253 625
1987			22 597	4 726		271 496
1988			25 201	4 997		291 700
1989			28 960	5 446		315 214
1990			33 616	5 930		342 899
1991			37 953	6 230		374 622
1992			39 314	6 898		407 038
1993			41 908	7 372		441 573
1994			47 673	7 908		481 338
1995			54 345	8 527		527 155
1996			62 232	9 160		580 228
1997			67 564	9 553		638 239
1998			43 554	8 307		673 486
1999*			34 731	8 304		699 913

Note: * Preliminary data.

APPENDIX C: IMPACT OF CHANGES IN THE TERMS OF TRADE ON GDP, 1900–99

The fundamental reasons for changes in the impact of terms of trade on real GDP are explained in Booth (1995). The main problem is that there is no price index for commodity imports before 1913. Booth (1995) did not acknowledge that the available import price index for 1913–39 is merely an unweighted index for only 20 products. An average price index of the export of manufactures from the United States and the United Kingdom up to 1932 was used to calculate the impact of changes in the net barter terms of trade (Lewis, 1952: 118; Schlote, 1952: 175–8). This is not entirely accurate, because Indonesia imported much more than only manufactured goods, for instance rice. The overlapping years 1913–32 in Figure 7.3 indicate that the difference is only marginal. An index based on only imported manufactures exaggerates the impact on GDY, it will not underestimate it.

The export price index for 1900–40 is the Paasche price index from Van Ark (1988). Both price indices were extended to 1941 with relevant price indices from *Economisch Weekblad voor Nederlandsch-Indië*. 1949–50 from *The Java Bank (De Javasche Bank): Report for the Financial Year 1950/51*, linked for 1950–72 to import and export price indices in US dollars from Rosendale (1978), which in themselves were linked in the overlapping years 1937–39 to the Van Ark export price index and the official import price index. The resulting indices were linked for 1973–99 to the linked implicit price indices of exports and imports of goods and services from the Indonesian national accounts, *Pendapatan Nasional Indonesia*. Note that the 1950–72 series may be somewhat artificial, because of Indonesia's multiple exchange rate system (Corden and Mackie, 1962). Foreign trade data were denominated in US dollars and recalculated to Rupiahs, using the appropriate exchange rates. Still, these exchange rates may not have been entirely representative, because exchange rates actually varied across different categories of imports and exports.

The principles of calculating GDY are explained in Sundrum (1986: 45–6). For 1900–39 and 1960–99 exports and imports of goods and services were used, and GDY was calculated in 1913 prices with Sundrum's equations 3 and 4:

$$GDY = GDP + [(X/P_x + M/P_m) \times (P_x - P_m)/(P_x + P_m)]$$

In which X = exports, M = imports, P_x = price index of exports, and P_m = price index of imports. The last term between squared brackets is the terms of trade effect of current transactions in adding to or subtracting from the resources available to the economy as a whole. GDY represents the resources available to the economy, net of capital transactions. The dotted line series in Figure 7.4 was calculated for 1900–41 and 1949–73 with only exports of goods according to Sundrum's equations 1 and 4:

$$GDY = GDP + [X \times (1/P_m + 1/P_x)]$$

The results differ slightly, but allow us to establish the GDY trend during the years not covered by the first series, i.e. 1940–41 and 1949–59.

REFERENCES

Akita, T. and R.A. Lukman (1995), 'Interregional Inequalities in Indonesia: A Sectoral Decomposition Analysis for 1975–92', *Bulletin of Indonesian Economic Studies*, 31, No. 2, pp. 61–81.

Athukorala, P.C. and B.H. Santosa (1997), 'Gains from Indonesian Export Growth: Do Linkages Matter?', *Bulletin of Indonesian Economic Studies*, 33, No. 2, pp. 73–95.

Booth, A. (1990a), 'Foreign Trade and Domestic Development in the Colonial Economy' in A. Booth et al. (eds), *Indonesian Economic History in the Dutch Colonial Era*, (New Haven: Yale University Southeast Asia Studies), pp. 363–98.

Booth, A. (1990b), 'The Evolution of Fiscal Policy and the Role of the Government in the Colonial Economy' in A. Booth et al. (eds), *Indonesian Economic History in the Dutch Colonial Era*, (New Haven: Yale Southeast Asia Studies), pp. 210–43.

Booth, A. (1992), 'International Trade and Domestic Economic Development: An Indonesian Case Study' in M. Arsjad Anwar et al. (eds), *Pemerikan, Pelaksanaan dan Perintisan Pembangunan Ekonomi*, (Jakarta: Gramedia), pp. 99–152.

Booth, A. (1995), 'The Real Domestic Product of Indonesia, 1880–1989: A Comment and An Estimate', *Explorations in Economic History*, 32, pp. 350–64.

BPS (1980), *Pendapatan Regional Propinsi-Propinsi di Indonesia, 1971–1977*. [Regional income of the provinces in Indonesia, 1971-77], Jakarta: Biro Pusat Statistik.

BPS (1986), *Penduduk Indonesia Tahun 1961, 1971 dan 1980 menurut Propinsi dan Kepulauan*. [The population of Indonesia in the years 1961, 1971 and 1980 by province and island] Jakarta: Biro Pusat Statistik.

BPS (1992a), *Penduduk Indonesia: Tabel Hasil Sensus Penduduk 1990. Seri S.2*. [The population of Indonesia: Table with the results of the 1990 population census] (Jakarta: Biro Pusat Statistik.

BPS (1992b), *Pendapatan Regional Propinsi-Propinsi di Indonesia menurut Lapangan Usaha, 1983–1990*. [Regional income of the provinces of Indonesia by economic sector, 1983-1990], Jakarta: Biro Pusat Statistik.

BPS (1996), *Penduduk Indonesia: Hasil Survei Penduduk antar Sensus 1995. Seri S2*. [The population of Indonesia: Table with the results of the 1995 inter-census population survey] Jakarta: Biro Pusat Statistik.

BPS (1997), *Produk Domestik Regional Bruto Propinsi-Propinsi di Indonesia menurut Lapangan Usaha, 1993–1996*. [Gross domestic regional product of Indonesia by economic sector, 1993-1996] Jakarta: Biro Pusat Statistik.

Census (1936), *Volkstelling 1930, Deel VIII*. [Population census 1930, Vol. 8] Batavia: Landsdrukkerij.

CKS (1939), 'Handelsstatistiek Nederlandsch-Indië 1874–1937'. [Trade statistics of the Dutch East Indies, 1874–1937] *Mededeeling van het Centraal Kantoor voor de Statistiek No. 161*. Batavia: CKS.

Corden, W.M. and J.A.C. Mackie (1962), 'The Development of the Indonesian Exchange Rate System', *Malayan Economic Review*, 7, pp. 37–60.

Creutzberg, P. (1976), *Changing Economy in Indonesia Vol. 2: Public Finance 1816–1939*. The Hague: Martinus Nijhoff.

Creutzberg, P. (1977), *Changing Economy in Indonesia Vol. 3: Expenditure on Fixed Assets*. The Hague: Nijhoff.

Dick, H.W. (1990), 'Interisland Trade, Economic Integration, and the Emergence of the National Economy' in A. Booth et al. (eds), *Indonesian Economic History in the Dutch Colonial Era*. (New Haven: Yale University Southeast Asia Studies), pp. 296–321.

Dick, H.W. (1993), 'Nineteenth-Century Industrialization: A Missed Opportunity?' in J.Th. Lindblad (ed.), *New Challenges in the Modern Economic History of Indonesia*, (Leiden: Programme of Indonesian Studies), pp. 123–49.

Dick, H.W. (1996), 'The Emergence of A National Economy, 1808–1990s' in J.T. Lindblad (ed.), *Historical Foundations of a National Economy in Indonesia, 1890s–1990*, (Amsterdam: North-Holland), pp. 21–51.

Djanin, A. (1962), 'Inflation, Capital Formation and Economic Development in Indonesia 1953–1958' in *Laporan Kongres Ilmu Pengatehuan Nasional Kedua 1962: Djilid Kesembilan Seksi E-3 Ekonomi.* (Jakarta: MIPI), pp. 191–207.

Dowling, M. (1997), 'Asia's Economic Miracle: An Historical Perspective', *The Australian Economic Review*, **30**, No. 1, pp. 113–23.

Dowling, M. and P.M. Summers (1998), 'Total Factor Productivity and Economic Growth: Issues for Asia', *Economic Record*, **74**, pp. 170–85.

Fruin, Th.A. (1947), *Het Economische Aspect van het Indonesische Vraagstuk.* [The economic side of the Indonesian issue], Amsterdam: Vrij Nederland.

Gordon, A. (1998), 'Industrial Development in Colonial Indonesia, 1921–1941', *Journal of Contemporary Asia*, **28**, No. 1, pp. 3–26.

Hill, H. (1988), *Foreign Investment and Industrialisation in Indonesia.* Oxford: Oxford UP.

Hill, H. (1991/92), 'Regional Development in a "Boom and Bust Petroleum Economy": Indonesia since 1970', *Economic Development and Cultural Change*, **40**, pp. 351–79.

Hill, H. (1992), 'Indonesia's Foreign Investment Regime since 1966: Balancing Economic Imperatives and Political Constraints' in M. Arsjad Anwar et al. (eds), *Pemerikan, Pelaksanaan dan Perintisan Pembangunan Ekonomi* (Jakarta: Gramedia), pp. 591–615.

Hill, H. (1996), *The Indonesian Economy since 1966: Southeast Asia's Emerging Giant.* Cambridge: CUP.

Hill, H. (1998), 'Introduction' in H. Hill and Thee Kian Wie (eds), *Indonesia's Technological Challenge,* (Singapore: ISEAS), pp. 1–52.

Hugo, G.J. et al. (1987), *The Demographic Dimension in Indonesian Development.* Singapore: Oxford UP.

Jap, K.S. (1964), 'Foreign Investment Policy and Taxation in Indonesia', *Bulletin for International Fiscal Documentation*, **13**, pp. 323–41.

Keuning, S.J. (1988), 'An Estimate of the Fixed Capital Stock by Industry and Type of Capital Good in Indonesia', *Statistical Analysis Capability Programme Working Paper Series No. 4*, The Hague: Institute of Social Studies.

Keuning, S.J. (1991), 'Allocation and Composition of Fixed Capital Stock in Indonesia: An Indirect Estimate Using Incremental Capital Value Added Ratios', *Bulletin of Indonesian Economic Studies*, **27**, No. 2, pp. 91–119.

Knaap, G.J. (1989), *Changing Economy in Indonesia, Vol. 9: Transport 1819–1940.* Amsterdam: Royal Tropical Institute.

Korthals Altes, W.L. (1987), *Changing Economy in Indonesia, Vol. 7: Balance of Payments 1822–1939.* Amsterdam: Royal Tropical Institute.

Korthals Altes, W.L. (1991), *Changing Economy in Indonesia, Vol. 12a: General Trade Statistics 1822–1940.* Amsterdam: Royal Tropical Institute.

Kravis, I.B. (1970), 'Trade as a Handmaiden of Growth: Similarities between the Nineteenth and Twentieth Centuries', *Economic Journal*, **80**, pp. 850–72.

Lewis, W.A. (1952), 'World Production, Prices and Trade, 1870–1960', *Manchester School*, **20**, pp. 105–38.

Maddison, A. (1995), *Monitoring the World Economy 1820–1992.* Paris: OECD Development Centre.

Mangkosuwondo, S. (1975), 'Indonesia' in S. Ichimura (ed.), *The Economic Development of East and Southeast Asia.* (Honolulu: UP of Hawaii), pp. 1–58.

Muljatno (1960), 'Perhitungan Pendapatan Nasional Indonesia untuk Tahun 1953 dan 1954' [The calculation of Indonesia's national income for 1953 and 1954], *Ekonomi dan Keuangan Indonesia*, **13**, pp. 162–211.

NIG (1947), *Hundred Pages Indonesian Economics.* Batavia: The Netherlands Indies Government, 1947.

Rosendale, Ph.B. (1975), 'The Indonesian Terms of Trade, 1950–73', *Bulletin of Indonesian Economic Studies*, **11**, No. 3, pp. 50–80.

Rosendale, Ph.B. (1978), *The Indonesian Balance of Payments, 1950–1976: Some New Estimates.* PhD Thesis, The Australian National University.

Schlote, W. (1952), *British Overseas Trade from 1700 to the 1930s.* Oxford: Blackwell.

Segers, W.A.I.M. (1988), *Changing Economy in Indonesia, Vol. 8: Manufacturing Industry 1870–1942*. Amsterdam: Royal Tropical Institute.

Sitsen, P.W. (1943), *Industrial Development of the Netherlands Indies*. New York: Institute of Pacific Relations.

Suhartono, R.B. (1967), *The Indonesian Economy: An Attempt in Econometric Model Analysis*. PhD thesis, Wayne State University, Detroit (Michigan).

Sundrum R.M. (1986), 'Indonesia's Rapid Economic Growth: 1968–81', *Bulletin of Indonesian Economic Studies*, **22**, No. 3, pp. 40–69.

Szirmai, A. (1994), 'Real Output and Labour Productivity in Indonesian Manufacturing, 1975–90', *Bulletin of Indonesian Economic Studies*, **30**, No. 2, pp. 49–90.

Tan, T.K. (ed.), (1967), *Sukarno's Guided Indonesia*. Brisbane: Jacaranda Press.

Timmer, M. (1999), 'Indonesia's Ascent on the Technology Ladder: Capital Stock and Total Factor Productivity in Indonesian Manufacturing, 1975–1995', *Bulletin of Indonesian Economic Studies*, **35**, No. 1, pp. 75–98.

Touwen, J. (1999), *Extremes in the Archipelago: Trade and Economic Development in the Outer Islands of Indonesia, 1900–1942*. Leiden: KITLV Press (forthcoming).

Van Ark, B. (1988), 'The Volume and Price of Indonesian Exports, 1823 to 1940: The Long-Term Trend and Its Measurement', *Bulletin of Indonesian Economic Studies*, **24**, No. 3, pp. 87–120.

Van der Eng, P. (1992), 'The Real Domestic Product of Indonesia, 1880–1989', *Explorations in Economic History*, **28**, pp. 343–73.

Van der Eng, P. (1993), 'The "Colonial Drain" from Indonesia, 1823–1990', *Research School of Pacific Studies, Economics Division Working Paper, Southeast Asia No. 93/2*. Canberra: Australian National University.

Van der Eng, P. (1996), *Agricultural Growth in Indonesia: Productivity Change and Policy Impact since 1880*. London: Macmillan.

Van der Eng, P. (1997), 'Gauging Growth: Development of National Accounting in Indonesia', *Newsletter of the Asian Historical Statistics Project*, No. 4 (1997), pp. 9–11.

Van der Eng, P. (1998), 'Exploring Exploitation: The Netherlands and Colonial Indonesia 1870–1940', *Revista de Historia Económica*, **16**, No. 1, pp. 291–321.

Van der Eng, P. (1999), 'Some Obscurities in Indonesia's New National Accounts', *Bulletin of Indonesian Economic Studies*, **35**, No. 2, pp. 91–106.

Van der Mandere, H.Ch.G.J. (1928), *De Javasuikerindustrie in Heden en Verleden*. [The Java Sugar Industry in Present and Past] Amsterdam: Bureau Industria.

Van Laanen, J.T.M. (1979), 'Het Bestedingspakket van de "Inheemse" Bevolking op Java (1921–1939)' [Consumptive expenditure of the native population in Java, 1921–1939] in F. van Anrooij et al. (eds), *Between People and Statistics. Essays in Modern Indonesian History*. (The Hague: Nijhoff), pp. 133–45.

Van Laanen, J.T.M. (1990), 'Between the Java Bank and the Chinese Moneylender: Banking and Credit in Colonial Indonesia' in A. Booth et al. (eds), *Indonesian Economic History in the Dutch Colonial Era*. (New Haven: Yale Southeast Asia Studies), pp. 244–66.

Westermann, J.C. (1945), 'The Conquest of Distance' in W.H. van Helsdingen (ed.), *Mission Interrupted: The Dutch in the East Indies and their Work in the XXth Century*. (Amsterdam: Elsevier), pp. 116–35.

Williamson, J.G. (1965), 'Regional Inequality and the Process of National Development', *Economic Development and Cultural Change*, **13**, pp. 3–45.

Van Oorschot, H.J. (1956), *De Ontwikkeling van de Nijverheid in Indonesië*. [The development of manufacturing in Indonesia] The Hague: Van Hoeve.

Zainuddin, A. (1970), 'Education in the Netherlands East Indies and the Republic of Indonesia' in R.J.W. Sellich (ed.), *Melbourne Studies in Education*. (Melbourne: Melbourne UP), pp. 17–82.

8. The Long-Term Performance of the Japanese Economy

Dirk Pilat

INTRODUCTION

Japan's successful economic development over the past century remains among the most impressive features in world economic history. It therefore continues to attract the attention of academics and policy makers, as they attempt to gain further insights in the factors that contribute to Japan's economic success and to draw lessons for other countries' economic policies.

This chapter aims to contribute to this work. It starts off with a brief overview of the Japanese growth experience. The third section looks at the historical origins and initial conditions for rapid post-war growth. The fourth section discusses economic growth in the post-war period, partly based on growth accounting. Section five presents a comparative perspective of Japanese economic growth and provides productivity estimates for the Japanese economy and its sub-sectors, while the final section draws some conclusions.

The chapter combines conventional growth analysis with a comparative perspective. Comparative studies can help in finding answers to some important questions, such as: are processes of catch-up and convergence important for all sectors of the economy; which sectors have been most important in the Japanese catch-up with productivity levels in the United States? The chapter updates some of my earlier work (Pilat, 1993, 1994) and also draws on analysis at OECD.

AN OVERVIEW OF JAPAN'S GROWTH EXPERIENCE

Japanese economic growth is very well documented. Relatively detailed statistics are available from 1885 onwards, and some indicators go back to the early 1870s. Before 1870, historians have made several estimates of economic growth in the Tokugawa period. Most of these suggest modest GDP per capita growth since 1600 of approximately 0.1 per cent annually (Hanley and Yamamura, 1977; Hanley, 1986; Yasuba, 1986, 1987). Growth only picked up substantially after the Meiji Restoration in 1868.

Figure 8.1 shows the growth phases of the Japanese economy from 1885 to the present. The data shown are calculated as five-year moving averages of annual growth rates of GDP. The graph indicates that pre-war growth was relatively modest at around 3 per cent annually, with two major exceptions. The first exception was the First World War, which substantially boosted growth. The second period of high growth was the immediate pre-war period, from 1930 to 1942, when GDP growth averaged almost 6 per cent annually.

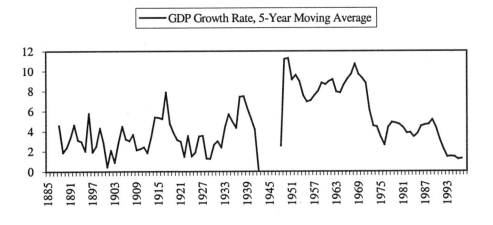

Source: Based on Pilat (1994) OECD National Accounts. OECD Economic Outlook, No. 63.

Figure 8.1   Phases of Growth in the Japanese Economy, 1885–1997

The Second World War had devastating effects on the economy. GDP plummeted and income levels fell substantially. The immediate post-war period, up to 1953, was characterised by relatively slow growth. After 1953 the tide turned. GDP growth from 1953 to 1973 averaged almost 9 per cent on an annual basis. This is the period of Japanese hypergrowth. After 1973, growth slowed down to about 4 per cent for 1973–1990. Since 1991 and the collapse of the bubble economy, Japanese economic growth has slowed down further and the years 1992 to 1995 saw growth of less than 1 per cent on average. The economy picked up somewhat in 1996, but deteriorated further over 1997.

Both Hanley (1986) and Yasuba (1986, 1987) have suggested that the Japanese standard of living prior to the start of economic growth in the 1850s was not that far removed from that in Western Europe, specifically that of the United Kingdom. However, Maddison's estimates (Maddison, 1995) suggest a large difference in per capita GDP levels between European countries and Japan. Figure 8.2 shows relative GDP per capita and relative GDP per person employed in Japan, compared with the United States. The graph is based on a comparison of productivity and price levels for 1985, and was extrapolated with time series to arrive at a long-term perspective (Pilat, 1993). According to the estimates in Figure 8.2, GDP per capita in 1870 was approximately 29 per cent of that in the United States. During the interwar period, Japan did not catch-up with US income levels, but neither did it fall behind. In the 1930s, there was a short period of catch-up, partly caused by the effects of the Great Depression on the US economy, which had only limited effects on Japanese economic growth. The Second World War caused an enormous drop in the Japanese income level to less than 10 per cent of the United States. After the war income levels rose fast. Into the 1950s, most growth was linked to reconstruction. In the middle of the 1950s, rapid growth emerged in Japan and there has been an almost continuous upward trend in relative income levels since. Japan has now reached an income level slightly over 70 per cent of that in the United States. For the pre-war period, productivity levels were substantially below relative income levels, as participation rates in Japan were much higher than in the United States. After the war, differences in labour force participation between the countries narrowed and income trends are currently a close reflection of productivity trends.

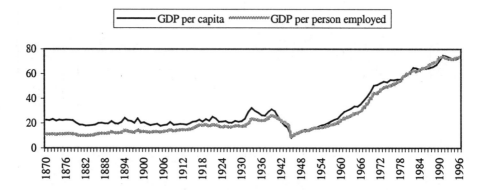

Source: Pilat (1994), updated with OECD Analytical Database. See Table A8.1 and A8.2.

Figure 8.2 Real Income and Productivity Levels, 1870–1995

Structural change in Japan followed the classical model (Chenery, Robinson and Syrquin, 1986). In the early 1870s, approximately 70 per cent of the workforce was engaged in agriculture (Pilat, 1994). Mining and manufacturing employed no more than 2 to 3 per cent of the workforce and the remaining part was employed in the service sector. Figure 8.3 shows the share of the three main sectors in employment from 1885 to 1995. Before the war, agriculture's share slowly dropped to some 40 per cent of total employment in the early 1940s. After the war, agriculture's share rose temporarily as post-war unemployment caused many workers to return to the countryside. In the high growth period, from the early 1950s to 1973, agriculture's share dropped rapidly from 44 per cent in 1953 to only 16 per cent in 1973. Since then its share has slowly declined to about 7 per cent of total employment today, which is still somewhat higher than in comparable high-income economies.

The share of mining and manufacturing rose slowly up to the early 1930s, when its growth rate accelerated due to the rapid growth of the military apparatus. In 1942, manufacturing's share was slightly less than 30 per cent, a proportion which was attained again in 1973. Since 1973, manufacturing's share in the economy has fallen and Japan has become a service economy. In 1995, about 70 per cent of the total workforce were engaged in services.

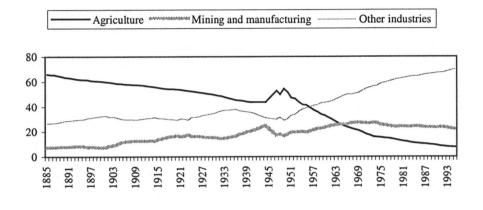

Source: Pilat (1994) updated with OECD National Accounts.

Figure 8.3   Structural Change in the Japanese Economy, 1885–1995

PRE-WAR ECONOMIC PERFORMANCE

Initial Conditions: The Tokugawa Period and the Meiji Restoration

The main impetus to modern economic growth came after the Meiji Restoration in 1868. The Restoration resulted in the overthrow of the Tokugawa Shogunate and its replacement by a modern government. It is usually seen as the starting point of economic growth. However, the Tokugawa period was characterised by some important achievements, which would be highly beneficial to the Meiji rulers (Hagen, 1962; Yasuba, 1987).

For instance, a reliable road system and large urban centres developed during the Tokugawa period. Commerce flourished and financial institutions were emerging. In agriculture, yields per acre were already quite high by international standards. There had also been important developments in land improvement, mainly through the extended use of irrigation. A large part of agricultural output was not for subsistence, but was sold on the market. In return for protection, the peasants were forced to provide large rice levies to their *daimyo*, that were subsequently sold to merchants (Rosovsky, 1966). This system generated a considerable surplus, which could be used for investment. Another important achievement of the Tokugawa period was the achievement of relatively – by Asian standards – high levels of literacy.

On the whole, however, Tokugawa Japan was a feudal society. The country was almost completely isolated from foreign influence, trade and commerce were restricted, even within the country itself, and there were significant constraints on change and modernisation. Some manufacturing had developed and there was some influence from 'Dutch learning', but this was all limited in scope. In the western part of Japan some *daimyo* had started relatively modern factories in the early nineteenth century. But these were isolated cases and were not representative of overall economic development.

After the overthrow of the Tokugawa government, the new Meiji government was politically motivated to retain Japanese sovereignty and keep foreigners out (Boserup, 1981). For that purpose Japan had to grow stronger, both militarily and economically. The government initiated a range of reforms which led the country to the start of an era of modern economic growth. The years up to 1885 are generally seen as a transition period. After the overthrow of the Tokugawa Shogunate the only possibility for change lay in the hands of the government. In this time of great uncertainty, the private sector chose to sit back and wait for change.

The new Meiji government carried out a series of sweeping reforms (Rosovsky, 1966). Between 1869 and 1871, there were significant changes in the class structure, leading to fewer regulations and much more mobility. Guilds were dissolved and trade and transport restrictions were lifted. The land tenure system was transformed, and the Meiji government provided government bonds to the *daimyo* in exchange for their land. Because of the successive inflation and the inexperience of the *daimyo* with financial matters, these bonds soon lost their real worth. The central role of the *daimyo* and *samurai* came to an end because of these measures.

The chaotic financial system, with several different currencies, was changed in the period 1869–74. One currency (the Yen) was introduced, and the government encouraged the development of a modern banking system. Several national banks and the government were allowed to take care of the money supply. The land tax system was changed drastically, from a system based on the actual harvest to one based on uniform rates. Furthermore, it was levied directly on the landowners thus resembling a modern system of private property. The government also introduced compulsory education in 1872.

The reforms were mainly institutional and helped to construct a framework within which modern economic growth could emerge. The government took further action in the development of infrastructure; telegraph, postal services and railways developed and some 'model factories' with modern Western technology were opened. Substantial economic progress was made in the Meiji period. The government promoted industrialisation and started some government enterprises. This was needed to generate foreign exchange to alleviate the balance of payment difficulties which arose through increased imports. Industrialisation was also required to find new occupations for the great number of *samurai* who lost their traditional function after the Meiji Restoration. In the first years of Meiji rule exports consisted mainly of agricultural commodities (silk, tea and rice). Some simple technological innovations were introduced from abroad, which mainly affected small-scale handicraft industry. Alongside the modern, partly government-subsidised industrial sector, another smaller-scale, and more traditional industrial sector developed.

The First Phase of Modern Economic Growth, 1885–1914

From 1885 onwards, economic growth really took hold. The structural transformation from an agricultural society to one dominated by industry and services was firmly in progress. In agriculture there was substantial growth through the introduction of fertilisers and chemicals, improvements in seeds and more efficient use of available land through reclamation and drainage. In the first part of this period, agriculture was important as a generator of foreign exchange. Raw silk, tea and rice were important export products, later supplemented with some mining products (copper, coal). Another important contribution of agriculture lay in its surplus labour. Partly on a seasonal basis, but increasingly on a fulltime basis, workers moved out of agriculture into industry and services. In times of industrial depression the agricultural sector would serve as a safety net into which industrial workers could return. Also important was the role of agriculture as a major source of savings. The Meiji government depended on agriculture for a large share of her tax base. In addition, agriculture was still able to feed the growing number of Japanese.

Over time, industry became more important as a source of foreign exchange. The Meiji government promoted silk reeling and other textile industries and set up some heavy industries (shipyards, iron industries). The light industries were able to use the few natural resources which Japan possessed and could utilise the abundant supply of (often female) labour. Furthermore, the textile industries were not too dependent on capital and imported inputs. It is therefore not surprising that the early success of Japanese industrial development was primarily confined to the textile industries. The heavy industries needed substantial capital inputs and were also partly dependent on imported iron ore and coal. Furthermore, although Japan was quite advanced in traditional metal working, the traditional methods differed too much from modern methods. In addition, the modernisation had not yet reached a level at which the heavy industries could optimally benefit from economies of scale.

In the Meiji period, Japan started to acquire substantial amounts of technology from abroad. Foreign engineers and teachers arrived to help construct railways, power plants and factories, and to give instruction on these projects. Fairly soon the Japanese themselves were able to do the same things and often slightly adjusted the technology to adapt it to their own wishes.

Foreign trade in the Meiji period was at first mainly carried out through the intermediation of foreign merchants and foreign trading companies. Over time, the Japanese learned from their methods and established their own trading companies, which also become closely linked to large manufacturing enterprises. Japanese foreign trade was especially successful in penetrating the Chinese and Indian markets for textile and silk goods. Also, a national merchant fleet was established in this period, partly backed by government support.

The Meiji government played an important role in the promotion of industry. It had a large share in overall capital formation in the economy and took part in some industries through the introduction of 'model' factories. Government expenditure in this period rose rapidly and taxes rose alongside it. Over the period 1885–1914 the government often ran a budget deficit and was forced to borrow. Domestic financial markets were not yet well developed and could not cope with the financial requirements of the government. For that reason, foreign borrowing came to be of considerable importance in this period.

Another characteristic of this period is the emergence of the dual structure of the economy, which would become even more marked after the First World War and is still apparent today. The main characteristics of this dual structure are:

1. a modern large-scale industrial sector on the one hand, with relatively high wages, a high capital intensity, a large numbers of skilled workers and high productivity levels;
2. on the other hand, agriculture and the more traditional small-scale industrial sector, with lower wages, lower capital intensity, lower educational levels and lower productivity

levels. In the post-war period, this small-scale sector would also include many of the subcontractors of large-scale manufacturing enterprises.

This period also witnessed an increase in Japan's imperial aspirations. The government devoted a large part of its budget to military expenditures. The Sino-Japanese War (1894–95) and the Russo-Japanese War (1904–5) demonstrated the military strength of Japan. As a consequence of the Sino-Japanese War the Japanese government was able to renegotiate treaties made with the Western Powers, and Formosa and the Pescadores were granted to Japan. The Chinese were also required to pay indemnities to the Japanese government, which served as a substantial contribution to its foreign exchange requirements. Tariff autonomy, an important instrument of industrial policy, was returned to the Japanese government. In 1910 the Japanese occupied Korea. The new colonies, Taiwan and Korea, became an integral part of the empire. They were important outlets for direct investment and also attracted immigrants.

The First World War and the Interwar Period, 1914–38

The First World War had favourable effects on the development of the economy (Figure 8.1). Japan did not become involved in the war and was able to benefit from some of its effects. It was able to expand its share on the Indian and Chinese markets in textiles (Maddison, 1969) and expanded its activities in shipping and the fabrication of ammunitions (Allen, 1981). The eruption of economic activity led to a huge export surplus and allowed the government to repay a large part of the debt accumulated in the previous period. The war seriously disrupted the cost and price system, however, and at the beginning of the 1920s the country suffered a depression.

In the interwar period the *zaibatsu*, manufacturing conglomerates with strong connections with banks and trading companies, emerged. The dual structure in the economy, which had already emerged before the war, now became more pronounced. Small industrial establishments became more closely linked to the *zaibatsu* through the system of subcontracting, in which the small establishments supplied parts and did contract work for their big partners. Scrapped machinery from the large companies was often sold to the smaller establishments, which was an efficient way of using the scarce capital resources.

The agricultural sector came under severe pressure in this period, especially due to cheap imports from the colonies of Korea and Taiwan. These imports were a disincentive to technological change, which levelled off anyway, because the biological and chemical improvements of the earlier period had already diffused to most parts of the country. There was also a lack of new land that could be reclaimed for farming. However, agriculture was able to attain sufficient growth to free surplus labour, and generated sufficient food to feed the slowly growing population.

In the second half of the interwar period the contradictions in society grew larger and larger. The modern industrial sector, dominated by the *zaibatsu*, with its much higher wages and government backing was quite distinct from the traditional sector. In the second half of the interwar period the *zaibatsu* had gained a position in which they had a major political influence.

From 1931 onwards the economy became more and more involved in military preparations. In 1931 the Japanese army occupied the Manchurian provinces and renamed them Manchukuo. From that time onwards, first in Manchukuo, the government took stricter control of the economy. Especially in Manchukuo, which was governed by the military, heavy industries were promoted to help prepare for war. The 1930s were also the period of the Great Depression. It hit Japan hard, especially in its export markets. Several countries used trade restrictions to curb the effects of the depression. In the late 1930s, in a period when Japan was already preparing for war, the possibilities for further economic expansion appeared limited (Allen, 1981). Military expansion was seen as a possible alternative.

Productivity Levels in Pre-War Japan

There was a considerable gap in per capita income between Japan and the United States in the pre-war period, and an underlying productivity gap. Detailed productivity estimates for 1939 – based on industry-specific purchasing power parities – are shown in Table 8.1 (Pilat, 1994).[1] Output per person engaged was 23 per cent of the United States in 1939. The available information on hours worked for this period is rather weak, especially for Japan, so no adjustment for hours can be made. The available levels for the whole economy (Maddison, 1991) suggest that Japanese productivity would be lower compared with the USA if adjustment for hours were made.

Table 8.1 Comparative Price Levels, Output and Productivity, 1939 (Japan as a percentage of the United States)

	Relative price level (USA = 100)	Real value added (USA = 100)	Relative employment (USA = 100)	Relative value added per employed (USA = 100)
Agriculture, forestry, fisheries	132.0	19.0	174.7	10.9
Mining	156.8	9.4	61.4	15.2
Manufacturing	94.6	16.1	64.8	24.8
Construction	104.8	24.4	53.0	46.0
Public utilities	63.4	15.2	30.7	49.3
Transport and communication	43.6	15.9	30.7	49.3
Transport	43.1	17.2	46.6	37.0
Communication	49.1	9.8	64.9	15.1
Wholesale and retail trade	27.9	25.3	42.6	59.5
Other services	34.5	2.6	40.3	6.4
Government	36.8	7.0	13.9	50.0
Total	65.1	15.1	65.4	23.2

Source: Pilat (1994).

Relatively high Japanese productivity was found in the service sectors, with the exception of communications. The lowest levels were those for agriculture and mining. Manufacturing took an intermediate position of 25 per cent of the US level. These findings indicate that Japan was well behind the US in 1939. There had been substantial growth in some sectors, especially in manufacturing, but Japan still had an extremely low level of productivity. Productivity in Japanese manufacturing was only half that in Germany and the United Kingdom (Broadberry, 1992). Within manufacturing, the variation in productivity was considerable (Pilat, 1994). Relatively high productivity was found in textiles, apparel and leather goods, non-metallic mineral products and basic and fabricated metal products. Productivity was very low in printing and other manufacturing.

The Second World War and its Effects

During the war the economy was heavily controlled and a strict guidance principle was followed. This principle remained of great importance after the war (Nakamura, 1981). Subcontracting also spread rapidly during this period. Some aspects of the post-war relations between labour and management were also shaped during the war. Firms set up organisations to promote industrial safety, rationing, and so on. These organisations became the forerunners of the post-war company trade unions. The government took an active hand in controlling wages during the war, and determined wage increases annually. Several elements of the system by which the government's decisions were made, such as lifetime employment and seniority wages, became of great importance in the post-war period.

The Second World War had devastating effects on the economy. Three million Japanese died, Japan lost its colonies Korea, Taiwan and Manchukuo and all the investments made in those countries. A quarter of all buildings and structures were destroyed (Kosai, 1986), the country had to repatriate approximately six million soldiers and expatriates and it lost its political autonomy to the US occupation forces.

The main purpose of the occupation authorities, mainly American forces, was to democratise and decentralise the economy. The occupation authorities forced the *zaibatsu* and large trading companies to disband and fostered the establishment of US-style trade unions. The pre-war power of the *zaibatsu* was seen by the allies as an important influence behind Japan's military expansion and therefore as an important obstacle to democratisation. The break-up of the *zaibatsu* may have been beneficial to Japanese economic growth, because it increased the degree of competition within the economy. The establishment of trade unions can also be seen as an effort to support democratic forces. The wartime company unions primarily turned into the new trade unions after the war. When strikes and labour unrest emerged in later years, the occupation authorities tried to reverse the trade union arrangements they had initiated.

Japan had to face restrictive trade policies after the war from most European countries. Furthermore, important markets in Asian countries, especially China, Taiwan and Korea were largely closed. These setbacks were huge and it took the economy up to 1952 to reach the pre-war GDP level. However, the occupation also had some favourable effects on economic development (Shinohara, 1970). Japan was forbidden to spend more than one per cent of its GDP on military expenditure, which released substantial amounts for productive investment. Furthermore, although the Japanese had lagged behind in the technological advances made during the war, there was now a new technological base available, which could be adopted almost instantaneously. Also, the war and the changes forced by the occupation authorities resulted in a new leadership in business, which was generally regarded as less conservative than its predecessors. In addition, a clearer distinction between ownership and management developed in this period.

The occupation had another favourable effect, because it allowed the Japanese to build up close ties with the United States, at that time the technological leader and one of the few major economies which was not in ruins after the war (Patrick and Rosovsky, 1976). External military security was assured by the United States in a security treaty, a huge export market for Japanese products was opened up, and the United States opened the way for integration into the international economic community by backing Japan's membership to various international organisations (IMF, OECD, GATT, World Bank). At a time when other markets were often closed to Japan, this relationship was of great importance.

Reconstruction and Recovery, 1945–53

The initial post-war period witnessed great problems in the economy. It had to assimilate six million expatriates, there were shortages of food and energy, a threat of large indemnities from the former occupied countries, strong inflationary pressures, and on top of this the country had suffered serious war damage. Surprisingly, high unemployment did not arise after the war, probably because people could simply not afford to be unemployed. The agricultural sector absorbed a large part of the labour surplus, and many workers took refuge in the informal economy. In the first two years the economy suffered from serious food and energy shortages. It seemed also that the occupation authorities would ask for large indemnities and that a large part of the remaining production facilities would be moved to the United States. This situation did not materialise, because with the outbreak of the Cold War, the United States gave priority to strengthening the Japanese economy.

In 1948, this American policy shift became clearer, when a number of restrictions on Japanese economic policy were lifted and the occupation authorities started planning for economic stabilisation and reconstruction. Up to 1950 the recovery of the economy progressed only slowly. A large, and much needed impulse to the recovery progress was given by the outbreak of the Korean War. This led to a world-wide economic boom, and affected the economy favourably. A combination of increased exports, partly for US military purposes, and additional income from expenditures by US military personnel in Japan, led to a large increase in foreign currency inflows. This was used for increased imports of foreign technology and large investments in capital goods. By the end of the Korean War the economy had been put firmly on the rapid growth path.

THE POST-WAR PERIOD

The Growth Accounts

Japanese economic growth in the post-war period has been the subject of a multitude of studies, from a wide range of scientific disciplines. Most of these have looked for the reasons of Japan's economic success in the five decades since the Second World War.

Several streams of thought can be distinguished (Johnson, 1982; Friedman, 1988; Lynn, 1989). The first school attributes Japan's success primarily to a highly successful interventionist policy by government, mainly by the Ministry of International Trade and Industry (MITI). The most convincing study in this respect is that by Johnson (1982). Less careful studies on these lines sometimes work with the concept of 'Japan Incorporated'. These studies see Japan as a planned economy, with forceful government guidance, and a limited role for market forces.

The second is what Johnson (1982) and Friedman (1988) call the market approach. This school finds Japanese development basically comparable to that of other industrialised countries. Its performance is explained within neo-classical production analysis, and the economy is seen principally as a competitive market. High rates of investment, advances in the stock of human capital through improved education and training, and acquisition of technology from abroad are the main engines of the economic process and can explain most of the success. Some important studies along these lines are Ohkawa and Rosovsky (1973), Denison and Chung (1976) and Patrick (1977).

The 'bureaucratic' and the market approaches are at the heart of most economic studies on Japanese development. Supplementary explanations are provided by two other schools. The 'cultural' approach sees Japanese development originating from a unique and dynamic culture, with a great emphasis on harmony and group values (Hofstede, 1984; Morishima, 1982; Dore, 1987; Hofstede and Bond, 1990). Hofstede (1984) and Hofstede and Bond (1990) have argued that the Confucian culture of Japan, like that of other East Asian countries, has made an extremely important contribution to economic growth. Particularly the long-term orientation of Confucian culture is stressed in these studies.

The final school relates Japan's success mainly to a set of unique features, such as the lifetime employment system and seniority wages. This view is found mostly among students of industrial organisation and business. Most studies of Japan's success take an eclectic approach, explaining growth from a mix of market and government (Okimoto, 1989).

What exactly is the phenomenon which needs explaining? Table 8.2 shows some indicators of economic growth in the post-war period. Before 1973 the economy was characterised by extremely high annual growth rates of 8.5 per cent on average. Several studies have drawn attention to the acceleration of growth in the period up to 1973 (Ohkawa and Rosovsky, 1973). After 1973 growth slowed down to less than 4 per cent annually. It has slowed down further since 1990. As population growth was fairly slow in the post-war period, GDP per capita rose only slightly less than GDP. Labour productivity rose slightly less than GDP per capita, due to an increase in the participation rate. For the period as a whole there is little difference between the growth of GDP per person employed and GDP per hour worked. However, before 1973 hours worked rose substantially, and GDP per person employed rose faster than GDP per hour worked. After 1973, hours worked were reduced and GDP per hour worked rose faster than GDP per person employed. Capital stock rose even faster than GDP, leading to a rise in the capital-output ratio. Especially in the period 1973–79 the difference between the growth of capital stock and the growth of GDP was large. The amount of capital per person employed rose by almost 7 per cent annually, and continued to rise even in the period 1990–96.

Table 8.3 shows GDP growth rates for the main sectors of the economy. There are huge differences between sectors. For all sectors, the period 1953–73 showed much higher growth than the period after 1973. However, for several sectors the period 1953–63 showed better performance than the period 1963–73. At the sectoral level, there is therefore only mixed evidence of trend acceleration. Surprisingly, the highest growth rate was not that of manufacturing, but for wholesale and retail trade. Within manufacturing the experiences of different branches differ widely, however, and the machinery and equipment branch in particular has experienced extremely high growth rates. Growth was also rapid in electricity, gas and water, and in transport and communication. Growth in agriculture was limited, with the exception of the period 1953–63. The recent slowdown in growth is broadly shared throughout the economy. GDP growth over the 1990–95 period was been negative in agriculture, mining and construction, and was substantially lower than previously in manufacturing, distribution, transport and communication, and finance, insurance and real estate.

Table 8.2 Main Indicators of Japanese Growth Experience, 1953–96 (annual average compound growth rates, in %)

	GDP at market prices	Popu-lation	GDP per capita	GDP per person employed	GDP per hour worked	Fixed non-residential capital stock	Fixed non-residential capital stock per person employed
1953–60	7.90	10.4	6.79	5.99	4.61	4.88	3.02
1960–73	8.83	1.12	7.63	7.43	7.65	12.89	11.44
1973–79	3.35	1.08	2.25	2.64	3.01	7.45	6.71
1979–90	4.33	0.58	3.73	3.08	3.28	7.02	5.73
1990–96	1.85	0.31	1.54	1.22	2.29	4.46	3.81
1953–73	8.51	1.09	7.33	6.92	6.58	10.02	8.42
1973–96	3.42	0.64	2.77	2.48	2.95	6.45	5.48
1953–96	5.76	0.85	4.87	4.52	4.62	8.10	6.84

Source: Pilat (1994), updated with OECD Analytical Database (ADB). See also Table A8.1

Growth accounting studies (Chung, 1970; Kosobud, 1974; Denison and Chung, 1976) have focused primarily on the explanation of the growth rate of GDP as a whole. Only a few studies (Nishimizu and Hulten, 1978; Uno, 1987) have concentrated on the explanation of sectoral growth rates. Most growth accounting studies cover the period before 1973 (Kanamori, 1972; Ohkawa and Rosovsky, 1973; Denison and Chung, 1976; Nishimizu and Hulten, 1978). The period after 1973 is covered by far fewer studies. The results of these studies show considerable differences, since there is little agreement in the growth accounting literature on the concepts and procedures used.

Table 8.4 shows growth accounting estimates (in the Denison tradition) for the whole economy, for the period 1953–90, by sub-period.[2] In all four sub-periods, more than 50 per cent of growth can be explained by increased factor inputs. In the period 1953–60, business labour input is the most important contributor to growth, with positive contributions from

Table 8.3 Annual Compound Growth Rates of GDP by Sector in Japan, 1953–95 (in %)

	Agriculture, forestry and fisheries	Mining	Manufacturing	Electricity, gas and water	Construction	Commerce	Transport, storage and communication	Finance, insurance and real estate	Services and government	Total economy
1953–63	4.68	8.77	12.67	12.19	9.83	13.48	13.00	7.3	5.12	8.26
1963–73	0.43	6.34	12.53	9.96	9.88	14.78	8.95	9.16	6.69	9.00
1973–79	−1.46	0.24	3.35	4.42	1.71	5.78	1.45	5.13	3.71	3.35
1979–90	0.76	0.34	5.91	4.25	2.62	4.52	4.27	4.93	3.74	4.30
1990–95	−2.58	−5.89	0.96	2.84	−0.19	1.06	1.47	1.33	2.59	1.40
1953–73	2.53	7.55	12.60	11.07	9.86	14.13	10.95	8.44	5.90	8.63
1973–95	−0.61	−1.14	4.06	3.97	1.73	4.06	2.86	4.16	3.47	3.38
1953–95	0.87	2.91	8.05	7.29	5.52	8.74	6.64	6.18	4.62	5.85

Source: Pilat (1994), updated with OECD (1997), National Accounts – Detailed Tables, 1983–95, Paris.

all four components. In this period, hours worked increased considerably, giving a strong positive effect on growth. Capital input, especially fixed capital, is also an important contributor in this sub-period. Improved resource allocation, i.e. a movement from sectors with low productivity levels to sectors with high productivity levels, contributed 0.45 percentage points to the overall growth rate. Also, the contribution of the residual – a measure of total factor productivity – is very high, with a share of almost 40 per cent in total growth.

Table 8.4 Growth of GDP and Contribution of Sources of Growth Whole Economy, 1953–90, by Sub-Period

	1953–60	1960–73	1973–79	1979–90	1953–73	1973–90	1953–90
GDP growth	8.25	8.83	3.35	4.30	8.63	3.97	6.46
Factor inputs	4.46	5.87	2.85	2.87	5.37	2.86	4.21
Business labour input	2.44	1.29	0.36	0.98	1.69	0.76	1.26
Employment	1.17	0.80	0.24	0.64	0.93	0.50	0.73
Hours worked	0.65	–0.19	–0.23	–0.11	0.10	–0.15	–0.01
Age-sex composition	0.29	0.39	–0.03	0.26	0.35	0.15	0.26
Education	0.30	0.28	0.37	0.19	0.29	0.25	0.27
Non-business labour input	0.24	0.26	0.23	0.09	0.25	0.14	0.20
Non-residential capital input	1.57	3.64	1.66	1.39	2.91	1.49	2.25
Fixed non-residential private capital	1.40	3.15	1.48	1.32	2.54	1.38	2.00
Residential capital input	0.16	0.59	0.57	0.39	0.44	0.45	0.44
Land	0.00	0.00	0.00	0.00	0.00	0.00	0.00
Output per unit of input	3.63	2.80	0.49	1.39	3.09	1.07	2.16
Improved resource allocation							
From agricultural inputs	0.45	0.44	0.16	0.28	0.44	0.24	0.35
From non-agricultural	0.37	0.39	0.16	0.16	0.38	0.16	0.28
Self employed	0.08	0.05	0.00	0.13	0.06	0.08	0.07
Residual	3.16	2.34	0.33	0.98	2.63	0.74	1.78

Source: Pilat (1994).

The second sub-period, 1960–73, is dominated by an increase in capital input, especially fixed non-residential capital stock. As indicated in Table 8.2, fixed capital stock grew with an annual growth rate of almost 12.5 per cent in this period. Residential capital also turned into a significant source of growth. The contribution of hours worked turned negative in this period, implying that average hours worked fell, and has ever since provided a negative contribution to growth. The other labour components all provided positive contributions to growth, with important effects from education and shifts in the age-sex composition of the labour force. The effect of improved resource allocation diminished somewhat, reflecting the reduced share of agriculture in the Japanese economy. This dropped from 18 per cent to 6 per cent of total GDP from 1953 to 1973, and from

35.5 to 10.8 per cent of total hours worked in the same period. The contribution of the residual dropped as well, although it remained an important source of growth.

After 1973, growth slowed down. In the period 1973–79, almost 90 per cent of growth was derived from increased factor inputs. The growth of total capital input explained almost 70 per cent of total growth. The effect of improved education was considerable and the contribution of improved resource allocation remained significant. The contribution of the residual was relatively small. In the period 1979–90, almost 70 per cent of growth can be explained from increased factor inputs. However, the share of the residual picked up considerably and contributed almost 30 per cent to growth. For the whole period 1953–90, the most important single factor in growth is fixed non-residential capital, explaining 32 per cent of growth. The next factor in importance is the residual, contributing about 28 per cent to growth. Important other factors are the growth of business employment (11.7 per cent), residential capital stock (7 per cent) and improved resource allocation (5.6 per cent).

A Further Look at Growth Causality

Growth accounting can identify proximate causes of growth, but gives little information about ultimate growth causality. Ultimate causes of growth are the basic underlying forces of the economy, such as culture, demography, history, institutions, international circumstances and economic policy. Ultimate causes influence proximate causes (the production process), but quite often the link between the two is indirect and difficult to quantify. For instance, Japan's Confucian culture is often seen as important because of the great stress given in Japan to schooling and training. Confucianism thus influences education and therefore the capacity to absorb new technology. But how important is this effect and would Japan's development have been different if it did not have a Confucian culture? Such questions are difficult to answer and impossible to quantify. The purpose of this section is threefold. First, to provide some further analysis of the most important proximate causes discussed in the previous section. Second, to discuss some factors in Japanese economic growth which were not covered explicitly in the growth accounting analysis. And third, to provide some links with ultimate causality. The discussion is not exhaustive, but covers four influences that have contributed to the Japanese success, namely capital formation, education and training, technological change and the organisation of production.

The role of capital

The first element of Japan's success was undoubtedly the rapid growth of the capital stock. Increases in the stock of capital explain more than 40 per cent of the GDP growth rate over the period 1953–90. Investment was the primary means to expand the productive capacity of the economy, and also an important way through which new technology was embodied in the production process. Investment in capital depends on a number of factors, including the availability of sufficient finance at low cost; a mechanism to channel financial means from savers to investors; and sufficient demand to absorb production generated by capacity expansion.

Capital investment in Japan has been financed mainly from domestic savings. Foreign savings played a very limited role. The shares of several sources of savings in total gross national expenditure (GNE) for the period 1955–95 are shown in Figure 8.4. Households are the main source of net savings, with a share of approximately 10 per cent of GNE for most of the period. Private savings include those of enterprises, financial institutions and other private entities besides households. Before 1975 the share of these other three groups was quite substantial, but in recent years their contribution to total savings has declined. The gap between private and net savings consists of government savings. For the whole period this has been important and positive. The final source derives from depreciation provisions, which amounted to 10 to 15 per cent of GNE.

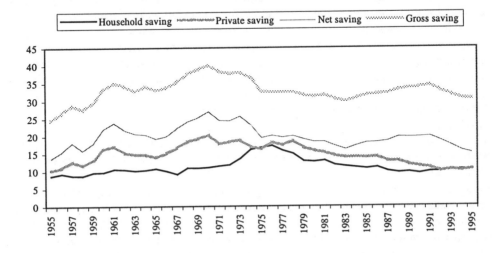

Source: Pilat (1994), updated with OECD National Accounts.

Figure 8.4 Savings in the Japanese Economy, 1955–95

Most studies have focused on net savings, thereby excluding depreciation as a source of capital. If net savings are the focus of analysis, it is obvious that households play the central role. A great number of surveys have been made by economists trying to explain the high rate of household savings in Japan. A survey by Shinohara (1970) pointed to the following factors. First, due to limited life insurance and social benefits, the Japanese have to save more for old age, sickness and schooling, than in most other industrialised countries. Second, households need to save considerably if they are to buy a house, prices being extremely high. A large part is saved out of bonuses, which constitute a large share of annual salaries. Furthermore, Japan has a relatively large number of self-employed persons, who save a greater share of their income than employees. Finally, the Japanese traditional consumption pattern has adjusted only slowly to high and fast-growing incomes. Except for bonuses, most of these causal influences have been criticised in empirical surveys (Sato, 1987; Ito, 1992), and several are also at odds with Japan's pre-war experience, when household savings were lower, but several of the factors mentioned by Shinohara had larger effects.

Horioka (1990) also surveys a large number of factors, and distinguishes between cultural, demographic and socio-economic, institutional, economic and government-induced factors. He finds that the age structure of the population, the bonus system and the high rate of growth explain a substantial part of the large gap between Japanese saving rates and those of other industrialised countries. Horioka (1991) suggested that the lifetime savings theory was the most important explanatory factor for Japan's high savings rate. In his view the small share of elderly and the low dependency ratio in the early post-war period have contributed substantially to the high savings rate. This argument is based on Modigliani's (1986) theory of the life-cycle hypothesis, which suggests that persons will save during their working life and dis-save when they retire. Changes in the composition of the population and an increasing share of elderly persons may therefore lead to a drop in saving rates. With the current ageing of the Japanese population, Horioka (1991) expects a decline in the savings rate.

Japanese companies depend more on external finance than their Western counterparts (Kosai and Ogino, 1984; Meerschwam, 1991). A large share of total finance is borrowed from banks or financial institutions. This is often called 'indirect financing'. Partly this was the result of the close ties between enterprises and financial institutions, especially within *keiretsu* groups. The Japanese government tried to keep interest rates low during the high growth period. This resulted in excess demand for funds and resulted in a policy of credit rationing by financial institutions (Wallich and Wallich, 1976; Sato, 1987). Financial institutions were forced to borrow from the central bank, which gave government some control over financial flows (Meerschwam, 1991). In addition, some funds, especially postal savings, were directly managed by government and could be targeted directly to certain industries. Uno (1987) has argued that government support for targeted industries also functioned as an indicator to financial institutions that these industries were seen as high growth areas by the government, thereby leveraging additional private funds as well. The preference for indirect financing is sometimes also related to the preference of Japanese enterprises for long-term market share and profits instead of short-term profit maximisation (Meerschwam, 1991). Direct financing at the stock exchange may be much more dependent on short-term considerations. Over the past decade, in particular during the 'bubble economy' period, the stock market has been a more important means for Japanese enterprises to acquire capital (Ito, 1992).

A related issue which has been discussed extensively in the literature is the cost of capital. Particularly in the United States it was argued that a major reason for the success of Japanese companies was the low cost of capital in Japan compared to that in the United States (Hatsopoulos, Krugman and Summers, 1988). Work by Ando and Auerbach (1988, 1990) also found considerable differences between the cost of capital in Japan and the United States. They related this to the much higher savings rate in Japan, compared with the United States, and imperfections in the flow of capital between the two countries. Frankel (1991) also concluded that there were differences in the cost of capital between Japan and the United States, especially during the 1970s and 1980s. He suggested that the main reason for this was the greater reliance of Japanese enterprises on indirect financing, which as a result of the low-interest policy followed by the Japanese government provided a cheap source of funds.

The collapse of the bubble economy in the early 1990s highlighted some of the problems of the Japanese financial system and its impact on economic performance. The fall in the stock market and the growing indebtedness of many of the major banks – due to many bad loans – severely affected the ability of the financial system to fund private investment and has lowered confidence in the Japanese economy. The Japanese system of corporate governance – with close ties between firms and main banks – has also come under threat (OECD, 1996). Increasing competition in the financial market has lowered banking profits, while a slowdown in economic activity has lowered the demand for investment funds by private enterprises. These developments have reduced the ability of banks to act as a monitor of private companies. Furthermore, the severe problems faced by many banks at this moment has made them reluctant to take risks.

The financial difficulties have highlighted another problem of the Japanese economy, namely the low and deteriorating productivity of investment in capital stock. The availability of cheap capital during the period of the bubble economy has contributed to overinvestment, leading to a high capital/output ratio and rapidly falling capital productivity (Figure 8.5). Estimates by Maddison (1995) suggest that Japan had the lowest level of capital productivity in 1992 among six industrialised economies (France, Germany, Japan, the Netherlands, the United Kingdom and the United States).

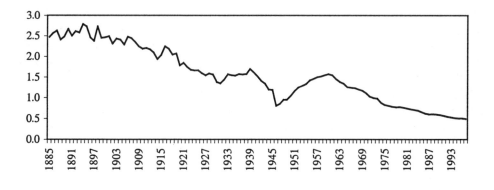

Source: Table A8.1.

Figure 8.5   GDP Per Unit of Fixed Capital Stock, 1885–1996

The role of technology

Investment in physical capital is the principal means by which new technology enters the production process. Technology acquisition and absorption from abroad is seen as the best way for follower countries to achieve rapid growth and catch-up with leader countries (Abramovitz, 1989; Nelson and Wright, 1992). It was realised early in Japan that technology was the primary means through which Japan would be able to catch-up with the West (Francks, 1992). Even during the late Tokugawa period Dutch technology acquired through contacts at the port of Deshima was an important source of learning. During the Meiji period and before the Second World War the search for Western technology intensified.

The Second World War increased the technological gap between Japan and the lead country, the United States. After the war, Japanese companies were extremely active in the search for new technology abroad, especially in the early post-war period (Peck and Tamura, 1976; Urata, 1990). Technology imports were highly regulated by MITI, and priority was given to targeted industries. Especially during the early post-war period, government controls were strictly enforced and only certain technologies were allowed. The government controls were not due to balance of payments problems, but seemed mainly influenced by a desire to achieve an industrial structure which offered high growth prospects in the long term (Peck and Tamura, 1976). MITI used two criteria in the evaluation of technology contracts (Urata, 1990), namely whether it would have a favourable impact on the balance of payments, and whether the proposed arrangement would contribute to the evolution of targeted industries. In the later years of the high growth period, technology imports were gradually liberalised, as were several other government policies during that time.

Japan's trade balance in technology has recently turned positive (OECD, 1997), but has been negative for a long time. However, a large part of Japanese payments for technology reflect old licences. On the other hand, a considerable share of receipts for technology also reflect old technology, exported to developing countries (Taylor and Yamamura, 1990). In new technology contracts Japan turned to a positive balance as early as 1972 (Okimoto and Saxonhouse, 1987).

As countries catch-up in technology with the leader, indigenous technology becomes important as well. Japan's performance in this respect has been somewhat different from that of other countries. First, its research has had an almost totally civilian character. In contrast to US research and development outlays, very little is spent on defence (Okimoto and Saxonhouse, 1987; Taylor and Yamamura, 1990). In general, defence research has a different character from civilian research. It is often aimed at high performance, but usually at high cost. Commercial applications are only secondary. In addition, defence research has often led to great waste and misdirected spending. Furthermore, the best engineers and researchers were not diverted to defence research, as was the case in the United States, but could work on civilian applications (Okimoto and Saxonhouse, 1987).

Partly related to this first aspect is that in the Japanese system of research and development government's role is much smaller than in most other industrialised countries. Most research is done in private companies, and government procurement, for instance for defence purposes, plays a limited role. Government's role is less direct. Especially in the early high growth period government played an important role in technology imports. Furthermore, government's long-term projections play an important role in the evolution of the Japanese economy and help to focus research on high growth areas.

In general, Japanese research is much more aimed at commercial application than in the United States. A large share of total research is aimed at modification and adaptation of technology (Mansfield, 1988), often with small improvements in terms of quality, cost and manufacturability. In Japanese companies, research and development are integrated within the production process, and there is considerable interaction between researchers and producers. Much more than in the United States, product designs have been aimed at simplicity and manufacturability (Dertouzos, Lester and Solow, 1989).

Japan has shown itself to be skilful in making technological progress in areas where the technology is predictable and incremental (Okimoto and Saxonhouse, 1987), for instance semiconductors. Japan has made much less progress in areas with technological uncertainty, such as software. These issues relate to the fact that Japanese research has been focused mainly on applied research and much less on basic research. As Japan has reached the edge of world technology in several areas, this has become a matter of great concern for Japanese companies.

A number of problems are involved here. First, the Japanese educational system, and especially its universities, has not produced sufficient innovative and creative researchers. It has been aimed to provide large numbers of highly educated people with general skills. Second, the mobility of researchers between enterprises is still limited, due to the lifetime employment system, thus leading to a slow spread of research findings between companies. A third problem is the reluctance of large companies to spend much on basic research, which has much less predictable results. There is some government participation in such long-term projects, but the lack of venture capital, which can be used to fund risky research and development projects, is also seen as a major obstacle (Taylor and Yamamura, 1990). Fourth, direct government involvement in the development of certain technologies has been problematic, reflecting the great uncertainties inherent in some fields (OECD, 1996). For instance, efforts to develop high-definition television based on analogue technology were bypassed by a more advanced digital system, while the results of a decade-long project on fifth-generation computers were also viewed as disappointing.

In 1953, Japan spent less than 0.5 per cent of GDP on research and development. Since 1953 the trend has been steadily upwards, with only a short interruption after the first oil crisis and the following recession. In 1995, Japan spent 2.8 per cent of GDP on research and development (OECD, 1997), which is more than Germany and the United States (2.3 and 2.6 per cent respectively in 1995). Most of R&D expenditure – 72 per cent in 1995 – is currently financed by private enterprises, but in the 1950s and 1960s the government played a more significant role. A major reason why Japanese companies were able to spend so much on research is their long-term perspective, which is partly related to their financial structure (see above). As they are much less focused on short-term profits than their US counterparts, they can focus on long-term efforts (Dertouzos, Lester and Solow, 1989).

Over the period 1991–95, the Japanese government significantly increased its contribution to research spending. Government-financed R&D rose by over 6 per cent on an annual basis over this period (OECD, 1997). In a time that most other OECD governments – and particularly the United States – were cutting back on R&D expenditures, the Japanese efforts reflect a desire to depend more on national sources for innovation and technological change. A greater emphasis on basic R&D may particularly be required at this time, as Japan remains quite weak in this area (OECD, 1996). Recent survey evidence indicates that several major centres of basic research, including universities and public laboratories, are limited by a lack of funds. A greater emphasis on basic research may particularly be required to support developments in certain areas, such as information technology and biotechnology.

However, technological change also continues to depend on diffusion across countries. Several large countries, including the United States, Germany, France and the United Kingdom, have increased their reliance on imported technology over the past two decades. Calculations on the basis of input–output tables (OECD, 1996a) show that the United States increased its reliance on imported technology in total acquired technology from less than 4 per cent in the early 1970s to over 13 per cent in 1993. France increased its reliance on imported technology from just over 20 per cent in the early 1970s to more than 35 per cent in 1993. Even more impressive changes were made in the United Kingdom, where the share of imported technology rose from less than 15 per cent in the early 1970s to over 50 per cent in 1993. During this period, Japan's reliance on imported technology remained relatively stable, suggesting that Japan has not been able to further enhance its reliance on technology from abroad.

Education and training
In the analysis of proximate causes of growth in the post-war period, increased education takes only a modest position. This is partly due to the fact that a number of educational improvements were already made before and during the war (Lincoln, 1988). The increase in the average standard of education of the workforce may underestimate the increased training of Japanese workers in their companies. In 1984, 82.5 per cent of all Japanese enterprises provided training to their employees, up from 76.7 per cent in 1976 (Ishikawa, 1991). From 1973 to 1983, the annual average increase of expenses for education and training in firms was almost 12 per cent (Ishikawa, 1991). However, such figures likely underestimate the importance of education and training. Education is closely related to the absorption capacity of an economy for new technology. Japan has a very high number of highly trained engineers per member of the population (Ergas, 1987), additional to the high average level of schooling of the Japanese workforce. Tests of international student achievement levels show Japanese students ahead of students in other industrialised countries in mathematics and most science subjects (IAEEA, 1991). The educational system is aimed at providing a large share of the population with high levels of general education. Once students leave the educational system and enter a company, more specific skills are learned through in-company training. In addition, new entrants to a firm are required to switch positions regularly during their first years, to acquire thorough knowledge of all aspects of the company.

The position of Japanese workers in their firm is quite different from that in US enterprises (Dertouzos, Lester and Solow, 1989). Workers are not trained for one task, but for a large number of tasks in a system of flexible production. By rotating workers on the shop-floor, they are taught all aspects of the production process. They are stimulated to think about improvements in the production process in the system of quality circles. Even for higher positions in the firm it is often required to spend some time in the production process, to gain understanding of all aspects of the firm. Within large companies the practice of lifetime employment has caused little mobility of workers between firms. Companies are therefore quite willing to spend on training of their employees, since most employees will stay a long time with the same company. This is also in contrast with the United States, where high job mobility has led to great reluctance of employers to invest in the training of workers.

Over the past decade, however, the Japanese system of education and training has also shown some problems. The current economic recession and growing problems in the labour markets have led many observers to question the ability of the Japanese educational framework to adjust to changing circumstances (OECD, 1996). Current developments suggest that the system of long-term employment is likely to become less widespread, which may imply that on-the-job training within firms may become less important. The rapid pace of structural change in the contemporary Japanese economy, combined with low growth, is likely to increase the number of redundant workers, many middle-aged, that will require training, both within and outside firms. The Japanese education system will also need to give greater emphasis on developing individual creativity and the ability to adapt to a changing working environment.

The organisation of production

Business economists tend to stress quite different causal influences than macro economists as crucial to the Japanese success. Their focus has been much more on the way production is organised and the differences from practices in American or European factories. The Japanese approach has been termed 'lean production' (Womack, Jones and Roos, 1990). It appears to be the Japanese answer to mass scale production, which originated in the United States (Nelson and Wright, 1992). The characteristic of lean production is that it economises on scarce resources. It uses fewer machines, workers, materials, parts, and less space and time to manufacture a product than does the mass scale production system. In addition, the system is able to manufacture a much wider range of products than the mass scale production system. It would go too far to discuss all the details of lean production, but some elements are discussed briefly.

Lean production was mainly a response to the shortages the Japanese economy had in several areas just after the Second World War and to some Japanese peculiarities, such as lifetime employment, which had developed already before the war. The main example of lean production is car production by Toyota. Looking at the huge American car factories at that time, Toyota found that it did not have the means to invest so much in machinery and new technology as did its US counterparts. It also did not have the scale to produce in the same way as the US car manufacturers. It had to be flexible with its scarce resources. Machinery had to be used for a large number of different tasks and had to be changed quickly from one task to another. The number of parts was reduced so as to reduce the complexity of the car and improve its manufacturability.

Lean production is not concerned only with the organisation of production on the shop floor. It also relates to product design, which is done in close co-operation between designers and the production department. Design periods in Japanese car companies are much shorter than in their US or European counterparts, and designs are prepared to be easy to manufacture. The lean production system even extends to relations with suppliers and consumers, which are based on long-term contracts. Suppliers are often closely integrated with the main producer, sometimes in a *keiretsu*. Other elements related to lean production are just-in-time delivery, quality circles, continuous product improvements and the Japanese system of subcontracting. However, the system's main applications lie in the manufacturing sector, and within manufacturing not all industries are equally affected by lean production. The importance of lean production in explaining the success of the Japanese economy as a whole may therefore be smaller than some studies have suggested.

Some conclusions on ultimate causality

The factors and issues discussed above provide some further background to the growth accounting results and may help to provide additional insights into the development of the Japanese economy. However, they do not provide the answer to the important question: Why has Japan succeeded where a lot of other countries have so far failed? Some factors made Japan special among other low-income countries in the middle of the nineteenth century. It was a unified country, with uninterrupted rule from 1603 onwards. It had a homogeneous culture and a single language. It had experienced gradual growth of per capita income for several centuries (Hanley, 1986; Yasuba, 1987), and was at somewhat higher levels of income than surrounding Asian countries (Maddison, 1994). This slow growth had led to a considerable savings surplus, which could be used for productive purposes. It had a significant social capability for development, expressed in high rates of literacy, a reasonably developed system of infrastructure, large and well-developed urban and commercial centres and a strong central government.

Japan had not been colonised, unlike several other Asian countries, and was therefore relatively free to pursue its own economic strategy of development. During its process of economic development it had several historical opportunities, which were highly beneficial to economic growth. The First World War offered an opportunity to increase market share in textiles in Asia, at the expense of the United Kingdom. The Korean War gave a much needed demand impetus to the manufacturing sector, and the move to free trade and the expanding world economy after the Second World War were of great importance as well. The free world system and the good relations with the United States allowed easy access to technology and gave a large catch-up potential. Combined with high savings rates, a large labour surplus and buoyant demand at home and abroad, the potential for growth was extremely high.

The Japanese success may also have been influenced by the government. Monetary and fiscal policy has helped to provide corporations with a stable supply of low-cost funding, by allowing them ample access to bank credit and by restricting the growth of government indebtedness (OECD, 1994). The government has also played a role in directing investment to high growth industries, and was an important actor in gaining access to modern technology, apart from its more classical roles in the development of education and infrastructure. However, Japan was not a planned economy and competition within the economy has been quite fierce in some markets. Decisions by private enterprises have mostly determined the success of the economy.

In recent years, structural problems and a low ability to adjust to changing circumstances have contributed to the slowdown in growth. The Japanese economy remains heavily regulated in many areas, although recent measures – such as the relaxation of the Large-Scale Retail Store Law – have helped to improve performance. Estimates by the Economic Planning Agency (EPA, 1996) and at OECD (Blondal and Pilat, 1997) suggest that considerable scope for deregulation remains, however. The turmoil in financial markets has also highlighted other structural problems of the Japanese economy, including the low productivity of investment in capital stock.

A COMPARATIVE PERSPECTIVE OF JAPANESE PERFORMANCE

Japan is still considered to be among the main challengers to the US leadership position in the world economy (van Ark and Pilat, 1993). How far has Japan really progressed in the post-war period and how does its performance vary between different sectors? To answer these questions it is necessary to compare Japan's achievement with that of other countries. Such a comparison can be made in a number of ways. The usual method is the comparison of growth rates. Another is the comparison of levels of achievement, such as income and productivity levels. The latter method is a useful complement to the comparison of growth rates, since countries may be able to achieve high growth rates if they start from a lower level. At lower levels of productivity there is a much larger stock of internationally available technology to be adopted, than if the country is already close to the levels achieved by the world productivity leader, i.e. the United States. This section presents some productivity comparisons for Japan, in a direct comparison with the United States.

Comparative Productivity in 1975 and 1985

The productivity comparisons presented in this section are based on sector-specific conversion factors. Exchange rates cannot be used to compare real output and productivity, as they are strongly affected by monetary factors, and generally do not reflect real price differences between countries. The sector-specific purchasing power parities used in the present exercise are based on detailed comparisons of prices and real output for each sector (Pilat, 1994). However, in many sectors – and particularly in certain services – measurement problems are huge and real price and output levels are difficult to derive.

Detailed benchmark comparisons were made for 1975 and 1985. In 1975, Japan had very low productivity levels in agriculture and mining. Japanese agriculture is characterised by a very small scale, and therefore has only limited benefits from economies of scale. In addition, a considerable share of farmers consists of part-timers who, because of high price levels, can still attain a reasonable income from inefficient holdings. The high degree of protection has led to excessive input use, which would be irrational at lower price levels. Furthermore, a general effect of protection has been that farmers are not open to competition from the world market and therefore do not rationalise production (van der Meer and Yamada, 1990). In mining, productivity was also relatively low, partly because the output structure of mining is quite different between Japan and the United States. In Japan, production consists mainly of coal mining and quarrying of gravel and stone, which are activities where value added per person is quite low. In the United States, oil and gas extraction are much more important. These are much more capital-intensive activities, where labour productivity is much higher.

For manufacturing, only the productivity results for the total sector are shown in Table 8.5. GDP per hour worked was 64 per cent of the US level in 1975. The variation within manufacturing was quite large, however, and more detailed results are discussed below. In electricity, gas and water, construction, and transport and communication Japan was still considerably behind US productivity levels. These are sectors which have long trailed in Japan's process of rapid growth. Productivity in utilities was only 27 per cent of the US level, in construction it was only 40 per cent, in transport 34 per cent, and in communication 38 per cent.

Japanese distribution is also a laggard in terms of productivity. Establishments are, on average, smaller than in the United States, partly due to regulations which have constrained their growth (Pilat, 1997). Distribution is usually regarded as a safety net, in which the least qualified workers can make a living. Productivity in wholesale trade was only 46 per cent of the US level, and in retail trade the level was only 37 per cent of that in the United States. Ito and Maruyama (1991) do not agree and argue that productivity in Japanese distribution is not very different from the United States. They measured productivity as sales per worker, converted with OECD PPPs for GDP. The main problem with their estimates is that they use sales as their indicator of output. An important aspect of the Japanese distribution system is that it has several layers. Products may move from the manufacturer through quite a few wholesalers before reaching the retailer. It is even possible that the product may move between retailers. Use of sales as the output concept for the distribution sector leads to double counting and therefore to an overstatement of relative output and productivity levels in this sector. This is especially the case for wholesale trade, where the difference between sales-based productivity measures and value added or GDP-based productivity measures is quite large in relative terms.

Table 8.5 Comparative Levels of Productivity and Prices, 1975 and 1985 (Japan as a percentage of the United States)

	1975			1985		
	GDP per person employed	GDP per hour worked	Relative price level	GDP per person employed	GDP per hour worked	Relative price level
Agriculture, forestry and fisheries	9	14	216	8	10	288
Mining	31	29	106	28	26	112
Manufacturing	70	64	78	84	74	75
Electricity, gas and water	29	27	201	53	51	172
Construction	49	40	110	51	45	126
Transport and communication						
Transport and storage	40	34	117	49	41	125
Communication	44	38	101	52	44	97
Wholesale and retail trade						
Wholesale trade	53	46	106	56	50	108
Retail trade	49	37	112	67	47	106
Finance, insurance and real estate						
Finance	153	138	83	106	96	99
Insurance	106	96	71	129	116	73
Services and Government						
Education	197	154	52	254	188	46
Health	154	122	48	182	138	47
Other services	67	54	99	74	58	98
Government	126	99	87	169	126	73
Total economy	53	46	106	65	53	101

Source: Pilat (1994).

In finance, insurance and real estate, spreads in productivity are also considerable. Japanese banks have grown to be among the largest in the world, handling enormous assets. In this respect the output of the financial sector is very large indeed. On the other hand, transactions in Japanese banks are often slow and there is a high level of inefficiency involved in simple withdrawals. Productivity in finance was estimated to be above the US level, at 138 per cent. In insurance, productivity was also very high, at 96 per cent of the United States. In real estate, productivity was much lower. Prices of dwellings in Japan are extremely high and the quality of housing is often much less than in the United States. The high price level partly reflects the extreme land scarcity in Japan, a situation which is aggravated by a strict set of regulations on the sale of land and regulations on the construction of multi-storey buildings.

In other services and government, productivity varies considerably as well, although output measurement in these sectors is faced with great uncertainties. Price levels in education and health were quite low, leading to very high productivity levels, of 150 per cent of the US level in education and 120 per cent of the United States in health. Other services consist of many activities, with an average productivity level of 54 per cent of the US level. In government, Japanese productivity was roughly the same as that in the United States. By 1985, Japan had made considerable progress in most industries, including some slow-growth industries. Large productivity gains were made in manufacturing, utilities, retail trade, real estate and non-market services. However, compared to 1975, Japan's productivity level dropped in agriculture, mining and financial services.

Manufacturing Productivity

Manufacturing is one of the sectors where Japan made most progress compared to the United States in the post-war period. It is also the sector where most of the Japanese challenge to US leadership has originated. The discussion of manufacturing productivity levels based on Table 8.5 was concerned mainly with the average productivity level. The results there were based on the national accounts and showed Japan still substantially behind US productivity levels.

However, Japan's performance in manufacturing shows a large variation across manufacturing branches (Pilat, 1997a). In a number of branches (basic metal products, machinery and transport equipment, electrical machinery), Japan is now at the same level as the United States or has surpassed US levels. In other branches, and particularly in the primary processing industries (food products, beverages and tobacco, wood and furniture), Japan is far removed from US productivity levels. It is no coincidence that the areas where Japanese productivity performance is relatively weak are also the areas where Japan has little international trade. Most of Japan's exports originate in the highly productive machinery and equipment and electrical machinery branches. Table 8.6 also demonstrates that US productivity leadership in several parts of the manufacturing sector is challenged by other countries, particularly the small but very open economies of the Netherlands and Sweden.

Comparative Productivity in the Post-war Period

Figure 8.6 shows the comparative performance of Japan and the United States since 1953. The graph consists of three components. The first one shows comparative productivity in agriculture, mining, manufacturing and the total economy. It is clear that Japanese agriculture has made no progress against the United States in the post-war period. Its productivity level has stagnated slightly below 10 per cent of the US level. This low productivity level of Japanese agriculture was a continuation of the situation before the war (see Table 8.1).

Table 8.6 Manufacturing Labour Productivity Levels in Major OECD Economies, 1987 and 1993 (Value Added per Hour Worked, Leader Country = 100)

Sectors	United States	Japan	Germany	France	United Kingdom	Canada	Australia	Netherlands	Sweden
Panel A: 1987									
Food, beverages and tobacco	100.0	32.3	75.3	65.3	46.1	59.6	45.9	95.4	57.3
Textiles, clothing and footwear	67.4	38.1	60.1	61.7	47.4	54.6	42.2	100.0	60.8
Wood products and furniture	69.5	15.6	50.2	52.4	38.1	63.8	32.7	100.0	64.1
Paper products and printing	97.2	47.5	61.2	65.0	64.7	81.4	53.2	62.7	100.0
Chemical products	80.8	52.9	60.1	58.0	59.5	68.0	44.9	100.0	72.4
Non-metallic mineral products	77.0	55.1	67.1	100.0	59.9	75.1	56.4	97.7	75.5
Basic metal products	94.4	100.0	80.3	77.0	74.2	89.3	57.1	80.3	93.3
Metal products	86.3	76.0	76.3	57.3	50.6	70.1	42.3	68.9	100.0
Machinery and equipment	99.0	85.6	73.8	100.0	65.4	64.2	61.1	59.1	66.5
Electrical machinery	100.0	82.7	67.6	90.0	51.3	66.4	35.8	93.7	75.6
Transport equipment	96.9	100.0	76.7	84.9	42.1	69.7	39.3	47.0	55.8
Other manufacturing	100.0	39.4	45.3	40.1	52.5	58.3	33.0	47.2	67.0
Total manufacturing	100.0	76.6	79.8	84.2	64.1	71.3	52.0	95.6	91.8
Panel B: 1993									
Food, beverages and tobacco	100.0	35.6	88.7	87.0	41.7	64.3	51.1	96.6	72.8
Textiles, clothing and footwear	78.3	41.9	72.1	67.1	51.5	46.3	32.3	100.0	66.5
Wood products and furniture	56.0	17.6	55.7	55.3	28.1	52.6	27.1	100.0	71.9
Paper products and printing	85.0	49.7	59.0	64.3	76.4	67.6	53.7	64.5	100.0
Chemical products	66.9	52.6	55.4	56.9	79.7	52.6	39.8	100.0	89.4
Non-metallic mineral products	81.8	62.9	79.5	99.4	70.6	78.4	77.4	100.0	81.0
Basic metal products	76.8	78.3	72.9	63.3	61.4	87.9	56.8	70.4	100.0
Metal products	68.9	67.6	64.6	46.4	42.5	54.8	35.9	54.0	100.0
Machinery and equipment	100.0	67.4	49.2	67.3	47.9	55.5	46.4	34.6	45.2
Electrical machinery	80.3	89.0	49.9	78.9	48.2	51.9	28.0	82.2	100.0
Transport equipment	88.4	100.0	68.0	85.0	47.8	71.9	45.5	41.8	49.5
Other manufacturing	100.0	41.4	43.1	31.4	43.5	33.5	22.1	27.0	47.4
Total manufacturing	100.0	76.6	79.8	84.2	64.1	71.3	52.0	95.6	91.8

Notes: a. The productivity level of the leader country in each industry is indicated in bold. b. The coefficient of variation is the standard deviation divided by the mean, expressed as a percentage. It is calculated over the 35 industries for which estimates are available (see Pilat, 1996).

Source: Pilat (1996; 1997).

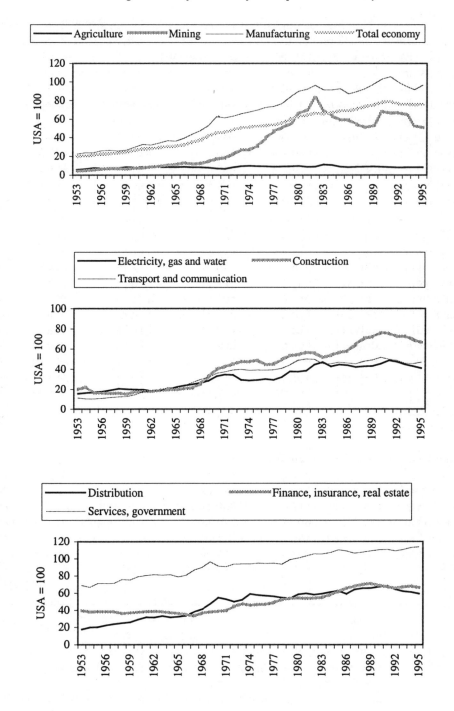

Source: Table A8.1.

Figure 8.6 Comparative Productivity in Main Sectors, 1953–95

Progress in mining has been much faster. Fast productivity growth in Japan as well as poor performance in US mining from the early 1970s to the early 1980s caused a very fast increase in relative productivity levels. During the 1980s the situation reversed and the Japanese productivity level dropped from some 75 per cent of that in the United States in 1982 to below 50 per cent in the early 1990s.

Much of the dynamism of Japan rests in the productivity growth of its manufacturing sector. Starting from a productivity level (measured as value added per employee) slightly above 20 per cent, Japan reached more than 90 per cent of the US level in 1990. During the 1980s and early 1990s, the productivity level stabilised due to improved productivity growth rates in the United States. The series for the economy as a whole show a steady upward trend from 20 per cent of the United States in 1953 to around 70 per cent in 1995. The second panel of Figure 8.6 shows productivity performance in utilities, transport and communication and construction. The construction sector rapidly improved productivity performance over the 1970–90 period, but has fallen back since. In utilities and transport and communication, productivity levels have stagnated at low levels.

The final panel of Figure 8.6 shows the service sectors. In finance, insurance and real estate post-war productivity levels were relatively high in 1953. In both countries productivity increases in this sector were small, but after 1973 productivity growth in this sector in the United States slowed down, whereas growth rates in Japan remained fairly high until the early 1990s. Services and government were at a substantially higher productivity level than other sectors, but still succeeded in making progress against the United States. The fast rate of catch-up in distribution, not usually regarded as a dynamic sector, is surprising. The slowdown in the increase in productivity levels in this sector in the late 1970s appears to correspond to the introduction of the Large-Scale Retail Store Law in Japan in 1979, which restricted the expansion of stores and the emergence of new and large outlets.

Productivity Levels in the Long Run

Detailed series for GDP per person for 1885 to 1995 are shown in Table 8.7. Only a few of these series could be backdated as far as 1885, most are available only from 1910 onwards. A number of interesting results emerge. First, the productivity of Japan's agricultural sector has been stagnant compared to the United States since 1885. The agricultural sector has been important in Japanese economic growth as a supplier of labour, as a market for industrial goods and as an early exporter. There has been considerable productivity growth, but not enough to catch-up with the United States. Land productivity is extremely high, but small land-holdings have been a constraint on fast productivity growth. Especially in the post-war period Japanese agriculture has fallen behind other sectors of the economy. To sustain agricultural incomes, the sector has been heavily protected, leading to extremely high price levels. In its turn, excessive protection has led to a lack of rationalisation in agriculture, expressed in excessive input use, inefficient part-time farming and slow productivity change (Van der Meer and Yamada, 1990).

The most spectacular development of productivity has been in manufacturing. Japan started from productivity levels of less than 10 per cent of the United States, which correspond to those in today's developing countries (Van Ark, 1991). Nowadays, manufacturing has reached productivity levels close to those in the United States, and in some manufacturing branches Japan has taken over the lead (Pilat, 1997a). Manufacturing has clearly been the leading sector in Japan's process of economic development. Most exports are and have been manufacturing products, changing from textile products in the early stages of development to machinery, electronics and transport equipment in the present situation.

Table 8.7 Comparative Labour Productivity Levels by Sector, 1885–95 (GDP per person engaged, Japan as a percentage of the United States)

	Agriculture, forestry and fisheries	Mining	Manufac-turing	Electricity, gas and water	Constru-ction	Transport and communi-cations	Other services and govern-ment	Whole economy
1885	8.4	7.4	7.9	n.a.	n.a.	n.a.	n.a.	12.9
1900	9.4	15.9	14.8	n.a.	n.a.	n.a.	n.a.	15.7
1910	10.2	19.6	11.5	22.3	10.2	36.7	38.9	16.4
1920	12.9	13.3	13.3	31.5	12.0	34.2	51.1	19.0
1929	10.9	16.9	15.9	62.5	16.4	47.6	41.8	19.4
1939	10.9	15.2	24.8	49.3	46.0	32.1	55.6	27.0
1953	5.8	4.5	22.5	15.5	19.8	11.4	42.6	19.8
1965	8.3	11.2	36.3	22.1	19.7	21.3	48.0	30.7
1975	9.4	31.2	69.7	29.2	49.0	39.2	67.9	52.5
1985	9.0	59.1	92.8	44.5	56.6	46.9	83.7	69.0
1995	8.2	50.8	96.6	40.9	66.1	46.9	89.5	75.9

Source: 1988–1939 based on 1939 benchmark comparisons; 1953–1995 based on 1975 benchmark comparison. See Pilat (1994).

The construction sector has been only slightly less dynamic than manufacturing, with extremely fast productivity growth. In transport and communication, and in electricity, gas and water there is still a substantial productivity gap between both countries. Rail transport is of high quality, but roads are relatively few and are heavily congested. The productivity of utility services is also still behind that in the United States. Sewerage connections are still not universal and heating facilities are generally poor.

In other services and government, where output measurement is most difficult, the available evidence suggests only a small remaining productivity gap. Within services, the spread in productivity levels is substantial. Productivity in distribution is still rather far behind US levels, partly due to the small size of retail outlets, but in services like education and health quality is quite high and price levels are below those in the United States.

On average, GDP per person engaged in Japan has risen from only 13 per cent of the United States in 1885 to almost 73 per cent in 1995, an almost six-fold increase in just over 100 years. Before the war, productivity had already doubled, but most of the catch-up with US levels took place in the post-war period. The war caused a sharp drop in productivity levels. Levels in 1953 were still behind those in 1939.

CONCLUDING REMARKS

The Japanese economy has made enormous progress over the past century. It has transformed from a low-income economy driven by the agricultural sector into one of the major economic centres in the world. Many factors have contributed to this success, including the historical background of the country, that had resulted in a strong social, institutional and technological capability for rapid economic growth. The historical background and the sustained pre-war economic growth ensured a strong capacity for Japan to catch-up with the US economy after the war. Catch-up may 'explain' a considerable share of Japan's rapid growth during the 1953–73 period, and the reduced growth rate after 1973 may partly be linked to the exhaustion of this catch-up potential. The technological and income gap with the United States has narrowed considerably and Japan is now at the edge of the production frontier in many areas of the economy.

However, productivity comparisons indicate that Japan still has very weak performance in many parts of the economy. Although its weak performance at the present is partly linked to the financial crisis and macro-economic instability over the past years, structural factors may also play an important role. The Japanese economy remains heavily regulated in several parts of the economy, its labour market appears not sufficiently able to adjust to changing circumstances, such as greater mobility and demands for individuality, and the technological base of the Japanese economy is lacking in some important areas, particularly those related to basic research. Addressing these concerns, while improving the performance of some of the trailing sectors of the economy, such as agriculture, will be a major challenge over the coming years.

NOTES

1. The industry-specific purchasing power parities are close or somewhat higher than the exchange rate in tradable sectors of the economy and substantially below the exchange rate for the service sectors. This pattern is often found for comparisons between developed and developing economies (Kravis, Heston and Summers, 1982). Comparisons of productivity levels are elaborated further in Section 5 of the chapter.
2. Detail on the methodology of the growth accounting exercise is available in Pilat (1994).

APPENDIX

Table A.8.1 Basic Time Series for Japan, 1885–1997

	Gross domestic product at market prices (1985 billion Yen)	Population (1 000 persons)	GDP per capita (1985 Yen)	Persons employed (1 000 persons)
1885	6 043	38 427	157 255	22 614
1886	6 558	38 622	169 791	22 656
1887	6 834	38 866	175 832	22 676
1888	6 536	39 251	166 510	22 857
1889	6 883	39 688	173 417	23 064
1890	7 507	40 077	187 321	23 251
1891	7 149	40 380	177 053	23 399
1892	7 630	40 684	187 535	23 549
1893	7 653	41 001	186 659	23 674
1894	8 560	41 350	207 024	23 801
1895	8 678	41 775	207 735	23 902
1896	8 206	42 196	194 466	24 042
1897	8 377	42 643	196 440	24 195
1898	9 973	43 145	231 152	24 360
1899	9 234	43 626	211 658	24 465
1900	9 623	44 103	218 194	24 574
1901	9 964	44 662	223 089	24 691
1902	9 454	45 255	208 894	24 806
1903	10 119	45 841	220 741	24 960
1904	10 193	46 378	219 776	25 092
1905	10 028	46 829	214 140	25 154
1906	11 339	47 227	240 087	25 259
1907	11 700	47 691	245 320	25 405
1908	11 778	48 260	244 054	25 491
1909	11 756	48 869	240 563	25 532
1910	11 941	49 518	241 150	25 602
1911	12 591	50 215	250 743	25 731
1912	13 048	50 941	256 136	25 913
1913	13 258	51 672	256 583	26 093
1914	12 855	52 396	245 339	26 287
1915	14 052	53 124	264 520	26 470
1916	16 226	53 815	301 518	26 737
1917	16 776	54 437	308 165	26 947
1918	16 950	54 886	308 818	27 112
1919	18 675	55 253	337 986	27 135
1920	17 509	55 818	313 672	27 261
1921	19 441	56 490	344 144	27 397

Table A.8.1 (continued)

	Gross domestic product at market prices (1985 billion Yen)	Population (1 000 persons)	GDP per capita (1985 Yen)	Persons employed (1 000 persons)
1922	19 379	57 209	338 749	27 616
1923	19 403	57 937	334 898	27 831
1924	19 945	58 686	339 851	28 076
1925	20 761	59 522	348 790	28 301
1926	20 951	60 490	346 348	28 565
1927	21 254	61 430	345 980	28 820
1928	22 985	62 361	368 576	29 062
1929	23 710	63 244	374 896	29 312
1930	21 983	64 203	342 404	29 620
1931	22 172	65 205	340 031	29 952
1932	24 029	66 189	363 029	30 215
1933	26 389	67 182	392 801	30 671
1934	26 438	68 090	388 278	31 084
1935	27 160	69 238	392 268	31 645
1936	29 142	70 171	415 302	32 059
1937	30 534	71 278	428 385	32 156
1938	32 572	71 879	453 146	32 290
1939	37 706	72 364	521 057	32 652
1940	38 811	72 967	531 894	32 942
1941	39 338	74 005	531 552	32 742
1942	39 172	75 029	522 091	32 542
1943	39 671	76 005	521 947	32 343
1944	37 842	77 178	490 318	32 143
1945	29 150	76 224	382 430	32 695
1946	20 459	77 199	265 016	33 248
1947	22 514	78 119	288 195	33 800
1948	26 192	80 155	326 764	34 510
1949	27 223	81 971	332 103	35 220
1950	30 555	83 563	365 651	35 930
1951	34 675	84 974	408 069	36 210
1952	38 306	86 293	443 912	37 280
1953	40 476	87 463	462 778	39 130
1954	42 963	88 752	484 075	39 630
1955	46 886	89 790	522 173	40 900
1956	49 840	90 727	549 338	41 710
1957	53 573	91 513	585 409	42 81
1958	56 961	92 349	616 805	42 980
1959	61 845	93 237	663 304	43 350
1960	68 927	94 053	732 857	44 360
1961	76 043	94 890	801 384	44 970

Table A.8.1 (continued)

	Gross domestic product at market prices (1985 billion Yen)	Population (1 000 persons)	GDP per capita (1985 Yen)	Persons employed (1 000 persons)
1962	81 160	95 797	847 208	45 560
1963	87 495	96 765	904 205	45 930
1964	95 854	97 793	980 167	46 540
1965	100 888	98 883	1 020 277	47 290
1966	110 856	99 790	1 110 894	48 270
1967	122 736	100 850	1 217 010	49 200
1968	135 988	102 050	1 332 566	49 970
1969	152 136	103 231	1 473 742	50 350
1970	167 937	104 334	1 609 607	50 860
1971	175 904	105 677	1 664 539	51 150
1972	191 278	107 179	1 784 657	51 190
1973	207 126	108 660	1 906 184	52 480
1974	203 684	110 160	1 848 986	52 260
1975	208 790	111 520	1 872 224	52 120
1976	217 751	112 770	1 930 926	52 610
1977	225 742	113 880	1 982 280	53 300
1978	235 591	114 920	2 050 040	53 980
1979	252 446	115 880	2 178 516	54 700
1980	264 964	116 800	2 268 525	55 230
1981	275 148	117 650	2 338 695	55 700
1982	283 372	118 450	2 392 330	56 220
1983	291 377	119 260	2 443 210	57 330
1984	304 584	120 020	2 537 778	57 660
1985	320 258	120 750	2 652 239	58 070
1986	325 480	121 490	2 679 064	58 530
1987	341 259	122 090	2 795 141	59 110
1988	363 122	122 610	2 961 600	60 110
1989	381 660	123 120	3 099 903	61 280
1990	402 456	123 540	3 257 698	62 490
1991	417 740	123 920	3 371 042	63 683
1992	422 009	124 320	3 394 542	64 360
1993	423 324	124 670	3 395 560	64 498
1994	426 053	124 960	3 409 514	64 526
1995	432 320	125 570	3 442 862	64 567
1996	449 280	125 864	3 569 567	64 859
1997	453 309	n.a.	n.a.	65 576

Table A.8.1 (continued)

	GDP per person employed (1985 Yen)	Participation rate	Gross fixed non-residential capital stock (1985 billion Yen)	Capital/output ratio (based on constant prices)
1885	267 216	58.8	2 444	0.40
1886	289 443	58.7	2 555	0.39
1887	301 370	58.3	2 597	0.38
1888	285 933	58.2	2 712	0.42
1889	298 414	58.1	2 770	0.40
1890	322 881	58.0	2 817	0.38
1891	305 539	57.9	2 851	0.40
1892	323 992	57.9	2 922	0.38
1893	323 271	57.7	2 967	0.39
1894	359 666	57.6	3 075	0.36
1895	363 066	57.2	3 179	0.37
1896	341 306	57.0	3 334	0.41
1897	346 218	56.7	3 524	0.42
1898	409 410	56.5	3 658	0.37
1899	377 421	56.1	3 769	0.41
1900	391 597	55.7	3 905	0.41
1901	403 539	55.3	3 998	0.40
1902	381 096	54.8	4 087	0.43
1903	405 417	54.4	4 158	0.41
1904	406 209	54.1	4 234	0.42
1905	398 664	53.7	4 374	0.44
1906	448 884	53.5	4 569	0.40
1907	460 514	53.3	4 799	0.41
1908	462 049	52.8	5 013	0.43
1909	460 442	52.2	5 242	0.45
1910	466 413	51.7	5 457	0.46
1911	489 334	51.2	5 715	0.45
1912	503 526	50.9	6 018	0.46
1913	508 106	50.5	6 331	0.48
1914	489 014	50.2	6 644	0.52
1915	530 876	49.8	6 914	0.49
1916	606 874	49.7	7 229	0.45
1917	622 527	49.5	7 678	0.46
1918	625 173	49.4	8 286	0.49
1919	688 209	49.1	9 017	0.48
1920	642 254	48.8	9 823	0.56
1921	709 592	48.5	10 519	0.54
1922	701 745	48.3	11 112	0.57
1923	697 185	48.0	11 564	0.60
1924	710 378	47.8	11 988	0.60

Table A.8.1 (continued)

	GDP per person employed (1985 Yen)	Participation rate	Gross fixed non-residential capital stock (1985 billion Yen)	Capital/output ratio (based on constant prices)
1925	733 565	47.5	12 467	0.60
1926	733 449	47.2	13 094	0.63
1927	737 453	46.9	13 771	0.65
1928	790 893	46.6	14 453	0.63
1929	808 878	46.3	15 170	0.64
1930	742 190	46.1	15 887	0.72
1931	740 245	45.9	16 400	0.74
1932	795 262	45.6	16 638	0.69
1933	860 403	45.7	16 794	0.64
1934	850 520	45.7	17 091	0.65
1935	858 268	45.7	17 670	0.65
1936	909 017	45.7	18 514	0.64
1937	949 568	45.1	19 509	0.64
1938	1 008 733	44.9	20 649	0.63
1939	1 154 766	45.1	22 217	0.59
1940	1 178 168	45.1	24 095	0.62
1941	1 201 442	44.2	25 973	0.66
1942	1 203 725	43.4	27 733	0.71
1943	1 226 572	42.6	29 554	0.74
1944	1 177 295	41.6	31 606	0.84
1945	891 577	42.9	24 563	0.84
1946	615 351	43.1	25 310	1.24
1947	666 081	43.3	26 336	1.17
1948	758 962	43.1	27 492	1.05
1949	772 936	43.0	28 502	1.05
1950	850 400	43.0	29 185	0.96
1951	957 616	42.6	29 783	0.86
1952	1 027 535	43.2	30 564	0.80
1953	1 034 397	44.7	31 390	0.78
1954	1 084 094	44.7	32 200	0.75
1955	1 146 355	45.6	32 983	0.70
1956	1 194 912	46.0	34 080	0.68
1957	1 251 402	46.8	35 688	0.67
1958	1 325 298	46.5	37 483	0.66
1959	1 426 632	46.5	39 939	0.65
1960	1 553 819	47.2	43 817	0.64
1961	1 690 978	47.4	49 250	0.65
1962	1 781 387	47.6	55 819	0.69
1963	1 904 973	47.5	63 078	0.72
1964	2 059 594	47.6	71 377	0.74

Table A.8.1 (continued)

	GDP per person employed (1985 Yen)	Participation rate	Gross fixed non-residential capital stock (1985 billion Yen)	Capital/output ratio (based on constant prices)
1965	2 133 392	47.8	80 278	0.80
1966	2 296 584	48.4	88 989	0.80
1967	2 494 624	48.8	99 690	0.81
1968	2 721 401	49.0	113 581	0.84
1969	3 021 567	48.8	129 883	0.85
1970	3 301 941	48.7	151 001	0.90
1971	3 438 974	48.4	171 068	0.97
1972	3 736 624	47.8	192 252	1.01
1973	3 946 761	48.3	211 916	1.02
1974	3 897 518	47.4	231 776	1.14
1975	4 005 955	46.7	251 549	1.20
1976	4 138 956	46.7	270 229	1.24
1977	4 235 310	46.8	288 591	1.28
1978	4 364 405	47.0	305 445	1.30
1979	4 615 108	47.2	326 106	1.29
1980	4 797 460	47.3	347 800	1.31
1981	4 939 811	47.3	370 419	1.35
1982	5 040 404	47.5	392 087	1.38
1983	5 082 456	48.1	414 396	1.42
1984	5 282 416	48.0	439 910	1.44
1985	5 515 030	48.1	493 132	1.54
1986	5 560 900	48.2	524 196	1.61
1987	5 773 284	48.4	565 580	1.66
1988	6 040 955	49.0	598 621	1.65
1989	6 228 133	49.8	640 929	1.68
1990	6 440 326	50.6	687 562	1.71
1991	6 559 708	51.4	738 205	1.77
1992	6 557 035	51.8	775 111	1.84
1993	6 563 415	51.7	805 404	1.90
1994	6 602 779	51.6	832 897	1.95
1995	6 695 704	51.4	861 511	1.99
1996	6 926 997	51.5	893 179	1.99
1997	6 912 782	n.a.	923 664	2.04

Source: Pilat (1994) updated with OECD Analytical Database (ADB).

Table A8.2 Basic Time Series for United States and Relative Position Japan/United States, 1885–1997

	Gross domestic product at prices (1982 million US$)	Population (1 000 persons)	GDP per capita (1982 US$)	Per sons employed (1 000 persons)
1885	141.7	56 879	2 491	19 216
1886	146.0	58 164	2 510	19 839
1887	150.4	59 448	2 530	20 481
1888	154.9	60 732	2 551	21 145
1889	159.6	62 016	2 573	21 829
1890	171.4	63 302	2 707	22 543
1891	178.9	64 612	2 769	23 112
1892	196.1	65 922	2 975	23 801
1893	186.7	67 231	2 777	23 726
1894	181.4	68 541	2 647	23 254
1895	203.1	69 851	2 907	24 443
1896	199.0	71 161	2 797	24 568
1897	218.0	72 471	3 008	25 282
1898	222.7	73 781	3 018	25 646
1899	242.7	75 091	3 232	27 121
1900	249.3	76 391	3 263	27 559
1901	277.6	77 888	3 564	28 700
1902	280.2	79 469	3 526	29 934
1903	293.8	80 946	3 630	30 821
1904	290.2	82 485	3 518	30 714
1905	311.6	84 147	3 703	32 122
1906	347.5	85 770	4 052	33 391
1907	353.1	87 339	4 043	34 176
1908	324.0	89 055	3 639	33 406
1909	363.6	90 845	4 002	35 122
1910	367.5	92 767	3 961	36 054
1911	379.4	94 234	4 026	36 625
1912	397.1	95 703	4 150	37 703
1913	412.8	97 606	4 229	38 263
1914	381.2	99 505	3 831	37 838
1915	391.6	100 941	3 880	38 034
1916	445.9	102 364	4 356	40 515
1917	434.9	103 817	4 189	41 933
1918	474.1	104 958	4 517	44 424
1919	477.9	105 473	4 531	42 723
1920	473.4	106 881	4 430	41 899
1921	462.6	108 964	4 245	39 742
1922	488.3	110 055	4 437	41 784
1923	552.6	112 387	4 917	44 363
1924	569.6	114 558	4 972	43 734

Table A8.2   (continued)

	Gross domestic product at prices (1982 million US$)	Population (1 000 persons)	GDP per capita (1982 US$)	Per sons employed (1 000 persons)
1925	583.0	116 284	5 013	44 943
1926	621.1	117 857	5 270	46 238
1927	627.1	119 502	5 247	46 344
1928	634.2	120 971	5 243	46 831
1929	672.7	122 245	5 503	48 072
1930	612.6	123 668	4 953	45 956
1931	576.6	124 633	4 627	43 130
1932	492.7	125 436	3 928	39 849
1933	478.8	126 180	3 795	41 363
1934	522.0	126 978	4 111	44 783
1935	590.6	127 859	4 619	46 276
1936	652.7	128 681	5 072	49 221
1937	706.1	129 464	5 454	50 252
1938	667.2	130 476	5 113	48 718
1939	718.1	131 539	5 459	49 958
1940	782.8	132 637	5 902	51 645
1941	897.8	133 922	6 704	55 935
1942	1001.7	135 386	7 399	60 224
1943	1102.8	137 272	8 034	65 510
1944	1189.4	138 937	8 561	66 612
1945	1172.6	140 474	8 347	65 027
1946	1072.1	141 940	7 553	59 670
1947	1061.6	144 688	7 337	60 212
1948	1102.5	147 203	7 490	61 611
1949	1103.4	149 770	7 367	60 516
1950	1197.4	152 271	7 864	62 506
1951	1320.3	154 878	8 525	66 253
1952	1371.7	157 553	8 706	67 495
1953	1427.4	160 184	8 911	68 564
1954	1407.8	163 026	8 635	66 940
1955	1485.5	165 931	8 953	68 471
1956	1515.0	168 903	8 970	70 078
1957	1539.7	171 984	8 953	70 378
1958	1529.7	174 882	8 747	68 700
1959	1619.1	177 830	9 105	70 277
1960	1654.1	180 671	9 155	71 265
1961	1696.6	183 691	9 236	71 326
1962	1785.6	186 538	9 572	72 824
1963	1858.5	189 242	9 821	73 574
1964	1957.1	191 889	10 199	75 162
1965	2070.6	194 303	10 657	77 424

Table A8.2 (continued)

	Gross domestic product at prices (1982 million US$)	Population (1 000 persons)	GDP per capita (1982 US$)	Per sons employed (1 000 persons)
1966	2192.5	196 560	11 154	81 004
1967	2255.0	198 712	11 348	82 861
1968	2347.9	200 706	11 698	84 962
1969	2406.2	202 677	11 872	87 312
1970	2399.1	205 052	11 700	87 120
1971	2464.1	207 661	11 866	86 980
1972	2584.9	209 896	12 315	89 111
1973	2711.8	211 909	12 797	92 824
1974	2693.5	213 854	12 595	94 414
1975	2665.7	215 973	12 343	92 878
1976	2793.7	218 035	12 813	95 228
1977	2921.2	220 239	13 264	98 515
1978	3073.0	222 585	13 806	103 259
1979	3136.6	225 055	13 937	106 515
1980	3131.7	227 726	13 752	107 084
1981	3193.6	229 966	13 887	107 982
1982	3114.8	232 188	13 415	106 781
1983	3231.2	234 307	13 790	107 907
1984	3457.5	236 348	14 629	112 714
1985	3581.9	238 466	15 021	115 343
1986	3687.4	240 651	15 323	117 329
1987	3820.0	242 804	15 733	121 853
1988	3970.4	245 021	16 204	125 252
1989	4070.8	247 342	16 458	128 130
1990	4104.1	249 911	16 422	129 829
1991	4066.0	252 643	16 094	128 645
1992	4176.4	255 407	16 352	129 492
1993	4273.4	258 120	16 556	131 428
1994	4421.4	260 682	16 961	134 499
1995	4509.2	263 168	17 134	136 503
1996	4633.8	265 557	17 449	138 476
1997	4808.0	n.a.	n.a.	141 589

Table A8.2 (continued)

	GDP per person employed (1982 US$)	Participation rate	GDP per capita	GDP per person employed
1885	7 374	33.8	18.8	10.8
1886	7 358	34.1	20.1	11.7
1887	7 342	34.5	20.3	12.0
1888	7 326	34.8	19.8	11.8
1889	7 310	35.2	19.8	12.0
1890	7 602	35.6	21.5	13.2
1891	7 742	35.8	19.9	12.3
1892	8 239	36.1	19.6	12.2
1893	7 869	35.3	20.9	12.8
1894	7 802	33.9	24.3	14.4
1895	8 307	35.0	22.2	13.6
1896	8 101	34.5	21.6	13.1
1897	8 622	34.9	20.3	12.5
1898	8 683	34.8	23.8	14.7
1899	8 949	36.1	20.3	13.1
1900	9 045	36.1	20.8	13.5
1901	9 673	36.8	19.5	13.0
1902	9 360	37.7	18.4	12.6
1903	9 534	38.1	18.9	13.2
1904	9 447	37.2	19.4	13.4
1905	9 700	38.2	18.0	12.8
1906	10 408	38.9	18.4	13.4
1907	10 332	39.1	18.9	13.9
1908	9 700	37.5	20.8	14.8
1909	10 351	38.7	18.7	13.8
1910	10 192	38.9	18.9	14.2
1911	10 358	38.9	19.4	14.7
1912	10 534	39.4	19.2	14.9
1913	10 789	39.2	18.9	14.6
1914	10 075	38.0	19.9	15.1
1915	10 296	37.7	21.2	16.0
1916	11 006	39.6	21.5	17.1
1917	10 371	40.4	22.9	18.7
1918	10 672	42.3	21.3	18.2
1919	11 186	40.5	23.2	19.1
1920	11 300	39.2	22.0	17.7
1921	11 640	36.5	25.2	18.9
1922	11 686	38.0	23.7	18.7
1923	12 456	39.5	21.2	17.4
1924	13 024	38.2	21.2	16.9
1925	12 971	38.6	21.6	17.6

Table A8.2 *(continued)*

	GDP per person employed (1982 US$)	Participation rate	GDP per capita	GDP per person employed
1926	13 432	39.2	20.4	17.0
1927	13 530	38.8	20.5	16.9
1928	13 543	38.7	21.9	18.2
1929	13 994	39.3	21.2	18.0
1930	13 329	37.2	21.6	17.4
1931	13 370	34.6	23.6	17.8
1932	12 364	31.8	29.3	20.4
1933	11 576	32.8	32.5	23.4
1934	11 657	35.3	30.0	23.2
1935	12 763	36.2	28.3	22.4
1936	13 261	38.3	26.4	22.1
1937	14 052	38.8	26.1	22.4
1938	13 695	37.3	29.1	24.2
1939	14 374	38.0	31.3	26.3
1940	15 158	38.9	29.8	25.7
1941	16 051	41.8	25.6	24.1
1942	16 633	44.5	21.3	21.9
1943	16 834	47.7	18.3	20.5
1944	17 856	47.9	16.1	18.6
1945	18 032	46.3	8.4	9.1
1946	17 968	42.0	11.3	11.0
1947	17 631	41.6	12.6	12.2
1948	17 895	41.9	13.9	13.5
1949	18 233	40.4	14.7	13.8
1950	19 157	41.0	14.9	14.2
1951	19 928	42.8	15.2	15.3
1952	20 323	42.8	16.4	16.2
1953	20 819	42.8	16.9	16.2
1954	21 031	41.1	18.2	16.7
1955	21 695	41.3	18.9	17.1
1956	21 619	41.5	20.0	18.1
1957	21 878	40.9	21.3	18.7
1958	22 266	39.3	22.9	19.3
1959	23 039	39.5	23.8	20.2
1960	23 211	39.4	26.6	22.2
1961	23 787	38.8	29.2	23.9
1962	24 519	39.0	30.4	25.0
1963	25 260	38.9	31.8	26.0
1964	26 038	39.2	33.6	27.7
1965	26 744	39.8	33.6	28.0
1966	27 067	41.2	35.5	30.2

Table A8.2 (continued)

	GDP per person employed (1982 US$)	Participation rate	GDP per capita	GDP per person employed
1967	27 214	41.7	38.6	33.0
1968	27 635	42.3	41.7	36.1
1969	27 559	43.1	45.5	40.2
1970	27 538	42.5	50.5	44.0
1971	28 330	41.9	51.0	44.1
1972	29 008	42.5	52.4	46.6
1973	29 214	43.8	53.8	48.8
1974	28 529	44.1	53.2	49.6
1975	28 701	43.0	55.1	50.7
1976	29 337	43.7	54.9	51.4
1977	29 652	44.7	55.4	52.9
1978	29 760	46.4	55.5	54.8
1979	29 447	47.3	57.4	57.5
1980	29 245	47.0	60.2	59.9
1981	29 575	47.0	61.3	60.8
1982	29 170	46.0	64.9	62.9
1983	29 944	46.1	64.5	61.8
1984	30 675	47.7	63.4	62.9
1985	31 054	48.4	64.2	64.5
1986	31 428	48.8	64.1	64.9
1987	31 349	50.2	64.7	67.1
1988	31 699	51.1	65.7	68.5
1989	31 771	51.8	67.3	70.0
1990	31 611	52.0	70.9	72.8
1991	31 606	50.9	74.9	74.2
1992	32 252	50.7	74.2	72.7
1993	32 515	50.9	73.3	72.2
1994	32 873	51.6	71.9	71.8
1995	33 034	51.9	71.8	72.5
1996	33 463	52.1	73.1	74.0
1997	33 957	n.a.	n.a.	n.a.

REFERENCES

Abramovitz, M. (1989), *Thinking About Growth*, Cambridge: Cambridge University Press.

Allen, G. (1981), A Short Economic History of Modern Japan, London: Macmillan.

Ando, A. and A.J. Auerbach (1988), 'The Cost of Capital in the United States and Japan: A Comparison', *Journal of the Japanese and International Economies*, **2**, 134–58.

Ando, A. and A.J. Auerbach (1990), 'The Cost of Capital in Japan: Recent Evidence and Further Results', *Journal of the Japanese and International Economies*, **4**, 323–50.

Ark, B. van and D. Pilat (1993), 'Productivity Levels in Germany, Japan and the United States: Differences and Causes', *Brookings Papers on Economic Activity (Microeconomics)*, (2), 1–69.

Baily, M.N. and H. Gersbach (1995), 'Efficiency in Manufacturing and the Need for Global Competition', *Brookings Papers on Economic Activity (Microeconomics)*, pp. 307–58.

Blondal, S. and D. Pilat (1997), 'The Economic Benefits of Regulatory Reform', *OECD Economic Studies*, **I** (28), forthcoming.

Boserup, E. (1981), *Population and Technology*, Oxford: Oxford University Press.

Broadberry, S.N. (1992), 'Manufacturing and the Convergence Hypothesis: What the Long Run Data Show', *CEPR Discussion Paper No. 708*, London.

Chenery, H., S. Robinson and M. Syrquin (1986), *Industrialization and Growth – A Comparative Study*, Washington: Oxford University Press.

Chung, W.K. (1970), *A Study of Economic Growth in Postwar Japan for the Period of 1952–1967*, Ph.D. Thesis, New York: New School for Social Research.

Denison, E.F. and W.K. Chung (1976), *How Japan's Economy Grew so Fast*, Washington, DC: The Brookings Institution.

Dertouzos, M.L., R.K. Lester and R. Solow (1989), *Made in America – Regaining the Productive Edge*, New York: HarperCollins.

Dore, R.P. (1987), *Taking Japan Seriously – A Confucian Perspective on Leading Economic Issues*, London: Athlone Press.

Economic Planning Agency (EPA) (1996), *Provisional Estimates of the Economic Effect of Recent Deregulations*, September, Tokyo.

Ergas, H. (1987), 'Does Technology Policy Matter', in B.R. Guile and H. Brooks (eds), *Technology and Global Industry*, Washington, DC: National Academy Press, pp. 191–245.

Feldstein, M. and C. Horioka (1980), 'Domestic Saving and International Capital Flows', *Economic Journal*, **90**, 314–29.

Francks, P. (1992), *Japanese Economic Development – Theory and Practice*, London: Routledge.

Frankel, J.A. (1991), 'Japanese Finance in the 1980s: A Survey', in P. Krugman (ed.), *Trade with Japan – Has the Door Opened Wider?*, Chicago: University of Chicago Press, pp. 225–70.

Friedman, D. (1988), *The Misunderstood Miracle: Industrial Development and Political Change in Japan*, Ithaca: Cornell University Press.

Hagen, E.E. (1962), *On the Theory of Social Change – How Economic Growth Begins*, Homewood: Dorsey Press.

Hanley, S.B. (1986), 'A High Standard of Living in Nineteenth Century Japan: Fact or Fantasy', *Journal of Economic History*, **46**, March, 183–92.

Hanley, S.B. and K. Yamamura (1977), *Economic and Demographic Change in Preindustrial Japan, 1600–1868*, Princeton: Princeton University Press.

Hatsopoulos, G., P.R. Krugman and L.H. Summers (1988), 'US Competitiveness: Beyond the Trade Deficit', *Science*, 15 July, 299–307.

Hayashi, F. (1986), 'Why is Japan's Saving Rate so Apparently High', *NBER Macroeconomics Annual 1986*, Cambridge: MIT Press, 147–234.

Hayashi, F. (1989), 'Japan's Saving Rate: New Date and Reflections', *NBER Working Paper No. 3205*, Cambridge.

Hofstede, G. (1984), *Culture's Consequences – International Differences in Work-Related Values*, Newbury Park: Sage Publications.

Hofstede, G. and M.H. Bond (1990), 'Confucius en Economische Groei', *Economisch Statistische Berichten*, (3744), February, 128–36.

Horioka, C.Y. (1990), 'Why is Japan's Household Saving Rate so High? A Literature Survey', *Journal of the Japanese and International Economies*, **4** (1), 49–92.

Horioka, C.Y. (1991), 'The Determinants of Japan's Saving Rate: The Impact of the Age Structure of the Population and Other Factors', *Economic Studies Quarterly*, **42** (3), 237–53, September.

Inoguchi, T. and D.I. Okimoto (eds) (1988), *The Political Economy of Japan – Vol. 2: The Changing International Context*, Stanford: Stanford University Press.

International Association for the Evaluation of Educational Achievement (IAEEA) (1991), *Science Achievement in 24 Countries*, Pergamon Press.

Ishikawa, T. (1991), 'Vocational Training', *Japanese Industrial Relations Series No. 7*, Tokyo: The Japan Institute of Labour.

Ito, T. (1992), *The Japanese Economy*, Cambridge: MIT Press.

Ito, T. and M. Maruyama (1991), 'Is the Japanese Distribution System Really Inefficient', in P. Krugman (ed.), *Trade with Japan – Has the Door Opened Wider?*, Chicago: University of Chicago Press, 149–73.

Johnson, C. (1982), *MITI and the Japanese Miracle*, Stanford: Stanford University Press.

Jorgenson, D.W. (1988), 'Productivity and Economic Growth in Japan and the United States', *American Economic Review*, **78**, May, 217–22.

Kanamori, H. (1972), 'What Accounts for Japan's High Rate of Economic Growth', *Review of Income and Wealth*, **18**, June, 155–71.

Kosai, Y. (1986), *The Era of High-Speed Growth – Notes on the Postwar Japanese Economy*, Tokyo: Tokyo University Press.

Kosai, Y. and Y. Ogino (1984), *The Contemporary Japanese Economy*, London: Macmillan.

Kosobud, R. (1974), 'Measured Productivity Growth in Japan, 1952–1968', *Japanese Economic Studies*, **2**, Spring, 80–118.

Lincoln, E.J. (1988), *Japan – Facing Economic Maturity*, Washington, DC: The Brookings Institution.

Lynn, L.H. (1989), Book Review of 'The Misunderstood Miracle: Industrial Development and Political Change in Japan', *Journal of Japanese Studies*, **15**, Summer, 490–94.

Maddison, A. (1969), *Economic Growth in Japan and the USSR*, New York: Norton.

Maddison, A. (1987), 'Growth and Slowdown in Advanced Capitalist Economies: Techniques of Quantitative Assessment', *Journal of Economic Literature*, **25**, 648–708.

Maddison, A (1991), *Dynamic Forces in Capitalist Development*, London: Oxford University Press.

Maddison, A (1994), 'Explaining the Economic Performance of Nations, 1820–1989', in W.J. Baumol, R.R. Nelson and E.N. Wolff (eds), *International Convergence of Productivity*, New York: Oxford University Press, forthcoming.

Maddison, A. (1995), *Monitoring the World Economy, 1820–1992*, Paris: OECD.

Mansfield, E. (1988), 'Industrial R&D in Japan and the United States: A Comparative Study', *American Economic Review*, **78**, May, 223–28.

Meer, C.L.J. van der and S. Yamada (1990), *Japanese Agriculture, A Comparative Economic Analysis*, London: Routledge.

Meerschwam, D.M. (1991), 'The Japanese Financial System and the Cost of Capital', in P. Krugman (ed.), *Trade with Japan – Has the Door Opened Wider?*, Chicago: University of Chicago Press, 191–224.

Modigliani, F. (1986), 'Life Cycle, Individual Thrift, and the Wealth of Nations', *American Economic Review*, **76**, June, 297–313.

Morishima, M. (1982), *Why Has Japan 'Succeeded'? Western Technology and the Japanese Ethos*, Cambridge.

Nakamura, T. (1981), *The Postwar Japanese Economy – Its Development and Structure*, Tokyo: University of Tokyo Press.

Nelson, R. and G. Wright (1992), 'The Rise and Fall of American Technological Leadership', *Journal of Economic Literature*, **XXX**, December, 1931–64.

Nishimizu, M. and C.R. Hulten (1978), 'The Sources of Japanese Economic Growth, 1955–1971', *The Review of Economics and Statistics*, **60**, 351–61.

OECD (1994), *Assessing Structural Reform: Lessons for the Future*, Paris.

OECD (1996), *OECD Economic Surveys – Japan*, Paris, December.

OECD (1996a), *Technology and Industrial Performance*, Paris.

OECD (1997), *Science, Technology and Industry: Scoreboard of Indicators 1997*, Paris.

Ohkawa, K. and H. Rosovsky (1973), *Japanese Economic Growth*, Stanford: Stanford University Press.

Ohkawa, K. and M. Shinohara (eds) (1979), *Patterns of Japanese Economic Development – A Quantitative Appraisal*, New Haven: Yale University Press.

Okimoto, D.I. (1989), *Between MITI and the Market: Japanese Industrial Policy for High Technology*, Stanford: Stanford University Press.

Okimoto, D.I. and G.R. Saxonhouse (1987), 'Technology and the Future of the Economy', in K. Yamamura and Y. Yasuba (eds) (1987), *The Political Economy of Japan – Vol. 1: The Domestic Transformation*, Stanford: Stanford University Press.

Patrick, H. (1977), 'The Future of the Japanese Economy: Output and Labour Productivity', *Journal of Japanese Studies*, **3**, Summer, 219–49.

Patrick, H. and H. Rosovksy (eds) (1976), *Asia's New Giant – How the Japanese Economy Works*, Washington, DC: Brookings Institution.

Peck, M. and S. Tamura (1976), 'Technology', in H. Patrick and H. Rosovsky (eds), *Asia's New Giant – How the Japanese Economy Works*, Washington, DC: Brookings Institution.

Pilat, D. (1993), 'The Sectoral Productivity Performance of Japan and the United States, 1885–1990', *Review of Income and Wealth*, **39** (4), 357–75.

Pilat, D. (1994), *The Economics of Rapid Growth: The Experience of Japan and Korea*, Aldershot: Edward Elgar.

Pilat, D. (1996), 'Labour Productivity Levels in OECD Countries: Estimates for Manufacturing and Selected Service Sectors', *OECD Economics Department Working Paper*, (169), Paris: OECD.

Pilat, D. (1997), 'Regulation and Performance in the Distribution Sector', *OECD Economics Department Working Paper*, (180), Paris: OECD.

Pilat, D. (1997a), 'Competition, Productivity and Efficiency', *OECD Economic Studies*, 1996, **II** (27), 107–146, Paris: OECD.

Rosovsky, H. (1966), 'Japan's Transition to Modern Economic Growth, 1868–1885', in H. Rosovsky (ed.), *Industrialisation in Two Systems: Essays in Honor of Alexander Gerschenkron*, New York: Wiley & Sons, pp. 91–139.

Sato, K. (1987), 'Saving and Investment', in K. Yamamura and Y. Yasuba (eds), *The Political Economy of Japan – Vol. 1: The Domestic Transformation*, Stanford: Stanford University Press.

Saxonhouse, G.R. (1987), 'Comparative Advantage, Structural Adaptation, and Japanese Performance', in T. Inoguchi and D.I. Okimoto, *The Political Economy of Japan – Vol. 2: The Changing International Context*, Stanford: Stanford University Press.

Shinohara, M. (1970), *Structural Changes in Japan's Economic Development*, Tokyo: Kinokuniya.

Taylor, S. and K. Yamamura (1990), in G. Heiduk and K. Yamamura (eds), *Technological Competition and Interdependence*, Seattle: University of Washington Press, pp. 25–63.

Uno, K. (1987), *Japanese Industrial Performance*, North Holland, Amsterdam.

Urata, S. (1990), 'The Impact of Imported Technologies on Japan's Economic Development', in C.H. Lee and I. Yamazawa (eds) (1990), *The Economic Development of Japan and Korea – A Parallel with Lessons*, New York: Praeger, pp. 73–86.

Wallich, H.C. and M.I. Wallich (1976), 'Banking and Finance', in H. Patrick and H. Rosovsky (eds), *Asia's New Giant – How the Japanese Economy Works*, Washington, DC: Brookings Institution.

Womack, J.P., D.T. Jones and D. Roos (1990), *The Machine that Changed the World – The Story of Lean Production*, New York: Harper Perennial.

World Bank (1993), *The East Asian Miracle – Economic Growth and Public Policy*, New York: Oxford University Press.

Yamamura, K. and Y. Yasuba (eds) (1987), *The Political Economy of Japan – Vol. 1: The Domestic Transformation*, Stanford: Stanford University Press.

Yasuba, Y. (1986), 'Standard of Living in Japan Before Industrialization: From What Level Did Japan Begin? A Comment', *Journal of Economic History*, **46**, March, 217–24.

Yasuba, Y. (1987), 'The Tokugawa Legacy: A Survey', *The Economic Studies Quarterly*, **38** (4) 290–322.

9. Realising Growth Potential: South Korea and Taiwan, 1960 to 1998

Bart van Ark and Marcel P. Timmer

1. INTRODUCTION

During the final quarter of the twentieth century South Korea (hereafter referred to as Korea) and Taiwan were among the most rapidly growing economies in the Asian region. Between 1960 and 1998 real GDP increased on average at 7.6 per cent per year in Korea and at 8.1 per cent per year in Taiwan, which was only matched by one other country in the region, namely Singapore at 7.9 per cent per year. Living standards improved rapidly as the average GDP per head of the population in these countries increased almost ten-fold over this period.

In this chapter we look at the determinants of the growth in these countries using a growth accounting framework. Table 9.1 summarises the contributions of labour input, capital input and total factor productivity to real GDP growth in Korea and Taiwan between 1960 and 1996. Between 62 and 64 per cent of GDP growth in both countries was realised through investment in physical capital. In Korea another 32 per cent of GDP growth originated from labour input growth, leaving only a 6 per cent for TFP growth. In Taiwan the labour input contribution to growth was less at 19 per cent, so that TFP growth accounted for 17 per cent of growth. In the remainder of this chapter we discuss these sources of growth in more detail.[1] Among other things, it appears that the contribution of capital input to GDP growth declined substantially over time, in particular since the middle of the 1980s, whereas the TFP contribution accelerated.

We also look at how much of the potential for growth has been realised since the early 1960s. The growth potential is defined as the gap in the labour productivity level between each country and the United States – the productivity leader in the world economy in the twentieth century. Realisation of potential is measured by the rate of catch-up in labour productivity with the level of the productivity leader. In 1960 GDP per hour worked was at 13 and 10 per cent of the US level for Korea and Taiwan respectively. By 1998 both countries had substantially caught up with the United States, as the GDP per hour worked was at 37 and 49 per cent of the US level for Korea and Taiwan respectively. According to Abramovitz (1979) the catch-up potential can be realised through diffusion of technological and organisational knowledge. In this respect one must distinguish between two mechanisms. One is through investment, i.e. reducing the initial gap in capital intensity (i.e., the amount of capital per worker) relative to the productivity leader. Another way of realising potential is by closing the gap in total factor productivity compared to the world technology leader. This gap indicates the gains that are made through diffusion of disembodied technology. In reality these two paths interact strongly (Abramovitz, 1986). We find that despite substantial catch-up, the remaining gaps in labour productivity and capital intensity are still large, leaving sufficient room for future catch-up growth in both countries.

Table 9.1 Growth Accounting Results, Korea and Taiwan, 1960–96

	Korea		Taiwan	
	Average annual compound growth rate	Contribution to real GDP growth (=1.00)	Average annual compound growth rate	Contribution to real GDP growth (=1.00)
Real GDP	8.1	1.00	8.3	1.00
Labour input	4.3	0.32	3.1	0.19
Persons Employed	3.1	0.23	2.8	0.16
Hours Worked	0.3	0.02	–0.4	–0.03
Education	0.9	0.07	0.8	0.05
Capital input	12.2	0.62	10.5	0.64
Capital Stock	11.8	0.60	9.8	0.60
Capital Quality	0.4	0.02	0.7	0.04
Total factor productivity	0.6	0.06	1.4	0.17

Sources: See Tables 9.2 to 9.7.

1.1 Per Capita Income, Labour Productivity and Labour Input

Between 1960 and 1998 GDP per capita in both Korea and Taiwan increased at 7.8 and 8.3 per cent respectively. During the 1960s GDP per capita still grew at somewhat higher rates than Japan, but since 1973 growth in Korea and Taiwan was faster. By 1998 the income gap with the United States had narrowed to 53 per cent for Korea and 43 per cent for Taiwan. Compared to Japan the income gap had reduced to 40 per cent for Korea and 29 per cent for Taiwan in 1998.

Compared to the estimates of per capita income, the bottom panel of Table 9.2 suggests somewhat slower growth in productivity in particular for Korea. In 1998 the productivity gap relative to the USA was larger than for per capita income. The difference between the faster decline in the per capita income gap relative to the labour productivity gap is due to the rapid rise in the ratio of total labour input to population in Korea and Taiwan. However, Table 9.3 shows that the increase in the ratio of persons employed to total population was not faster in Korea and Taiwan than in the United States. The employment/population ratios also remained substantially below the level in the United States. This is partly due to the larger share of children (below 15 years old) in Korea and Taiwan and the lower participation rates of women compared to the United States.

However, lower labour force participation was largely offset by the much higher annual working hours per person employed. The lower panel of Table 9.3 shows that working hours in Korea increased from 2 235 hours in 1960 to 2 497 in 1998. Taiwanese hours fell from 2 772 hours in 1960 and declined to 2 369 hours in 1998.

Table 9.2 GDP Per Capita and Labour Productivity in 1990 US$, 1960–98

	Korea	Taiwan	Japan	USA
GDP per capita (in 1990 US$)				
1960	1 302	1 399	3 879	11 193
1973	2 840	3 669	11 017	16 607
1985	5 777	7 187	15 237	20 050
1998	11 823	14 457	19 841	25 159
GDP per hour worked (in 1990 US$)				
1960	2.13	1.68	3.58	16.78
1973	3.63	3.90	11.15	23.60
1985	6.07	7.45	15.82	27.33
1998	11.77	15.45	20.80	31.69

Source: GDP and population from 1960 to 1990 calculated from Maddison (1995a), updated to 1998 on the basis of Asian Development Bank, *Key Indicators of Developing Asian and Pacific Countries* (various issues). Employment for Taiwan from 1975 also from Asian Development Bank (various issues); before 1975 from DGBAS, *Statistical Yearbook of the Republic of China* (various issues). Employment for Japan, Korea and Taiwan from OECD, *Labour Force Statistics* (various issues). Hours per person see Table 9.3.

Table 9.3 Employment/Population Ratios and Annual Hours Worked Per Person
          Employed, 1960–98

	Korea	Taiwan	Japan	USA
Employment/population ratios				
1960	0.27	0.30	0.47	0.37
1973	0.32	0.35	0.48	0.41
1985	0.37	0.39	0.48	0.45
1998	0.40	0.40	0.52	0.49
Hours worked per person employed				
1960	2 235	2 772	2 318	1 795
1973	2 428	2 728	2 042	1 717
1985	2 593	2 485	2 003	1 612
1998	2 497	2 369	1 849	1 620

Source: Employment and population see Tables 9.2 and 9.3. Average hours for Korea and Taiwan from Crafts (1997). For Korea hours in 1960 were assumed the same as in 1963. For Korea and Taiwan hours in 1998 were assumed the same as in 1995. Hours per person for Japan and United States from Maddison (1991 and 1995a) with geometric interpolation and extrapolation to recent years with OECD, *Employment Outlook* (various issues).

Apart from the substantial rise in labour quantity, the quality of labour improved as well due to the rapid rise in the level of schooling of the working population in Korea and Taiwan. Table 9.4 shows a comparison of the shares of the labour force according to different levels of educational attainment. It appears that the share of secondary and tertiary educated workers increased rapidly between 1963 and 1996. Weighting the attainment shares at relative wages for workers with tertiary or secondary education compared to those with only primary education provides a labour quality index.

Table 9.4 Educational Attainment as Percentage of the Labour Force, 1963–96

	Primary (a)		Secondary (b)		Higher (c)	
	Korea	Taiwan	Korea	Taiwan	Korea	Taiwan
1963	76	80	20	16	4	3
1973	61	69	32	25	7	5
1985	38	43	52	44	10	13
1996	20	24	60	54	20	22

Notes: (a) Primary school or below; (b) Middle and high school; (c) Above high school.

Sources: Korea for 1980–96: EPB, *Economically Active Population Survey*, various issues. 1966, 1970 and 1975 based on EPB, *Report on Population and Housing Census in Korea*, various issues. Years in between intrapolated; Taiwan from DGBAS, *Yearbook of Manpower Survey Statistics*, various issues, and *Social Indicators in Taiwan Area*, various issues.

Figure 9.1 shows the rise in labour quantity, measured as total hours worked and the rise in labour quality for Korea and Taiwan between 1963 and 1996. Korea shows a strikingly faster growth in total hours worked, which is mainly caused by the rise in average working hours (see Table 9.4). In Taiwan average hours declined, as they started from very high levels in 1963 so that the labour quantity grew more slowly. Labour quality in Korea also increased somewhat faster than in Taiwan as the share of workers with only primary education remained relatively high in the latter country.

The rapid growth in labour input has substantially contributed to growth in both countries. For example, between 1960 and 1985 the rise in ratio of total hours worked to total population accounted about 23 per cent of the growth in GDP per capita in Korea and for about 10 per cent in Taiwan. But since 1985 this contribution has significantly declined. Probably most of the growth effects from labour input in Korea and Taiwan are already realised. Even though there is still scope for greater labour participation within the 15–64 age group, projections for population growth suggest a decrease in the share of the working-age population in the total population for these countries. It is also unlikely that working hours per employee can be increased much beyond about 2 500 hours per year. Hence, other sources of growth will need to play a larger role in future growth in these countries.

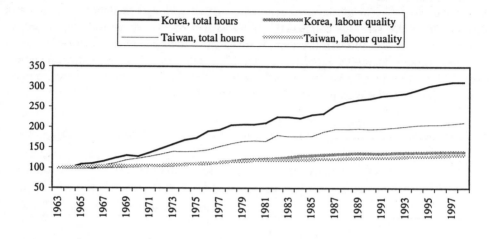

Source: See Tables 9.2 to 9.4.

Figure 9.1   Total Hours Worked and Weighted Average of Educational Attainment of the Labour Force, 1963–96 (1963 = 100)

1.2 Physical Capital Stock and Capital-Labour Ratios

Labour productivity growth can be realised by a greater use of factor inputs other than labour or by greater efficiency in their use. In this section we focus on the growth contribution of machinery, equipment and non-residential structures, using comparable estimates of the capital stock for Korea and Taiwan.

In this section we first present measures of gross non-residential capital stock using the perpetual inventory method (PIM), which was pioneered by Goldsmith (1951).[2] The gross capital stock is measured as the sum of past investments corrected for retirements but with no adjustment for wear and tear during their service life. An important characteristic of our procedure is that we use investment series for Korea and Taiwan going back to the beginning of the twentieth century to obtain a benchmark capital stock figure for the early 1950s (see the Appendix for a brief description of sources). The retirement pattern depends on the average lifetime and the range of years around the average service life during which retirements occur. In the simplest version, assets are discarded in one stroke at the end of their service lives. In this case, the gross capital stock can be measured as:

$$K_{i,T} = \sum_{T-d_i+1}^{T} I_{i,t} \tag{9.1}$$

with $I_{i,t}$ investment at constant prices in asset type i at time t and d_i the service lifetime of asset i.

An important problem in comparing perpetual inventory estimates of the capital stock across countries is that the assumptions concerning the asset lives can differ substantially.

For example, even within the OECD, asset lives for non-residential structures vary between 39 years in the United States, 57 years in Germany and 66 years in the United Kingdom (Maddison, 1995). The (limited) direct and indirect evidence that is available does not support these large differences. As a second-best approach, until internationally comparable asset lives are available, we used standardised asset lives across countries. Maddison (1995) pioneered the standardisation method for France, Germany, Japan, Netherlands, UK and the USA. Hofman (1998) applied the standardisation procedure to six Latin American countries.

Clearly the standardisation procedure may be sensitive to the assumptions made concerning asset lives. Blades (1993) argues that international differences may exist for a variety of reasons, including variations in composition of the capital stock, in tax incentives for new investment, and in maintenance costs. A recalculation of the standardised estimates using alternative assumptions for asset lives, shows that small variations in lifetimes have only a limited impact on the estimated growth rates of gross capital stock. We also compared our gross capital stock estimates with official stock estimates for Korea and Taiwan, which are based on national wealth surveys. Our estimates are up to 30 per cent lower than those from the wealth surveys, but in particular in the case of Taiwan this difference declines over time.[3]

If one assumes that repair and maintenance keep the physical production capabilities of an asset constant until it is retired, the gross capital stock can be used for measuring its contribution to growth of output and productivity. In practice, however, it is likely that assets undergo some efficiency decline as they age due to wear and tear. The productive capital stock takes into account declines in efficiency alongside retirements. Using a geometric age-efficiency pattern appears to be the most suitable pattern given evidence from, for example, used asset price studies.[4] As can be seen from the Appendix to this chapter, which shows both gross and productive capital stock, the level of the productive stock is systematically lower at 70 to 85 per cent of the gross stock. However, growth of the productive capital stock is rather similar to that for gross stock, especially for the more recent periods.

To compare the intensity of capital use across countries, the capital stocks were converted to 1990 US dollars using investment PPPs for 1990 for Korea and Taiwan from Penn World Tables (version 5.6). The investment PPPs were adjusted for the relative price levels of investment to GDP in the USA when expressed in international prices.[5] The investment PPPs indicate a relative investment price level of 133 per cent and 126 per cent of the US level for Korea and Taiwan in 1990, respectively.

Table 9.5 compares the ratios of non-residential productive capital stock to GDP and to total labour input. The Table shows a continuous rise in the capital-output ratio, but the rise is faster in Korea than in Taiwan in particular in Korea. Even though Korea started at lower capital output ratios in 1963 it had overtaken Taiwan by 1985. The amount of capital per working increased very rapidly in both countries, but throughout the period capital intensity remained somewhat higher in Taiwan than in Korea.

An adjustment for the quality of the capital stock can be made by measuring the capital services delivered by the various types of assets. As the service flow approach requires user cost of capital, it is necessary to estimate rental prices of the different asset types. These are difficult to observe in practice. For this study we apply the opportunity-cost approach in which the cost of capital is approximated by a standard cost-of-capital formulation:

$$\frac{p_k}{P_k} = i + \delta_k - \frac{\Delta P_k}{P_k} \tag{9.2}$$

with i the nominal interest rate, δ_k the depreciation rate and P_k the purchase price of asset type k. The last term is included to represent capital gains.[6] By applying the user cost of capital, a dollar invested in buildings will yield a lower annual revenue than a dollar invested in machinery because the formers depreciation rate is much lower. Similarly a dollar invested in a personal computer will deliver larger services than a dollar invested in a benchworking machine, because the former is depreciated more rapidly and its prices decline rapidly to the average change in prices of capital goods.

Table 9.5 Productive Capital Stock per Unit of Output and Per Hour Worked, in 1990 US$

	Korea		Taiwan	
	Capital-output ratio 1990 US$	Capital-labour ratio 1990 US$	Capital-output ratio 1990 US$	Capital-labour ratio 1990 US$
1963	0.39	0.88	0.67	1.28
1973	0.60	2.17	0.72	2.81
1985	1.11	6.77	1.03	7.71
1996	1.44	16.37	1.23	17.31

Note: Productive non-residential capital stock is the gross capital stock adjustment for efficiency decline due to wear and tear. Using a geometric age-efficiency pattern implies that the productive capital here equals the net capital stock. 'Output' refers to Gross Domestic Product and 'Labour' refers to total number of hours worked.

Source: See Appendix. Converted to 1990 US$ on the basis of 1990 Geary Khamis purchasing power parities for investment, adjusted for US price difference between investment and GDP, from Penn World Tables 5.6. Output and labour inputs: see Tables 9.2 and 9.3.

Figure 9.2 shows the index of capital quantity and capital quality on a logarithmic scale. Compared to labour input, the acceleration in quantity is much faster than in quality. Moreover, the growth of capital quality is slower than the growth in labour quality. In Korea labour quality increased by 40 per cent compared to 16 per cent for capital quality. In Taiwan the rise in labour quality was 31 per cent compared to 26 per cent for capital quality. Strikingly the capital quality improvement was faster in Taiwan whereas the labour improvement was faster in Korea.

1.3 Total Factor Productivity

Total factor productivity (TFP) growth measures the growth of output relative to that of the combined factor inputs. For the calculation of TFP growth we use the translog formula:

$$\ln \frac{A_{t+1}}{A_t} = \ln \frac{Y_{t+1}}{Y_t} - \sum_j \overline{v}_{t+1}^{\,j} \ln \frac{X_{t+1}^{\,j}}{X_t^{\,j}} \qquad (9.3)$$

with $\overline{v}_{t+1}^{\,j} = 1/2\,(v_t^{\,j} + v_{t+1}^{\,j})$ and $v_t^{\,j}$ the value share of input X_j in output at t. Here we consider the contributions to growth from the quantity and quality of labour and capital input as discussed in the previous sections. The columns in Table 9.6 with the growth estimates for capital and labour confirm the previous observation of faster growth in factor inputs in Korea than in Taiwan, except that Taiwan was somewhat ahead of Korea in terms of improving capital quality most of which was realised before 1973. We also find that the share of capital in total factor income was somewhat higher for Taiwan and that, in contrast to Korea, the capital share did not decline over time. For both countries the growth of factor inputs have slowed down in particular since the middle of the 1980s.

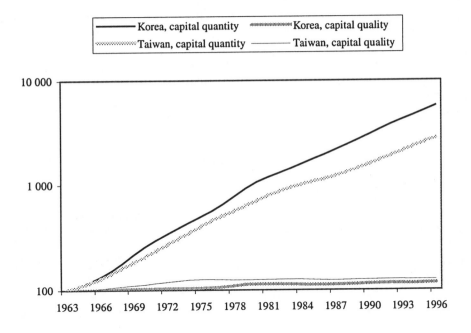

Source: Table 9.5 and Appendix.

Figure 9.2   Total Non-residential Capital Stock and Capital Services, 1963–96 (1963 = 100) (semi-logarithmic scale)

The TFP growth rates are shown in the final column of Table 9.6. These show substantial differences between the two countries and between sub-periods. Up to 1985, TFP growth was substantially faster in Taiwan than in Korea. Between 1973 and 1985 TFP growth in Korea was even negative, as Korea pursued very capital-intensifying industrialisation policies during that period (Pilat, 1994; Timmer, 2000). After 1985 TFP in Korea recovered and became faster than in Taiwan. In both cases there are clear indications that the contribution of TFP to GDP growth improved after 1985.

Table 9.6 Total Factor Productivity (TFP) Growth, 1960–96 (average annual growth rates, %)

	Real GDP	Labour Input			
		Number of persons employed	Hours worked per person employed	Quality: educational attainment	Total
Korea					
1960–73	8.4	3.6	0.6	0.5	4.8
1973–85	7.5	2.6	0.5	1.7	4.9
1985–96	8.3	3.0	−0.3	0.6	3.2
1960–96	8.1	3.1	0.3	0.9	4.3
Taiwan					
1960–73	9.9	3.5	−0.1	0.7	4.1
1973–85	7.4	2.8	−0.8	1.0	3.0
1985–96	7.2	1.8	−0.4	0.7	2.0
1960–96	8.3	2.8	−0.4	0.8	3.1

	Capital Input				
	Quantity: aggregate productive capital stock	Quality: aggregate service flows	Total	Capital share in gross value added	Total factor productivity
Korea					
1960–73	11.9	0.3	12.3	0.46	0.3
1973–85	12.7	0.6	13.3	0.39	−0.7
1985–96	10.7	0.4	11.0	0.36	2.3
1960–96	11.8	0.4	12.2	0.41	0.6
Taiwan					
1960–73	10.2	1.7	11.8	0.51	1.9
1973–85	10.4	0.2	10.6	0.51	0.5
1985–96	8.8	0.0	8.8	0.50	1.8
1960–96	9.8	0.7	10.5	0.51	1.4

Sources: Tables 9.2 to 9.5 and Appendix. Capital share in value added for Korea from Pilat (1994, Annex Table I.7) assuming no change after 1990. Capital share in value added for Taiwan from DGBAS (1994, Table 7) assuming no change before 1978 and after 1993.

Table 9.7 summarises the percentage contribution of total labour and capital input and total factor productivity to GDP growth. It shows that the growth contribution of TFP growth to output growth since 1985 was higher than during the periods before. Clearly, Korea has created more output growth by way of increased labour input, whereas Taiwan, at least up to 1985 has showed a larger TFP contribution to growth.

Table 9.7 Contribution of Total Labour Input, Total Capital Input and Total Factor Productivity to Real GDP Growth, in Per Cent, 1960–96

	Korea			Taiwan		
	Total labour input	Total capital input	Total factor productivity	Total labour input	Total capital input	Total factor productivity
1960–73	0.31	0.68	0.02	0.21	0.58	0.20
1973–85	0.40	0.69	–0.09	0.20	0.71	0.09
1985–96	0.25	0.48	0.28	0.14	0.61	0.25
1960–96	0.32	0.62	0.06	0.19	0.63	0.18

Source: Calculated from Table 9.6.

Our TFP results for Korea differ from previous growth accounting results as presented in Kim and Hong (1997) and Pilat (1994). Both studies show much faster growth in TFP for the 1960s and 1970s. This is mainly explained by the difference in the growth rate of capital. Both previous studies use capital stock data based on wealth surveys without an adjustment for the rise in quality of capital. Young (1995) uses a similar approach as ours, but he excludes the agricultural sector from his analysis. His TFP results for Korea and Taiwan are comparable to ours showing a clear improvement during the 1980s compared to the 1970s. Young's TFP growth rates for the 1960s are higher than ours due to his short-cut method to estimate investment growth in the pre-1953 period, necessitated by his lack of historical series. A similar improvement in TFP growth for Taiwan is found by Liang and Jorgenson (1999) who apply a gross-output approach to growth accounting and take account of changes in the use of intermediate and energy inputs, apart from factor inputs.

It should be emphasised that the TFP calculations in this section are not meant to provide an estimate of technological change. Technological change is at least partly embodied in inputs. In its most extreme form all technological change, as far as captured by the investors in terms of higher returns, is embodied in the inputs. The TFP residual then solely represents non-pecuniary spillovers (Jorgenson, 1995). Others, like Denison (1967) and Maddison (1987), argue that after accounting for various residual factors, such as improved resource allocation, economies of scale, etc., the final residual may represent advances in knowledge, as a form of disembodied technological change.[7]

1.4 Has the Growth Potential been Fully Realised?

Well before the start of the crisis of the late 1990s, a vigorous debate emerged on the role of capital accumulation in the growth process of East Asian countries. Krugman (1994) suggested that growth in these countries had become extensive, and that future growth is likely to slow down because of diminishing returns to capital. Some scholars report rapid accumulation in combination with low total factor productivity growth (Kim and Lau, 1994; Young, 1995). This might indicate that Asian countries, including Taiwan and Korea, have realised most of their potential for factor input growth and that further needs to come from TFP to a much larger extent than before. Above we showed that TFP growth was quite reasonable in particular during the most recent period in this study, 1985–96.

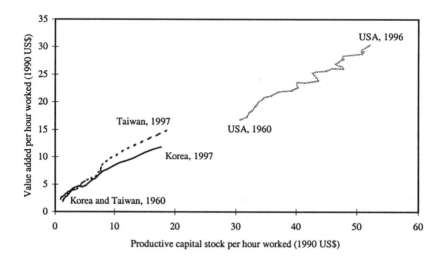

Sources: Labour productivity, see Table 9.2. Capital intensity see Table 9.5.

Figure 9.3   Labour Productivity and Capital Intensity, Total Economy, 1990 US$

One way to check what the potential for further growth in these countries is by comparing the change in levels of labour productivity and capital intensity. Figure 9.1 shows the relation between the non-residential productive capital stock per hour worked and GDP per hour worked in 1990 US dollars. The figure clearly shows the rapid catching-up of Korea and Taiwan with the USA but also indicates the remaining potential for further growth in these countries through narrowing of the two mentioned gaps: one through increasing capital intensity and another one through a rise in productivity. Hence the conclusion that continued growth in East Asia on the basis of expansion of inputs is 'inevitably subject to diminishing returns' (Krugman, 1994, p. 63) seems highly doubtful. There remains substantial scope for further investment in East Asia, but it must be accompanied with measures that help to realise the potential of productivity improvements through disembodied technical change.

ACKNOWLEDGEMENT

The authors wish to thank Barbara Fraumeni, Kyoji Fukao, Masahiro Kuroda, Angus Maddison, Konosuke Odaka, Hak Pyo, Ngo Tak-Wing and participants at seminars at the

University of Leiden, University of Amsterdam, Tilburg University, Hitotsubashi University, National University of Seoul, National University Taiwan, Academia Sinica and the 26th General conference of the IARIW (Cracow) for their comments on previous versions of this chapter. We also thank Saskia van Bergen, Andries Hof, Andrea van Kolmeschate and Erik J. Monnikhof for their assistance.

NOTES

1. The determinants of the rapid catch-up process in these two countries were also documented in various other studies, including Galenson (1979), Kim and Park (1985), Kuznets (1988), Maddison (1989), Ranis (1992), Pilat (1994), Cha, Kim and Perkins (1997), Asian Productivity Organization (1999) and Timmer (2000). Our main contribution lies in the construction of new capital stock series.
2. The non-residential fixed capital stock includes non-residential buildings and other construction (except land improvement), machinery and equipment and transport equipment.
3. See Timmer and Van Ark (2000) for more details on these comparisons. The Korean wealth series were obtained from Pyo (1998) for Korea and from the Directorate General of Budget, Accounting and Statistics for Taiwan (DGBAS, 1999). The DGBAS series are not fully comparable with ours as capital formation in agriculture is excluded from these figures. It is not clear whether residential buildings are included in the DGBAS estimates. As they are based on a wealth survey amongst firms, probably part of the residential buildings stock will be included.
4. See Timmer and van Ark (2000) for a more detailed discussion. It is emphasised that in principle the productive capital stock differs from the net capital stock. The latter does not only adjust for a loss in the productive capacity of the assets but also for their loss in value. The net capital stock concept understates the productive capital stock when economic depreciation is faster than the efficiency decline. However, when using a geometric age-efficiency patterns, as in the present study, the productivity capital stock equals the net capital stock. See Triplett (1998) for an extensive discussion of these issues.
5. These estimates are obtained from Penn World Tables (version 5.6; described in Summers and Heston, 1991) and are consistent with Maddison's PPP estimates for total GDP. The division of the investment PPP by the US relative price level for investment to GDP is far from trivial. In international prices, investments in the US are 'cheap' relative to total GDP and hence the investment PPP is considerably lower than 1.
6. As a variety of interest rates exist, we chose the discount rate which is the lower limit for most other interest rates a rate but for which long time series are available and which reflect general interest rate movements. For the depreciation rate we took the ratio of the declining balance rate and the asset lifetime. For the real capital gains formulation we adjusted the price change in asset type i by the overall asset price change.
7. See also studies of this nature for Korea, in particular Kim and Park (1985), Pilat (1994) and Kim and Hong (1997).

APPENDIX: CONSTRUCTION OF CAPITAL STOCK ESTIMATES

Korea

For the period 1953–97 two series on capital formation were obtained from the Korean national accounts, namely one for non-residential buildings and the other construction (except land improvement) and one for transport equipment and machinery and equipment. For the period 1914–40, we obtained similar series from Pyo (1996). To bridge the period 1940–53, we estimated capital formation on the basis of output series assuming investment-output ratios at 0.10 for the period 1940–44, at 0.00 for 1945 and 1946, at 0.05 for 1947–50 and at 0.00 for 1951 and 1952. After linking, the investment series was expressed in 1990 Won. As the 1940–53 figures were not divided into a series for non-residential structures and machinery and equipment, we used an average of the pre- and post- five-year period share. Next we applied the perpetual inventory method, by using the standardised asset lives of 39 years for structures and 14 years for equipment from Maddison (1995). Moreover we discounted all pre-1953 investment by 40 per cent to account for war damage (Maddison, 1998, Table 3.10, p. 66). The first cumulated benchmark estimate is provided for 1953. The estimates are adjusted from end-year to mid-year basis.

Taiwan

The procedure for the estimation of the capital stock of the Taiwanese economy was similar to that used for Korea. For the period 1951–97 two series on capital formation were obtained from the Directorate-General of Budget, Accounting and Statistics (DGAS) for non-residential structures and for plant and equipment. For the period 1912–38, we obtained similar figures from Mizoguchi (1997). To bridge the period 1938–51, we estimated capital formation on the basis of output series assuming investment-output ratios at 0.10 for the period 1939–44, at 0.00 for 1945 and 1946 and at 0.05 for 1947–50. After linking, the whole investment series was expressed in 1991 Taiwanese dollars. As the 1938–51 figures were not divided into series for non-residential structures and machinery and equipment, we used an average of the pre-five year period share and the post-five year period share. Next we applied the perpetual inventory method, by using the standardised asset lives of 39 years for structures and 14 years for equipment from Maddison (1995). The first cumulated benchmark estimate could be provided for 1951. The estimates were adjusted from end-year to mid-year basis. In contrast to the measures for Korea, we judged that no adjustment for war damage was necessary for Taiwan.

Table A9.1 *Non-residential Gross Fixed Capital Formation and Non-residential Gross Fixed Capital Stock in Korea, Total Economy (billion 1990 won)*

	Gross Fixed Capital Formation			Gross Fixed Capital Stock			Productive Fixed Capital Stock		
	Struc-tures	Equip-ment	Total	Struc-tures	Equip-ment	Total	Struc-tures	Equip-ment	Total
1913	58	33	92						
1914	67	32	99						
1915	73	24	97						
1916	67	25	91						
1917	83	42	125						
1918	102	72	174						
1919	106	79	185						
1920	116	43	159						
1921	133	47	181						
1922	189	46	235						
1923	181	52	234						
1924	151	56	207						
1925	184	50	233						
1926	221	74	295						
1927	251	101	352						
1928	250	134	384						
1929	281	160	441						
1930	272	184	456						
1931	245	142	387						
1932	233	135	368						
1933	295	163	458						
1934	381	225	606						
1935	438	276	714						
1936	498	212	709						
1937	492	189	681						
1938	580	227	807						
1939	658	369	1 028						
1940	692	490	1 182						
1941	803	395	1 198						
1942	798	393	1 191						
1943	810	399	1 209						
1944	775	382	1 156						
1945									
1946									
1947	226	112	338						
1948	244	120	364						
1949	262	129	391						
1950	282	139	421						
1951									
1952									
1953	266	88	354	6 976	1 690	8 666	4 913	736	5 649
1954	280	125	405	7 207	1 539	8 746	5 071	756	5 827
1955	369	158	527	7 490	1 415	8 904	5 277	808	6 085
1956	317	218	535	7 788	1 366	9 154	5 497	901	6 398
1957	420	231	651	8 101	1 353	9 454	5 737	1 020	6 757
1958	432	212	644	8 465	1 341	9 805	6 030	1 121	7 150

Table A9.1 (continued)

	Gross Fixed Capital Formation			Gross Fixed Capital Stock			Productive Fixed Capital Stock		
	Struc-tures	Equip-ment	Total	Struc-tures	Equip-ment	Total	Struc-tures	Equip-ment	Total
1959	497	189	686	8 863	1 427	10 289	6 353	1 189	7 543
1960	415	217	632	9 244	1 629	10 873	6 661	1 252	7 913
1961	523	229	752	9 616	1 819	11 435	6 975	1 328	8 302
1962	706	303	1 009	10 119	2 016	12 135	7 426	1 437	8 864
1963	887	399	1 286	10 816	2 292	13 108	8 049	1 619	9 668
1964	861	306	1 167	11 590	2 564	14 154	8 736	1 780	10 516
1965	1 135	379	1 514	12 467	2 865	15 331	9 530	1 913	11 443
1966	1 400	802	2 203	13 593	3 455	17 048	10 576	2 278	12 854
1967	1 640	1 059	2 699	14 963	4 342	19 305	11 850	2 940	14 789
1968	2 303	1 384	3 687	16 775	5 457	22 232	13 545	3 815	17 360
1969	3 272	1 678	4 950	19 397	6 846	26 243	16 016	4 897	20 913
1970	3 309	1 604	4 913	22 533	8 299	30 832	18 933	5 961	24 894
1971	3 197	1 974	5 171	25 642	9 864	35 506	21 744	7 047	28 791
1972	3 304	2 199	5 503	28 734	11 729	40 463	24 487	8 303	32 790
1973	4 178	2 652	6 830	32 272	13 954	46 226	27 657	9 750	37 407
1974	3 968	3 181	7 149	36 100	16 667	52 767	31 084	11 517	42 602
1975	4 443	3 484	7 927	40 024	19 777	59 801	34 564	13 493	48 057
1976	5 307	4 717	10 024	44 602	23 611	68 213	38 633	16 003	54 636
1977	6 616	6 312	12 928	50 242	28 775	79 017	43 693	19 632	63 325
1978	7 789	9 387	17 176	57 073	36 273	93 346	49 876	25 168	75 044
1979	8 846	10 875	19 720	64 985	46 061	111 047	57 030	32 333	89 362
1980	8 725	8 859	17 584	73 322	55 338	128 660	64 484	38 389	102 873
1981	8 639	8 900	17 539	81 524	63 287	144 811	71 661	42 744	114 406
1982	9 977	8 937	18 914	90 349	70 984	161 333	79 297	46 625	125 922
1983	11 936	9 695	21 631	100 830	78 769	179 599	88 403	50 446	138 849
1984	13 497	11 312	24 808	113 314	87 631	200 945	99 057	55 004	154 061
1985	14 225	11 860	26 085	127 175	97 428	224 602	110 606	60 107	170 713
1986	13 934	14 677	28 611	141 187	108 609	249 796	122 105	66 291	188 396
1987	16 467	17 483	33 950	156 246	122 264	278 510	134 457	74 558	209 014
1988	18 301	19 766	38 067	173 479	137 971	311 450	148 703	84 395	233 098
1989	21 147	22 567	43 713	193 039	155 805	348 844	164 957	95 615	260 572
1990	25 028	26 845	51 873	216 042	176 410	392 452	184 196	109 052	293 247
1991	28 284	30 088	58 372	242 698	199 361	442 059	206 553	124 666	331 219
1992	29 102	29 767	58 868	271 257	221 439	492 696	230 427	139 900	370 327
1993	31 419	29 722	61 140	301 244	241 052	542 297	255 310	153 156	408 466
1994	33 650	36 726	70 376	333 454	264 409	597 863	281 887	168 329	450 217
1995	36 613	42 521	79 134	368 243	295 153	663 396	310 441	188 114	498 555
1996	39 920	46 094	86 013	406 140	330 541	736 682	341 464	210 251	551 714
1997	42 245	40 868	83 112	446 796	364 706	811 502	374 578	228 952	603 530

Sources and Notes: Total gross capital formation (excluding residential and land improvement) for 1914–40 Pyo (1996) and for 1953–97 from Bank of Korea, *National Accounts* (various issues). Capital formation from 1940–53 on the basis of output series assuming investment-output ratios at 0.10 for the period 1939–44, at 0.00 for 1945 and 1946, at 0.05 for 1947–50 and at 0.00 for 1951 and 1952. Output from Maddison (1995), *Monitoring the World Economy, 1820–1992* (OECD Development Centre). After linking, the whole investment series was expressed in 1990 Won. 1940–53 figures were divided into series for non-residential structures and machinery and equipment using an average of the pre- and post-war period share of 67 per cent for structures. Moreover we discounted all pre-1953 investment by 40 per cent for war damage (Maddison, 1998, Table 3.10, p. 66). For gross stock, investment was accumulated by using the standardised asset lives of 39 years for structures and 14 years for equipment from Maddison (1995). For productive stock a geometric efficiency pattern is assumed with similar lifetimes and a declining balance rate of 1.65 for equipment and 0.91 for structures. Stocks adjusted to mid-year.

Table A9.2 *Non-residential Gross Fixed Capital Formation and Non-residential Gross and Productive Fixed Capital Stock in Taiwan, Total Economy, in Million 1991 NT$*

	Gross Fixed Capital Formation			Gross Fixed Capital Stock			Productive Fixed Capital Stock		
	Struc- tures	Equip- ment	Total	Struc- tures	Equip- ment	Total	Struc- tures	Equip- ment	Total
1912	3 177	849	4 026						
1913	2 818	439	3 257						
1914	2 314	394	2 708						
1915	1 858	384	2 242						
1916	1 919	348	2 268						
1917	3 448	538	3 986						
1918	2 793	508	3 301						
1919	4 138	847	4 986						
1920	6 579	867	7 445						
1921	5 924	982	6 906						
1922	4 834	675	5 509						
1923	4 841	743	5 585						
1924	3 955	570	4 525						
1925	5 475	745	6 220						
1926	5 456	898	6 355						
1927	6 474	1 051	7 525						
1928	7 767	1 377	9 144						
1929	8 291	1 360	9 651						
1930	7 265	1 560	8 825						
1931	7 104	1 289	8 393						
1932	8 807	1 259	10 066						
1933	9 579	1 554	11 133						
1934	10 314	2 198	12 512						
1935	13 269	2 816	16 085						
1936	14 247	2 974	17 221						
1937	10 564	3 099	13 663						
1938	11 411	3 633	15 043						
1939	13 481	4 494	17 975						
1940	13 432	4 477	17 909						
1941	14 777	4 926	19 702						
1942	15 864	5 288	21 151						
1943	10 814	3 605	14 419						
1944	7 427	2 476	9 902						
1945									
1946									
1947	4 710	1 570	6 280						
1948	5 097	1 699	6 796						
1949	5 518	1 839	7 357						
1950	5 973	1 991	7 964						
1951	7 337	2 783	10 120	273 794	38 937	312 731	189 713	18 633	208 346
1952	8 779	4 160	12 938	278 854	39 043	317 897	193 344	19 908	213 252
1953	11 654	4 974	16 628	286 504	39 546	326 050	199 049	22 128	221 178
1954	12 086	4 848	16 934	296 288	39 972	336 260	206 275	24 431	230 706
1955	10 404	4 279	14 683	305 645	39 834	345 479	212 707	26 116	238 822
1956	11 018	5 921	16 939	313 672	39 828	353 499	218 454	28 138	246 592
1957	10 121	6 353	16 474	321 120	41 518	362 639	223 927	30 959	254 885
1958	12 392	7 723	20 115	328 911	45 516	374 428	229 958	34 348	264 306

Table A9.2 (continued)

	Gross Fixed Capital Formation			Gross Fixed Capital Stock			Productive Fixed Capital Stock		
	Struc-tures	Equip-ment	Total	Struc-tures	Equip-ment	Total	Struc-tures	Equip-ment	Total
1959	14 997	9 371	24 368	337 248	52 825	390 073	238 288	38 847	277 134
1960	18 769	10 428	29 196	347 880	62 724	410 604	249 611	44 168	293 778
1961	19 153	12 277	31 431	361 462	73 292	434 754	262 747	50 315	313 062
1962	22 297	11 301	33 598	377 350	83 447	460 797	277 342	56 174	333 516
1963	25 077	13 019	38 096	396 638	93 838	490 476	294 557	61 714	356 271
1964	28 455	15 011	43 466	418 690	105 937	524 627	314 450	68 455	382 905
1965	29 736	23 115	52 852	442 320	122 614	564 934	336 209	79 450	415 659
1966	34 764	31 097	65 861	468 606	146 248	614 854	360 615	97 192	457 807
1967	42 166	38 862	81 029	499 950	176 661	676 612	390 666	120 717	511 383
1968	50 172	46 661	96 833	538 091	214 512	752 603	427 719	149 251	576 971
1969	53 667	56 034	109 700	582 232	261 296	843 528	469 659	183 009	652 667
1970	54 302	73 919	128 221	629 032	321 172	950 204	512 684	226 416	739 101
1971	57 600	94 585	152 186	677 028	399 287	1 076 315	556 673	283 984	840 657
1972	70 091	113 064	183 155	731 680	496 074	1 227 755	607 529	354 339	961 869
1973	72 636	130 785	203 421	793 097	609 452	1 402 549	664 717	434 502	1 099 219
1974	82 001	153 130	235 131	858 624	741 510	1 600 134	726 526	525 250	1 251 776
1975	116 709	164 760	281 470	944 221	889 103	1 833 324	808 929	622 291	1 431 220
1976	128 531	162 158	290 689	1 054 436	1 040 773	2 095 208	912 674	712 409	1 625 083
1977	146 938	149 732	296 671	1 181 183	1 184 558	2 365 741	1 029 113	784 392	1 813 505
1978	160 022	173 566	333 588	1 322 217	1 332 192	2 654 409	1 158 581	853 594	2 012 175
1979	170 747	212 233	382 980	1 474 145	1 506 028	2 980 173	1 296 932	945 891	2 242 823
1980	184 580	261 437	446 017	1 637 705	1 715 757	3 353 462	1 444 334	1 071 246	2 515 580
1981	181 567	280 945	462 512	1 805 458	1 951 968	3 757 426	1 593 706	1 216 183	2 809 889
1982	184 863	279 846	464 709	1 975 334	2 189 602	4 164 936	1 739 734	1 353 243	3 092 977
1983	181 788	278 575	460 362	2 149 539	2 417 465	4 567 004	1 882 466	1 472 964	3 355 429
1984	194 208	279 031	473 238	2 333 823	2 631 291	4 965 114	2 026 539	1 578 167	3 604 706
1985	203 696	239 452	443 148	2 532 774	2 806 280	5 339 055	2 178 205	1 651 410	3 829 615
1986	210 091	268 717	478 808	2 737 313	2 956 540	5 693 853	2 334 274	1 710 864	4 045 138
1987	246 986	344 289	591 275	2 960 949	3 141 118	6 102 067	2 508 346	1 815 730	4 324 076
1988	277 737	402 569	680 306	3 218 003	3 372 590	6 590 593	2 712 179	1 975 162	4 687 342
1989	307 768	483 570	791 338	3 505 010	3 656 714	7 161 724	2 941 648	2 185 445	5 127 092
1990	351 629	524 174	875 803	3 828 053	3 997 128	7 825 180	3 202 708	2 431 747	5 634 454
1991	416 769	548 503	965 271	4 204 194	4 377 521	8 581 715	3 512 177	2 681 486	6 193 663
1992	459 567	653 339	1 112 905	4 632 145	4 816 792	9 448 938	3 868 394	2 966 375	6 834 768
1993	522 251	667 796	1 190 047	5 111 184	5 284 460	10 395 645	4 269 040	3 277 333	7 546 373
1994	593 028	714 258	1 307 287	5 657 579	5 738 653	11 396 232	4 727 069	3 582 103	8 309 172
1995	641 714	796 995	1 438 709	6 264 239	6 223 089	12 487 328	5 234 141	3 915 554	9 149 695
1996	645 289	857 285	1 502 574	6 897 171	6 769 833	13 667 004	5 755 513	4 281 218	10 036 731
1997	676 282	1 031 064	1 707 346	7 546 700	7 434 797	14 981 497	6 282 003	4 720 820	11 002 823
1998	721 803	1 152 470	1 874 273	8 232 047	8 247 762	16 479 809	6 834 465	5 256 205	12 090 671

Sources and Notes: Total gross capital formation (excluding residential and land improvement) for 1912–38 Mizoguchi (1997), and for 1951–98 from DGBAS, *National Income in the Taiwan Area of the Republic of China* (1998). Capital formation from 1938–51 on the basis of output series assuming investment-output ratios at 0.10 for the period 1939–44, at 0.00 for 1945 and 1946 and 0.05 for 1947–50. Output from Maddison (1995), *Monitoring the World Economy, 1820–92* (OECD Development Centre). After linking, the whole investment series was expressed in 1991 Taiwanese dollars. Pre-1951 figures were divided into series for non-residential structures and machinery and equipment using an average of the pre- and post-war period share of 75 per cent for structures. For gross stock, investment was accumulated by using the standardised asset lives of 39 years for structures and 14 years for equipment from Maddison (1995). For productive stock a geometric efficiency pattern is assumed with similar lifetimes and a declining balance rate of 1.65 for equipment and 0.91 for structures. Stocks adjusted to mid-year.

REFERENCES

Abramovitz, M. (1979), 'Rapid Growth Potential and Its Realization: the Experience of Capitalist Economies in the Postwar Period', in E. Malinvaud (ed.), *Economic Growth and Resources. Proceedings of the Fifth World Congress of the International Economic Association held in Tokyo, Japan, 1977, vol. 1, The Major Issues,* London: Macmillan, 1–30.

Abramovitz, M. (1986), 'Catching Up, Forging Ahead and Falling Behind', *Journal of Economic History,* **46** (2), 385–406.

Asian Productivity Organization (1999), *APO Productivity Journal,* Theme: Total Factor Productivity, edited by Linda Low, Tokyo: APO

Blades, D. (1993), 'Comparing Capital Stocks', in A. Szirmai, B. van Ark and D. Pilat (eds), *Explaining Economic Growth. Essays in Honour of Angus Maddison,* Amsterdam: North Holland, 399–412.

Cha, Dong-se, Kwang Suk Kim and Dwight H. Perkins (eds, 1997), The Korean economy 1945–1995: Performance and Vision for the 21st Century, Seoul: Korea Development Institute Press.

Crafts, N.F.R. (1997), 'Economic Growth in East Asia and Western Europe since 1950: Implications for Living Standards', *National Institute Economic Review,* London, 75–84.

DGBAS (1999), *The Trends in Multifactor Productivity,* Taiwan Area, Republic of China, Taipei.

Galenson, W., ed. (1979), *Economic Growth and Structural Change in Taiwan: the Postwar Experience of the Republic of China,* Ithaca, NY: Cornell University Press.

Goldsmith, R.W. (1951), 'A Perpetual Inventory of National Wealth', *Studies in Income and Wealth,* **14**, New York: NBER.

Hofman, A. (1998), *Latin-American Economic Development. A Causal Analysis in Historical Perspective,* Monograph series no. 3, Groningen: Groningen Growth and Development Centre.

Jorgenson, D.W. (1995) *Productivity. Volumes 1 and 2,* Cambridge, MA, MIT Press.

Kim, J.-I. and L.J. Lau (1994), 'The Sources of Economic Growth of the East Asian Newly Industrialized Countries', *Journal of the Japanese and International Economies,* **8**, 235–71

Kim, K.-S. and J.K. Park (1985), *Sources of Economic Growth in Korea, 1963–1982,* Seoul: Korea Development Institute.

Kim, K.-S. and S.-D. Hong (1997), *Accounting for Rapid Economic Growth in Korea, 1963–1995,* Seoul: Korea Development Institute.

Krugman, P. (1994), 'The Myth of Asia's Miracle', *Foreign Affairs,* November/December, 62–78

Kuznets, P.W. (1977), *Economic Growth and Structure in the Republic of Korea,* New Haven: Yale University Press.

Liang, C-Y and D.W. Jorgenson (1999), 'Productivity Growth in Taiwan's Manufacturing Industry, 1961–1993', in T-T Fu, C.J. Huang and C.A. Knox Lovell (eds), *Economic Efficiency and Productivity Growth in the Asia-Pacific Region,* Cheltenham: Edward Elgar, 265–85.

Maddison, A. (1987), 'Growth and Slowdown in Advanced Capitalist Countries: Techniques of Quantitative Assessment', *Journal of Economic Literature,* **25** (2), June.

Maddison, A. (1995), 'Standardised Estimates of Fixed Capital Stock: A Six Country Comparison', in *Explaining the Economic Performance of Nations. Essays in Time and Space,* Cheltenham: Edward Elgar.

Maddison, A. (1995a), *Monitoring the World Economy 1820–1992,* OECD Development Centre, Paris

Maddison, A. (1998), *Chinese Economic Performance in the Long Run,* OECD Development Centre, Paris

Mizoguchi, T. (1997), 'Revising Long-Term National Accounts Statistics of Taiwan 1912–1990: A Comparison of Estimates of Production Accounts to Expenditure Accounts', *Discussion Papers No. D97-8,* Institute of Economic Research, Hitotsubashi University, Tokyo.

Pilat, D. (1994), *The Economics of Rapid Growth. The Experience of Japan and Korea,* Aldershot, UK and Brookfield, US: Edward Elgar.

Pyo, H.K. (1996), *Historical Statistics of Korea: Investment and Capital Stock,* Jewon Historical Statistics Series No. 2, Institute of Economic Research, Seoul National University, Seoul 1996.

Pyo, H.K. (1998), 'Estimates of Fixed Reproducible Tangible Assets in the Republic of Korea, 1953–1996', *KDI Working Paper No. 9810,* Korea Development Institute, Seoul.

Ranis, G. (1992), *Taiwan: From Developing to Mature Economy*, Boulder: Westview Press.

Summers, R. and A. Heston (1991), 'The Penn World Table (Mark 5): an Expanded Set of International Comparisons, 1950–1988', *Quarterly Journal of Economics,* **106**, 327–68.

Timmer, M.P. (2000), *The Dynamics of Asian Manufacturing. A Comparative Perspective in the Late Twentieth Century,* Edward Elgar, Cheltenham.

Timmer, M.P. and B. van Ark (2000), 'Capital Formation and Productivity Growth in South Korea and Taiwan: Beating Diminishing Returns through Realising the Catch-Up Potential', mimeographed.

Triplett, J. (1998), *A Dictionary of Usage for Capital Measurement Issues,* presented at the Second Meeting of the Canberra Group on Capital Stock Statistics.

Young, A. (1995), 'The Tyranny of Numbers: Confronting the Statistical Realities of the East Asian Growth Experience', *The Quarterly Journal of Economics,* **110**, 641–80.

Index